REVOLT
IN THE DESERT

```
C  R
C  B
```

After a portrait by Augustus John

T. E. LAWRENCE

REVOLT
IN THE DESERT

T. E. LAWRENCE

CONTENTS

LIST OF ILLUSTRATIONS

FOREWORD

Revolt in the Desert is an abridgment, by T. E. Lawrence's own hand, of *Seven Pillars of Wisdom*, the author's mammoth account of his role in the Arab revolt against the Turks as World War I engulfed Europe. From the outset, *Revolt* was devised as a popular volume with a specific purpose: to pay the cost of the larger work, which Lawrence planned as a lavish, elegantly illustrated (by John Singer Sargent, among others), very limited publication—"a richly-produced edition, with many portrait drawings," as Lawrence put it, "to be published by subscription at a stiff price." Writing in the foreword to the original issue of *Revolt*, Lawrence continues: "The stiff price, though it covered the cost of printing, was not stiff enough to pay the artists adequately. Some of the richer artists agreed to work for nominal fees: and I raised money to pay the others by selling to Jonathan Cape the right to bring out this abridgment. It amounts to less than half of the original text . . ., but half a calamity is better than a whole one, and this fairly represents all sides of the story."

The publishing history of Lawrence's Arabian writing is a complicated affair that, even in outline, sheds some light on its notoriously diffident and enigmatic creator. He was a famous figure by the time he returned to England after the war, the flames of his legend fanned by the efforts of the American journalist Lowell Thomas, whose romanticized film-and-lecture reports on Lawrence's adventures captivated large audiences in both New York and London. As we learn from John E. Mack's excellent biography, *A Prince of Our Disorder*, Lawrence—urged by Rudyard Kipling and others—began to compose his own chronicle of his exploits as early as January 1919. By May 1922, Mack relates, Lawrence had written three manuscripts of *Seven Pillars*, of which only the last survives.

The first text, comprising 250,000 words, was lost around Christmas 1919, when Lawrence left it on a train. The second, written in intense bursts of concentration and worked on throughout 1920, ended up sixty percent longer than its predecessor. "Naturally," Lawrence wrote, alluding to the speed of its composition, "the style was careless." The third manuscript, nearly 330,000 words, was "composed with great care" during 1921 and 1922. Upon its completion, the author—with the peculiar fierceness that was the flip side of his preternatural sensitivity—burned "all but one page" of the second version.

Still resisting distribution of his book, Lawrence at least took the precaution of having eight copies of the third manuscript printed in sheets by the *Oxford Times* in 1922. Over the course of the next four years, with the help of criticism from George Bernard Shaw and E. M. Forster, Lawrence labored to perfect *Seven Pillars*, eventually cutting 50,000 words from the text set in the Oxford proofs. At the same time, he concerned himself with the details of the book's deluxe production and concocted perverse publishing schemes. For instance, in 1925, he signed a contract with George Doran in New York for the printing of twenty-two copies, of which the publisher was to keep four and the author six; of the remaining dozen, two would go to the Library of Congress and ten were to be offered for sale at $20,000 each—at which price, of course, they would never sell. As Mack explains,

> It appears that Doran was willing to make such an outlandish arrangement because he knew that an abridgment of *Seven Pillars* that would be sold to the general public was in the offing. When in fact the abridgment, entitled *Revolt in the Desert*, was published — in 1927 by Doran in the United States — it sold handsomely at $3.00 a copy, the earlier

publicity attending the publication of the "$20,000 edition" having done an excellent job of advance promotion.

The elaborate limited edition of *Seven Pillars of Wisdom* was finally distributed to subscribers at the very end of 1926, "so printed and assembled," as Lawrence mysteriously explained, "that nobody but myself knew how many copies were produced" (Mack puts the figure at over 200). At the same time, *Revolt in the Desert*, which stripped the larger book of its introspective passages to create a thrilling epic of action, was serialized in a London newspaper. In March 1927 it appeared in book form, becoming an immediate sensation in England and America and quickly retiring the debts Lawrence incurred in creating *Seven Pillars*. Once the abridgment's financial mission had been accomplished, the author asked that the book be withdrawn in England; and despite the fact that its British publisher had more than 50,000 copies on hand, *Revolt in the Desert* was declared out of print.

In America, the book sold more than 120,000 copies in its first three months alone, becoming a bestseller for George Doran, whose perspicacity in floating the "$20,000 edition" was well rewarded, as was the interest of readers drawn to this unparalleled tale of brave deeds and heroic energy.

James Mustich, Jr.
August 2004

INTRODUCTION

"*ARABS could be swung on an idea as on a cord; for the unpledged allegiance of their minds made them obedient servants. None of them would escape the bond till success had come, and with it responsibility and duty and engagements. Then the idea was gone and the work ended— in ruins. Without a creed they could be taken to the four corners of the world (but not to heaven) by being shown the riches of earth and the pleasures of it; but if on the road, led in this fashion, they met the prophet of an idea, who had nowhere to lay his head and who depended for his food on charity or birds, then they would all leave their wealth for his inspiration. They were incorrigibly children of the idea, feckless and colour-blind, to whom body and spirit were for ever and inevitably opposed. Their mind was strange and dark, full of depressions and exaltations, lacking in rule, but with more of ardour and more fertile in belief than any other in the world. They were a people of starts, for whom the abstract was the strongest motive, the process of infinite courage and variety, and the end nothing. They were as unstable as water, and like water would perhaps finally prevail. Since the dawn of life, in successive waves they had been dashing themselves against the coasts of flesh. Each wave was broken, but, like the sea, wore away ever so little of the granite on which it failed, and some day, ages yet, might roll unchecked over the place where the material world had been, and God would move upon the face of those waters. One such wave (and not the least) I raised and rolled before the breath of an idea, till it reached its crest, and toppled over and fell at Damascus. The wash of that wave, thrown back by the resistance of vested things, will provide the matter of the following wave, when in fullness of time the sea shall be raised once more.*"

The strange and still mysterious figure of T. E. Lawrence has become, if not the best known, certainly one of the most famous in all the small gallery of true heroes of the war. An unimpressive, rather studious, young man of twenty-six, he was rejected in the opening days of the war as physically unfit for military service. The authorities who rejected him can be forgiven; for not even Lawrence himself had guessed that he added, to the unusual combination of archæologist, philosopher, diplomat and student of military affairs, the genius of a surpassing leader of irregular cavalry. After his failure to enlist, his knowledge of Arabic and the Arabian peoples brought him a commission as a subaltern in the Intelligence Service of the British command at Cairo. For his subsequent single-handed organisation and leadership of the Arab revolt, through two years of bitter and weird adventure, in an atmosphere of incredible romance and under a veil of profound secrecy, the authorities were not to blame. It was his own masterpiece, and it was one of the miracles of the war.

In 1914, T. E. Lawrence was serving as a more or less unnoticed assistant in the British Museum's excavation of Carchemish on the Euphrates. Under the appearance of a brilliant and somewhat eccentric student of archæology, he concealed a lively initiative, a sympathetic understanding of the country, and a relationship to more than one soldier prominent in British history, including—it is supposed—a Sir Robert Lawrence who fought as a crusader under Richard Cœur de Lion. Casual travellers found him unobtrusively digging Hittite remains out of the banks of the Euphrates; he left them reassured by his tactfulness with the Arab labourers as to the future of the British Empire. He knew the Near East intimately. His first direct knowledge of the complicated peoples of Arabia had been gained while he was still an undergraduate at Oxford, when he is said to have undertaken, alone and in native dress, a two-year expedition among the tribes behind Syria, in order to gather material for his thesis on the military history of the Crusades. Such experience placed him, obviously, in the direct line of those remarkable British Orientalists like Doughty and Burton who have done so much to enrich British letters. It could hardly have been anticipated that it was preparing him for the very different and more romantic achievements in reckless leadership and masterful strategy which are described in these pages.

Lawrence was not the author of the revolt; his was the more difficult, and also more dangerous, task of being its inspiration. A subaltern officer with no respect for his superiors, with a sensitive and vigorous mind, undisturbed either by military regulations or a desire for glory, and with a scholarly taste in reading, he was clearly an unexpected figure among the soldiery and camp followers at Cairo. Since then he has allowed very little to be known of himself. After his triumph in Syria, the famous guerilla leader (who nevertheless remained an ethnological expert) served in the British peace delegation at Versailles, and was later a member of a special commission on Near Eastern affairs headed by the Colonial Secretary. But an almost passionate dislike of notoriety and a seemingly deliberate eccentricity have continued to conceal his character; and he is now [February, 1927] actually serving as a private soldier in the British Army, while the mists of a gathering legend have cloaked him in the obscurity of an almost mythological hero.

However, in 1919, he wrote out in a 400,000-word book the whole bitter account of his adventure and of his disappointment over the conclusion which the Peace Conference seemed to put to it. He left the book, together with some of his notes and many photographs, in a handbag in the Reading railway station; a few minutes later it had disappeared. There was a flurry of rumour to the effect that it had been stolen by high authorities; subsequently it has seemed more likely that the bag was taken by a casual sneak-thief, but Lawrence at any rate sat down with an heroic effort of memory to rewrite the account. He never intended it, however, for publication. He had it printed on a newspaper press in Oxford, in an edition limited characteristically to eight copies, of which three, in what seems almost an excess of reticence, were afterward destroyed.

Of all the honours that an astonished government tried to force upon him, the war-time rank of Lieutenant-Colonel was the only one which he accepted, and that largely because of the necessity for maintaining his status with the Arabs. The latter called him simply "El-Orens," or else by the more picturesque title of "Wrecker of Engines." The titles which the newspapers afterwards invented only annoyed him; and not long ago the astonishing discovery was made that he had enlisted under an assumed name in the Royal Air Force, presumably to avoid attention. There was, of course, another wave of notoriety, and it is understood that he is now occupying the even less explicable position of a private in the Tank Corps.

The re-written book, with which Lawrence himself was never quite satisfied, was a purely personal record. His impregnable reticence was, however, broken down to the extent of allowing a lengthy abridgment for publication by "a friendly man of letters." The book in its present form opens abruptly with Lawrence's arrival with the Arabian armies, long after he had taken up, along with others of the more brilliant younger men in the intelligence service at Cairo, the enthusiastic advocacy of the Arabian revolt.

At the very outset of the war British diplomacy had remembered the unrest among the Arab-speaking populations of Turkey, and its possible value in the defence of the Suez Canal. A revolutionary movement, fostered both by powerful secret societies and the repressive measures of the Turks, had been growing ever since the Young Turk revolution of 1908. It included many high civil and military officers of the Turkish Government, while a third of the Turkish Army was Arabic-speaking and consequently disaffected. Even before Turkey declared war, Sir Henry McMahon, the representative of British civil power in Egypt, had written to Hussein, the Grand Sherif of Mecca, to promise British support for the independence of the Arabs. The secret societies did not agree that the Allies' cause against the Central Powers was identical with the Arabs' cause against Turkey; many of their members were still loyally commanding Turkish troops at the end of the war, and a doubt among the Arabs as to the disinterestedness of the British explains many of Lawrence's later difficulties. The Arabs, however, did plan a revolution on their own account, under the banner of Hussein and his four sons, but it came to nothing.

Meanwhile Lawrence had taken up his modest duties in the Intelligence Service at Cairo.

"I had been many years," he has said, *"going up and down the Semitic East before the war, learning the manners of the villagers and tribesmen and citizens of Syria and Mesopotamia. My poverty had constrained me to mix with the humbler classes, those seldom met by European travellers, and thus my experiences gave me an unusual angle of view, which enabled me to understand and think for the ignorant many as well as for the more enlightened whose rare opinions mattered, not so much for the day, as for the morrow. In addition I had seen something of the political forces working in the minds of the Middle East, and especially had noted everywhere sure signs of the decay of imperial Turkey."*

There were other archæologists, orientalists, and younger experts of the political service, who, although wearing the unfamiliar uniforms of the army and navy, believed in the Arabian revolt as much for the sake of the Arabs as for the sake of the Allies. Lawrence was united with them in their interest in Sir Henry McMahon's correspondence with Hussein, although the more orthodox minds among the military found it difficult to understand such unconventional methods of warfare. As Lawrence adds:

"We called ourselves 'Intrusive' as a band; for we meant to break into the accepted halls of English foreign policy, and build a new people in the East, despite the rails laid down for us by our ancestors. Therefore, from our hybrid Intelligence office in Cairo (a jangling place which for its incessant bells and bustle and running to and fro was likened by Aubrey Herbert to an Oriental railway station) we began to work upon all our chiefs, far and near."

It is a process of which chiefs seldom approve; but Sir Henry continued both his correspondence and his promises. The long agony of the Dardanelles was played out and ended, the British came to disaster at Kut-el-Amara, and the Turks were as close across the Suez Canal as ever. But in the summer of 1916 Sir Henry triumphed, and at the beginning of June Hussein proclaimed the revolt of the Arab people, with British money and support.

Both Jidda and Mecca fell in the first rush of the Sherifian armies, but Feisal's attack upon Medina, the Turkish strong-point at the end of the Hejaz Railway, failed, and the revolt began to go rather precariously astray amid the simplicities of Arab patriotism and the complex departmental and international jealousies at Cairo. The military authorities still seemed incapable of grasping the value of a war started by the civilians; and a staff perturbed by the eccentric brilliancy of an Intelligence Service made up of experts began to show tendencies toward suppressing them. Sir Henry was recalled to England, and the Sherifian forces, led by Hussein's son Feisal and his three brothers, Ali, Abdulla and Zeid, got neither the supplies nor the advice which they needed.

Lawrence (he was only twenty-eight years old) had never regarded himself as a soldier; he liked his work of making maps and running a secret Arab newspaper, and he felt it meanness in him to pretend to be a man of action. Yet his Arab revolt was in serious difficulties. The Turks had sent out a formal attacking column from Medina, and the Arab levies were in danger of being jammed—by the inapplicable principles of orthodox war—into the area around Mecca, instead of using their dash and mobility in the irregular combat for which they were supremely fitted. Meanwhile Lawrence found himself in danger of being politely eliminated, as an upstart, while other men ruined the plans for which he was largely responsible.

His reply was, first to make himself as obnoxious as possible to his military superiors, and then to ask for leave. It was granted with alacrity, in the hope that he could be gently put out of the way on his return. But he did not intend to be put out of the way. He boarded a naval vessel on the way down the Red Sea, ostensibly as a "joy-ride" with Sir Ronald Storrs, another of the "Intrusives," who was making an official trip to Jidda. He was without authority or passes, and Feisal, the principal commander, was in the interior, from which as a Christian he was debarred by order. But it was his precocious intention to see what he, a staff-captain on leave, could do for the confused armies of Arabia.

"Storrs and I then marched off together, happily. In the East they swore that by three sides was the decent way across a square; and my trick to escape was in this sense oriental. But I justified myself by my confidence in the final success of the Arab revolt if properly advised. I had been a mover in its beginning; my hopes lay in it. The fatalistic subordination of a professional soldier (intrigue being unknown in the British army) would have made a proper officer sit down and watch his plan of campaign wrecked by men who thought nothing of it, and to whose spirit it made no appeal. Non nobis, Domine."

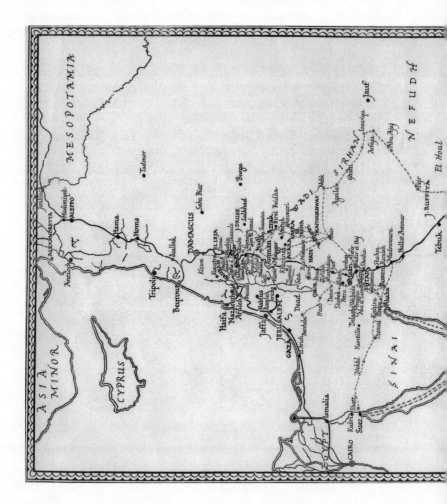

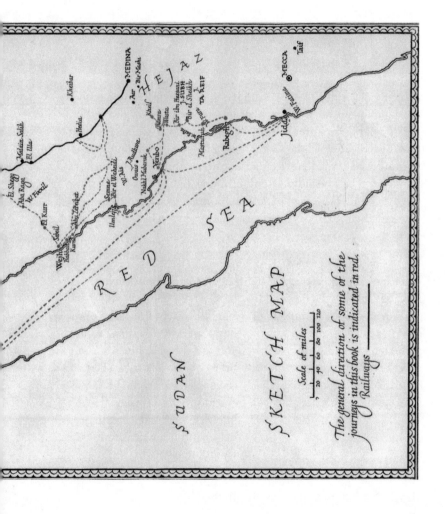

SKETCH MAP

Scale of miles

0   20   40   60   80   100   120

The general direction of some of the
journeys in this book is indicated in red.

Railways

RED SEA

SUDAN

HEJAZ

Taif

MECCA

Jidda
Wasima

TA KEIF
SUBH
Bir Ibn Hassani
Bir el Shaikh

Rabegh

Masturah

Wasta
Bir
Hamra

Khuff

Aar
Bir Nazh

MEDINA

Khedar

Hedia

Medain Salih
El Ula

E. Stagg
Abu Raga
W. Fwciz

El Kurr

Ghail
Jedil

Wejh
Habra
Kurd

Abu Zereibat

Umlejj

Semna
Bir el Wahcidi

W. Ais

Rudlwa

Owais
Nabsi Mubarak

Kribo

PUBLISHER'S NOTE

It seems necessary to explain that the spelling of Arabic names throughout this book varies according to the whim of the author.

The publisher's proof-reader objected strongly to the apparent inconsistencies which he found, and a long and entertaining correspondence ensued between author and publisher. The author's attitude can best be judged from the following extracts which show questions and answers in parallel columns.

Q.	A.
I attach a list of queries raised by F. who is reading the proofs. He finds these very clean, but full of inconsistencies in the spelling of proper names, a point which reviewers often take up. Will you annotate it in the margin, so that I can get the proofs straightened?	Annotated: not very helpfully perhaps. Arabic names won't go into English, exactly, for their consonants are not the same as ours, and their vowels, like ours, vary from district to district. There are some 'scientific systems' of transliteration, helpful to people who know enough Arabic not to need helping, but a wash-out for the world. I spell my names anyhow, to show what rot the systems are.
Slip 1. Jeddah and Jidda used impartially throughout. Intentional?	Rather!

Q.	A.
Slip 16. Bir Wahei*da*, was Bir Wahei*di*.	Why not? All one place.
Slip 20. Nuri, Emir of the Ruwalla, belongs to the 'chief family of the Rualla.' On Slip 33 'Rualla horse,' and Slip 38, 'killed one Rueili.' In all later slips 'Rualla.'	Should have also used Ruwala and Ruala.
Slip 28. The Bisaita is also spelt Biseita.	Good.
Slip 47. Jedha, the she camel, was Jedhah on Slip 40.	She was a splendid beast.
Slip 53. 'Meleager, the immoral poet.' I have put 'immortal' poet, but the author may mean immoral after all.	Immorality I know. Immortality I cannot judge. As you please: Meleager will not sue us for libel.
Slip 65. Author is addressed 'Ya Auruns,' but on Slip 56 was 'Aurans.'	Also Lurens and Runs: not to mention 'Shaw.' More to follow, if time permits.
Slip 78. Sherif Abd el Mayin of Slip 68 becomes el Main, el Mayein, el Muein, el Mayin, and el Muyein.	Good egg. I call this really ingenious.

In the face of such replies to the publisher's well-intentioned questions, further expostulation was clearly impossible.

AUTHOR'S NOTE

THIS book, written in 1919, was printed on a newspaper press in Oxford shortly after, not for publication, but as a convenience to myself and friends. Some of them asked for copies of their own: and from that demand gradually grew the idea of a richly-produced edition, with many portrait drawings, to be published by subscription at a stiff price.

The stiff price, though it covered the cost of printing, was not stiff enough to pay the artists adequately. Some of the richer artists agreed to work for nominal fees: and I raised money to pay the others by selling to Jonathan Cape the right to bring out this abridgment. It amounts to less than half of the original text (which occupied the reading hours of my friends for months), but half a calamity is better than a whole one, and this fairly represents all sides of the story.

If I am asked why I have abridged an unsatisfactory book, instead of recasting it as a history, I must plead that to do so nice a job in the barracks which have been my home since 1922 would need a degree of concentration amounting in an airman to moroseness: and an interest in the subject which was exhausted long ago in the actual experience of it.

'T. E. L.'

CHAPTER I

STORRS GOES TO JIDDAH

WHEN AT last we anchored in Jeddah's outer harbour, off the white town hung between the blazing sky and its reflection in the mirage which swept and rolled over the wide lagoon, then the heat of Arabia came out like a drawn sword and struck us speechless. It was a midday of October of 1916; and the noon sun had, like moonlight, put to sleep the colours. There were only lights and shadows, the white houses and black gaps of streets: in front, the pallid lustre of the haze shimmering upon the inner harbour: behind, the dazzle of league after league of featureless sand, running up to an edge of low hills, faintly suggested in the far away mist of heat.

Just north of Jidda was a second group of black-white buildings, moving up and down like pistons in the mirage, as the ship rolled at anchor and the intermittent wind shifted the heat waves in the air.

Colonel Wilson, British representative with the new Arab state, had sent his launch to meet us; and we had to go ashore to learn the reality of the men levitating in that mirage. We walked past the white masonry of the still-building water gate, and through the oppressive alley of the food market on our way to the Consulate.

In the air, from the men to the dates and back to the meat, squadrons of flies like particles of dust danced up and down the sun-shafts which stabbed into the darkest corners of the booths through torn places in the wood and sackcloth awnings overhead. The atmosphere was like a bath.

We reached the Consulate; and there in a shaded room with an open lattice behind him sat Wilson, prepared to welcome the sea breeze, which had lagged these last few days. He told us that Sherif Abdulla, second son of Hussein, Grand Sherif of Mecca, was just then entering the town. Ronald Storrs and myself had come down the Red Sea from Cairo to meet Abdulla. It was auspicious that we had arrived together, for Mecca, the Sherifian capital, was inaccessible to Christians, and such business as Storrs' could not well be transacted by telephone. My presence must be put down to joy-riding: but Storrs, Oriental Secretary to the Residency in Cairo, was the confidential assistant of Sir Henry McMahon in all the delicate negotiations with the Sherif of Mecca. The happy union of his local knowledge, with the experience and acumen of Sir Henry, and the sympathy of Clayton, so impressed the Sherif, that that very difficult person accepted their guarded undertakings as sufficient assurance for beginning his Revolt against Turkey, and kept faith with the British authorities throughout a war-history which teemed with doubtful and hazardous situations. Sir Henry was England's right-hand man in the Middle East till the Arab Revolt was an established event. Sir Mark Sykes was the left hand: and if the Foreign Office had kept itself and its hands mutually informed our reputation for honesty would not have suffered as it did.

Abdulla, on a white mare, came to us softly, with a bevy of richly-armed slaves on foot about him, through the silent respectful salutes of the town. He was flushed with his success at Taif, and happy. I was seeing him for the first time, while Storrs was an old friend, and on the best of terms; yet, before long, as they spoke together, I began to suspect him of a constant cheerfulness. His eyes had a confirmed twinkle; and though only thirty-five, he was putting on flesh. It might be due to too much laughter. He jested with all comers in most easy fashion: yet, when we fell into serious talk, the veil of humour seemed to fade away, as he chose his words, and argued shrewdly. Of course, he was in discussion with Storrs, who demanded a high standard from his opponent.

I was playing for effect, watching, criticizing him. The Sherif's rebellion had been unsatisfactory for the last few months (standing still, which, with an irregular war, was the prelude to disaster); and my suspicion was that its lack was leadership: not intellect, nor judgment, nor political wisdom, but the flame of enthusiasm, that would set the desert on fire. My visit was mainly to find the yet unknown master-spirit of the affair, and measure his capacity to carry the revolt to the goal I had conceived for it. As our conversation continued, I became more and more sure that Abdulla was too balanced, too cool, too humorous to be a prophet: especially the armed prophet who, if history be true, succeeded in revolutions. His value would come perhaps in the peace after success.

Storrs brought me into the discussion by asking his views on the state of the campaign. Abdulla at once grew serious, and said that he wanted to urge upon the British their immediate and very personal concern in the matter, which he tabulated so:—

By our neglect to cut the Hejaz Railway, the Turks had been able to collect transport and supplies for the reinforcement of Medina.

Feisal had been driven back from the town; and the enemy was preparing a mobile column of all arms for an advance on Rabegh.

The Arabs in the hills across their road were by our neglect too weak in supplies, machine-guns and artillery to defend them long.

Hussein Mabeirig, chief of the Rabegh Harb, had joined the Turks. If the Medina column advanced, the Harb would join it.

It would only remain for his father to put himself at the head of his own people of Mecca, and to die fighting before the Holy City.

At this moment the telephone rang: the Grand Sherif wanted to speak to Abdulla. He was told of the point our conversation had reached, and at once confirmed that he would so act in the extremity. The Turks would enter Mecca over his dead body. The telephone rang off; and Abdulla, smiling a little, asked, to prevent such a disaster, that a British brigade, if possible of Moslem troops, be kept at Suez, with transport to rush it to Rabegh as soon as the Turks debouched from Medina in their attack. What did we think of the proposal?

I said that I would represent his views to Egypt, but that the British were reluctant to spare troops from the vital defence of Egypt (though he was not to imagine that the Canal was in any danger from the Turks) and, still more, to send Christians to defend the people of the Holy City against their enemies; as some Moslems in India, who considered the Turkish Government had an imprescriptable right to the Haramein, would misrepresent our motives and action. I thought that I might perhaps urge his opinions more powerfully if I was able to report on the Rabegh question in the light of my own knowledge of the position and local feeling. I would also like to see Feisal, and talk over with him his needs and the prospects of a prolonged defence of his hills by the tribesmen if we strengthened them materially. I would like to ride from Rabegh up the Sultani road towards Medina as far as Feisal's camp.

Storrs then came in and supported me with all his might, urging the vital importance of full and early information from a trained observer for the British Commander-in-Chief in Egypt. Abdulla went to the telephone and tried to get his father's consent to my going up country. The Sherif viewed the proposal with grave distrust. Abdulla argued the point, made some advantage, and transferred the mouthpiece to Storrs, who turned all his diplomacy on the old man. Storrs in full blast was a delight to listen to in the mere matter of Arabic speech, and also a lesson to every Englishman alive of how to deal with suspicious or unwilling Orientals. It was nearly impossible to resist him for more than a few minutes, and in this case also he had his way. The Sherif asked again for Abdulla, and authorized him to write to Ali, and suggest that if he thought fit, and if conditions were normal, I might be allowed to visit Feisal; and Abdulla, under Storrs' influence, transformed this guarded message into direct written instructions to Ali to mount me as well and as quickly as possible, and convey me, by sure hand, to Feisal's camp. This being all I wanted and half what Storrs wanted, we adjourned for lunch.

Jeddah had pleased us, on our way to the Consulate: so after lunch, when it was a little cooler, or at least when the sun was not so high, we wandered out to see the sights under guidance of Young, Wilson's assistant, a man who found good in many old things, but little good in things now being made.

It was indeed a remarkable town. The streets were alleys, wood roofed in the main bazaar, but elsewhere open to the sky in the little gap between the tops of the lofty white-walled houses. These were built four or five stories high, of coral rag tied with square beams and decorated by wide bow-windows running from ground to roof in grey wooden panels. There was no glass in Jidda, but a profusion of good lattices, and some very delicate shallow chiselling on the panels of window casings. The doors were heavy two-leaved slabs of teak-wood, deeply carved, often with wickets in them; and they had rich hinges and ring-knockers of hammered iron. There was much moulded or cut plastering, and on the older houses fine stone heads and jambs to the windows looking on the inner courts.

The style of architecture was like crazy Elizabethan half-timber work, in the elaborate Cheshire fashion, but gone gimcrack to an incredible degree. House-fronts were fretted, pierced and pargetted till they looked as though cut out of cardboard for a romantic stage-setting. Every story jutted, every window leaned one way or other; often the very walls sloped. It was like a dead city, so clean underfoot, and so quiet. Its winding, even streets were floored with damp sand solidified by time and as silent to the tread as any carpet. The lattices and wall-returns deadened all reverberation of voice. There were no carts, nor any streets wide enough for carts, no shod animals, no bustle anywhere. Everything was hushed, strained, even furtive. The doors of houses shut softly as we passed. There were no loud dogs, no crying children: indeed, except in the bazaar, still half asleep, there were few wayfarers of any kind; and the rare people we did meet, all thin, and as it were wasted by disease, with scarred, hairless faces and screwed-up eyes, slipped past us quickly and cautiously, not looking at us. Their skimp, white robes, shaven polls with little skull-caps, red cotton shoulder-shawls, and bare feet were so same as to be almost a uniform.

The atmosphere was oppressive, deadly. There seemed no life in it. It was not burning hot, but held a moisture and sense of great age and exhaustion such as seemed to belong to no other place: not a passion of smells like Smyrna, Naples or Marseilles, but a feeling of long use, of the exhalations of many people, of continued bath-heat and sweat. One would say that for years Jidda had not been swept through by a firm breeze: that its streets kept their air from year's end to year's end, from the day they were built for so long as the houses should endure. There was nothing in the bazaars to buy.

In the evening the telephone rang; and the Sherif called Storrs to the instrument. He asked if we would not like to listen to his band. Storrs, in astonishment, asked What band? and congratulated his holiness on having advanced so far towards urbanity. The Sherif explained that the headquarters of the Hejaz Command under the Turks had had a brass band, which played each night to the Governor-General; and when the Governor-General was captured by Abdulla at Taif his band was captured with him. The other pris-oners were sent to Egypt for internment; but the band was excepted. It was held in Mecca to give music to the victors. Sherif Hussein laid his receiver on the table of his reception hall, and we, called solemnly one by one to the telephone, heard the band in the Palace at Mecca forty-five miles away. Storrs expressed the general gratifi-cation; and the Sherif, increasing his bounty replied that the band should be sent down by forced march to Jidda, to play in our court-yard also, "And," said he, "you may then do me the pleasure of ringing me up from your end, that I may share your satisfaction."

Next day Storrs visited Abdulla in his tent out by Eve's Tomb; and together they inspected the hospital, the barracks, the town offices, and partook of the hospitality of the Mayor and the Governor. In the intervals of duty they talked about money, and the Sherif's title, and his relations with the other Princes of Arabia, and the general course of the war: all the commonplaces that should pass between envoys of two Governments. It was tedious, and for the most part I held myself excused, as I had made up my mind that Abdulla was not the necessary leader.

The company of Sherif Shakir, Abdulla's cousin and best friend, proved more exciting. Shakir, a grandee of Taif, had been playmate from boyhood of the Sherif's sons: and he played yet, publicly and privately, in the enormous fashion which his wealth and courage and self-confidence united to make possible. Never before had I met so sudden a man, passing instantly from a frozen dignity to a whirlwind of jesting life, strident, intense, athletic, magnificent. His face, eaten away by small-pox so that hardly a hair-root remained, mirrored like the window of a speeding car at once what passed without and within it. Abdulla had commanded at the siege of Taif: but it was Shakir who led the troops with a headlong dash that defeated its own purpose by excess of danger. The Arabs dared not support him into the very breach of the wall: and Shakir had to return, alone and unscathed, cursing his fellows, laughing at them, and jeering wildly at the discomfited enemy: whose revenge was to pour petrol over his great house, and burn it, with its famous library of Arabic manuscripts.

That evening Abdulla came to dine with Colonel Wilson. We received him in the courtyard on the house steps. Behind him were his brilliant household servants and slaves, and behind them a pale crew of bearded, emaciated men with woe-begone faces, wearing tatters of military uniform, and carrying tarnished brass instruments of music. Abdulla waved his hand towards them and crowed with delight, "My Band." We sat them on benches in the forecourt, and Wilson sent them cigarettes, while we went up to the dining-room, where the shuttered balcony was opened right out, hungrily, for a sea breeze. As we sat down, the band, under the guns and swords of Abdulla's retainers, began, each instrument apart, to play heart-broken Turkish airs. Our ears ached with noise; but Abdulla beamed.

We got tired of Turkish music, and asked for German. An aide-de-camp stepped out on the balcony and called down to the bandsmen in Turkish to play us something foreign. They struck shakily into "Deutschland über Alles" just as the Sherif came to his telephone in Mecca to listen to the music of our feast. We asked for more German music; and they played "Ein'feste Burg." Then in the midst they died away into flabby discords of drums. The parchment had stretched in the damp air of Jidda. They cried for fire; and Wilson's servants and Abdulla's bodyguard brought them piles of straw and packing cases. They warmed the drums, turning them round and round before the blaze, and then broke into what they said was the Hymn of Hate, though no one could recognize a European progression in it all. Some one turned to Abdulla and said, "It is a death march." Abdulla's eyes widened; but Storrs who spoke in quickly to the rescue turned the moment to laughter; and we sent out rewards with the leavings of the feast to the sorrowful musicians, who could take no pleasure in our praises, but begged to be sent home.

CHAPTER II

RIDING UP TO FEISAL

NEXT MORNING I left Jidda by ship for Rabegh, the headquarters of Sherif Ali, Abdulla's elder brother. When Ali received his father's "order" to send me at once up to Feisal, he was staggered, but could not help himself. So he prepared for me his own splendid riding-camel, saddled with his own saddle, and hung with luxurious housings and cushions of Nejd leather-work pieced and inlaid in various colours, with plaited fringes and nets embroidered with metal tissues. As a trustworthy man he chose out Tafas, a Hawazim Harb tribesman, with his son, to guide me to Feisal's camp.

Ali would not let me start till after sunset, lest any of his followers see me leave the camp. He kept my journey a secret even from his slaves, and gave me an Arab cloak and headcloth to wrap round myself and my uniform, that I might present a proper silhouette in the dark upon my camel. I had no food with me; so he instructed Tafas to get something to at at Bir el Sheikh, the first settlement, some sixty miles out, and charged him most stringently to keep me from questioning and curiosity on the way, and to avoid all camps and encounters.

We marched through the palm-groves which lay like a girdle about the scattered houses of Rabegh village, and then out under the stars along the Tehama, the sandy and featureless strip of desert bordering the western coast of Arabia between sea-beach and littoral hills, for hundreds of monotonous miles. In daytime this low plain was insufferably hot, and its waterless character made it a forbidding road; yet it was inevitable, since the more fruitful hills were too rugged to afford passage north and south for loaded animals.

The cool of the night was pleasant after the day of checks and discussions which had so dragged at Rabegh. Tafas led on without speaking, and the camels went silently over the soft flat sand. My thoughts as we went were how this was the Pilgrim Road, down which, for uncounted generations, the people of the north had come to visit the Holy City, bearing with them gifts of faith for the shrine; and it seemed that the Arab Revolt might be in a sense a return pilgrimage, to take back to the north, to Syria, an ideal for an ideal, a belief in liberty for their past belief in a revelation.

We endured for some hours, without variety except at times when the camels plunged and strained a little and the saddles creaked: indications that the soft plain had merged into beds of drift-sand, dotted with tiny scrub, and therefore uneven going, since the plants collected little mounds about their roots, and the eddies of the sea-winds scooped hollows in the intervening spaces. Camels appeared not sure-footed in the dark, and the starlit sand carried little shadow, so that hummocks and holes were difficult to see. Before midnight we halted, and I rolled myself tighter in my cloak, and chose a hollow of my own size and shape, and slept well in it till nearly dawn.

As soon as he felt the air growing chill with the coming change, Tafas got up, and two minutes later we were swinging forward again. An hour after and it grew bright, as we climbed a low neck of lava drowned nearly to the top with blown sand. This joined a small flow near the shore to the main Hejaz lava-field, whose western edge ran up upon our right hand, and caused the coast road to lie where it did. The neck was stony, but brief: on each side the blue lava humped itself into low shoulders, from which, so Tafas said, it was possible to see ships sailing on the sea. Pilgrims had built cairns here by the road. Sometimes they were individual piles, of just three stones set up one above the other: sometimes they were common heaps, to which any disposed passer-by might add his stone—not reasonably nor with known motive, but because others did, and perhaps they knew.

Beyond the ridge the path descended into a broad open place, the Masturah, or plain by which Wadi Fura flowed into the sea. Seaming its surface with innumerable interwoven channels of loose stone, a few inches deep, were the beds of the flood water, on those rare occasions when there was rain in the Tareif and the courses raged like rivers to the sea. The delta here was about six miles wide. Down some part of it water flowed for an hour or two, or even for a day or two, every so many years. Underground there was plenty of moisture, protected by the overlying sand from the sun-heat; and thorn trees and loose scrub profited by it and flourished. Some of the trunks were a foot through: their height might be twenty feet. The trees and bushes stood somewhat apart, in clusters, their lower branches cropped by the hungry camels. So they looked cared for, and had a premeditated air, which felt strange in the wilderness, more especially as the Tehama hitherto had been a sober bareness.

In the early sunlight we lifted our camels to a steady trot across the good going of these shingle-beds among the trees, making for Masturah well, the first stage out from Rabegh on the pilgrim road. There we would water and halt a little. My camel was a delight to me, for I had not been on such an animal before. There were no good camels in Egypt; and those of the Sinai Desert, while hardy and strong, were not taught to pace fair and softly and swiftly, like these rich mounts of the Arabian princes.

Yet her accomplishments were to-day largely wasted, since they were reserved for riders who had the knack and asked for them, and not for me, who expected to be carried, and had no sense of how to ride. It was easy to sit on a camel's back without falling off, but very difficult to understand and get the best out of her so as to do long journeys without fatiguing either rider or beast. Tafas gave me hints as we went: indeed, it was one of the few subjects on which he would speak. His orders to preserve me from contact with the world seemed to have closed even his mouth. A pity, for his dialect interested me.

Quite close to the north bank of the Masturah, we found the well. Beside it were some decayed stone walls which had been a hut, and opposite it some little shelters of branches and palm-leaves, under which a few Beduin were sitting. We did not greet them. Instead, Tafas turned across to the ruinous walls, and dismounted; and I sat in their shade while he and Abdulla watered the animals, and drew a drink for themselves and for me. The well was old, and broad, with good stone steyning, and a strong coping round the top. It was about twenty feet deep; and for the convenience of travellers without ropes, like ourselves, a square chimney had been contrived in the masonry, with foot and hand holds in the corners, so that a man might descend to the water, and fill his goat-skin.

Idle hands had flung so many stones down the shaft, that half the bottom of the well was choked, and the water not abundant. Abdulla tied his flowing sleeves about his shoulders; tucked his gown under his cartridge belt; and clambered nimbly down and up, bringing each time four or five gallons which he poured for our camels into a stone trough beside the well. They drank about five gallons each, for they had been watered at Rabegh a day back. Then we let them moon about a little, while we sat in peace, breathing the light wind coming off the sea. Abdulla smoked a cigarette as reward for his exertions.

Some Harb came up, driving a large herd of brood camels, and began to water them, having sent one man down the well to fill their large leather bucket, which the others drew up hand over hand with a loud staccato chant.

As we watched them two riders, trotting light and fast on thoroughbred camels, drew towards us from the north. Both were young.

One was dressed in rich Cashmere robes and heavy silk embroidered headcloth. The other was plainer, in white cotton, with a red cotton head-dress. They halted beside the well; and the more splendid one slipped gracefully to the ground without kneeling his camel, and threw his halter to his companion, saying, carelessly, "Water them while I go over there and rest." Then he strolled across and sat down under our wall, after glancing at us with affected unconcern. He offered a cigarette, just rolled and licked, saying, "Your presence is from Syria?" I parried politely, suggesting that he was from Mecca, to which he likewise made no direct reply. We spoke a little of the war and of the leanness of the Harb she-camels.

Meanwhile the other rider stood by, vacantly holding the halters, waiting perhaps for the Harb to finish watering their herd before taking his turn. The young lord cried, "What is it, Mustafa? Water them at once." The servant came up to say dismally, "They will not let me." "God's mercy!" shouted his master furiously, as he scrambled to his feet and hit the unfortunate Mustafa three or four sharp blows about the head and shoulders with his riding-stick. "Go and ask them." Mustafa looked hurt, astonished, and angry as though he would hit back, but thought better of it, and ran to the well.

The Harb, shocked, in pity made a place for him, and let his two camels drink from their water-trough. They whispered, "Who is he?" and Mustafa said, "Our Lord's cousin from Mecca." At once they ran and untied a bundle from one of their saddles, and spread from it before the two riding camels fodder of the green leaves and buds of the thorn trees. They were used to gather this by striking the low bushes with a heavy staff, till the broken tips of the branches rained down on a cloth stretched over the ground beneath.

The young Sherif watched them contentedly. When his camel had fed, he climbed slowly and without apparent effort up its neck into the saddle, where he settled himself leisurely, and took an unctuous farewell of us, asking God to requite the Arabs bountifully. They wished him a good journey; and he started southward, while Abdulla brought our camels, and we went off northward. Ten minutes later I heard a chuckle from old Tafas, and saw wrinkles of delight between his grizzled beard and moustache.

"What is upon you, Tafas?" said I.

"My Lord, you saw those two riders at the well?"

"The Sherif and his servant?"

"Yes; but they were Sherif Ali ibn el Hussein of Modhig, and his cousin, Sherif Mohsin, lords of the Harith, who are blood enemies of the Masruh. They feared they would be delayed or driven off the water if the Arabs knew them. So they pretended to be master and servant from Mecca. Did you see how Mohsin raged when Ali beat him? Ali is a devil. While only eleven years old he escaped from his father's house to his uncle, a robber of pilgrims by trade; and with him he lived by his hands for many months, till his father caught him. He was with our lord Feisal from the first day's battle in Medina, and led the Ateiba in the plains round Aar and Bir Derwish. It was all camel-fighting; and Ali would have no man with him who could not do as he did, run beside his camel, and leap with one hand into the saddle, carrying his rifle. The children of Harith are children of battle." For the first time the old man's mouth was full of words.

While he spoke we scoured along the dazzling plain, now nearly bare of trees, and turning slowly softer under foot. At first it had been grey shingle, packed like gravel. Then the sand increased and the stones grew rarer, till we could distinguish the colours of the separate flakes, porphyry, green schist, basalt. At last it was nearly pure white sand, under which lay a harder stratum. Such going was like a pile-carpet for our camels' running. The particles of sand were clean and polished, and caught the blaze of sun like little diamonds in a reflection so fierce, that after a while I could not endure it. I frowned hard, and pulled the head-cloth forward in a peak over my eyes, and beneath them, too, like a beaver, trying to shut out the heat which rose in glassy waves off the ground, and beat up against my face. Eighty miles in front of us, the huge peak of Rudhwa behind

SIR A. H. MCMAHON, *High Commissioner in Egypt*

Yenbo was looming and fading in the dazzle of vapour which hid its foot. Quite near in the plain little shapeless hills seemed to block the way. To our right the steep ridge of Beni Ayub, toothed and narrow like a saw-blade, fell away on the north into a blue series of smaller hills, soft in character, behind which lofty range after range in a jagged stairway, red now the sun grew low, climbed up to the towering central mass of Jebel Subh with its fantastic granite spires.

A little later we turned to the right, off the pilgrim road, and took a short cut across gradually rising ground of flat basalt ridges, buried in sand till only their topmost piles showed above the surface.

Along this we held our way till sunset, when we came into sight of the hamlet of Bir el Sheikh. In the first dark as the supper fires were lighted we rode down its wide open street and halted. Tafas went into one of the twenty miserable huts, and in a few whispered words and long silences bought flour, of which with water he kneaded a dough cake two inches thick and eight inches across. This he buried in the ashes of a brushwood fire, provided for him by a Subh woman whom he seemed to know. When the cake was warmed he drew it out of the fire, and clapped it to shake off the dust: then we shared it together, while Abdulla went away to buy himself tobacco.

They told me the place had two stone-lined wells at the bottom of the southward slope, but I felt disinclined to go and look at them, for the long ride that day had tired my unaccustomed muscles, and the heat of the plain had been painful. My skin was blistered by it, and my eyes ached with the glare of light striking up at a sharp angle from the silver sand, and from the shining pebbles. The last two years I had spent in Cairo, at a desk all day or thinking hard in a little overcrowded office full of distracting noises, with a hundred rushing things to say, but no bodily need except to come and go each day between office and hotel. In consequence the novelty of this change was severe, since time had not been given me gradually to accustom myself to the pestilent beating of the Arabian sun, and the long monotony of camel pacing. There was to be another stage to-night, and a long day to-morrow before Feisal's camp would be reached.

So I was grateful for the cooking and the marketing, which spent one hour, and for the second hour of rest after it which we took by common consent; and sorry when it ended, and we remounted, and rode in pitch darkness up valleys and down valleys, passing in and out of bands of air, which were hot in the confined hollows, but fresh and stirring in the open places. The ground under foot must have been sandy, because the silence of our passage hurt my straining ears, and smooth, for I was always falling asleep in the saddle, to wake a few seconds later suddenly and sickeningly, as I clutched by instinct at the saddle post to recover my balance which had been thrown out by some irregular stride of the animal. It was too dark, and the forms of the country were too neutral, to hold my heavy-lashed, peering eyes. At length we stopped for good, long after midnight; and I was rolled up in my cloak and asleep in a most comfortable little sand-grave before Tafas had done knee-haltering my camel.

Three hours later we were on the move again, helped now by the last shining of the moon. We marched down Wadi Mared, the night of it dead, hot, silent, and on each side sharp-pointed hills standing up black and white in the exhausted air. There were many trees. Dawn finally came to us as we passed out of the narrows into a broad place, over whose flat floor an uneasy wind span circles, capriciously, in the dust. The day strengthened always, and now showed Bir ibn Hassani just to our right. The trim settlement of absurd little houses, brown and white, holding together for security's sake, looked doll-like and more lonely than the desert, in the immense shadow of the dark precipice of Subh, behind. While we watched it, hoping to see life at its doors, the sun was rushing up, and the fretted cliffs, those thousands of feet above our heads, became outlined in hard refracted shafts of white light against a sky still sallow with the transient dawn.

We rode on across the great valley. A camel-rider, garrulous and old, came out from the houses and jogged over to join us. He named himself Khallaf, too friendly-like. His salutation came after a pause in a trite stream of chat; and when it was returned he tried to force us into conversation. However, Tafas grudged his company, and gave him short answers. Khallaf persisted, and finally, to improve his footing, bent down and burrowed in his saddle pouch till he found a small covered pot of enamelled iron, containing a liberal portion of the staple of travel in the Hejaz. This was the unleavened dough cake of yesterday, but crumbled between the fingers while still warm, and moistened with liquid butter till its particles would fall apart only reluctantly. It was then sweetened for eating with ground sugar, and scooped up like damp sawdust in pressed pellets with the fingers.

I ate a little, on this my first attempt, while Tafas and Abdulla played at it vigorously; so for his bounty Khallaf went half-hungry: deservedly, for it was thought effeminate by the Arabs to carry a provision of food for a little journey of one hundred miles. We were now fellows, and the chat began again while Khallaf told us about the last fighting, and a reverse Feisal had had the day before. It seemed he had been beaten out of the head of Wadi Safra, and was now at Hamra, only a little way in front of us; or at least Khallaf thought he was there: we might learn for sure in the next village on our road. The fighting had not been severe; but the few casualties were all among the tribesmen of Tafas and Khallaf; and the names and hurts of each were told in order.

We rode seven miles, to a low watershed, crossed by a wall of granite slivers, now little more than a shapeless heap, but once no doubt a barrier. It ran from cliff to cliff, and even far up the hill-sides, wherever the slopes were not too steep to climb. In the centre, where the road passed, had been two small enclosures like pounds. I asked Khallaf the purpose of the wall. He replied that he had been in Damascus and Constantinople and Cairo, and had many friends among the great men of Egypt. Did I know any of the English there? Khallaf seemed curious about my intentions and my history. He tried to trip me in Egyptian phrases. When I answered in the dialect of Aleppo he spoke of prominent Syrians of his acquaintance. I knew them, too; and he switched off into local politics, asking care-ful questions, delicately and indirectly, about the Sherif and his sons, and what I thought Feisal was going to do. I understood less of this than he, and parried inconsequentially. Tafas came to my rescue, and changed the subject. Afterwards we knew that Khallaf was in

Turkish pay, and used to send frequent reports of what came past Bir ibn Hassani for the Arab forces.

We turned to the right, across another saddle, and then down-hill for a few miles to a corner of tall cliffs. We rounded this and found ourselves suddenly in Wadi Safra, the valley of our seeking, and in the midst of Wasta, its largest village. Wasta seemed to be many nests of houses, clinging to the hill-sides each side the tor-rent-bed on banks of alluvial soil, or standing on detritus islands between the various deep-swept channels whose sum made up the parent valley.

Riding between two or three of these built-up islands, we made for the far bank of the valley. On our way was the main bed of the winter floods, a sweep of white shingle and boulders, quite flat. Down its middle, from palm-grove on the one side to palm-grove on the other, lay a reach of clear water, perhaps two hundred yards long and twelve feet wide, sand-bottomed, and bordered on each brink by a ten-foot lawn of thick grass and flowers. On it we halted a moment to let our camels put their heads down and drink their fill, and the relief of the grass to our eyes after the day-long hard glitter of the pebbles was so sudden that involuntarily I glanced up to see if a cloud had not covered the face of the sun.

We rode up the stream to the garden from which it ran sparkling in a stone-lined channel; and then we turned along the mud wall of the garden in the shadow of its palms, to another of the detached hamlets. Tafas led the way up its little street (the houses were so low that from our saddles we looked down upon their clay roofs), and near one of the larger houses stopped and beat upon the door of an uncovered court. A slave opened to us, and we dismounted in pri-vacy. Tafas haltered the camels, loosed their girths, and strewed before them green fodder from a fragrant pile beside the gate. Then he led me into the guest room of the house, a dark clean little mud-brick place, roofed with half palm-logs under hammered earth. We sat down on the palm-leaf mat which ran along the dais. The day in this stifling valley had grown very hot; and gradually we lay back side by side. Then the hum of the bees in the gardens without, and of the flies hovering over our veiled faces within, lulled us into sleep.

Before we awoke, a meal of bread and dates had been prepared for us by the people of the house. The dates were new, meltingly sweet and good, like none I had ever tasted. Afterwards we mounted again, and rode up the clear, slow rivulet till it was hidden within the palm-gardens, behind their low boundary walls of sun-dried clay. In and out between the tree roots were dug little canals a foot or two deep, so contrived that the stream might be let into them from the stone channel, and each tree watered in its turn. The head of water was owned by the community, and shared out among the landowners for so many minutes or hours daily or weekly according to the traditional use. The water was a little brackish, as was needful for the best palms; but it was sweet enough in the wells of private water in the groves. These wells were very frequent, and found water three or four feet below the surface.

Our way took us through the central village and its market street. There was little in the shops; and all the place felt decayed. A generation ago Wasta was populous (they said by a thousand houses); but one day there rolled a huge wall of water down Wadi Safra, the embankments of many palm gardens were breached, and the palm trees swept away. Some of the islands on which houses had stood for centuries were submerged, and the mud houses melted back again into mud, killing or drowning the unfortunate slaves within. The men could have been replaced, and the trees, had the soil remained; but the gardens had been built up of earth carefully won from the normal freshets by years of labour, and this wave of water— eight feet deep, running in a race for three days—reduced the plots in its track to their primordial banks of stones.

A little above Wasta the valley widened somewhat, to an average of perhaps four hundred yards, with a bed of fine shingle and sand, laid very smooth by the winter rains. The walls were of bare red and black rock, whose edges and ridges were sharp as knife blades, and reflected the sun like metal. They made the freshness of the trees and grass seem luxurious. We now saw parties of Feisal's soldiers, and grazing herds of their saddle camels. Before we reached Hamra every nook in the rocks or clump of trees was a bivouac. They cried cheery greetings to Tafas, who came to life again, waving back and calling to them, while he pressed on quickly to end his duty towards me.

Hamra opened on our left. It seemed a village of about one hundred houses, buried in gardens among mounds of earth some twenty feet in height. We forded a little stream, and went up a walled path between trees to the top of one of these mounds, where we made our camels kneel by the yard-gate of a long, low house. Tafas said something to a slave who stood there with silver-hilted sword in hand. He led me to an inner court, on whose further side, framed between the uprights of a black doorway, stood a white figure waiting tensely for me. I felt at first glance that this was the man I had come to Arabia to seek—the leader who would bring the Arab Revolt to full glory. Feisal looked very tall and pillar-like, very slender, in his long white silk robes and his brown headcloth bound with a brilliant scarlet and gold cord. His eyelids were dropped; and his black beard and colourless face were like a mask against the strange, still watchfulness of his body. His hands were crossed in front of him on his dagger.

I greeted him. He made way for me into the room, and sat down on his carpet near the door. As my eyes grew accustomed to the shade, they saw that the little room held many silent figures, looking at me or at Feisal steadily. He remained staring down at his hands, which were twisting slowly about his dagger. At last he inquired softly how I had found the journey. I spoke of the heat, and he asked how long from Rabegh, commenting that I had ridden fast for the season.

"And do you like our place here in Wadi Safra?"

"Well; but it is far from Damascus."

The word had fallen like a sword into their midst. There was a quiver. Then everybody present stiffened where he sat, and held his breath for a silent minute. Some, perhaps, were dreaming of far off success: others may have thought it a reflection on their late defeat. Feisal at length lifted his eyes, smiling at me, and said, "Praise be to God, there are Turks nearer us than that." We all smiled with him; and I rose and excused myself for the moment.

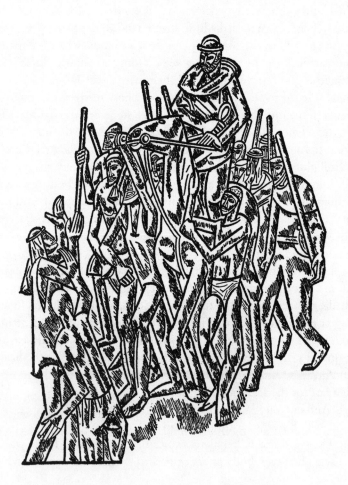

CHAPTER III

FEISAL AND HIS LEVIES

UNDER TALL arcades of palms with ribbed and groined branches, in a soft meadow, I found the trim camp of Egyptian Army soldiers with Nafi Bey, their Egyptian major, sent lately from the Sudan by Sir Reginald Wingate to help the Arab rebellion. They comprised a mountain battery and some machine-guns. Nafi himself was an amiable fellow, kind and hospitable to me.

Feisal was announced with Maulud el Mukhlus, the Arab zealot of Tekrit, who, for rampant nationalism, had been twice degraded in the Turkish Army, and had spent an exile of two years in Nejd as a secretary with ibn Rashid. He had commanded the Turkish cavalry before Shaiba, and had been taken by us there. As soon as he heard of the rebellion of the Sherif he had volunteered for him, and had been the first regular officer to join Feisal. He was now nominally his A.D.C.

Bitterly he complained that they were in every way ill-equipped. This was the main cause of their present plight. They got thirty thousand pounds a month from the Sherif, but little flour and rice, little barley, few rifles, insufficient ammunition, no machine-guns, no mountain guns, no technical help, no information.

I stopped Maulud there and said that my coming was expressly to learn what they lacked and to report it, but that I could work with them only if they would explain to me their general situation. Feisal agreed, and began to sketch to me the history of their revolt from its absolute beginning.

The first rush on Medina had been a desperate business. The Arabs were ill-armed and short of ammunition, the Turks in great force. At the height of the crisis the Beni Ali broke; and the Arabs were thrust out beyond the walls. The Turks then opened fire on them with their artillery; and the Arabs, unused to this new arm, became terrified. The Ageyl and Ateiba got into safety and refused to move out again.

Sections of Beni Ali tribesmen approached the Turkish command with an offer to surrender, if their villages were spared. Fakhri played with them, and in the ensuing lull of hostilities surrounded the Awali suburb with his troops: whom suddenly he ordered to carry it by assault and to massacre every living thing within its walls. Hundreds of the inhabitants were raped and butchered, the houses fired, and living and dead alike thrown back into the flames. Fakhri and his men had served together and had learned the arts of both the slow and the fast kill upon the Armenians in the North.

This bitter taste of the Turkish mode of war sent a shock across Arabia; for the first rule of Arab war was that women were inviolable: the second that the lives and honour of children too young to fight with men were to be spared: the third, that property impossible to carry off should be left undamaged. The Arabs with Feisal perceived that they were opposed to new customs, and fell back out of touch to gain time to readjust themselves. There could no longer be any question of submission: the sack of Awali had opened blood-feud upon blood-feud, and put on them the duty of fighting to the end of their force: but it was plain now that it would be a long affair, and that with muzzle-loading guns for sole weapons, they could hardly expect to win.

So they fell back from the level plains about Medina into the hills where they rested, while Ali and Feisal sent messenger after messenger down to Rabegh, their sea-base, to learn when fresh stores and money and arms might be expected. The revolt had begun haphazard, on their father's explicit orders, and the old man, too independent to take his sons into his full confidence, had not worked out with them any arrangements for prolonging it. So the reply was only a little food. Later some Japanese rifles, most of them broken, were received. Such barrels as were still whole were so foul that the too-eager Arabs burst them on the first trial. No money was sent up at all: to take its place Feisal filled a decent chest with stones, had it locked and corded carefully, guarded on each daily march by his own slaves, and introduced meticulously into his tent each night. By such theatricals the brothers tried to hold a melting force.

At last Ali went down to Rabegh to inquire what was wrong with the organization. He found that Hussein Mabeirig, the local chief, had made up his mind that the Turks would be victorious (he had tried conclusions with them twice himself and had the worst of it), and accordingly decided theirs was the best cause to follow. As the stores for the Sherif were landed by the British he appropriated them and stored them away secretly in his own houses. Ali made a demonstration, and sent urgent messages for his half-brother Zeid to join him from Jidda with reinforcements. Hussein, in fear, slipped off to the hills, an outlaw. The two Sherifs took possession of his villages. In them they found great stores of arms, and food enough for their armies for a month. The temptation of a spell of leisured ease was too much for them: they settled down in Rabegh.

This left Feisal alone up country, and he soon found himself isolated, in a hollow situation, driven to depend upon his native resources. He bore it for a time, but in August took advantage of the visit of Colonel Wilson to the newly-conquered Yenbo, to come down and give a full explanation of his urgent needs. Wilson was impressed with him and his story, and at once promised him a battery of mountain guns and some maxims, to be handled by men

and officers of the Egyptian Army garrison in the Sudan. This
explained the presence of Nafi Bey and his units.

The Arabs rejoiced when they came, and believed they were now
equals of the Turk; but the four guns were twenty-year-old
Krupps, with a range of only three thousand yards; and their crews
were not eager enough in brain and spirit for irregular fighting.
However, they went forward with the mob and drove in the Turkish outposts, and then their supports, until Fakhri becoming seriously
alarmed, came down himself, inspected the front, and at once reinforced the threatened detachment at Bir Abbas to some three thousand
strong. The Turks had field guns and howitzers with them, and the
added advantage of high ground for observation. They began to
worry the Arabs by indirect fire, and nearly dropped a shell on Feisal's
tent while all the head men were conferring within. The Egyptian
gunners were asked to return the fire and smother the enemy guns.
They had to plead that their weapons were useless, since they could
not carry the nine thousand yards. They were derided; and the Arabs
ran back again into the defiles.

Feisal was deeply discouraged. His men were tired. He had lost
many of them. His only effective tactics against the enemy had been
to chase in suddenly upon their rear by fast mounted charges, and
many camels had been killed, or wounded or worn out in these
expensive measures. He demurred to carrying the whole war upon
his own neck while Abdulla delayed in Mecca, and Ali and Zeid at
Rabegh. Finally he withdrew the bulk of his forces, leaving the Harb
sub-tribes to keep up pressure on the Turkish supply columns and
communications by a repeated series of such raids as those which
he himself found impossible to maintain.

Yet he had no fear that the Turks would again come forward
against him suddenly. His failure to make any impression on them
had not imbued him with the smallest respect for them. His late
retirement to Hamra was not forced: it was a gesture of disgust,
because he was bored by his obvious impotence, and was determined for a little while to have the dignity of rest.

I asked Feisal what his plans were now. He said that till Medina fell they were inevitably tied down there in Hejaz dancing to Fakhri's tune. In his opinion the Turks were aiming at the recapture of Mecca. The bulk of their strength was now in a mobile column, which they could move towards Rabegh by a choice of routes which kept the Arabs in constant alarm. A passive defence of the Subh hills had shown that the Arabs did not shine as passive resisters. When the enemy moved they must be countered by an offensive.

Maulud, who had sat fidgeting through our long, slow talk, could no longer restrain himself and cried out, "Don't write a history of us. The needful thing is to fight and fight and kill them. Give me a battery of Schneider mountain guns, and machine-guns, and I will finish this off for you. We talk and talk and do nothing." I replied as warmly; and Maulud, a magnificent fighter, who regarded a battle won as a battle wasted if he did not show some wound to prove his part in it, took me up. We wrangled while Feisal sat by and grinned delightedly at us.

This talk had been for him a holiday. He was encouraged even by the trifle of my coming; for he was a man of moods, flickering between glory and despair, and just now dead-tired. He looked years older than thirty-one; and his dark, appealing eyes, set a little sloping in his face, were bloodshot, and his hollow cheeks deeply lined and puckered with reflection. His nature grudged thinking, for it crippled his speed in action: the labour of it shrivelled his features into swift lines of pain. In appearance he was tall, graceful and vigorous, with the most beautiful gait, and a royal dignity of head and shoulders. Of course he knew it, and a great part of his public expression was by sign and gesture.

His movements were impetuous. He showed himself hot-tempered and sensitive, even unreasonable, and he ran off soon on tangents. Appetite and physical weakness were mated in him, with the spur of courage. His personal charm, his imprudence, the pathetic hint of frailty as the sole reserve of this proud character made him the idol of his followers. One never asked if he were scrupulous; but

later he showed that he could return trust for trust, suspicion for
suspicion. He was fuller of wit than of humour.

His training in Abdul Hamid's entourage had made him past-
master in diplomacy. His military service with the Turks had given
him a working knowledge of tactics. His life in Constantinople and
in the Turkish Parliament had made him familiar with European
questions and manners. He was a careful judge of men. If he had
the strength to realize his dreams he would go very far, for he was
wrapped up in his work and lived for nothing else; but the fear was
that he would wear himself out by trying to seem to aim always a
little higher than the truth, or that he would die of too much action.
His men told me how, after a long spell of fighting, in which he had
to guard himself, and lead the charges, and control and encourage
them, he had collapsed physically and was carried away from his
victory, unconscious, with the foam flecking his lips.

Meanwhile, here, as it seemed, was offered to our hand, which
had only to be big enough to take it, a prophet who, if veiled, would
give cogent form to the idea behind the activity of the Arab revolt.
It was all and more than we had hoped for, much more than our
halting course deserved. The aim of my trip was fulfilled.

My duty was now to take the shortest road to Egypt with the
news: and the knowledge gained that evening in the palm wood
grew and blossomed in my mind into a thousand branches, laden
with fruit and shady leaves, beneath which I sat and half-listened
and saw visions, while the twilight deepened, and the night; until
a line of slaves with lamps came down the winding paths between
the palm trunks, and with Feisal and Maulud we walked back
through the gardens to the little house, with its courts still full of
waiting people, and to the hot inner room in which the familiars
were assembled; and there we sat down together to the smoking
bowl of rice and meat set upon the food-carpet for our supper by
the slaves.

Next morning I was up early and out among Feisal's troops
towards the side of Kheif, by myself, trying to feel the pulse of their

opinions in a moment. Time was of the essence of my effort, for it was necessary to gain in ten days the impressions which would ordinarily have been the fruit of weeks of observing in my crab-fashion, that sideways-slipping affair of the senses. Normally I would go along all day, with the sounds immediate, but blind to every detail, only generally aware that there were things red, or things grey, or clear things about me. To-day my eyes had to be switched straight to my brain, that I might note a thing or two the more clearly by contrast with the former mistiness. Such things were nearly always shapes: rocks and trees, or men's bodies in repose or movement: not small things like flowers, nor qualities like colour.

Yet here was strong need of a lively reporter. In this drab war the least irregularity was a joy to all, and McMahon's strongest course was to exploit the latent imagination of the General Staff. I believed in the Arab movement, and was confident, before ever I came, that in it was the idea to tear Turkey into pieces; but others in Egypt lacked faith, and had been taught nothing intelligent of the Arabs in the field. By noting down something of the spirit of these romantics in the hills about the Holy Cities I might gain the sympathy of Cairo for the further measures necessary to help them.

The men received me cheerfully. Beneath every great rock or bush they sprawled like lazy scorpions, resting from the heat, and refreshing their brown limbs with the early coolness of the shaded stone. Because of my khaki they took me for a Turk-trained officer who had deserted to them, and were profuse in good-humoured but ghastly suggestions of how they should treat me.

They were in wild spirits, shouting that the war might last ten years. It was the fattest time the hills had ever known. The Sherif was feeding not only the fighting men, but their families, and paying two pounds a month for a man, four for a camel. Nothing else would have performed the miracle of keeping a tribal army in the field for five months on end.

The actual contingents were continually shifting, in obedience to the rule of flesh. A family would own a rifle, and the sons serve in turn for a few days each. Married men alternated between camp and wife, and sometimes a whole clan would become bored and take a rest. Feisal's eight thousand men were one in ten camel-corps and the rest hill-men. They served only under their tribal sheikhs, and near home, arranging their own food and transport.

Blood feuds were nominally healed, and really suspended in the Sherifian area: Billi and Juheina, Ateiba and Ageyl living and fighting side by side in Feisal's army. All the same, the members of one tribe were shy of those of another, and within the tribe no man would quite trust his neighbour. Each might be, usually was, whole-hearted against the Turk, but perhaps not quite to the point of failing to work off a family grudge upon a family enemy in the field.

Their acquisitive recklessness made them keen on booty, and whetted them to tear up railways, plunder caravans, and steal camels; but they were too free-minded to endure command, or to fight in team. A man who could fight well by himself made generally a bad soldier, and these champions seemed to me no material for our drilling; but if we strengthened them by light automatic guns of the Lewis type, to be handled by themselves, they might be capable of holding their hills.

The Hejaz war was the fight of a rocky, mountainous, barren country (reinforced by a wild horde of mountaineers) against an enemy so enriched in equipment by the Germans as almost to have lost virtue for rough-and-tumble war. The hill-belt was a paradise for snipers. The valleys, which were the only practicable roads, for miles and miles were not so much valleys as chasms or gorges, sometimes two hundred yard across, but sometimes only twenty, full of twists and turns, one thousand or four thousand feet deep, barren of cover, and flanked each side by pitiless granite, basalt and porphyry, not in polished slopes, but serrated and split and piled up in thousands of jagged heaps of fragments as hard as metal and nearly as sharp.

It seemed to my unaccustomed eyes impossible that, without treachery on the part of the mountain tribes, the Turks could dare to break their way through.

The sole disquieting feature was the very real success of the Turks in frightening the Arabs by artillery. The sound of a fired cannon sent every man within earshot behind cover. They thought weapons destructive in proportion to their noise. They were not afraid of bullets, nor indeed overmuch of dying: just the manner of death by shell-fire was unendurable. It seemed to me that their moral confidence was to be restored only by having guns, useful or useless, but noisy, on their side. From the magnificent Feisal down to the most naked stripling in the army the theme was artillery, artillery, artillery.

At these close quarters the bigness of the revolt impressed me. This well-peopled province had suddenly changed its character from a rout of casual nomad pilferers to an eruption against Turkey, fighting her, not certainly in our manner, but fiercely enough, in spite of the religion which was to raise the East against us in a holy war. There was among the tribes in the fighting zone a nervous enthusiasm common, I suppose, to all national risings, but strangely disquieting to one from a land so long delivered that national freedom had become like the water in our mouths, tasteless.

Later I saw Feisal again, and promised to do my best for him. My chiefs would arrange a base at Yenbo, where the stores and supplies he needed would be put ashore for his exclusive use. We would try to get him officer-volunteers from among the prisoners of war captured in Mesopotamia or on the Canal. We would form gun crews and machine-gun crews from the rank and file in the internment camps, and provide them with such mountain guns and light machine-guns as were obtainable in Egypt. Lastly, I would advise that British Army officers, professionals, be sent down to act as advisers and liaison officers with him in the field.

This time our talk was of the pleasantest, and ended in warm thanks from him, and an invitation to return as soon as might be. I explained that my duties in Cairo excluded field work, but perhaps my chiefs would let me pay a second visit later on, when his present wants were filled and his movement was going forward prosperously.

Meanwhile I would ask him for facilities to return to the coast, for Egypt.

Feisal's care gave me an escort of local Sherifs, who guided me to Yenbo, through other miles of stark hills, with the hair lines of irrigated valleys threading their barrenness. Yenbo, a village Jeddah, proved hospitable. Its governor, a Javanese from Mecca, fed me and lodged me for many days till the *Suva*, Captain Boyle, put in to harbour, and granted me passage down the coast. "Granted me": for I was in a very soiled condition after days of riding light, and I had a native head-cloth on my head: and to the Royal Navy all native things seemed crapulous. Boyle, as the senior naval officer in the Red Sea, should have been the exemplar of his type, but he sat on the shadow side of his bridge, reading Bryce's *American Constitution* too intently to spare me more than fourteen words a day.

In Jidda was the *Euryalus*, with Admiral Wemyss, bound for Port Sudan that he might visit Sir Reginald Wingate at Khartoum. Sir Reginald, as Sirdar of the Egyptian Army, had been put in command of the British military side of the Arab adventure; and it was necessary for me to impart my impressions to him. So I begged the Admiral for a passage over sea, and a place in his train to Khartoum. This he readily granted, after cross-questioning me himself at length.

I found that his active mind and broad intelligence had engaged his interest in the Arab Revolt from the beginning. He had come down again and again in his flagship to lend a hand when things were critical, and had gone out of his way twenty times to help the shore, which properly was Army business. He had given the Arabs guns and machine-guns, landing parties and technical help, with unlimited transport and naval co-operation, always making a real pleasure of requests, and fulfilling them in overflowing measure.

Khartoum felt cool after Arabia, and nerved me to show Sir Reginald Wingate my long reports, in which I urged that the situation seemed full of promise. The main need was skilled assistance; and the campaign should go prosperously if some regular British

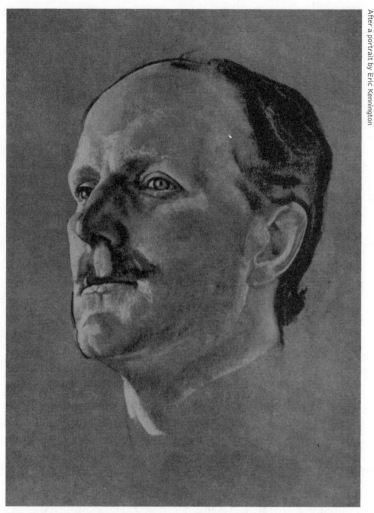

After a portrait by Eric Kennington

SIR RONALD STORRS, *Governor of Jerusalem, Governor of Cyprus*

officers, professionally competent and speaking Arabic, were attached
to the Arab leaders as technical advisers, to keep us in proper touch.

Wingate was glad to hear a hopeful view. The Arab Revolt had been his dream for years. So after two or three days in Khartoum, I went down towards Cairo, feeling that the responsible person had accepted all my news. The Nile trip became a holiday.

CHAPTER IV

CHECKS AROUND YENBO

AFTER I had been a few days in Cairo, my chief, General Clayton, told me to return to Arabia and Feisal. This being much against my grain I urged my complete unfitness for the job: said I hated responsibility—obviously the position of a conscientious adviser would be responsible—and that in all my life objects had been gladder to me than persons, and ideas than objects. So the duty of succeeding with men, of disposing them to any purpose, would be doubly hard to me. I was unlike a soldier: hated soldiering: whereas the Sirdar had telegraphed to London for certain regular officers competent to direct the Arab war.

Clayton replied that they might be months arriving, and meanwhile Feisal must be linked to us, and his needs promptly notified to Egypt. So I had to go; leaving to others the Arab Bulletin I had founded, the maps I wished to draw, and the file of the war-changes of the Turkish Army, all fascinating activities in which my training helped me; to take up a rôle for which I felt no inclination. As our revolt succeeded, onlookers have praised its leadership: but behind the scenes lay all the vices of amateur control, experimental councils, divisions, whimsicality.

My journey was to Yenbo, now the special base of Feisal's army. As I was starting thence up country to visit Feisal again, news came in of a Turkish repulse. A reconnaissance of their cavalry and camel corps had been pushed too far into the hills, and the Arabs had caught it and scattered it. So I made a happy start with my sponsor for the journey, Sherif Abd el Kerim. With him were three or four of his men, all well mounted; and we had a rapid journey, for Abd el Kerim was a famous rider who took pride in covering his stages at three times the normal speed. It was not my camel, and the weather was cool and clouded, with a taste of rain. So I had no objection.

After starting, we cantered for three unbroken hours. That had shaken down our bellies far enough for us to hold more food, and we stopped and ate bread and drank coffee till sunset, while Abd el Kerim rolled about his carpet in a dog-fight with one of the men. When he was exhausted he sat up; and they told stories and japed, till they were breathed enough to get up and dance. Everything was very free, very good-tempered, and not at all dignified.

When we re-started, an hour's mad race in the dusk brought us to the foot of a low range. We crossed it, going up a narrow, winding, sandy valley. Because this had run in flood a few days earlier, the going was firm for our panting camels; but the ascent was steep and we had to take it at walking pace. This pleased me, but so angered Abd el Kerim, that when, in a short hour, we reached the water-shed he thrust his mount forward again and led us at breakneck speed down hill in the yielding night (a fair road, fortunately, with sand and pebbles underfoot) for half an hour, when the land flattened out, and we came to the outlying plantations of Nakhl Mubarak, chief date-gardens of the southern Juheina.

As we got near we saw through the palm trees flame, and the flame-lit smoke of many fires, while the hollow ground re-echoed with the roaring of thousands of excited camels, and volleying of shots or shoutings in the darkness of lost men, who sought through the crowd to rejoin their friends. As we had heard in Yenbo that the Nekhl were deserted, this tumult meant something strange, perhaps hostile. We crept quietly past an end of the grove and along a narrow street between man-high mud walls, to a silent group of houses. Abd el Kerim forced the courtyard door of the first on our left, led the camels within, and hobbled them down by the walls that they might remain unseen. Then he slipped a cartridge into the breech of his rifle and stole off on tiptoe down the street towards the noise to find out what was happening. We waited for him, the sweat of the ride slowly drying in our clothes as we sat there in the chill night, watching.

He came back after half an hour to say that Feisal with his camel corps had just arrived, and we were to go down and join him. So we led the camels out and mounted; and rode in file down another lane on a bank between houses, with a sunk garden of palms on our right. Its end was filled with a solid crowd of Arabs and camels, mixed together in the wildest confusion, and all crying aloud. We pressed through them, and down a ramp suddenly into the bed of the Wadi Yenbo, a broad, open space: how broad could only be guessed from the irregular lines of watchfires glimmering over it to a great distance. Also it was very damp; with slime, the relic of a shallow flood two days before, yet covering its stones. Our camels found it slippery under foot and began to move timidly.

We had no opportunity to notice this, or indeed anything, just now, except the mass of Feisal's army, filling the valley from side to side. There were hundreds of fires of thornwood, and round them were Arabs making coffee or eating, or sleeping muffled like dead men in their cloaks, packed together closely in the confusion of camels. So many camels in company made a mess indescribable, couched as they were or tied down all over the camping ground, with more ever coming in, and the old ones leaping up on three legs to join them, roaring with hunger and agitation. Patrols were going out, caravans being unloaded, and dozens of Egyptian mules bucking angrily over the middle of the scene.

We ploughed our way through this din, and in an island of calm at the very centre of the valley-bed found Sherif Feisal. We halted our camels by his side. On his carpet, spread barely over the stones, he was sitting between Sherif Sharraf, the Kaimmakam both of the Imaret and of Taif, his cousin, and Maulud, the rugged, slashing old Mesopotamian patriot, now acting as his A.D.C. In front of him knelt a secretary taking down an order, and beyond him another reading reports aloud by the light of a silvered lamp which a slave was holding. The night was windless, the air heavy, and the unshielded flame poised there stiff and straight.

Feisal, quiet as ever, welcomed me with a smile until he could finish his dictation. After it he apologized for my disorderly reception, and waved the slaves back to give us privacy. As they retired with the onlookers, a wild camel leaped into the open space in front of us, plunging and trumpeting. Maulud dashed at its head to drag it away; but it dragged him instead; and, its load of grass ropes for camel fodder coming untied, there poured down over the taciturn Sharraf, the lamp, and myself, an avalanche of hay. "God be praised," said Feisal gravely, "that it was neither butter nor bags of gold." Then he explained to me what unexpected things had happened in the last twenty-four hours on the battle front.

The Turks had slipped round the head of the Arab barrier forces in Wadi Safra by a side road in the hills, and had cut their retreat. The Harb, in a panic, had melted into the ravines on each side, and escaped through them in parties of twos and threes. The Turkish mounted men poured down the empty valley and over the Dhifran Pass to Bir Said, where Emir Zeid, Feisal's young half-brother was camped with a Harb contingent. The Turks took Zeid by surprise and routed him. His force melted into a loose mob of fugitives riding wildly through the night towards Yenbo.

Thereby the road to Yenbo was laid open to the Turks, and Feisal had rushed down here only an hour before our arrival, with five thousand men, to protect his base until something properly defensive could be arranged. The situation was serious: but Feisal's presence here might attract the enemy, and cause them to lose more days trying to catch his field army while we strengthened Yenbo. Meanwhile, he was doing all he could, quite cheerfully; so I sat down and listened to the news; or to the petitions, complaints and difficulties being brought in and settled by him summarily.

This lasted till half-past four in the morning. It grew very cold as the damp of the valley rose through the carpet and soaked our clothes. The camp gradually stilled as the tired men and animals went one by one to sleep; a white mist collected softly over them and in it the fires became slow pillars of smoke.

Feisal at last finished the urgent work. We ate half-a-dozen dates, a frigid comfort, and curled up on the wet carpet. As I lay there in a shiver, I saw the Biasha guards creep up and spread their cloaks gently over Feisal, when they were sure that he was sleeping.

An hour later we got up stiffly in the false dawn (too cold to go on pretending and lying down) and the slaves lit a fire of palm-ribs to warm us, while Sharraf and myself searched for food and fuel enough for the moment. Messengers were still coming in from all sides with evil rumours of an immediate attack; and the camp was not far off panic. So Feisal decided to move to another position, partly because we should be washed out of this one if it rained anywhere in the hills, and partly to occupy his men's minds.

When his drums began to beat, the camels were loaded hurriedly. After the second signal every one leaped into the saddle and drew off to left or right, leaving a broad lane up which Feisal rode, on his mare, with Sharraf a pace behind him, and then Ali, the standard-bearer, a splendid wild man from Nejd, with his hawk's face framed in long plaits of jet-black hair falling downward from his temples. Ali was dressed garishly, and rode a tall camel. Behind him were all the mob of Sherifs and sheikhs and slaves—and myself—pell mell. There were eight hundred in the bodyguard that morning.

The next two days I spent in Feisal's company, and so got a deeper experience of his method of command, at an interesting season when the morale of his men was suffering heavily from the scare reports brought in, and from the defection of the Northern Harb. Feisal, fighting to make up their lost spirits, did it most surely by lending of his own to every one within reach. He was accessible to all who stood outside his tent and waited for notice; and he never cut short petitions, even when men came in chorus with their grief in a song of many verses, and sang them around us in the dark. He listened always, and, if he did not settle the case himself, called Sharraf or Faiz to arrange it for him. This extreme patience was a further lesson to me of what native headship in Arabia meant.

His self-control seemed equally great. When Mirzuk el Tikheimi, his guest-master, came in from Zeid to explain the shameful story of their rout, Feisal just laughed at him in public and sent him aside to wait while he saw the sheikhs of the Harb and the Ageyl whose carelessness had been mainly responsible for the disaster. These he rallied gently, chaffing them for having done this or that, for having inflicted such losses, or lost so much. Then he called back Mirzuk and lowered the tent-flap: a sign that there was private business to be done. I thought of the meaning of Feisal's name (the sword flashing downward in the stroke) and feared a scene, but he made room for Mirzuk on his carpet, and said, "Come! tell us more of your 'nights' and marvels of the battle: amuse us."

Feisal, in speaking, had a rich musical voice, and used it carefully upon his men. To them he talked in tribal dialect, but with a curious, hesitant manner, as though faltering painfully among phrases, looking inward for the just word. His thought, perhaps, moved only by a little in front of his speech, for the phrases at last chosen were usually the simplest, which gave an effect emotional and sincere. It seemed possible, so thin was the screen of words, to see the pure and very brave spirit shining out.

The routine of our life in camp was simple. Just before daybreak the army Imam used to utter an astounding call to prayer. His voice was harsh and very powerful, and we were effectually roused, whether we prayed or cursed. As soon as he ended, Feisal's Imam cried gently and musically from just outside the tent. In a minute, one of Feisal's five slaves came round with sweetened coffee. Sugar for the first cup in the chill of dawn was considered fit.

An hour or so later, the flap of Feisal's sleeping-tent would be thrown back: his invitation to callers from the household. There would be four or five present; and after the morning's news a tray of breakfast would be carried in. The staple of this was dates, but sometimes Hejris, the body slave, would give us odd biscuits and cereals of his own trying. After breakfast we would play with bitter coffee and sweet tea in alternation, while Feisal's correspondence was dealt with by dictation to his secretaries. One of these was Faiz the adventurous; another was the Imam, a sad-faced person made conspicuous in the army by the baggy umbrella hanging from his saddle-bow. Occasionally a man was given private audience at this hour, but seldom; as the sleeping-tent was strictly for the Sherif's own use. It was an ordinary bell-tent, furnished with cigarettes, a camp-bed, a fairly good Kurd rug, a poor Shirazi, and the delightful old Baluch prayer carpet on which he prayed.

At about eight o'clock in the morning Feisal would buckle on his ceremonial dagger and walk across to the reception tent. He would sit down at the end of the tent facing the open side, and we with our backs against the wall, in a semicircle out from him. The slaves brought up the rear, and clustered round the open wall of the tent to control the besetting suppliants who lay on the sand in the tent-mouth, or beyond, waiting their turn. If possible, business was got through by noon, when the Emir liked to rise.

We of the household, and any guests, then reassembled in the living-tent; and Hejris and Salem carried in the luncheon-tray, on which were as many dishes as circumstances permitted. Feisal was an inordinate smoker, but a very light eater, and he used to make-believe with his fingers or a spoon among the beans, lentils, spinach, rice, and sweet cakes, till he judged that we had had enough, when at a wave of his hand the tray would disappear, as other slaves walked forward to pour water for our fingers at the tent door. Fat men, like Mohammed Ibn Shefia, made a comic grievance of the Emir's quick and delicate meals, and would have food of their own prepared for them when they came away. After lunch we would talk a little, while sucking up two cups of coffee, and savouring two glasses full of syrup-like green tea. Then till two in the afternoon the curtain of the living-tent was down, signifying that Feisal was sleeping, or reading, or doing private business. Afterwards he would sit again in the reception-tent till he had finished with all who wanted him. I never saw an Arab leave him dissatisfied or hurt—a tribute to his tact and to his memory; for he seemed never to halt for loss of a fact, nor to stumble over a relationship.

If there were time after second audience, he would walk with his friends. Between six and seven there was brought in the evening meal, to which all present in headquarters were called by the slaves. It resembled the lunch.

This meal ended our day, save for the stealthy offering by a bare-footed slave of a tray of tea-glasses at protracted intervals. Feisal did not sleep till very late, and never betrayed a wish to hasten our going. In the evening he relaxed as far as possible and avoided avoidable work. Very rarely he would play chess, with the unthinking directness of a fencer, and brilliantly. Sometimes, perhaps for my benefit, he told stories of what he had seen in Syria, and scraps of Turkish secret history, or family affairs. I learned much of the men and parties in the Hejaz from his lips.

Suddenly Feisal asked me if I would wear Arab clothes like his own while in the camp. I should find it better for my own part, since it was a comfortable dress in which to live Arab-fashion as we must do. Besides, the tribesmen would then understand how to take me. The only wearers of khaki in their experience had been Turkish officers, before whom they took up an instinctive defence. If I wore Meccan clothes, they would behave to me as though I were really one of the leaders; and I might slip in and out of Feisal's tent without making a sensation which he had to explain away each time to strangers.

I agreed at once, very gladly. Hejris was pleased, too, and exercised his fancy in fitting me out in splendid white silk and gold-embroidered wedding garments which had been sent to Feisal lately (was it a hint?) by his great-aunt in Mecca. I took a stroll in the new looseness of them round the palm-gardens, to accustom myself to their feel.

Feisal's stand in Nakhl Mubarak could in the nature of things only be a pause, and I felt that I had better get back to Yenbo, to think seriously about our amphibious defence of this port, the Navy having promised its every help. We settled that I should consult Zeid, and act with him as seemed best. Feisal gave me a magnificent bay camel for the trip back. We marched through the Agida hills by a new road, Wadi Messarih, because of a scare of Turkish patrols on the more direct line. Bedr ibn Shefia was with me; and we did the distance gently in a single stage of six hours, getting to Yenbo before dawn. Being tired after three strenuous days of little sleep among constant alarms and excitements I went straight to Garland's empty house (he was living on board ship in the harbour) and fell asleep on a bench; but afterwards I was called out again by the news that Sherif Zeid was coming, and went down to the walls to see the beaten force ride in.

There were about eight hundred of them, quiet, but in no other way mortified by their shame. Zeid himself seemed finely indifferent. As he entered the town he turned and cried to Abd el Kadir, the Governor, riding behind him, "Why, your town is ruinous! I must telegraph to my father for forty masons to repair the public buildings." And this actually he did. I had telegraphed to Captain Boyle (the British senior naval officer in the Red Sea) that Yenbo was gravely threatened, and Boyle at once replied that his fleet would be there in time. This readiness was an opportune consolation: worse news came along next day. The Turks, by throwing a strong force forward from Bir Said against Nakhl Mubarak, had closed with Feisal's levies while they were yet unsteady. After a short fight, Feisal had broken off, yielded his ground, and was retreating here. Our war seemed entering its last act. I took my camera, and from the parapet of the Medina gate got a fine photograph of the brothers coming in. Feisal had nearly two thousand men with him, but none of the Juheina tribesmen. It looked like treachery and a real defection of the tribes, things which both of us had ruled out of court as impossible.

I called at once at his house and he told me the history. The Turks had come on with three battalions and a number of mule-mounted infantry and camelry. They got across Wadi Yenbo to the groves in their first onset, and thus threatened the Arab communications with Yenbo. They were also able to shell Nakhl Mubarak freely with their seven guns. Feisal was not a whit dismayed, but threw out the Juheina on his left to work down the great valley. His centre and right he kept in Nakhl Mubarak, and he sent the Egyptian artillery to deny the Yenbo road to the Turks. Then he opened fire with his own two fifteen pounders.

Rasim, a Syrian officer, formerly a battery commander in the Turkish Army, was fighting these two guns; and he made a great demonstration with them. They had been sent down as a gift from Egypt, anyhow, old rubbish thought serviceable for the wild Arabs. So Rasim had no sights, nor range-finder, no range tables, no high explosive.

His distance might have been six thousand yards; but the fuses of his shrapnel were Boer War antiquities, full of green mould, and, if they burst, it was sometimes short in the air, and sometimes grazing. However, he had no means of getting his ammunition away if things went wrong, so he blazed off at speed, shouting with laughter at this fashion of making war; and the tribesmen seeing the commandant so merry took heart of grace themselves. "By God," said one, "those are the real guns: the Importance of their noise!" Rasim swore that the Turks were dying in heaps; and the Arabs charged forward warmly, at his word.

Things were going well; and Feisal had the hope of a decisive success when suddenly his left wing in the valley wavered, halted; finally it turned its back on the enemy and retired tumultuously to the camping ground. Feisal, in the centre, galloped to Rasim and cried that the Juheina had broken and he was to save the guns. Rasim yoked up the teams and trotted away. After him streamed the levies. Feisal and his household composed the rear, and in deliberate procession they moved down towards Yenbo, leaving the Juheina under their leader, Sherif Abd el Kerim, my old guide, with the Turks on the battlefield.

As I was still hearing of this sad end, and cursing with him the traitor Beidawi brothers, there was a stir about the door, and Abd el Kerim broke through the slaves, swung up to the dais, kissed Feisal's head-rope in salutation, and sat down beside us. Feisal with a gasping stare at him said, "How?" and Abd el Kerim explained their dismay at the sudden flight of Feisal, and how he with his brother and their gallant men had fought the Turks for the whole night, alone, without artillery, till the palm-groves became untenable and they too had been driven back. His brother, with half the manhood of the tribe, was just entering the gate. The others had vanished up Wadi Yenbo for water.

"And why did you retire to the camp-ground behind us during the battle?" asked Feisal. "Only to make ourselves a cup of coffee," said Abd el Kerim. "We had fought from sunrise and it was dusk: we were very tired and thirsty." Feisal and I lay back and laughed: then we went to see what could be done to save the town.

Yenbo, on the top of its flat reef of coral rose perhaps twenty feet above the sea, and was compassed by water on two sides. The other two sides looked over flat stretches of sand, soft in places, destitute of cover for miles, and with no fresh water upon them anywhere. In daylight, if defended by artillery and machine-gun fire, the place should be impregnable.

The artillery was arriving every minute; for Boyle, as usual, better than his word, had concentrated five ships on us in less than twenty-four hours. He put the monitor *M.*31, whose shallow draught fitted her for the job, in the end of the south-eastern creek of the harbour, whence she could rake the probable direction of a Turkish advance with her six-inch guns. Crocker, her captain, was very anxious to let off those itching guns. The larger ships were moored to fire over the town at longer range, or to rake the other flank from the northern harbour. The searchlights of *Dufferin* and *M. *31 crossed on the plain beyond the town.

The Arabs, delighted to count up the quantity of vessels in the harbour, were prepared to contribute their part to the night's entertainment. They gave us good hope there would be no further panic: but to reassure them fully they needed some sort of rampart to defend, mediæval fashion. So we took the crumbling, salt-riddled wall of the place, doubled it with a second, packed earth between the two, and raised them till our sixteenth-century bastions were rifle-proof at least, and probably proof against the Turkish mountain guns. Outside the bastions we put barbed wire, festooned between cisterns on the rain catchments beyond the walls. We dug in machine-gun nests in the best angles, and manned them with Feisal's regular gunners. The Egyptians, like every one else given a place in the scheme, were gratifyingly happy. Garland, an ordnance officer lent us by the Sirdar, was engineer-in-chief and chief adviser.

After sun-down the town quivered with suppressed excitement. So long as the day lasted there had been shouts and joy-shots and wild bursts of frenzy among the workmen; but when dark came they went back to feed and a hush fell. Nearly every one sat up that night. There was one alarm about eleven o'clock. Our outposts had met the enemy only three miles outside the town. Garland, with a crier, went through the few streets and called the garrison. They tumbled straight out and went to their places in dead silence without a shot or a loose shout. The seamen on the minaret sent warning to the ships, whose combined searchlights began slowly to traverse the plain in complex intersections, drawing pencils of wheeling light across the flats which the attacking force must cross. However, no sign was made and no cause given us to open fire.

Afterwards, we heard the Turks' hearts had failed them at the silence and the blaze of lighted ships from end to end of the harbour, with the eerie beams of the searchlights revealing the bleakness of the glacis they would have to cross. So they turned back: and that night, I believe, they lost their war. Personally, I was on the *Suva*, to be undisturbed, and sleeping splendidly at last; so I was grateful to the prudence of the enemy, as, though we might perhaps have won a glorious victory, I was ready to give much more for just that eight hours' unbroken rest.

CHAPTER V

FEISAL STRIKES NORTH

COLONEL WILSON came up to Yenbo to persuade us of the necessity of an immediate operation against Wejh, the next port after Yenbo, going northward, and a point from which the Turks were threatening Feisal's rear. If we swung round at it suddenly, the initiative would pass to us.

Feisal was a fine, hot workman, whole-heartedly doing a thing when he had agreed to it. He pledged his word that he would go at once, so he and I sat down together on New Year's Day for consideration of what this move meant to us and to the Turks.

Feisal suggested taking nearly all the Juheina to Wejh with him and adding to them enough of the Harb and Billi, Ateiba and Ageyl to give the mass a many-tribed character. We wanted this march, which would be in its way a closing act of the war in Northern Hejaz, to send a rumour through the length and breadth of Western Arabia.

Feisal was nervous over abandoning Yenbo, hitherto his indispensable base, and the second sea-port of Hejaz: and when casting about for further expedients to distract the Turks from its occupation we suddenly remembered Sidi Abdulla. He had some five thousand irregulars, and a few guns and machine-guns. Feisal suggested that he move to Wadi Ais, a historic valley of springs which lay just one hundred kilometres north of Medina, a direct threat on Fakhri's railway communications with Damascus.

The proposal was obviously an inspiration and we sent off Raja el Khuluwi at once to put it to Abdulla. So sure were we of his adopting it that we urged Feisal to move away from Wadi Yenbo northward on the first stage to Wejh, without waiting a reply.

He agreed, and on January 3, 1917, we took the wide upper road through Wadi Messarih, for Owais, a group of wells about fifteen miles to the north of Yenbo. The hills were beautiful to-day. The rains of December had been abundant, and the warm sun after them had deceived the earth into believing it was spring. So a thin grass had come up in all the hollows and flat places. The blades (single, straight and very slender) shot up between the stones. If a man bent over from his saddle and looked downward he would see no new colour in the ground; but, by looking forward, and getting a distant slope at a flat angle with his eye, he could feel a lively mist of pale green here and there over the surface of slate-blue and brown-red rock. In places the growth was strong, and our painstaking camels had become prosperous, grazing on it.

The starting signal went, but only for us and the Ageyl. The other units of the army, standing each man by his couched camel, lined up beside our road, and, as Feisal came near, saluted him in silence. He called back cheerfully, "Peace upon you," and each head sheikh returned the phrase. When we had passed they mounted, taking the time from their chiefs, and so the forces behind us swelled till there was a line of men and camels winding along the narrow pass towards the watershed for as far back as the eye reached.

Feisal's greetings had been the only sounds before we reached the crest of the rise where the valley opened out and became a gentle forward slope of soft shingle and flint bedded in sand: but there ibn Dakhil, the keen sheikh of Russ, who had raised this contingent of Ageyl two years before to aid Turkey, and had brought it over with him intact to the Sherif when the revolt came, dropped back a pace or two, marshalled our following into a broad column of ordered ranks, and made the drums strike up. Every one burst out singing a full-throated song in honour of Emir Feisal and his family.

The march became rather splendid and barbaric. First rode Feisal in white, then Sharraf at his right in red head-cloth and henna-dyed tunic and cloak, myself on his left in white and scarlet, behind us three banners of faded crimson silk with gilt spikes, behind them the drummers playing a march, and behind them again the wild mass of twelve hundred bouncing camels of the bodyguard, packed as closely as they could move, the men in every variety of coloured clothes and the camels nearly as brilliant in their trappings. We filled the valley to its banks with our flashing stream.

The risk of the fall of Yenbo while we hunted Wejh was great, and it would be wise to empty it of stores. Boyle gave me an opportunity by signalling that *Hardinge* would be made available for transport. She was an Indian troopship, and her lowest troop-deck had great square ports along the water level. Captain Linberry opened these for us, and we stuffed straight in eight thousand rifles, three million rounds of ammunition, thousands of shells, quantities of rice and flour, a shed-full of uniforms, two tons of high explosive, and all our petrol, pell-mell. It was like posting letters in a box. In no time she had taken a thousand tons of stuff.

Boyle came in eager for news. He promised the *Hardinge* as depot ship throughout, to land food and water whenever needed, and this solved the main difficulty. The Navy were already collecting. Half the Red Sea Fleet would be present. The admiral was expected and landing parties were being drilled on every ship. Every one was dyeing white duck khaki-coloured, or sharpening bayonets, or practising with rifles.

I hoped silently, in their despite, that there would be no fighting. Feisal had nearly ten thousand men, enough to fill the whole Billi country with armed parties and carry off everything not too heavy or too hot. It was sure that we would take Wejh: the fear was lest numbers of Feisal's host die of hunger or thirst on the way. However, the country to Um Lejj, half way, was friendly: nothing tragic could happen so far as that: therefore, Feisal started on the very day that Abdulla replied welcoming the Ais plan. The same day came news of my relief. Newcombe, the regular colonel being sent to Hejaz as chief of our military mission, had arrived in Egypt, and his two staff officers, Cox and Vickery, were actually on their way down the Red Sea, to join this expedition.

Boyle took me to Um Lejj in the *Suva*, and we went ashore to get the news. The sheikh told us that Feisal would arrive to-day, at Bir el Waheidi, the water supply, four miles inland. We sent up a message for him and then walked over to the fort which Boyle had shelled some months before from the *Fox*. It was just a rubble barrack, and Boyle looked at the ruins and said: "I'm rather ashamed of myself for smashing such a potty place." He was a very professional officer, alert, businesslike and official; sometimes a little intolerant of easy-going things and people. Red-haired men are seldom patient. "Ginger Boyle," as they called him, was warm.

While we were looking over the ruins four grey ragged elders of the village came up and asked leave to speak. They said that some months before a sudden two-funnelled ship had come up and destroyed their fort. They were now required to re-build it for the police of the Arab Government. Might they ask the generous captain of this peaceable one-funnelled ship for a little timber, or for other material help towards the restoration? Boyle was restless at their long speech, and snapped at me, "What is it? What do they want?" I said, "Nothing; they were describing the terrible effect of the *Fox's* bombardment." Boyle looked round him for a moment and smiled grimly, "It's a fair mess."

Next day Vickery arrived. He was a gunner, and in his ten years' service in the Sudan had learned Arabic, both literary and colloquial, so well that he would quit us of all need of an interpreter. We arranged to go up with Boyle to Feisal's camp to make the time-table

After a portrait by Eric Kennington

REAR-ADMIRAL W. E. D. BOYLE, *S.N.O., Red Sea*

for the attack, and after lunch Englishmen and Arabs got to work and discussed the remaining march to Wejh.

We decided to break the army into sections: and that these should proceed independently to our concentration place of Abu Zereibat in Hamdh, after which there was no water before Wejh; but Boyle agreed that the *Hardinge* should take station for a single night in Sherm Habban—supposed to be a possible harbour—and land twenty tons of water for us on the beach. So that was settled.

For the attack on Wejh we offered Boyle an Arab landing party of several hundred Harb and Juheina peasantry. He decided to put them on another deck of the many-stomached *Hardinge*. They, with the naval party, would land north of the town, where the Turks had no post to block a landing, and whence Wejh and its harbour were best turned.

Boyle would have at least six ships, with fifty guns to occupy the Turks' minds, and a seaplane ship to direct the guns. We would be at Abu Zereibat on the twentieth of the month: at Habban for the *Hardinge's* water on the twenty-second: and the landing party should go ashore at dawn on the twenty-third, by which time our mounted men would have closed all roads of escape from the town.

The news from Rabegh was good; and the Turks had made no attempt to profit by the nakedness of Yenbo. These were our hazards, and when Boyle's wireless set them at rest we were mightily encouraged. Abdulla was almost in Ais: we were half-way to Wejh: the initiative had passed to the Arabs. I was so joyous that for a moment I forgot my self-control, and said exultingly that in a year we would be tapping on the gates of Damascus. A chill came over the feeling in the tent and my hopefulness died: but it was not an impossible dream, for five months later I was in Damascus, and a year after that I was its *de facto* Governor.

The army at Bir el Waheida amounted to five thousand one hundred camel-riders, and five thousand three hundred men on foot, with four Krupp mountain guns, and ten machine-guns: and for transport we had three hundred and eighty baggage camels.

Our start was set for January the eighteenth just after noon, and punctually by lunch-time Feisal's work was finished. After lunch the tent was struck. We went to our camels, where they were couched in a circle, saddled and loaded, each held short by the slave standing on its doubled fore-leg. The kettle-drummer, waiting beside ibn Dakhil, who commanded the bodyguard, rolled his drum seven or eight times, and everything became still. We watched Feisal. He got up from his rug, on which he had been saying a last word to Abd el Kerim, caught the saddle-pommels in his hands, put his knee on the side and said aloud, "Make God your agent." The slave released the camel, which sprang up. When it was on its feet Feisal passed his other leg across its back, swept his skirts and his cloak under him by a wave of the arm, and settled himself in the saddle.

As his camel moved we had jumped for ours, and the whole mob rose together, some of the beasts roaring, but the most quiet, as trained she-camels should be. They took their first abrupt steps, and we riders had quickly to hook our legs round the front cantles, and pick up the headstalls to check the pace. We then looked where Feisal was, and tapped our mounts' heads gently round, and pressed them on the shoulders with our bare feet till they were in line beside him. Ibn Dakhil came up, and after a glance at the country and the direction of march passed a short order for the Ageyl to arrange themselves in wings, out to right and left of us.

There came a warning patter from the drums and the poet of the right wing burst into strident song, a single invented couplet, of Feisal and the pleasures he would afford us at Wejh. The right wing listened to the verse intently, took it up and sang it together once, twice and three times, with pride and self-satisfaction and derision. However, before they could brandish it a fourth time the poet of the left wing broke out in extempore reply, in the same metre, in answering rhyme, and capping the sentiment. The left wing cheered it in a roar of triumph, the drums tapped again, the standard-bearers threw out their great crimson banners, and the whole guard, right, left and centre, broke together into the rousing regimental chorus,

"I've lost Britain and I've lost Gaul,
I've lost Rome, and, worst of all,
I've lost Lalage—"

only it was Nejd they had lost, and the women of the Maabda, and
their future lay from Jidda towards Suez. Yet it was a good song,
with a rhythmical beat which the camels loved, so that they put
down their heads, stretched their necks out far and with lengthened
pace shuffled forward musingly while it lasted.

Our road to-day was easy for them, since it was over firm sand
slopes, long, slowly-rising waves of dunes, bare-backed, but for scrub
in the folds, or barren palm-trees solitary in the moist depressions.
Afterwards in a broad flat, two horsemen came cantering across
from the left to greet Feisal. I knew the first one, dirty old blear-
eyed Mohammed Ali el Beidawi, Emir of the Juheina: but the second
looked strange. When he came nearer I saw he was in khaki uniform, with a cloak to cover it and a silk head-cloth and head-rope,
much awry. He looked up, and there was Newcombe's red and peel-
ing face, with straining eyes and vehement mouth, a strong, humorous
grin between the jaws. He had arrived at Um Lejj this morning, and
hearing we were only just off, had seized Sheikh Yusuf's fastest horse
and galloped after us.

I offered him my spare camel and an introduction to Feisal, whom
he greeted like an old school-friend; and at once they plunged into
the midst of things, suggesting, debating, planning at lightning speed.
Newcombe's initial velocity was enormous, and the freshness of the
day and the life and happiness of the Army gave inspiration to the
march and brought the future bubbling out of us without pain.

The route was not easy to decide with the poor help of the Musa
Juheina, our informants. They seemed to have no unit of time smaller than the half-day, or of distance between the span and the stage:
and a stage might be from six to sixteen hours according to the man's
will and camel. Intercommunication between our units was hindered because often there was no one who could read or write, in

either. Delay, confusion, hunger and thirst marred this expedition. These might have been avoided had time let us examine the route beforehand. The animals were without food for nearly three days, and the men marched the last fifty miles on half a gallon of water, with nothing to eat. It did not in any way dim their spirit, and they trotted into Wejh gaily enough, hoarsely singing, and executing mock charges: but Feisal said that another hot and barren mid-day would have broken both their speed and their energy.

When business ended, Newcombe and I went off to sleep in the tent Feisal had lent us as a special luxury. Baggage conditions were so hard and important for us that we rich took pride in faring like the men, who could not transport unnecessary things: and never before had I had a tent of my own. We pitched it at the very edge of a bluff of the foot-hills; a bluff no wider than the tent and rounded, so that the slope went straight down from the pegs of the door-flap. There we found sitting and waiting for us Abd el Kerim, the young Beidawi Sherif, wrapped up to the eyes in his head-cloth and cloak, since the evening was chill and threatened rain. He had come to ask me for a mule, with saddle and bridle. The smart appearance of our M.I. company in breeches and puttees, and their fine new animals had roused his desire.

I played with his eagerness, and put him off, advancing a condition that he should ask me after our successful arrival at Wejh; and with this he was content. We hungered for sleep, and at last he rose to go, but, chancing to look across the valley, saw the hollows beneath and about us winking with the faint campfires of the scattered contingents. He called me out to look, and swept his arm round, saying half-sadly, "We are no longer Arabs but a People."

During the morning it rained persistently; and we were glad to see more water coming to us, and so comfortable in the tents at Semna that we delayed our start till the sun shone again in the early afternoon. Then we rode westward down the valley in the fresh light. First behind us came the Ageyl. After them Abd el Kerim led his Gufa men, about seven hundred of them mounted, with more than that number following afoot. They were dressed in white, with large head-shawls of red and black striped cotton, and they waved green palm branches instead of banners.

Next to them rode Sherif Mohammed Ali abu Sharrain, an old patriarch with a long, curling grey beard and an upright carriage of himself. His three hundred riders were Ashraf, of the Aiaishi (Juheina) stock, known Sherifs, but only acknowledged in the mass, since they had not inscribed pedigrees. They wore rusty-red tunics henna-dyed, under black cloaks, and carried swords. Each had a slave crouched behind him on the crupper to help him with rifle and dagger in the fight, and to watch his camel and cook for him on the road. The slaves, as befitted slaves of poor masters, were very little dressed. Their strong, black legs gripped the camels' woolly sides as in a vice, to lessen the shocks inevitable on their bony perches, while they had knotted up their rags of shirts into the plaited thong about their loins to save them from the fouling of the camels and their staling on the march. Semna water was medicinal, and our animals' dung flowed like green soup down their hocks that day.

Behind the Ashraf came the crimson banner of our last tribal detachment, the Rifaa, under Owdi ibn Zuweid, the old wheedling sea-pirate who had robbed the Stotzingen Mission and thrown their wireless and their Indian servants into the sea at Yenbo. The sharks presumably refused the wireless, but we had spent fruitless hours dragging for it in the harbour. Owdi still wore a long, rich, fur-lined German officer's great-coat, a garment little suited to the climate but, as he insisted, magnificent booty. He had about a thousand men, three-quarters of them on foot, and next him marched Rasim, the gunner commandant, with his four old Krupp guns on the pack-mules, just as we had lifted them from the Egyptian Army.

Rasim was a sardonic Damascene, who rose laughing to every crisis and slunk about sore-headed with grievances when things went well. On this day there were dreadful murmurings, for alongside him rode Abdulla el Deleimi, in charge of machine-guns, a quick, clever, superficial but attractive officer, much of the professional type, whose great joy was to develop some rankling sorrow in Rasim till it discharged full blast on Feisal or myself. To-day I helped him by smiling to Rasim that we were moving at intervals of a quarter-day in echelon of sub-tribes. Rasim looked over the new-washed underwood, where raindrops glistened in the light of the sun setting redly across the waves below a ceiling of clouds, and looked too at the wild mob of Beduins racing here and there on foot after birds and rabbits and giant lizards and jerboas and one another: and assented sourly, saying that he too would shortly become a sub-tribe, and echelon himself half a day to one side or other, and be quit of flies.

At first starting a man in the crowd had shot a hare from the saddle, but because of the risk of wild shooting Feisal had then forbidden it, and those later put up by our camels' feet were chased with sticks. We laughed at the sudden commotion in the marching companies: cries, and camels swerving violently, their riders leaping off and laying out wildly with their canes to kill or be pickers-up of a kill. Feisal was happy to see the army win so much meat, but disgusted at the shameless Juheina appetite for lizards and jerboas.

We rode over the flat sand, among the thorn trees, which here were plentiful and large, till we came out on the sea-beach and turned northward along a broad, well-beaten track, the Egyptian pilgrim road. It ran within fifty yards of the sea, and we could go up it thirty or forty singing files abreast. An old lava-bed half buried in sand jutted out from the hills four or five miles inland, and made a promontory. The road cut across this, but at the near side were some mud flats, on which shallow reaches of water burned in the last light of the west. This was our expected stage, and Feisal signalled the halt. We got off our camels and stretched ourselves, sat down or walked before supper to the sea and bathed by hundreds, a splashing, screaming, mob of fish-like naked men of all earth's colours.

Supper was to look forward to, as a Juheini that afternoon had shot a gazelle for Feisal. Gazelle meat was found better than any other in the desert, because this beast, however barren the land and dry the water-holes, seemed to own always a fat juicy body.

Next day we rode easily. The journey was pleasant, for it was cool; there were a lot of us; and we two Englishmen had a tent in which we could shut ourselves up and be alone. A weariness of the desert was the living always in company, each of the party hearing all that was said and seeing all that was done by the others day and night. To have privacy, as Newcombe and I had, was ten thousand times more restful than the open life, but the work suffered by the creation of such a bar between leaders and men. Among the Arabs there were no distinctions, traditional or natural, except the unconscious power given a famous sheikh by virtue of his accomplishment; and they taught me that no man could be their leader except he ate the ranks' food, wore their clothes, lived level with them, and yet appeared better in himself.

In the morning we pressed towards Abu Zereibat over a sweeping fall of bare, black gravel. Once we halted and began to feel that a great depression lay in front of us; but not till two in the afternoon after we had crossed a basalt outcrop did we look out over a trough fifteen miles across, which was Wadi Hamdh, escaped from the hills. To our eyes, sated with small things, it was a fair sight, this end of a dry river longer than the Tigris; the greatest valley in Arabia, first understood by Doughty, and as yet unexplored.

Full of expectation we rode down the gravel slopes, on which tufts of grass became more frequent, till at three o'clock we entered the Wadi itself, a bed about a mile wide, filled with clumps of *asla* bushes, round which clung sandy hillocks each a few feet high. Their sand was not pure, but seamed with lines of dry and brittle clay, last indications of old flood levels. These divided them sharply into layers, rotten with salty mud and flaking away, so that our camels sank in, fetlock-deep, with a crunching noise like breaking pastry. The dust rose up in thick clouds, thickened yet more by the sunlight held in them; for the dead air of the hollow was a-dazzle.

The ranks behind could not see where they were going, which was difficult for them, as the hillocks came closer together, and the river bed split into a maze of shallow channels, the work of partial floods year after year. Before we gained the middle of the valley everything was overgrown by brushwood, which sprouted sideways from the mounds and laced one to another with tangled twigs as dry, dusty and brittle as old bone. We tucked in the streamers of our gaudy saddle-bags, to prevent their being jerked off by the bushes, drew cloaks tight over our clothes, bent our heads down to guard our eyes and crashed through like a storm amongst reeds. The dust was blinding and choking, and the snapping of the branches, grumbles of the camels, shouts and laughter of the men, made a rare adventure.

Before we quite reached the far bank the ground suddenly cleared at a clay bottom, in which stood a deep brown water pool, eighty yards long and about fifteen yards wide. This was the flood-water of Abu Zereibat, our goal. We went a few yards farther, through the last scrub, and reached the open north bank where Feisal had appointed the camp. So we stopped our camels, and the slaves unloaded them and set up the tents; while we walked back to see the mules, thirsty after their long day's march, rush with the foot-soldiers into the pond, kicking and splashing with pleasure in the sweet water. The abundance of fuel was an added happiness, and in whatever place they chose to camp each group of friends had a roaring fire— very welcome, as a wet evening mist rose eight feet out of the ground and our woollen cloaks stiffened and grew cold with its silver beads in their coarse woof.

It was a black night, moonless, but above the fog very brilliant with stars. On a little mound near our tents we collected and looked over the rolling white seas of fog. Out of it rose tent-peaks, and tall spires of melting smoke, which became luminous underneath when the flames licked higher into the clean air, as if driven by the noises of the unseen army. Old Owdi ibn Zuweid corrected me gravely when I said this to him, telling me, "It is not an army, it is a world which is moving on Wejh." I rejoiced at his insistence, for it had been to create this very feeling that we had hampered ourselves with an unwieldy crowd of men on so difficult a march.

Then, without warning or parade, Sherif Nasir of Medina came in. Feisal leaped up, embraced him, and led him over to us. Nasir made a splendid impression, much as we had heard, and much as we were expecting of him. He was the opener of roads, the fore-runner of Feisal's movement, the man who had fired his first shot in Medina, and who was to fire our last shot at Muslimieh beyond Aleppo on the day that Turkey asked for an armistice: and from beginning to end all that could be told of him was good.

He was a man of gardens, whose lot had been unwilling war since boyhood. He was now about twenty-seven. His low, broad forehead matched his sensitive eyes, while his weak pleasant mouth and small chin were clearly seen through a clipped black beard.

We slept late the following day, to brace ourselves for the nec-essary hours of talk. Feisal carried most of this upon his own shoulders. Nasir supported him as second in command, and the Beidawi broth-ers sat by to help. The day was bright and warm, threatening to be hot later, and Newcombe and I wandered about looking at the water-ing, the men, and the constant affluence of new-comers.

We were already two days behind our promise to the Navy, and Newcombe decided to ride ahead this night to Habban. There he would meet Boyle and explain that we must fail the *Hardinge* at the rendezvous, but would be glad if she could return there on the evening of January the twenty-fourth, when we should arrive much in need of water. He would also see if the naval attack could not be delayed till the twenty-fifth to preserve the joint scheme.

In the morning, early, we marched in a straggle for three hours down Wadi Hamdh. Then the valley went to the left, and we struck out across a hollow, desolate, featureless region. To-day was cold: a hard north wind drove into our faces down the grey coast. As we marched we heard intermittent heavy firing from the direction of Wejh, and feared that the Navy had lost patience and were acting without us. However, we could not make up the days we had wast-ed, so we pushed on for the whole dull stage, crossing affluent after affluent of Hamdh. The plain was striped with these wadies, all shallow and straight and bare, as many and as intricate as the veins in a leaf. At last we re-entered Hamdh, at Kurna, and though its clay bottoms held only mud, decided to camp.

While we were settling in there was a sudden rush. Camels had been seen pasturing away to the East, and the energetic of the Juheina streamed out, captured them, and drove them in. Feisal was furious, and shouted to them to stop, but they were too excited to hear him. He snatched his rifle, and shot at the nearest man; who, in fear, tumbled out of his saddle, so that the others checked their course. Feisal had them up before him, laid about the principals with his camel-stick, and impounded the stolen camels and those of the thieves till the whole tally was complete. Then he handed the beasts back to their Billi owners. Had he not done so it would have involved a private war with the local people, our allies of the morrow, and might have checked extension beyond Wejh. Our success lay in bond to such trifles.

Next morning we made for the beach, and up it to Habban at four o'clock. The *Hardinge* was duly there, to our relief, and landing water: although the shallow bay gave little shelter, and the rough sea rolling in made boat-work hazardous. We reserved first call for the mules, and gave what water was left to the more thirsty of the footmen; but it was a difficult night, and crowds of suffering men lingered jostling about the tanks in the rays of the searchlight, hoping for another drink, if the sailors should venture in again.

I went on board, and heard that the naval attack had been carried out as though the land army were present, since Boyle feared the Turks would run away if he waited. As a matter of fact, the day we reached Abu Zereibat, Ahmed Tewfik Bey, Turkish Governor, had addressed the garrison, saying that Wejh must be held to the last drop of blood. Then at dusk he had got on to his camel and ridden off to the railway with the few mounted men fit for flight. The two hundred infantry determined to do his abandoned duty against the landing party; but they were out-numbered three to one, and the naval gun-fire was too heavy to let them make proper use of their positions. So far as the *Hardinge* knew, the fighting was not ended, but Wejh town had been occupied by seamen and Arabs.

Profitable rumours excited the army, which began to trickle off northward soon after midnight. At dawn we rallied the various contingents, and advanced in order, meeting a few scattered Turks, of whom one party put up a short resistance. The Ageyl dismounted, to strip off their cloaks, headcloths and shirts; and went on in brown half-nakedness, which they said would ensure clean wounds if they were hit: also their precious clothes would not be damaged.

It was pretty to look at the neat, brown men in the sunlit sandy valley, with the turquoise pool of salt water in the midst to set off the crimson banners which two standard bearers carried in the van. They went along in a steady lope, covering the ground at nearly six miles an hour, dead silent, and reached and climbed the ridge without a shot fired. So we knew the work had been finished for us by the navy and its landing parties.

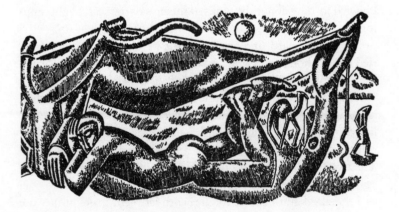

CHAPTER VI

TACTICS AND POLITICS

IN CAIRO the yet-hot authorities promised gold, rifles, mules, more machine-guns, and mountain-guns; but these last, of course, we never got. The gun question was an eternal torment. It was maddening to be unequal to many enterprises and to fail in others, for the technical reason that we could not keep down the Turkish artillery because its guns outranged ours by three or four thousand yards.

We received a great reinforcement to our cause in Jaafar Pasha, a Bagdadi officer from the Turkish Army. After distinguished service in the German and Turkish armies, he had been chosen by Enver to organize the levies of the Sheikh el Senussi. He went there by submarine, made a decent force of the wild men, and showed tactical ability against the British in two battles. Then he was captured and lodged in the Citadel at Cairo with the other officer prisoners of war. He escaped one night, slipping down a blanket-rope towards the moat; but the blankets failed under the strain, and in the fall he hurt his ankle, and was retaken helpless. In hospital he gave his parole and was enlarged after paying for the torn blanket. But one day he read in an Arabic newspaper of the Sherif's revolt, and of the execution by the Turks of prominent Arab Nationalists—his

friends—and realized that he had been on the wrong side. Feisal had
heard of him, of course, and wanted him as commander-in-chief of
his regular troops, whose improvement was now our main effort.

In Cairo were Hogarth and George Lloyd, Storrs and Deedes,
and many old friends. Beyond them the circle of Arabian well-wish-
ers was now strangely increased. Sir Archibald Murray realized with
a sudden shock that more Turkish troops were fighting the Arabs
than were fighting him, and began to remember how he had always
favoured the Arab revolt. Admiral Wemyss was as ready to help now
as he had been in our hard days round Rabegh. Sir Reginald Wingate,
High Commissioner in Egypt, was happy in the success of the work
he had advocated for years. I grudged him this happiness; for McMahon, who took the actual risk of starting it, had been broken just
before prosperity began.

I returned to Wejh where life was interesting. We had now set
our camp in order. Feisal pitched his tents (here an opulent group:
living tents, reception tents, staff tents, guest tents, servants') about
a mile from the sea, on the edge of the coral shelf which ran up gently from the beach till it ended in a steep drop facing east and south
over broad valleys radiating star-like from the land-locked harbour.
The tents of soldiers and tribesmen were grouped in these sandy
valleys, leaving the chill height for ourselves; and very delightful in
the evening we northerners found it when the breeze from the sea
carried us a murmur of the waves, faint and far off, like the echo of
traffic up a by-street in London.

Immediately beneath us were the Ageyl, an irregular close group
of tents. South of these were Rasim's artillery; and by him for company, Abdulla's machine gunners, in regular lines, with their animals
picketed out in those formal rows which were incense to the professional officer and convenient if space were precious. Further out the
market was set plainly on the ground, a boiling swell of men always
about the goods. The scattered tents and shelters of the tribesmen
filled each gully or windless place. Beyond the last of them lay open
country, with camel-parties coming in and out by the straggling palms

of the nearest, too-brackish well. As background were the foothills, reefs and clusters like ruined castles, thrown up craggily to the horizon of the coastal range.

As it was the custom in Wejh to camp wide apart, very wide apart, my life was spent in moving back and forth, to Feisal's tents, to the English tents, to the Egyptian Army tents, to the town, the port, the wireless station, tramping all day restlessly up and down these coral paths in sandals or barefoot, hardening my feet, getting by slow degrees the power to walk with little pain over sharp and burning ground, tempering my already trained body for greater endeavour.

Poor Arabs wondered why I had no mare; and I forbore to puzzle them by incomprehensible talk of hardening myself, or confess I would rather walk than ride for sparing of animals: yet the first was true and the second true. Something hurtful to my pride, disagreeable, rose at the sight of these lower forms of life. Their existence struck a servile reflection upon our human kind: the style in which a God would look on us; and to make use of them, to lie under an avoidable obligation to them, seemed to me shameful. It was as with the negroes, tom-tom playing themselves to red madness each night under the ridge. Their faces, being clearly different from our own, were tolerable; but it hurt that they should possess exact counterparts of all our bodies.

Feisal, within, laboured day and night at his politics, in which so few of us could help. Outside, the crowd employed and diverted us with parades, joy-shooting, and marches of victory. Also there were accidents. Once a group, playing behind our tents, set off a seaplane bomb, dud relic of Boyle's capture of the town. In the explosion their limbs were scattered about the camp, marking the canvas with red splashes which soon turned a dull brown and then faded pale. Feisal had the tents changed and ordered the bloody ones to be destroyed: the frugal slaves washed them. Another day a tent took fire, and part-roasted three of our guests. The camp crowded round and roared with laughter till the fire died down, and then, rather shamefacedly, we cared for their hurts. The third day, a mare was wounded by a falling joy-bullet, and many tents were pierced.

One night the Ageyl mutinied against their commandant, ibn Dakhil, for fining them too generally and flogging them too severely. They rushed his tent, howling and shooting, threw his things about and beat his servants. That not being enough to blunt their fury, they began to remember Yenbo, and went off to kill the Ateiba. Feisal from our bluff saw their torches and ran barefoot amongst them, laying on with the flat of his sword like four men. His fury delayed them while the slaves and horsemen, calling for help, dashed downhill with rushes and shouts and blows of sheathed swords. One gave him a horse on which he charged down the ringleaders, while we dispersed groups by firing Very lights into their clothing. Only two were killed and thirty wounded. Ibn Dakhil resigned next day.

Fakhri Pasha was still playing our game. He held an entrenched line around Medina, just far enough out to make it impossible for the Arabs to shell the city. (Such an attempt was never made or imagined.) The other troops were being distributed along the railway, in strong garrisons at all water stations between Medina and Tebuk, and in smaller posts between these garrisons, so that daily patrols might guarantee the track. In short, he had fallen back on as stupid a defensive as could be conceived. Garland had gone southeast from Wejh, and Newcombe north-east, to pick holes in it with high explosives. They would cut rails and bridges, and place automatic mines for running trains.

The Arabs had passed from doubt to violent optimism, and were promising exemplary service. Feisal enrolled most of the Billi, who made him master of Arabia between the railway and the sea. He then sent the Juheina to Abdulla in Wadi Ais.

He could now prepare to deal solemnly with the Hejaz Railway; but I begged him first to delay in Wejh and set marching an intense movement among the tribes beyond us, that in the future our revolt might be extended, and the railway threatened from Tebuk (our present limit of influence) northward as far as Maan.

MUDOWWARA: *From the air*

With his northern neighbours, the coastal Howeitat, he had already made a beginning: but we now sent to the Beni Atiyeh, a stronger people to the north-east; the chief, Asi ibn Atiyeh, came in and swore allegiance. He gave us freedom of movement across his tribe's territory. Beyond lay various tribes owning obedience to Nuri Shaalan, the great Emir of the Ruwalla, who, after the Sherif and ibn Saud and ibn Rashid, was the fourth figure among the precarious princes of the desert.

Nuri was an old man, who had ruled his Anazeh tribesmen for thirty years. His was the chief family of the Rualla, but Nuri had no precedence among them at birth, nor was he loved, nor a great man of battle. His headship had been acquired by sheer force of character. To gain it he had killed two of his brothers. Later he had added Sherarat and others to the number of his followers, and in all their desert his word was absolute law. He had none of the wheedling diplomacy of the ordinary sheikh; a word, and there was an end of opposition, or of his opponent. All feared and obeyed him; to use his roads we must have his countenance.

Fortunately, this was easy. Feisal had secured it years ago, and had retained it by interchange of gifts from Medina and Yenbo. Now, from Wejh, Faiz el Ghusein went up to him and on the way crossed ibn Dughmi, one of the chief men of the Ruwalla, coming down to us with the desirable gift of some hundreds of good baggage camels. Nuri, of course, still kept friendly with the Turks. Damascus and Bagdad were his markets, and they could have halfstarved his tribe in three months, had they suspected him; but we knew that when the moment came we should have his armed help, and till then anything short of a breach with Turkey.

His favour would open to us the Sirhan, a famous roadway, camping ground, and chain of water holes, which in a series of linked depressions extended from Jauf, Nuri's capital, in the south-east, northwards to Azrak, near Jebel Druse, in Syria. It was the freedom of the Sirhan we needed to reach the tents of the Eastern Howeitat, those famous abu Tayi, of whom Auda, the greatest fighting

man in northern Arabia, was chief. Only by means of Auda abu
Tayi could we swing the tribes from Maan to Akaba so violently in
our favour that they would help us take Akaba and its hills from
their Turkish garrisons: only with his active support could we venture to thrust out from Wejh on the long trek to Maan. Since our
Yenbo days we had been longing for him and trying to win him to
our cause.

We made a great step forward at Wejh; ibn Zaal, his cousin and
a war-leader of the abu Tayi, arrived on the seventeenth of February, which was in all respects a fortunate day. At dawn there came
in five chief men of the Sherarat from the desert east of Tebuk, bringing a present of eggs of the Arabian ostrich, plentiful in their
little-frequented desert. After them, the slaves showed in Dhaif-
Allah, abu Tiyur, a cousin of Hamd ibn Jazi, paramount of the
central Howeitat of the Maan plateau. These were numerous and
powerful; splendid fighters; but blood enemies of their cousins, the
nomad abu Tayi, because of an old-grounded quarrel between Auda
and Hamd. We were proud to see them coming thus far to greet us,
yet not content, for they were less fit than the abu Tayi for our purposed attack against Akaba.

On their heels came a cousin of Nawwaf, Nuri Shaalan's eldest
son, with a mare sent by Nawwaf to Feisal. The Shaalan and the
Jazi, being hostile, hardened eyes at one another; so we divided the
parties and improvised a new guest-camp. After the Rualla, was
announced the abu Tageiga chief of the sedentary Howeitat of the
coast. He brought his tribe's respectful homage and the spoils of
Dhaba and Moweilleh, the two last Turkish outlets on the Red Sea.
Room was made for him on Feisal's carpet, and the warmest thanks
rendered him for his tribe's activity; which carried us to the borders
of Akaba, by tracks too rough for operations of force, but convenient for preaching, and still more so for getting news.

In the afternoon, ibn Zaal arrived, with ten other of Auda's chief
followers. He kissed Feisal's hand once for Auda and then once for
himself, and, sitting back, declared that he came from Auda to

present his salutations and to ask for orders. Feisal, with policy, controlled his outward joy, and introduced him gravely to his blood-enemies, the Jazi Howeitat. Ibn Zaal acknowledged them distantly. Later, we held great private conversations with him and dismissed him with rich gifts, richer promises, and Feisal's own message to Auda that his mind would not be smooth till he had seen him face to face in Wejh. Auda was an immense chivalrous name, but an unknown quantity to us, and in so vital a matter as Akaba we could not afford a mistake. He must come down that we might weigh him, and frame our future plans actually in his presence, and with his help.

When the sun had declined across the sea, and the cool of evening drew down, a great cavalcade issued from the ridges masking Abu Zereibat and closed on us. Forth from its front at wild speed shot three or four mounted specks crossing each other's and their own tracks in mimic battle, while the main body began to chant a deep Ateiba melody. This was Sherif Shakir, my astonishment of Jeddah, coming attended to visit Feisal from Sherif Abdulla's camp at Wadi Ais, near Medina. Shakir was a prince in the eyes of the great Ateiba tribe, to whom his riding (the man was a very centaur on horse-back), his shooting, his bravery, his recklessness, his wealth were alike wonderful. In return, Shakir played the Bedawi. His simple clothes, simple living, his arts and manners were all nomadic: even his appearance, from the horny feet to the braided hair; and the hair was Beduin also, in its population: "Only a niggard," laughed Shakir, "would want his whole head to himself."

Except that all its events were happy, this day was not essential-ly unlike Feisal's every day. The rush of news made my diary fat. The roads to Wejh swarmed with envoys and volunteers and great sheikhs riding in to swear allegiance. The contagion of their con-stant passage made the lukewarm Billi ever more profitable to us. Feisal swore new adherents solemnly on the Koran between his hands, "to wait while he waited, march when he marched, to yield obedience to no Turk, to deal kindly with all who spoke Arabic (whether Bagdadi, Aleppine, Syrian, or pure blooded) and to put independence above life, family, and goods."

He also began to confront them at once, in his presence, with their tribal enemies, and to compose their feuds. An account of profit and loss would be struck between the parties, with Feisal modulating and interceding between them, and often paying the balance, or contributing towards it from his own funds, to hurry on the pact. During two years Feisal so laboured daily, putting together and arranging in their natural order the innumerable tiny pieces which made up Arabian society, and combining them into his one design of war against the Turks. There was no blood feud left active in any of the districts through which he had passed, and he was Court of Appeal, ultimate and unchallenged, for western Arabia.

He showed himself worthy of this achievement. He never gave a partial decision, nor a decision so impracticably just that it must lead to disorder. No Arab ever impugned his judgments, or questioned his wisdom and competence in tribal business. By patiently sifting out right and wrong, by his tact, his wonderful memory, he gained authority over the nomads from Medina to Damascus and beyond. He was recognized as a force transcending tribe, superseding blood-chiefs, greater than jealousies. The Arab movement became in the best sense national, since within it all Arabs were at one, and for it private interests must be set aside; and in this movement chief place, by right of application and by right of ability, had been properly earned by the man who filled it for those few weeks of triumph and longer months of disillusion after Damascus had been set free.

The Bedu were odd people. For an Englishman, sojourning with them was unsatisfactory unless he had patience wide and deep as the sea. They were absolute slaves of their appetite, with no stamina of mind, drunkards for coffee, milk or water, gluttons for stewed meat, shameless beggars of tobacco. They dreamed for weeks before and after their rare sexual exercises, and spent the intervening days titillating themselves and their hearers with bawdy tales. Had the circumstances of their lives given them opportunity they would have been sheer sensualists. Their strength was the strength of men geographically beyond temptation: the poverty of Arabia made them simple, continent, enduring. If forced into civilized life they would have succumbed like any savage race to its diseases, meanness, luxury, cruelty, crooked dealing, artifice; and, like savages, they would have suffered them exaggeratedly for lack of inoculation.

If they suspected that we wanted to drive them either they were mulish or they went away. If we comprehended them, and gave time and trouble to make things tempting to them, then they would go to great pains for our pleasure. Whether the results achieved were worth the effort, no man could tell. Englishmen, accustomed to greater returns, would not, and, indeed, could not, have spent the time, thought and tact lavished every day by Sheikhs and Emirs for such meagre ends. Arab processes were clear, Arab minds moved logically as our own, with nothing radically incomprehensible or different, except the premises: there was no excuse or reason, except our laziness and ignorance, whereby we could call them inscrutable or Oriental, or leave them misunderstood.

Militarily we were now firmly assured in Wejh. Allenby sent us down two Rolls Royce armoured cars, veterans of General Smuts' campaign in German East Africa. Their officers and crews were English and enterprising. They began to learn the arts of sand driving. Yenbo was emptied of its last soldiers and stores.

Rabegh also was being abandoned. The aeroplanes from it had flown up here and were established. Their Egyptian troops had been shipped after them, with Joyce and Goslett and the Rabegh staff, who were now in charge of things at Wejh. Newcombe and Hornby were up country tearing at the railway day and night, almost with their own hands: all seemed already for the best, when one afternoon, Suleiman, the guest-master, hurried in and whispered to Feisal, who turned to me with shining eyes, trying to be calm, and said, "Auda is here." I shouted "Auda abu Tayi," and at that moment the tent-flap was drawn back, before a deep voice which boomed salutations to Our Lord, the Commander of the Faithful. There entered a tall, strong figure, with a haggard face, passionate and tragic. This was Auda, and after him followed Mohammed, his son, a child in looks, and only eleven years old in truth.

Feisal had sprung to his feet. Auda caught his hand and kissed it, and they drew aside a pace or two and looked at each other—a splendidly unlike pair, typical of much that was best in Arabia, Feisal the prophet, and Auda the warrior, each filling his part to perfection, and immediately understanding and liking the other. They sat down. Feisal introduced us one by one, and Auda with a measured word seemed to register each person.

We had heard much of Auda, and were banking to open Akaba with his help; and after a moment I knew, from the force and directness of the man, that we would attain our end. He had come down to us like a knight-errant, chafing at our delay in Wejh, anxious only to be acquiring merit for Arab freedom in his own lands. If his performance was one half his desire, we should be prosperous and fortunate. The weight was off all minds before we went to supper.

We were a cheerful party; Nasib, Faiz, Mohammed el Dheilan, Auda's politic cousin, Zaal his nephew, and Sherif Nasir, resting in Wejh for a few days between expeditions. I told Feisal odd stories of Abdulla's camp, and the joy of breaking railways. Suddenly Auda scrambled to his feet with a loud "God forbid," and flung from the tent. We stared at one another, and there came a noise of hammering outside. I went after to learn what it meant, and there was Auda bent over a rock pounding his false teeth to fragments with a stone. "I had forgotten," he explained, "Jemal Pasha gave me these. I was eating my Lord's bread with Turkish teeth!" Unfortunately he had few teeth of his own, so that henceforward eating the meat he loved was difficulty and after-pain, and he went about half-nourished till we had taken Akaba, and Sir Reginald Wingate sent him a dentist from Egypt to make an Allied set.

Auda was very simply dressed, northern fashion, in white cotton with a red Mosul head cloth. He might be over fifty, and his black hair was streaked with white; but he was still strong and straight, loosely built, spare, and as active as a much younger man. His face was magnificent in its lines and hollows. On it was written how truly the death in battle of Annad, his favourite son, cast sorrow over all his life when it ended his dream of handing on to future generations the greatness of the name of Abu Tayi. He had large eloquent eyes, like black velvet in richness. His forehead was low and broad, his nose very high and sharp, powerfully hooked: his mouth rather large and mobile: his beard and moustaches had been trimmed to a point in Howeitat style, with the lower jaw shaven underneath.

Centuries ago the Howeitat came from Hejaz, and their nomad clans prided themselves on being true Bedu. Auda was their master type. His hospitality was sweeping; except to very hungry souls, inconvenient. His generosity kept him always poor, despite the profits of a hundred raids. He had married twenty-eight times, had been wounded thirteen times; whilst the battles he provoked had seen all his tribesmen hurt and most of his relations killed. He himself had slain seventy-five men, Arabs, with his own hand in battle: and never a man except in battle. Of the number of dead Turks he could give no account: they did not enter the register. His Toweiha under him had become the first fighters of the desert, with a tradition of desperate courage, a sense of superiority which never left them while there was life and work to do: but which had reduced them from twelve hundred men to less than five hundred, in thirty years, as the standard of nomadic fighting rose.

Auda raided as often as he had opportunity, and as widely as he could. He had seen Aleppo, Basra, Wejh, and Wadi Dawasir on his expeditions: and was careful to be at enmity with nearly all tribes in the desert, that he might have proper scope for raids. After his robber-fashion, he was as hard-headed as he was hot-headed, and in his maddest exploits there would be a cold factor of possibility to lead him through. His patience in action was extreme: and he received and ignored advice, criticism, or abuse, with a smile as constant as it was very charming. If he got angry his face worked uncontrollably, and he burst into a fit of shaking passion, only to be assuaged after he had killed: at such times he was a wild beast, and men escaped his presence. Nothing on earth would make him change his mind or obey an order or do the least thing he disapproved; and he took no heed of men's feelings when his face was set.

He saw life as a saga. All the events in it were significant: all personages in contact with him heroic. His mind was stored with poems of old raids and epic tales of fights, and he overflowed with them on the nearest listener. If he lacked listeners he would very likely sing them to himself in his tremendous voice, deep and resonant and loud. He had no control over his lips, and was therefore terrible to his own interests and hurt his friends continually. He spoke of himself in the third person, and was so sure of his fame that he loved to shout out stories against himself. At times he seemed taken by a demon of mischief, and in public assembly would invent and utter on oath appalling tales of the private life of his hosts or guests: and yet with all this he was modest, as simple as a child, direct, honest, kind hearted, and warmly loved even by those to whom he was most embarrassing—his friends.

The long pause after Wejh fell had an important effect on my mind, for I was sent on detached duty and had solitude for thinking, and a remote point from which to regard our activities. Every effort was still directed against the railway. Newcombe and Garland were near Muadhdham with Sherif Sharraf and Maulud. They had many Billi, the mule-mounted infantry, and guns and machine-guns, and hoped to take the fort and railway station there. Newcombe meant then to move all Feisal's men forward very close to Medain Salih, and, by taking and holding a part of the line, to cut off Medina and compel its early surrender. Wilson was coming up to help in this operation, and Davenport would take as many of the Egyptian army as he could transport, to reinforce the Arab attack.

All this programme was what I had believed necessary for the further progress of the Arab Revolt when we took Wejh. I had planned and arranged some of it myself. But now, to my leisure, it seemed that not merely the details, but the essence of this plan were wrong. It therefore became my business to explain my changed ideas, and if possible to persuade my chiefs to follow me into the new theory.

So I began with three propositions. Firstly, that irregulars would not attack places, and so remained incapable of forcing a decision. Secondly, that they were as unable to defend a line or point as they were to attack it. Thirdly, that their virtue lay in depth, not in face.

The Arab war was geographical, and the Turkish Army an accident. Our aim was to seek the enemy's weakest material link and bear only on that till time made their whole length fail. Our largest resources, the Beduin on whom our war must be built, were unused to formal operations, but had assets of mobility, toughness, self-assurance, knowledge of the country, intelligent courage. With them dispersal was strength. Consequently we must extend our front to its maximum, to impose on the Turks the longest possible passive defence, since that was, materially, their most costly form of war.

Our duty was to attain our end with the greatest economy of life, since life was more precious to us than money or time. If we were patient and superhuman-skilled, we could follow the direction of Saxe and reach victory without battle, by pressing our advantages mathematical and psychological. Fortunately our physical weakness was not such as to demand this. We were richer than the Turks in transport, machine-guns, cars, high explosive. We could develop a highly mobile, highly equipped striking force of the smallest size, and use it successively at distributed points of the Turkish line, to make them strengthen their posts beyond the defensive minimum of twenty men. This would be a short cut to success.

We must not take Medina. The Turk was harmless there. In prison in Egypt he would cost us food and guards. We wanted him to stay at Medina, and every other distant place, in the largest numbers. Our ideal was to keep his railway just working, but only just, with the maximum of loss and discomfort. The factor of food would confine him to the railways, but he was welcome to the Hejaz Railway, and the Trans-Jordan railway, and the Palestine and Syrian railways for the duration of the war, so long as he gave us the other nine hundred and ninety-nine thousandths of the Arab world. If he tended to evacuate too soon, as a step to concentrating in the small area which his numbers could dominate effectually, then we should have to restore his confidence by reducing our enterprises against him. His stupidity would be our ally, for he would like to hold, or to think he held, as much of his old provinces as possible. This pride in his imperial heritage would keep him in his present absurd position—all flanks and no front.

In detail I criticized the ruling scheme. To hold a middle point of the railway would be expensive, for the holding force might be threatened from each side. The mixture of Egyptian troops with tribesmen was a moral weakness. If there were professional soldiers present, the Beduin would stand aside and watch them work, glad to be excused the leading part. Jealousy, superadded to inefficiency, would be the outcome. Further, the Billi country was very dry, and the maintenance of a large force up by the line technically difficult.

Neither my general reasoning, however, nor my particular objections had much weight. The plans were made, and the preparations advanced. Every one was too busy with his own work to give me specific authority to launch out on mine. All I gained was a hearing, and a qualified admission that my counter-offensive might be a useful diversion. I was working out with Auda abu Tayi a march to the Howeitat in their spring pastures of the Syrian desert. From them we might raise a mobile camel-force, and rush Akaba from the eastward without guns or machine-guns.

The eastern was the unguarded side, the line of least resistance, the easiest for us. Our march would be an extreme example of a turning movement, since it involved a desert journey of six hundred miles to capture a trench within gun fire of our ships: but there was no practicable alternative. Auda thought all things possible with dynamite and money, and that the smaller clans about Akaba would join us. Feisal, who was already in touch with them, also believed that they would help if we won a preliminary success up by Maan and then moved in force against the port. The Navy raided it while we were thinking, and their captured Turks gave us such useful information that I became eager to go off at once.

CHAPTER VII

SETTING OUT FOR SYRIA

By MAY the ninth, 1917, all things were ready, and in the glare of mid-afternoon we left Feisal's tent, his good wishes sounding after us from the hill-top as we marched away. Sherif Nasir led us: his lucent goodness made him the only leader (and a benediction) for forlorn hopes.

Our short stage was to the fort of Sebeil, inland Wejh, where the Egyptian pilgrims used to water. We camped by their great brick tank, in shade of the fort's curtain-wall, or of the palms, and put to rights the deficiencies which this first march had shown. Auda and his kinsmen were with us; also Nesib el Bekri, the politic Damascene, to represent Feisal to the villagers of Syria. Nesib had brains and position, and the character of a previous, successful, desert-journey: his cheerful endurance of adventure, rare among Syrians, marked him out as our fellow, as much as his political mind, his ability, his persuasive good-humoured eloquence, and the patriotism which often overcame his native passion for the indirect. Nesib chose Zeki, a Syrian officer, as his companion. For escort we had thirty-five Ageyl, under ibn Dgheithir, a man walled into his own temperament: remote, abstracted, self-sufficient. Feisal made up a purse of twenty thousand pounds in gold—all he could afford and more than we asked for—to pay the wages of the new men we hoped to enrol, and to make such advances as should stimulate the Howeitat to swiftness.

My Ageyl—Mukheymer, Merjan, Ali—had been supplemented by Mohammed, a blowsy, obedient peasant boy from some village in Hauran, and by Gasim, of Maan, a fanged and yellow-faced outlaw, who fled into the desert to the Howeitat, after killing a Turkish official in a dispute over cattle tax. Crimes against tax-gatherers had a sympathetic aspect for all of us, and this gave Gasim a specious rumour of geniality, which actually was far from truth.

After dark we loaded up, and started. Nasir, our guide, had grown to know this country nearly as well as he did his own. While we rode through the moonlit and starry night, his memory was dwelling very intimately about his home. He told me of their stone-paved house whose sunk halls had vaulted roofs against the summer heat, and of the gardens planted with every kind of fruit tree, in shady paths about which they could walk at ease, mindless of the sun. He told me of the wheel over the well, with its machinery of leathern trip-buckets, raised by oxen upon an inclined path of hard-trodden earth; and of how the water from its reservoir slid in concrete channels by the borders of the paths; or worked fountains in the court beside the great vine-trellised swimming tank, lined with shining cement, within whose green depth he and his brother's household used to plunge at midday.

Nasir, though usually merry, had a quick vein of suffering in him, and, to-night he was wondering why he, an Emir of Medina, rich and powerful and at rest in that garden-palace, had thrown up all to become the weak leader of desperate adventures in the desert. For two years he had been outcast, always fighting beyond the front line of Feisal's armies, chosen for every particular hazard, the pioneer in each advance; and, meanwhile, the Turks were in his house, wasting his fruit trees and chopping down his palms. Even, he said, the great well, which had sounded with the creak of the bullock wheels for six hundred years, had fallen silent; the garden, cracked with heat, was becoming waste as the blind hills over which we rode.

After four hours' march we slept for two, and rose with the sun. The baggage camels, weak with the cursed mange of Wejh, moved slowly, grazing all day as they went. We riders, light-mounted, might have passed them easily; but Auda, who was regulating our marches, forbade, because of the difficulties in front, for which our animals would need all the fitness we could conserve in them. So we plodded soberly on for six hours in great heat. The summer sun in this country of white sand behind Wejh could dazzle the eyes cruelly, and the bare rocks each side our path threw off waves of heat which made our heads ache and swim. Consequently, by eleven of the forenoon we were mutinous against Auda's wish still to hold on. So we halted and lay under trees till half-past two, each of us trying to make a solid, though shifting shadow for himself by means of a doubled blanket caught across the thorns of over-hanging boughs.

We rode again, after this break, for three gentle hours over level bottoms, approaching the walls of a great valley; and found the green garden of El Kurr lying just in front of us. White tents peeped from among the palms. While we dismounted, Rasim and Abdulla, Mahmud, the doctor, and even old Maulud, the cavalryman, came out to welcome us. They told us that Sherif Sharraf, whom we wished to meet at Abu Raga, our next stopping place, was away raiding for a few days. This meant that there was no hurry, so we made holi-day at El Kurr for two nights.

The inhabitant of Kurr, the only sedentary Belluwi, hoary Dhaif-Allah, laboured day and night with his daughters in the little terraced plot which he had received from his ancestors. It was built out of the south edge of the valley in a bay defended against flood by a massive wall of unhewn stone. In its midst opened the well of clear cold water, above which stood a balance-cantilever of mud and rude poles. By this Dhaif-Allah, morning and evening when the sun was low, drew up great bowls of water and spilled them into clay runnels contrived through his garden among the tree roots. He grew low palms, for their spreading leaves shaded his plants from the sun which otherwise might in that stark valley wither them, and raised young tobacco (his most profitable crop); with smaller plots of beans and melons, cucumbers and egg-plants, in due season.

The old man lived with his women in a brushwood hut beside the well, and was scornful of our politics, demanding what more to eat or drink these sore efforts and bloody sacrifices would bring. We gently teased him with notions of liberty; with freedom of the Arab countries for the Arabs. "This Garden, Dhaif-Allah, should it not be your very own?" However, he would not understand, but stood up to strike himself proudly on the chest, crying, "I— I am Kurr."

Still we were grateful to him, for, besides that he showed an example of contentment to us slaves of unnecessary appetite, he sold vegetables; and on them, and on the tinned bounty of Rasim and Abdulla and Mahmud, we lived richly. Each evening round the fires they had music, not the monotonous open-throated roaring of the tribes, nor the exciting harmony of the Ageyl, but the falsetto quarter tones and trills of urban Syria. Maulud had musicians in his unit; and bashful soldiers were brought up each evening to play guitars and sing café songs of Damascus or the love verses of their villages.

The soldier camp would grow dead silent till the stanza ended, and then from every man would come a sighing, longing echo of the last note. Only old Dhaif-Allah went on splashing out his water, sure that after we had finished with our silliness some one would yet need and buy his greenstuff.

To townsmen this garden was a memory of the world before we went mad with war and drove ourselves into the desert: to Auda there was an indecency of exhibition in the plant-richness, and he longed for an empty view. So we cut short our second night in paradise, and at two in the morning went on up the valley. It was pitch dark, the very stars in the sky being unable to cast light into the depths where we were wandering. Auda was guide, and to make us sure of him he lifted up his voice in an interminable "ho, ho, ho" song of the Howeitat; an epic chanted on three bass notes, up and down, back and forward, in so round a voice that the words were indistinguishable. After a little we thanked him for the singing, since the path went away to the left, and our long line followed his turn by the echoes of his voice rolling about the torn black cliffs in the moonlight.

We marched until the early sun, very trying to those who had ridden all night, opposed us. Breakfast was off our own flour, thus lightening at last, after days of hospitality, our poor camels' food-load. Sharraf being not yet in Abu Raga, we made no more haste than water-difficulties compelled; and, after food, again put up our blanket roofs and lay till afternoon, fretfully dodging after their unstable shadow, getting moist with heat and the constant pricking of flies.

In the morning we rode at five. Our valley pinched together, and we went round a sharp spur, ascending steeply. The track became a bad goat-path, zigzagging up a hill-side too precipitous to climb except on all fours. We dropped off our camels and led them by the headstalls. Soon we had to help each other, a man urging the camels from behind, another pulling them from the front, encouraging them over the worst places, adjusting their loads to ease them.

Parts of the track were dangerous, where rocks bulged out and narrowed it, so that the near half of the load grazed and forced the animal to the cliff-edge. We had to re-pack the food and explosives; and, in spite of all our care, lost two of our feeble camels in the pass. The Howeitat killed them where they lay broken, stabbing a keen dagger into the throat-artery near the chest, while the neck was strained tight by pulling the head round to the saddle. They were at once cut up and shared out as meat.

Then we came to the first break of surface, a sharp passage to the bottom of a shrub-grown, sandy valley, on each side of which sandstone precipices and pinnacles, gradually growing in height as we went down, detached themselves sharply against the morning sky. We wound on, ever deeper into the earth until, half an hour later, by a sharp corner, we entered Wadi Jizil, a deep gorge some two hundred yards in width.

Our camp was on some swelling dunes of weedy sand in an elbow of the valley, where a narrow cleft had set up a backwash and scooped out a basin in which a remnant of last winter's flood was caught. We sent a man for news up the valley to an oleander thicket where we saw the white peaks of Sharraf's tents. They expected him next day; so we passed two nights in this strange-coloured, echoing place. The brackish pool was fit for our camels, and in it we bathed at noon. Then we ate and slept generously, and wandered in the nearer valleys to see the horizontal stripes of pink and brown and cream and red which made up the general redness of the cliffs, delighting in the varied patterns of thin pencillings of lighter or darker tint which were drawn over the plain body of rock. One afternoon I spent behind some shepherd's fold of sandstone blocks in warm soft air and sunlight, with a low burden of the wind plucking at the rough wall-top above my head. The valley was instinct with peace, and the wind's continuing noise made even it seem patient.

My eyes were shut and I was dreaming, when a youthful voice made me see an anxious Ageyli, a stranger, Daud, squatting by me. He appealed for my compassion. His friend Farraj had burned their tent in a frolic, and Saad, captain of Sharraf's Ageyl, was going to beat him in punishment. At my intercession he would be released. Saad happened, just then, to visit me, and I put it to him, while Daud sat watching us, his mouth slightly, eagerly open, his eyelids narrowed over large, dark eyes, and his straight brows furrowed with anxiety. Daud's pupils, set a little in from the centre of the eyeball, gave him an air of acute readiness.

Saad's reply was not comforting. The pair were always in trouble, and of late so outrageous in their tricks that Sharraf, the severe, had ordered an example to be made of them. All he could do for my sake was to let Daud share the ordained sentence. Daud leaped at the chance, kissed my hand and Saad's, and ran off up the valley; while Saad, laughing, told me stories of the famous pair. They were an instance of the eastern boy and boy affection which the segregation of women made inevitable. Such friendships often led to manly loves of a depth and force beyond our flesh-steeped conceit. When innocent they were hot and unashamed. If sexuality entered, they passed into a give and take, unspiritual relation, like marriage.

Next day Sharraf did not come. Our morning passed with Auda talking of the march in front, while Nasir with forefinger and thumb flicked sputtering matches from the box across his tent at us. In the midst of our merriment two bent figures, with pain in their eyes, but crooked smiles upon their lips, hobbled up and saluted. These were Daud the hasty and his love-fellow, Farraj; a beautiful, soft-framed girlish creature, with innocent, smooth face and swimming eyes. They said they were for my service. I had no need of them; and objected that after their beating they could not ride. They replied they had now come bare-backed. I said I was a simple man who disliked servants about him. Daud turned away, defeated and angry; but Farraj pleaded that we must have men, and they would follow me for company and out of gratitude. While the harder Daud revolted, he went over to Nasir and knelt in appeal, all the woman of him evident in his longing. At the end, on Nasir's advice, I took them both, mainly because they looked so young and clean.

Sharraf delayed to come until the third morning. He had captured prisoners on the line and blown up rails and a culvert. One piece of his news was that in Wadi Diraa, on our road, were pools of rainwater, new fallen and sweet. This would shorten our waterless march to Fejr by fifty miles.

Next day we left Abu Raga. Auda led us up a tributary valley which soon widened into the plain of the Shegg—a sand flat. About it, in scattered confusion, sat small islands and pinnacles of red sandstone, grouped like seracs, wind-eroded at the bases till they looked very fit to fall and block the road; which wound in and out between them, through narrows seeming to give no passage, but always opening into another bay of blind alleys. Through this maze Auda led unhesitatingly; digging along on his camel, elbows out, hands poised swaying in the air by his shoulders.

There were no footmarks on the ground, for each wind swept like a great brush over the sand surface, stippling the traces of the last travellers till the surface was again a pattern of innumerable tiny virgin waves. Only the dried camel droppings, which were lighter than the sand and rounded like walnuts, escaped over its ripples. They rolled about, to be heaped in corners by the skirling winds. It was perhaps by them, as much as by his unrivalled road sense, that Auda knew the way.

In the mid-march we perceived five or six riders coming from the railway. I was in front with Auda, and we had that delicious thrill "Friend or enemy?" of meeting strangers in the desert, whilst we circumspectly drew across the vantage side which kept the rifle-arm free for a snap shot; but when they came nearer we saw they were of the Arab forces. The first, riding loosely on a hulking camel, with the unwieldy Manchester-made timber saddle of the British Camel Corps, was a fair-haired, shaggy-bearded Englishman in tattered uniform. This we guessed must be Hornby, Newcombe's pupil, the wild engineer who vied with him in smashing the railway. After we had exchanged greetings, on this our first meeting, he told me that Newcombe had lately gone to Wejh to talk over his difficulties with Feisal and make fresh plans to meet them.

At sunset we reached the northern limit of the ruined sandstone land, and rode up to a new level, sixty feet higher than the old, blue-black and volcanic, with a scattered covering of worn basalt-blocks, small as a man's hand, neatly bedded like cobble paving over a floor of fine, hard, black cinder-debris of themselves.

It was very dark; a pure night enough, but the black stone underfoot swallowed the light of the stars, and at seven o'clock, when at last we halted, only four of our party were with us. We had reached a gentle valley, with a yet damp, soft, sandy bed, full of thorny brush-wood, unhappily useless as camel food. We ran about tearing up these bitter bushes by the roots and heaping them in a great pyre, which Auda lit. When the fire grew hot a long black snake wormed slowly out into our group; we must have gathered it, torpid, with the twigs. The flames went shining across the dark flat, a beacon to the heavy camels which had lagged so much to-day that it was two hours before the last group arrived, the men singing their loudest, partly to encourage themselves and their hungry animals over the ghostly plain, partly so that we might know them friends.

In the night some of our camels strayed and our people had to go looking for them so long, that it was nearly eight o'clock, and we had baked bread and eaten, before again we started. Our track lay across more lava field, but to our morning strength the stones seemed rarer, and waves or hard surfaces of laid sand often drowned them smoothly with a covering as good to march on as a tennis court.

We marched steadily till noon, and then sat out on the bare ground till three; an uneasy halt made necessary by our fear that the dejected camels, so long accustomed only to the sandy tracks of the coastal plain, might have their soft feet scorched by the sun-baked stones, and go lame with us on the road. After we mounted, the going became worse, and we had continually to avoid large fields of piled basalt, or deep yellow water-courses which cut through the crust into the soft stone beneath. After a while red sandstone again cropped out in crazy chimneys, from which the harder layers pro-jected knife-sharp in level shelves beyond the soft, crumbling rock. At last these sandstone ruins became plentiful, in the manner of yesterday, and stood grouped about our road in similar chequered yards of light and shade. Again we marvelled at the sureness with which Auda guided our little party through the mazy rocks.

They passed, and we re-entered volcanic ground. Little pimply craters stood about, often two or three together, and from them spines of high, broken basalt led down like disordered causeways. Between craters the basalt was strewn in small tetrahedra, with angles rubbed and rounded, stone tight to stone like tesseræ upon a bed of pink-yellow mud. The ways worn across such flats by the constant passage of camels were very evident, since the slouching tread had pushed the blocks to each side of the path, and the thin mud of wet weather had run into these hollows and now inlaid them palely against the blue. Less-used roads for hundreds of yards were like narrow ladders across the stone-fields, for the tread of each foot was filled in with clean yellow mud, and ridges or bars of the blue-grey stone remained between each stepping place. After a stretch of such stone-laying would be a field of jet-black basalt cinders, firm as concrete in the sun-baked mud, and afterwards a valley of soft, black sand, with more crags of weathered sandstone rising from the blackness, or from waves of the wind-blown red and yellow grains of their own decay.

At last Auda pointed ahead to a fifty-foot ridge of large twisted blocks, lying coursed one upon the other as they had writhed and shrunk in their cooling. There was the limit of lava; and he and I rode on together and saw in front of us an open rolling plain (Wadi Aish) of fine scrub and golden sand, with green bushes scattered here and there. It held a very little water in holes which some one had scooped after the rainstorm of three weeks ago. We camped by them and drove our unladen camels out till sunset, to graze for the first adequate time since Abu Raga.

While they were scattered over the land, mounted men appeared on the horizon to the east, making towards the water. They came on too quickly to be honest, and fired at our herdsmen; but the rest of us ran at once upon the scattered reefs and knolls, shooting or shouting. Hearing us so many they drew off as fast as their camels would go; and from the ridge in the dusk we saw them, a bare dozen in all, scampering away towards the line. We were glad to see them avoid us so thoroughly. Auda thought they were a Shammar patrol.

COLONEL C. E. WILSON, *H.M. Diplomatic Agent, Jidda*

CHAPTER VIII

THE VERITABLE DESERT

AT DAWN we saddled up for the short stage to Diraa, the water pools of which Sharraf had told us. We halted there till afternoon; for we were now quite near the railway, and had to drink our stomachs full and fill our few water skins, ready for the long dash to Fejr.

In the halt Auda came to see Farraj and Daud dress my camel with butter for relief against the intolerable itch of mange which had broken out recently on its face. The dry pasturage of the Billi country and the infected ground of Wejh had played havoc with our beasts. In all Feisal's stud of riding camels there was not one healthy; in our little expedition every camel was weakening daily. Nasir was full of anxiety lest many break down in the forced march before us and leave their riders stranded in the desert.

We had no medicines for mange and could do little for it in spite of our need. However, the rubbing and anointing did make my animal more comfortable, and we repeated it as often as Farraj or Daud could find butter in our party. These two boys were giving me great satisfaction. They were brave and cheerful, active, good riders, and willing workmen.

By a quarter to four we were in the saddle, going down Wadi Diraa, into steep and high ridges of shifting sand, sometimes with a cap of harsh red rock jutting from them. After a while, three or four of us, in advance of the main body, climbed a sandpeak on hands and knees to spy out the railway. There was no air, and the exercise was more than we required; but our reward was immediate, for the line showed itself quiet and deserted-looking. We were to have an unmolested crossing.

Our heavy camels marched over the valley, the line, and the farther flat, till sheltered in the sand and rock mouths of the country beyond the railway. Meanwhile the Ageyl fixed guncotton or gelatine charges to as many of the rails as we had time to reach, and began, in proper order, to light the fuses, filling the hollow valley with the echoes of repeated bursts.

Auda had not before known dynamite, and with a child's first pleasure was moved to a rush of hasty poetry on its powerful glory. We cut three telegraph wires, and fastened the free ends to the saddles of six riding camels of the Howeitat. The astonished team struggled far into the eastern valleys with the growing weight of twanging, tangling wire and the bursting poles dragging after them. At last they could no longer move. So we cut them loose and rode in the falling dusk laughing after the caravan.

In the morning Auda had us afoot before four, going uphill, till at last we climbed a ridge to a plain, with an illimitable view down hill to the east, where one gentle level after another slowly modulated into a distance only to be called distance because it was a sober blue, and more hazy. The rising sun flooded this falling plain with a perfect level of light, throwing up long shadows of almost imperceptible ridges, and the whole life and play of a complicated ground-system—but a transient one; for, as we looked at it, the shadows drew in towards the dawn, quivered a last moment behind their mother-banks, and went out as though at a common signal. Full morning had begun: the river of sunlight, sickeningly in the full-face of us moving creatures, poured impartially on every stone of the desert.

The Fejr Bedouin, whose property it was, called our plain El
Houl because it was desolate; and to-day we rode without seeing
signs of life; no tracks of gazelle, no lizards, no burrowing of rats,
not even any birds. We, ourselves, felt tiny in it, and our urgent
progress across its immensity was a stillness or immobility of futile
effort. The only sounds were the hollow echoes, like the shutting
down of pavements over vaulted places, of rotten stone slab on stone
slab when they tilted under our camels' feet; and the low but pierc-
ing rustle of the sand, as it crept slowly westward before the hot
wind along the worn sandstone, under the harder overhanging caps
which gave each reef its eroded rind-like shape.

It was a breathless wind, with the furnace taste sometimes known
in Egypt when a khamsin came; and, as the day went on and the
sun rose in the sky it grew stronger, more filled with the dust of the
Nefudh, the great sand desert of Northern Arabia, close by us over
there, but invisible through the haze. By noon it blew a half-gale,
so dry that our shrivelled lips cracked open, and the skin of our faces
chapped; while our eyelids, gone granular, seemed to creep back
and bare our shrinking eyes. The Arabs drew their headcloths tightly across their noses, and pulled the brow-folds forward like vizors
with only a narrow, loose-flapping slit of vision.

We plodded on all the day (even without the wind forbidding
us there could have been no more luxury-halts under the shadow
of blankets, if we would arrive unbroken men with strong camels
at el Fejr), and nothing made us widen an eye or think a thought
till evening, calm and black and full of stars, had come down on us.
We had covered about fifty miles, so we halted.

Before dawn the following day we started, and at the height of
noon reached the well of our desire. It was about thirty feet deep,
stone-steyned, seemingly ancient. The water was slightly brackish,
but not ill-tasting when drunk fresh: though it soon grew foul in
a skin. The valley had flooded in some burst of rain the year before,
and therefore contained much dry and thirsty pasturage: to this
we loosed our camels, to crop industriously till nightfall, then we

watered them again, and pounded them under the bank a half-mile from the water, for the night: thus leaving the well unmolested in case raiders should need it in the dark hours. Yet our sentries heard no one.

As usual we were off before dawn and reached our stage, Khabr Ajaj, just before sunset, after a dull ride over a duller plain. The pool was of this year's rain, good for camels and just possible for men to drink. We had thought to find Howeitat here; but the ground was grazed bare and the water fouled by their animals, while they themselves were gone. Auda searched for their tracks, but could find none: the wind-storms had swept the sand face into clean new ripples. However, if we went away northward, we should find them.

The following day, despite the interminable lapse of time, was only our fourteenth from Wejh; and its sun rose upon us again marching, over flats of limestone and sand, towards a distant corner of the Great Nefudh, the famous belts of sanddune which cut off Jebel Shammar from the Syrian Desert. Palgrave, the Blunts, and Gertrude Bell amongst the storied travellers had crossed it, and I begged Auda to bear off a little and let us enter it, and their company: but he growled that men went to the Nefudh only of necessity, when raiding, and that the son of his father did not raid on a tottering, mangy camel. Our business was to reach Arfaja alive.

So we wisely marched on, over monotonous, glittering sand; and over those worse stretches, "Giaan," of polished mud, nearly as white and smooth as laid paper, and often whole miles square. They blazed back the sun into our faces with glassy vigour, so we rode with its light raining direct arrows upon our heads, and its reflection glancing up from the ground through our inadequate eyelids. It was not a steady pressure, but a pain ebbing and flowing; at one time piling itself up and up till we nearly swooned; and then falling away coolly, in a moment of false shadow like a black web crossing the retina: these gave us a moment's breathing space to store new capacity for suffering, like the struggles to the surface of a drowning man. We grew short-answered to one another; but relief came toward six o'clock, when we halted for supper, and baked ourselves fresh bread.

After dark we crawled for three hours, reaching the top of a sand ridge. There we slept thankfully, after a bad day of burning wind, dust blizzards, and drifting sand which stung our inflamed faces, and at times, in the greater gusts, wrapped the sight of our road from us and drove our complaining camels up and down. But Auda was anxious about the morrow, for another hot head-wind would delay us a third day in the desert, and we had no water left: so he called us early in the night, and we marched down into the plain of the Bisaita (so called in derision, for its huge size and flatness), before day broke. Its fine surface-litter of sun-browned flints was restfully dark after sunrise for our streaming eyes, but hot and hard going for our camels, some of which were already limping with sore feet.

Camels brought up on the sandy plains of the Arabian coast had delicate pads to their feet; and if such animals were taken suddenly inland for long marches over flints or other heat-retaining ground, their soles would burn, and at last crack in a blister; leaving quick flesh, two inches or more across, in the centre of the pad. In this state they could march as ever over sand; but if, by chance, the foot came down on a pebble, they would stumble, or flinch as though they had stepped on fire, and in a long march might break down altogether unless they were very brave. So we rode carefully, picking the softest way, Auda and myself in front.

As we went, some little puffs of dust scurried into the eye of the wind. Auda said they were ostriches. A man ran up to us with two great ivory eggs. We settled to breakfast on this bounty of the Biseita, and looked for fuel; but in twenty minutes found only a wisp of grass. The barren desert was defeating us. The baggage train passed, and my eye fell on the loads of blasting gelatine. We broached a packet, shredding it carefully into a fire beneath the egg propped on stones, till the cookery was pronounced complete. Nasir and Nesib, really interested, dismounted to scoff at us. Auda drew his silver-hilted dagger and chipped the top of the first egg. A stink like a pestilence went across our party. We fled to a clean spot, rolling the second hot egg before us with gentle kicks. It was fresh enough, and hard as a stone. We dug out its contents with the dagger on to the flint flakes which were our platters, and ate it piece-meal; persuading even Nasir, who in his life before had never fallen so low as egg-meat, to take his share. The general verdict was:—tough and strong, but good in the Biseita.

Zaal saw an oryx; stalked it and killed it. The better joints were tied upon the baggage camels for the next halt, and our march continued. Afterwards the greedy Howeitat saw more oryx in the distance and went after the beasts, who foolishly ran a little; then stood still and stared till the men were near, and, too late, ran away again. Their white shining bellies betrayed them; for, by the magnification of the mirage, they winked each move to us from afar.

I was too weary, and too little sporting, to go out of the straight way for all the rare beasts in the world; so I rode after the caravan, which my camel overhauled quickly with her longer stride. At the tail of it were my men, walking. They feared that some of their animals would be dead before evening, if the wind blew stronger, but were leading them by hand in hope of getting them in. I admired the contrast between Mohammed the lusty, heavy-footed peasant, and the lithe Ageyl, with Farraj and Daud dancing along, barefooted, delicate as thoroughbreds. Only Gasim was not there: they thought him among the Howeitat, for his surliness offended the laughing soldiery and kept him commonly with the Beduin, who were more of his kidney.

There was no one behind, so I rode forward wishing to see how his camel was: and at last found it, riderless, being led by one of the Howeitat. His saddlebags were on it, and his rifle and his food, but he himself nowhere; gradually it dawned on us that the miserable

man was lost. This was a dreadful business, for in the haze and
mirage the caravan could not be seen two miles, and on the iron
ground it made no tracks: afoot he would never overtake us.

Every one had marched on, thinking him elsewhere in our loose
line; but much time had passed and it was nearly mid-day, so he
must be miles back. His loaded camel was proof that he had not
been forgotten asleep at our night halt. The Ageyl ventured that
perhaps he had dozed in the saddle and fallen, stunning or killing
himself: or perhaps some one of the party had borne him a grudge.
Anyway they did not know. He was an ill-natured stranger, no charge
on any of them, and they did not greatly care.

True: but it was true also that Mohammed, his countryman and
fellow, who was technically his road-companion, knew nothing of
the desert, had a foundered camel, and could not turn back for him.

I looked weakly at my trudging men, and wondered for a
moment if I could change with one, sending him back on my
camel to the rescue. My shirking the duty would be understood,
because I was a foreigner: but that was precisely the plea I did not
dare set up, while I yet presumed to help these Arabs in their own
revolt. It was hard, anyway, for a stranger to influence another
people's national movement, and doubly hard for a Christian and
a sedentary person to sway Moslem nomads. I should make it
impossible for myself if I claimed, simultaneously, the privileges
of both societies.

So, without saying anything, I turned my unwilling camel round,
and forced her, grunting and moaning for her camel friends, back
past the long line of men, and past the baggage into the emptiness
behind. My temper was very unheroic, for I was furious with my
other servants, with my own play-acting as a Beduin, and most of
all with Gasim, a gap-toothed, grumbling fellow, skrimshank in all
our marches, bad-tempered, suspicious, brutal, a man whose engagement I regretted, and of whom I had promised to rid myself as soon
as we reached a discharging place. It seemed absurd that I should
peril my weight in the Arab adventure for a single worthless man.

My camel seemed to feel it also, by her deep grumbling; but that was a constant recourse of ill-treated camels. After a mile or two, she felt better, and began to go forward less constrainedly, but still slowly. I had been noting our direction all these days with my oil compass, and hoped, by its aid, to return nearly to our starting place, seventeen miles away.

I had ridden about an hour and a half, easily, for the following breeze had let me wipe the crust from my red eyes and look forward almost without pain: when I saw a figure, or large bush, or at least something black ahead of me. The shifting mirage disguised height or distance; but this thing seemed moving, a little east of our course. On chance I turned my camel's head that way, and in a few minutes saw that it was Gasim. When I called he stood confusedly; I rode up and saw that he was nearly blinded and silly, standing there with his arms held out to me, and his black mouth gaping open. The Ageyl had put our last water in my skin, and this he spilled madly over his face and breast, in haste to drink. He stopped babbling, and began to wail out his sorrows. I sat him, pillion, on the camel's rump; then stirred her up and mounted.

At our turn the beast seemed relieved, and moved forward freely. In spite of our double weight she began to stride out, and at times even put her head down and for a few paces developed that fast and most comfortable shuffle to which the best animals, while young, were broken by skilled riders. This proof of reserve spirit in her rejoiced me, as did the little time lost in search.

Gasim was moaning impressively about the pain and terror of his thirst: I told him to stop; but he went on, and began to sit loosely; until at each step of the camel he bumped down on her hinder quarters with a crash, which, like his crying, spurred her to greater pace. There was danger in this, for we might easily founder her so. Again I told him to stop, and when he only screamed the louder, hit him and swore that for another sound I would throw him off. The threat, to which my general rage gave colour, worked. After it he clung on grimly without sound.

Not four miles had passed when again I saw a black bubble, lunging and swaying in the mirage ahead. It split into three, and swelled. I wondered if they were enemy. A minute later the haze unrolled with the disconcerting suddenness of illusion; and it was Auda with two of Nasir's men come back to look for me. I yelled jests and scoffs at them for abandoning a friend in the desert. Auda pulled his beard and grumbled that had he been present I would never have gone back. Gasim was transferred with insults to a better rider's saddle-pad, and we ambled forward together.

In an hour we rejoined Nasir and Nesib in the van. Nesib was vexed with me for perilling the lives of Auda and myself on a whim. It was clear to him that I reckoned they would come back for me. Nasir was shocked at his ungenerous outlook, and Auda was glad to rub into a townsman the paradox of tribe and city; the collective responsibility and group-brotherhood of the desert, contrasted with the isolation and competitive living of the crowded districts.

Over this little affair hours had passed, and the rest of the day seemed not so long; though the heat became worse, and the sand-blast stiffened in our faces till the air could be seen and heard, whistling past our camels like smoke. The ground was flat and featureless till five o'clock, when we saw low mounds ahead, and a little later found ourselves in comparative peace, amid sand-hills coated slenderly with tamarisk. These were the Kaseim of Sirhan. The bushes and the dunes broke the wind, it was sunset, and the evening mellowed and reddened on us from the west. So I wrote in my diary that Sirhan was beautiful.

Having not a mouthful of water we of course ate nothing: which made it a continent night. Yet the certainty of drink on the morrow let us sleep easily, lying on our bellies to prevent the inflation of foodlessness. Arab habit was to fill themselves to vomiting point at each well, and either to go dry to the next; or, if they carried water, to use it lavishly at the first halt, drinking and bread-making.

Next morning we rode down slopes, over a first ridge, and a second, and a third; each three miles from the other; till at eight o'clock we dismounted by the wells of Arfaja, the sweet-smelling bush, so called, being fragrant all about us. The unlined wells were dug about eighteen feet, to water creamy to the touch with a powerful smell and brackish taste. We found it delicious, and since there was greenstuff about, good for camel food, decided to stay here the day.

CHAPTER IX

FEASTS OF THE TRIBES

NEXT MORNING we did a fast march of five hours (our camels being full of life after their ease of yesterday) to an oasis-hollow of stunted palm trees, with tamarisk clumps here and there, and plentiful water, about seven feet underground, tasting sweeter than the water of Arfaja. Yet this also upon experience proved "Sirhan water," the first drink of which was tolerable, but which refused a lather to soap, and developed (after two days in closed vessels) a foul smell and a taste destructive to the intended flavour of coffee, tea, or bread.

Verily we were tiring of Wadi Sirhan, though Nesib and Zeki still designed works of plantation and reclamation here for the Arab Government when by them established. Such vaulting imagination was typical of Syrians, who easily persuaded themselves of possibilities, and as quickly reached forward to lay their present responsibilities on others. "Zeki," said I one day, "your camel is full of mange." "Alas, and alack," agreed he mournfully, "in the evening, very quickly, when the sun is low, we shall dress her skin with ointment."

During our next ride, I mentioned mange once more. "Aha," said Zeki, "it has given me a full idea. Conceive the establishment of a Veterinary Department of State for Syria when Damascus is ours. We shall have a staff of skilled surgeons, with a school of probationers and students, in a central hospital, or rather central hospitals, for camels and for horses, and for donkeys and cattle, even (why not?) for sheep and goats. There must be scientific and bacteriological branches to make researches into universal cures for animal disease. And what about a library of foreign books? . . . and district hospitals to feed the central, and travelling inspectors. . . ." With Nesib's eager collaboration he carved Syria into four inspectorates-general, and many sub-inspectorates.

Again on the morrow there was mention of mange. They had slept on their labour, and the scheme was rounding out. "Yet, my dear, it is imperfect; and our nature stops not short of perfection. We grieve to see you thus satisfied to snatch the merely opportune. It is an English fault." I dropped into their vein. "O Nesib," said I, "and O Zeki, will not perfection, even in the least of things, entail the ending of this world? Are we ripe for that? When I am angry I pray God to swing our globe into the fiery sun, and prevent the sorrows of the not-yet-born: but when I am content, I want to lie for ever in the shade, till I become a shade myself." Uneasily they shifted the talk to stud farms, and on the sixth day the poor camel died. Very truly "Because," as Zeki pointed out, "you did not dress her." Auda, Nasir, and the rest of us kept our beasts going by constant care. We could, perhaps, just stave the mange off till we should reach the camp of some well-provided tribe, and be able to procure medicines, with which to combat the disease whole-heartedly.

A mounted man came bearing down upon us. Tension there was, for a moment; but then the Howeitat hailed him. He was one of their herdsmen, and greetings were exchanged in an unhurried voice, as was proper in the desert, where noise was a low-bred business at the best, and urban at its worst.

He told us the Howeitat were camped in front, from Isawiya to Nebk, anxiously waiting our news. All was well with their tents. Auda's anxiety passed and his eagerness kindled. We rode fast for an hour to Isawiya and the tents of Ali abu Fitna, chief of one of

Auda's clans. Old Ali, rheumy-eyed, red and unkempt, into whose jutting beard a long nose perpetually dripped, greeted us warmly and urged us to the hospitality of his tent. We excused ourselves as too many, and camped near by under some thorns, while he and the other tent-holders made estimate of our numbers, and prepared feasts for us in the evening, to each group of tents its little batch of visitors. The meal took hours to produce, and it was long after dark when they called us to it. I woke and stumbled across, ate, made my way back to our couched camels and slept again.

Our march was prosperously over. We had found the Howeitat: our men were in excellent fettle: we had our gold and our explosives still intact. So we drew happily together in the morning to a solemn council on action. There was agreement that first we should present six thousand pounds to Nuri Shaalan, by whose sufferance we were in Sirhan. We wanted from him liberty to stay while enrolling and preparing our fighting men; and when we moved off we wanted him to look after their families and tents and herds.

These were great matters. It was determined that Auda himself should ride to Nuri on embassy, because they were friends. Meanwhile we would stay with Ali abu Fitna, moving gently northward with him towards Nebk, where Auda would tell all the Abu Tayi to collect. He would be back from Nuri before they were united. This was the business, and we laded six bags of gold into Auda's saddlebags, and off he went. Afterwards the chiefs of the Fitenna waited on us, and said that they were honoured to feast us twice a day, forenoon and sunset, so long as we remained with them; and they meant what they said. Howeitat hospitality was unlimited—no three-day niggardliness for them of the nominal desert law—and importunate, and left us no honourable escape from the entirety of the nomad's dream of well-being.

Each morning between eight and ten, a little group of blood mares under an assortment of imperfect saddlery would come to our camping place, and on them Nasir, Nesib, Zeki and I would mount, and with perhaps a dozen of our men on foot would move solemnly across the valley by the sandy paths between the bushes. Our horses were led by our servants, since it would be immodest to ride free or fast. So eventually we would reach the tent which was to be our feast-hall for that time; each family claiming us in turn, and bitterly offended if Zaal, the adjudicator, preferred one out of just order.

As we arrived, the dogs would rush out at us, and be driven off by onlookers—always a crowd had collected round the chosen tent—and we stepped in under the ropes to its guest half, made very large for the occasion and carefully dressed with its wall-curtain on the sunny side to give us shade. The bashful host would murmur and vanish again out of sight. The tribal rugs, lurid red things from Beyrout, were ready for us, arranged down the partition curtain, along the back wall and across the dropped end, so that we sat down on three sides of an open dusty space. We might be fifty men in all.

The host would reappear, standing by the pole; our local fellow-guests, el Dheilan, Zaal and other sheikhs, reluctantly let themselves be placed on the rugs between us, sharing our elbow-room on the pack-saddles, padded with folded felt rugs, over which we leaned. The front of the tent was cleared, and the dogs were frequently chased away by excited children, who ran across the empty space pulling yet smaller children after them. Their clothes were less as their years were less, and their pot-bodies rounder. The smallest infants of all, out of their fly-black eyes, would stare at the company, gravely balanced on spread legs, stark-naked, sucking their thumbs and pushing out expectant bellies towards us.

Then would follow an awkward pause, which our friends would try to cover, by showing us on its perch the household hawk (when possible a sea-bird taken young on the Red Sea coast) or their watch-cockerel, or their greyhound. Once a tame ibex was dragged in for our admiration: another time an oryx. When these interests were exhausted they would try and find a small-talk to distract us from the household noises, and from noticing the urgent whispered cookery-directions wafted through the dividing curtain with a powerful smell of boiled fat and drifts of tasty meat-smoke.

After a silence the host or a deputy would come forward and whisper, "Black or white?" an invitation for us to choose coffee or tea. Nasir would always say "Black," and the slave would be beckoned forward with the beaked coffee pot in one hand, and three or four clinking cups of white ware in the other. He would dash a few drops of coffee into the uppermost cup, and proffer it to Nasir, then pour the second for me, and the third for Nesib; and pause while we turned the cups about in our hands, and sucked them carefully, to get appreciatively from them the last richest drop.

As soon as they were empty his hand was stretched to clap them noisily one above the other, and toss them out with a lesser flourish for the next guest in order, and so on round the assembly till all had drunk. Then back to Nasir again. This second cup would be tastier than the first, partly because the pot was yielding deeper from the brew, partly because of the heel-taps of so many previous drinkers, present in the cups; whilst the third and fourth rounds, if the serving of the meat delayed so long, would be of surprising flavour.

However, at last, two men came staggering through the thrilled crowd, carrying the rice and meat on a tinned copper tray or shallow bath, five feet across, set like a great brazier on a foot. In the tribe there was only this one food-bowl of the size, and an incised inscription ran round it in florid Arabic characters: "To the glory of God, and in trust of mercy at the last, the property of His poor suppliant, Auda abu Tayi." It was borrowed by the host who was to entertain us for the time; and, since my urgent brain and body made me wakeful, from my blankets in the first light I would see the dish going across country, and by marking down its goal would know where we were to feed that day.

The bowl was now brim-full, ringed round its edge by white rice in an embankment a foot wide and six inches deep, filled with legs and ribs of mutton till they toppled over. It needed two or three victims to make in the centre a dressed pyramid of meat such as honour prescribed. The centre-pieces were the boiled, upturned heads, propped on their severed stumps of neck, so that the ears, brown like old leaves, flapped out on the rice surface. The jaws gaped emptily upward, pulled open to show the hollow throat with the tongue, still pink, clinging to the lower teeth and the long incisors whitely crowned the pile, very prominent above the nostrils' pricking hair and the lips which sneered away blackly from them.

This load was set down on the soil of the cleared space between us, where it steamed hotly, while a procession of minor helpers bore the small cauldrons and copper vats in which the cooking had been done. From them, with much-bruised bowls of enamelled iron, they ladled out over the main dish all the inside and outside of the sheep; little bits of yellow intestine, the white tail-cushion of fat, brown muscles and meat and bristly skin, all swimming in the liquid butter and grease of the seething. The bystanders watched anxiously, muttering satisfactions when a very juicy scrap plopped out.

The fat was scalding. Every now and then a man would drop his baler with an exclamation, and plunge his burnt fingers, not reluctantly, in his mouth to cool them: but they persevered till at last their scooping rang loudly on the bottoms of the pots; and, with a gesture of triumph, they fished out the intact livers from their hiding place in the gravy and topped the yawning jaws with them.

Two raised each smaller cauldron and tilted it, letting the liquid splash down upon the meat till the rice-crater was full, and the loose grains at the edge swam in the abundance: and yet they poured till, amid cries of astonishment from us, it was running over, and a little pool congealing in the dust. That was the final touch of splendour, and the host called us to come and eat.

We feigned a deafness, as manners demanded: at last we heard him, and looked surprised at one another, each urging his fellow to move first; till Nasir rose coyly, and after him we all came forward to sink on one knee round the tray, wedging in and cuddling up till the twenty-two for whom there was barely space were grouped around the food. We turned back our right sleeves to the elbow, and, taking lead from Nasir with a low "In the name of God the merciful, the loving-kind," we dipped together.

The first dip, for me, at least, was always cautious, since the liquid fat was so hot that my unaccustomed fingers could seldom bear it: and so I would toy with an exposed and cooling lump of meat till others' excavations had drained my rice-segment. We would knead between the fingers (not soiling the palm), neat balls of rice and fat and liver and meat cemented by gentle pressure, and project them by leverage of the thumb from the crooked forefinger into the mouth. With the right trick and the right construction the little lump held together and came clean off the hand; but when surplus butter and odd fragments clung, cooling, to the fingers, they had to be licked carefully to make the next effort slip easier away.

Our host stood by the circle, encouraging the appetite with pious ejaculations. At top speed we twisted, tore, cut and stuffed: never speaking, since conversation would insult a meal's quality; though it was proper to smile thanks when an intimate guest passed a select fragment, or when Mohammed el Dheilan gravely handed over a huge barren bone with a blessing. On such occasion I would return the compliment with some hideous, impossible lump of guts, a flippancy which rejoiced the Howeitat, but which the gracious, aristocratic Nasir saw with disapproval.

At length some of us were nearly filled, and began to play and pick; glancing sideways at the rest till they too grew slow, and at last ceased eating, elbow on knee, the hand hanging down from the wrist over the tray edge to drip, while the fat, butter and scattered grains of rice cooled into a stiff white grease which gummed the fingers together. When all had stopped, Nasir meaningly cleared his throat, and we rose up together in haste with an explosive "God requite it you, O host," to group ourselves outside among the tent-ropes while the next twenty guests inherited our leaving.

Those of us who were nice would go to the end of the tent where the flap of the roof-cloth, beyond the last poles, drooped down as an end curtain; and on this clan handkerchief (whose coarse goat-hair mesh was pliant and glossy with much use), would scrape the thickest of the fat from the hands. Then we would make back to

From a portrait by Augustus John

D. G. HOGARTH

our seats, and retake them sighingly; while the slaves, leaving aside their portion, the skulls of the sheep, would come round our rank with a wooden bowl of water, and a coffee-cup as dipper, to splash over our fingers, while we rubbed them with the tribal soap-cake.

Meantime the second and third sittings by the dish were having their turn, and then there would be one more cup of coffee, or a glass of syrup-like tea; and at last the horses would be brought and we would slip out to them, and mount, with a quiet blessing to the hosts as we passed by. When our backs were turned the children would run in disorder upon the ravaged dish, tear our gnawed bones from one another, and escape into the open with valuable fragments to be devoured in security behind some distant bush: while the watch dogs of all the camp prowled round snapping, and the master of the tent fed the choicest offal to his greyhound.

We feasted on the first day once, on the second twice, on the third twice; at Isawiya: and then, on the thirtieth of May, we saddled and rode easily for three hours, past an old sanded lava field to a valley in which seven-foot wells of the usual brackish water lay all about us. The Abu Tayi struck camp when we struck, and journeyed at our side, and camped around us: so today for the first time I was spectator from the midst of an Arab tribe, and actor in the routine of its march.

It was strangely unlike the usual desert-constancy. All day the grey-green expanse of stones and bushes quivered like a mirage with the movement of men on foot; and horsemen; men on camels; camels bearing the hunched black loads which were the goat-hair tent-cloths; camels, swaying curiously, like butterflies, under the winged and fringed howdahs of the women; camels tusked like mammoths or tailed like birds with the cocked or dragging tent-poles of silvery poplar. There was no order nor control nor routine of march, other than the wide front, the self-contained parties, the simultaneous start, which the insecurity of countless generations had made instinctive. The difference was that the desert, whose daily sparseness gave value to every man, to-day seemed with their numbers suddenly to come alive.

The pace was easy; and we, who had been guarding our own lives for weeks, found it a relaxation beyond feeling to know ourselves so escorted as to share the light liability of danger with a host. Even our most solemn riders let themselves go a little, and the wilder ones became licentious. First amongst these, of course, were Farraj and Daud, my two imps, whose spirits not all the privations of our road had quelled for a moment. About their riding places in our line of march centred two constant swirls of activity or of accident, according as their quenchless mischief found a further expression. On my dry patience they grated a little, because the plague of snakes which had been with us since our first entry into Sirhan, to-day rose to memorable height, and became a terror. In ordinary times, so the Arabs said, snakes were little worse here than elsewhere by water in the desert: but this year the valley seemed creeping with horned vipers and puff-adders, cobras and black snakes. By night movement was dangerous: and at last we found it necessary to walk with sticks, beating the bushes each side while we stepped warily through on bare feet.

A strange thing was the snakes' habit, at night, of lying beside us, probably for warmth, under or on the blanket. When we learned this our rising was with infinite care, and the first up would search round his fellows with a stick till he could pronounce them unencumbered. Our party of fifty men killed perhaps twenty snakes daily; at last they got so on our nerves that the boldest of us feared to touch ground; while those who, like my self, had a shuddering horror of all reptiles, longed that our stay in Sirhan might end.

Not so Farraj and Daud. To them, this was a new and splendid game. They troubled us continually with alarms, and furious beatings upon the head of every harmless twig or root which caught their fancy. At last, in our noon-halt, I charged them strictly not to let the cry of snake again pass their lips aloud; and then, sitting by our traps upon the sand, we had peace. To live on the floor, whence it was so far to arise and walk, disposed to inaction, and there was much to think about: so that it may have been an hour afterwards before I noticed the offending pair smiling and nudging one another. My eyes idly followed their eyes to the neighbouring bush under which a brown snake lay coiled, glittering at me.

Quickly I moved myself, and cried to Ali, who jumped in with his riding-cane and settled it. I told him to give the two boys a swinging half-dozen each, to teach them not again to be literal at my expense. Nasir, slumbering behind me, heard and with joy shouted to add six from himself. Nesib copied him, and then Zeki, and then ibn Dgheithir, till half the men were clamouring for revenge. The culprits were abashed when they saw that all the hides and all the sticks in the party would hardly expiate their account: however, I saved them the weight of it, and instead we proclaimed them moral bankrupts, and set them under the women to gather wood and draw water for the tents.

We were very weary of Sirhan. The landscape was of a hopelessness and sadness deeper than all the open deserts we had crossed. Sand, or flint, or a desert of bare rocks was exciting sometimes, and in certain lights had the monstrous beauty of sterile desolation: but there was something sinister, something actively evil in this snake-devoted Sirhan, proliferant of salt water, barren palms, and bushes which served neither for grazing nor for firewood.

Accordingly we marched one day, and another, beyond Ghutti, whose weak well was nearly sweet. When we got near Ageila, we saw that it was held by many tents, and presently a troop came out to meet us. They were Auda abu Tayi, safely back from Nuri Shaalan, with the one-eyed Durzi ibn Dughmi, our old guest at Wejh. His presence proved Nuri's favour, as did their strong escort of Rualla horse; who, bareheaded and yelling, welcomed us to Nuri's empty house with a great show of spears and wild firing of rifles and revolvers at full gallop through the dust.

Affairs looked well, and we set three men to make coffee for the visitors, who came in to Nasir one by one or group by group, swearing allegiance to Feisal and to the Arab Movement, in the Wejh formula; and promising to obey Nasir, and to follow after him with their contingents. Besides their formal presents, each new party deposited on our carpet their privy, accidental gift of lice; and long before sunset Nasir and I were in a fever, with relay after relay of irritation. Auda had a stiff arm, the effect of an old wound in the elbow joint, and so could not scratch all of himself; but experience had taught him a way of thrusting a cross-headed camel-stick up his left sleeve and turning it round and round inside against his ribs, which method seemed to relieve his itch more than our claws did ours.

CHAPTER X

NOMADS AND NOMAD LIFE

WE WERE now five weeks out from Wejh; we had spent nearly all the money we had brought with us: we had eaten all the Howeitat sheep: we had rested or replaced all our old camels: nothing hindered the start. The freshness of the adventure in hand consoled us for everything; and Auda, importing more mutton, gave a farewell feast, the greatest of the whole series, in his huge tent the eve before we started. Hundreds were present, and five fills of the great tray were eaten up in relay as fast as they were cooked and carried in.

Sunset came down, delightfully red, and after the feast the whole party lay round the outside coffee hearth lingering under the stars, while Auda and others told us stories. In a pause I remarked casually that I had looked for Mohammed el Dheilan in his tent that afternoon, to thank him for the milch camel he had given me, but had not found him. Auda shouted for joy, till everybody looked at him; and then, in the silence which fell that they might learn the joke, he pointed to Mohammed sitting dismally beside the coffee mortar, and said in his huge voice:—

"Ho! Shall I tell why Mohammed for fifteen days has not slept in his tent?" Everybody chuckled with delight, and conversation stopped; all the crowd stretched out on the ground, chins in hands, prepared to take the good points of the story which they had heard perhaps twenty times. The women, Auda's three wives, Zaal's wife, and some of Mohammed's, who had been cooking, came across, straddling their bellies in the billowy walk which came of carrying burdens on their heads, till they were near the partition-curtain; and there they listened like the rest while Auda told at length how Mohammed had bought publicly in the bazaar at Wejh a costly string of pearls, and had not given it to any of his wives, and so they were all at odds, except in their common rejection of him.

The story was, of course, a pure invention—Auda's elvish humour heightened by the stimulus of Revolt—and the luckless Mohammed, who had dragged through the fortnight guesting casually with one or other of the tribesmen, called upon God for mercy, and upon me for witness that Auda lied. I cleared my throat solemnly. Auda asked for silence, and begged me to confirm his words.

I began with the introducing phrase of a formal tale: "In the name of God the merciful, the loving-kind. We were six in Wejh. There were Auda, and Mohammed, and Zaal, Gasim el Shimt, Mufaddhi and the poor man (myself); and one night just before dawn, Auda said, 'Let us make a raid against the market.' And we said, 'in the name of God.' And we went; Auda in a white robe and a red headcloth, and Kasim sandals of pieced leather; Mohammed in a silken tunic of 'seven kings' and barefoot; Zaal . . . I forget Zaal. Gasim wore cotton, and Mufaddhi was in silk of blue stripes with an embroidered headcloth. Your servant was as your servant."

My pause was still with astonishment. This was a close parody of Auda's epic style; and I mimicked also his wave of the hand, his round voice, and the rising and dropping tone which emphasized the points, or what he thought were points, of his pointless stories. The Howeitat sat silent as death, twisting their full bodies inside their sweat-stiffened shirts for joy, and staring hungrily at Auda; for they all recognized the original, and parody was a new art to them and to him. The coffee man, Mufaddhi, a Shammar refugee from the guilt of blood, himself a character, forgot to pile fresh thorns on his fire for fixity of listening to the tale.

I told how we left the tents, with a list of the tents, and how we walked down towards the village, describing every camel and horse we saw, and all the passers-by, and the ridges, "all bare of grazing, for by God that country was barren. And we marched: and after we had marched the time of a smoked cigarette, we heard something, and Auda stopped and said, 'Lads, I hear something.' And Mohammed stopped and said, 'Lads, I hear something.' And Zaal, 'By God, you are right.' And we stopped to listen, and there was nothing, and the poor man said, 'By God, I hear nothing.' And Zaal said, 'By God, I hear nothing.' And Mohammed said, 'By God, I hear nothing.' And Auda said, 'By God, you are right.'

"And we marched and we marched, and the land was barren, and we heard nothing. And on our right hand came a man, a negro, on a donkey. The donkey was grey, with black ears, and one black foot, and on its shoulder was a brand like this" (a scrabble in the air), "and its tail moved and its legs: Auda saw it, and said, 'By God, a donkey.' And Mohammed said, 'By the very God, a donkey and a slave.' And we marched. And there was a ridge, not a great ridge, but a ridge as great as from the here to the what-do-you-call-it (*lil biliyeh el hok*) that is yonder: and we marched to the ridge and it was barren. That land is barren: barren: barren.

"And we marched: and beyond the what-do-you-call-it there was a what-there-is as far as hereby from thence, and thereafter a ridge: and we came to that ridge, and went up that ridge: it was barren, all that land was barren: and as we came up that ridge, and were by the head of that ridge, and came to the end of the head of that ridge, by God, by my God, by very God, the sun rose upon us."

It ended the session. Every one had heard that sunrise twenty times, in its immense bathos; an agony piled up of linked phrases, repeated and repeated with breathless excitement by Auda to carry over for hours the thrill of a raiding story in which nothing happened; and the trivial rest of it was exaggerated the degree which made it like one of Auda's tales; and yet, also, the history of the walk to market at Wejh which many of us had taken. The tribe was in waves of laughter on the ground.

Auda laughed the loudest and longest, for he loved a jest upon himself; and the fatuousness of my epic had shown him his own sure mastery of descriptive action. He embraced Mohammed, and confessed the invention of the necklace. In gratitude Mohammed invited the camp to breakfast with him in his regained tent on the morrow, an hour before we started for the swoop on Akaba. We should have a sucking camel-calf boiled in sour milk by his wives: famous cooks, and a legendary dish!

We started an hour before noon on June 19, 1917. Nasir led us, riding his Ghazala—a camel vaulted and huge-ribbed as an antique ship; towering a good foot above the next of our animals, and yet perfectly proportioned, with a stride like an ostrich's—a lyrical beast, noblest and best bred of the Howeitat camels, a female of nine remembered dams. Auda was beside him, and I skirmished about their gravities on Naama, "the hen-ostrich," a racing camel and my last purchase. Behind me rode my Ageyl, with Mohammed, the clumsy. Mohammed was now companioned by Ahmed, another peasant, who had been for six years living among the Howeitat by force of his thews and wits—a knowing eager ruffian.

Our present party totalled more than five hundred strong; and the sight of this jolly mob of hardy, confident northerners chasing gazelle wildly over the face of the desert, took from us momentarily all sorry apprehension as to the issue of our enterprise. We felt it was a rice-night, and the chiefs of the Abu Tayi came to sup with us. Afterwards, with the embers of our coffee fire pleasantly red between us against the cool of this upland northcountry, we sat about on the carpets chatting discursively of this remote thing and that.

Nasir rolled over on his back, with my glasses, and began to study the stars, counting aloud first one group and then another; crying out with surprise at discovering little lights not noticed by his unaided eye. Auda set us on to talk of telescopes—of the great

ones—and of how man in three hundred years had so far advanced
from his first essay that now he built glasses as long as a tent, through
which he counted thousands of unknown stars, "And the stars—
what are they?" We slipped into talk of suns beyond suns, sizes and
distance beyond wit. "What will now happen with this knowledge?"
asked Mohammed. "We shall set to, and many learned and some
clever men together will make glasses as more powerful than ours,
as ours than Galileo's; and yet more hundreds of astronomers will
distinguish and reckon yet more thousands of now unseen stars,
mapping them, and giving each one its name. When we see them
all, there will be no night in heaven."

"Why are the Westerners always wanting all?" provokingly said
Auda. "Behind our few stars we can see God, who is not behind
your millions." "We want the world's end, Auda." "But that is God's"
complained Zaal, half angry. Mohammed would not have his subject turned. "Are there men on these greater worlds?" he asked. "God
knows." "And has each the Prophet and heaven and hell?" Auda
broke in on him, "Lads, we know our districts, our camels, our
women. The excess and the glory are to God. If the end of wisdom
is to add star to star our foolishness is pleasing." And then he spoke
of money, and distracted their minds till they all buzzed at once.
Afterwards he whispered to me that I must get him a worthy gift
from Feisal when he won Akaba.

We marched at dawn, and presently Auda told me he was riding ahead to Bair, and would I come? We went fast, and in two
hours came upon the place suddenly, under a knoll. Auda had hurried on to visit the tomb of his son Annad, who had been waylaid
by five of his Motalga cousins in revenge for Abtan, their champi-
on, slain by Annad in single combat. Auda told me how Annad had
ridden at them, one against five, and had died as he should; but it
left only little Mohammed between him and childlessness. He had
brought me along to hear him greatly lament his dead.

However, as we rode down towards the graves, we were astonished to see smoke wreathing from the ground about the wells. We

changed direction sharply, and warily approached the ruins. It seemed there was no one there; but the thick dungcake round the well-brink was charred, and the well itself shattered at the top. The ground was torn and blackened as if by an explosion; and when we looked down the shaft we saw its steyning stripped and split, and many blocks thrown down the bore half choking it and the water in the bottom. I sniffed the air and thought the smell was dynamite.

Auda ran to the next well, in the bed of the valley below the graves; and that, too, was ragged about the head and choked with fallen stones. "This," said he, "is Jazi work." We walked across the valley to the third—the Beni Sakhr—well. It was only a crater of chalk. Zaal arrived, grave at sight of the disaster. We explored the ruined khan, in which were night-old traces of perhaps a hundred horse. There was a fourth well, north of the ruins in the open flat, and to it we went hopelessly, wondering what would become of us if Bair were all destroyed. To our joy it was uninjured.

This was a Jazi well, and its immunity gave strong colour to Auda's theory. We were disconcerted to find the Turks so ready, and began to fear that perhaps they had also raided El Jefer, east of Maan, the wells at which we planned to concentrate before we attacked. Their blocking would be a real embarrassment. Meanwhile, thanks to the fourth well, our situation, though uncomfortable, was not dangerous. Yet its water facilities were altogether insufficient for five hundred camels; so it became imperative to open the least damaged of the other wells—that in the ruins, about whose lip the turf smouldered. Auda and I went off with Nasir to look again at it.

An Ageyli brought us an empty case of Nobel's gelignite, evidently the explosive which the Turks had used. From scars in the ground it was clear that several charges had been fired simultaneously round the well-head, and in the shaft. Staring down it till our eyes were adjusted to its dark, we suddenly saw many niches cut in the shaft less than twenty feet below. Some were still tamped, and had wires hanging down.

Evidently there was a second series of charges, either inefficiently wired, or with a very long time-fuse. Hurriedly we unrolled our bucket-ropes, twined them together, and hung them freely down the middle of the well from a stout cross-pole, the sides being so tottery that the scrape of a rope might have dislodged their blocks. I then found that charges were small, not above three pounds each, and had been wired in series with field telephone cable. But something had gone wrong. Either the Turks had scamped their job or their scouts had seen us coming before they had had time to re-connect.

So we soon had two fit wells, and a clear profit of thirty pounds of enemy gelignite. We determined to stay a week in this fortunate Bair. A third object—to discover the condition of the Jefer wells— was now added to our needs for food, and for news of the state of mind of the tribes between Maan and Akaba. We sent a man to Jefer. We prepared a little caravan of pack-camels with Howeitat brands and sent them across the line to Tafileh with three or four obscure clansmen—people who would never be suspected of association with us. They would buy all the flour they could and bring it back to us in five or six days' time.

As for the tribes about the Akaba road, we wanted their active help against the Turks to carry out the provisional plan we had made at Wejh. Our idea was to advance suddenly from El Jefer, to cross the railway-line and to crown the great pass—Nagb el Shtar— down which the road dipped from the Maan plateau to the red Guweira plain. To hold this pass we should have to capture Aba el Lissan, the large spring at its head, about sixteen miles from Maan; but the garrison was small, and we hoped to overrun it with a rush. We would then be astride the road, whose posts at the end of the week should fall from hunger; though probably before that the hill tribes, hearing of our successful beginning, would join us to wipe them out.

The crux of our plan was the attack on Aba el Lissan, lest the force in Maan have time to sally out, relieve it, and drive us off the head of Shtar. If, as at present, they were only a battalion, they would hardly dare move; and should they let it fall while waiting for reinforcements to arrive, Akaba would surrender to us, and we should be based on the sea and have the advantageous gorge of Itm between us and the enemy. So our insurance for success was to keep Maan careless and weak, not suspecting our malevolent presence in the neighbourhood.

It was never easy for us to keep our movements secret, as we lived by preaching to the local people, and the unconvinced would tell the Turks. Our long march into Wadi Sirhan was known to the enemy, and the most civilian owl could not fail to see that the only fit objective was Akaba. The demolition of Bair (and Jefer, too, for we had it confirmed that the seven wells of Jefer were destroyed) showed that the Turks were to that extent on the alert.

It might be that Jefer really was denied to us; but we were not without hope that there too we should find the technical work of demolition ill-done by these pitiful Turks. Dhaif-Allah, a leading man of the Jazi Howeitat, one who came down to Wejh and swore allegiance, had been present in Jefer when the King's Well was fired by dynamite placed about its lip; and sent us secret word from Maan that he had heard the upper stones clap together and key over the mouth of the well. His conviction was that the shaft was intact, and the clearing of it a few hours' work. We hoped so; and rode away from Bair all in order, on the twenty-eighth of June, to find out.

Quickly we crossed the weird plain of Jefer. Next day by noon we were at the wells. They seemed most thoroughly destroyed; and the fear grew that we might find in them the first check to our scheme of operations, a scheme so much too elaborate that a check might be far reaching.

However, we went to the well—Auda's family property—of which Dhaif-Allah had told us the tale, and began to sound about it. The ground rang hollow under our mallet, and we called for volunteers able to dig and build. Some of the Ageyl came forward, led by the Mirzugi, a capable camel boy of Nasir's. They started with the few tools we had. The rest of us formed a ring round the well-depression and watched them work, singing to them and promising rewards of gold when they had found the water.

It was a hot task in the full glare of the summer sun; for the Jefer plain was of hard mud, flat as the hand, blinding white with salt, and twenty miles across; but time pressed, because if we failed we might have to ride fifty miles in the night to the next well. So we pushed the work by relays at speed through the midday heat, turning into labourers all our amenable fellows. It made easy digging, for the explosion which shifted the stones had loosened the soil.

As they dug and threw out the earth, the core of the well rose up like a tower of rough stones in the centre of the pit. Very carefully we began to take away the ruined head of the pile: difficult work, for the stones had become interlocked in their fall; but this was the better sign, and our spirits rose. Before sunset the workers shouted that there was no more packing soil, that the interstices between the blocks were clear, and that they heard the mud fragments which slipped through splashing many feet below.

Half an hour later came a rush and rumble of stones in the mouth, followed by a heavy splash and yells. We hurried down, and by the Mirzugi's torch saw the well yawning open, no longer a tube, but a deep bottle-shouldered pit, twenty feet across at the bottom, which was black with water and white in the middle with spray where the Ageyli who had been clearing when the key slipped, was striking out lustily in the effort not to drown. Everybody laughed down the well at him, till at last Abdulla lowered him a noose of rope, and we drew him up, very wet and angry, but in no way damaged by his fall.

We rewarded the diggers, and feasted them on a weak camel, which had failed in the march to-day; and then all night we watered, while a squad of Ageyl, with a long chorus, steyned up to ground-level an eight-foot throat of mud and stones. At dawn the earth was stamped in round this, and the well stood complete, as fit in appearance as ever. Only the water was not very much. We worked it the twenty-four hours without rest, and ran it to a cream; and still some of our camels were not satisfied.

From Jefer we took action. Riders went forward into the Dhumaniyeh tents to lead their promised attack against Fuweilah, the block-house which covered the head of the pass of Aba el Lissan. Our attack was planned for two days before the weekly caravan which, from Maan, replenished the client garrisons. Starvation would make reduction of these distant places easier, by impressing on them how hopelessly they were cut off from their friends.

We sat in Jefer meanwhile, waiting to hear the fortune of the attack. On its success or failure would depend the direction of our next march. The halt was not unpleasant, for our position had its comic side. We were within sight of Maan, during those minutes of the day in which the mirage did not make eyes and glasses useless; and yet we strolled about admiring our new well-lip in complete security, because the Turkish garrison believed water impossible here or at Bair, and were hugging the pleasant idea that we were now desperately engaged with their cavalry in Sirhan.

I hid under some bushes near the well for hours, against the heat, very lazy, pretending to be asleep, the wide silk sleeve of my pillow-arm drawn over my face as veil against the flies. Auda sat up and talked like a river, telling his best stories in great form. At last I reproved him with a smile, for talking too much and doing too little. He sucked his lips with pleasure of the work to come.

In the following dawn a tired horseman rode into our camp with news that the Dhumaniyeh had fired on the Fuweilah post the afternoon before as soon as our men had reached them. The surprise had not been quite complete; the Turks manned their dry stone breastworks and drove them off. The crestfallen Arabs drew back into cover, and the enemy, believing it only an ordinary tribal affray had made a mounted sortie upon the nearest encampment.

One old man, six women and seven children were its only occupants. In their anger at finding nothing actively hostile or able-bodied, the troopers smashed up the camp and cut the throats of its helpless ones. The Dhumaniyeh on the hill-tops heard and saw nothing till it was too late; but then, in their fury, they dashed down across the return road of the murderers and cut them off almost to the last man. To complete their vengeance they assaulted the now weakly-garrisoned fort, carried it in the first fierceness of their rush, and took no prisoners.

We were ready saddled; and within ten minutes had loaded and marched for Ghadir el Haj, the first railway station south of Maan, on our direct road for Aba el Lissan. Simultaneously, we detached a small party to cross the railway just above Maan and create a diversion on that side. Especially they were to threaten the great herds of sick camels, casualties of the Palestine front, which the Turks pastured in the Shobek plains till once more fit for service.

We calculated that the news of their Fuweilah disaster would not have reached Maan till the morning, and that they could not drive in these camels (supposing our northern party missed them) and fit out a relief expedition, before nightfall; and if we were then attacking the line at Ghadir el Haj, they would probably divert the relief thither, and so let us move on Akaba unmolested.

With this hope we rode steadily through the flowing mirage till afternoon, when we descended on the line; and, having delivered a long stretch of it from guards and patrols, began on the many bridges of the captured section. The little garrison of Ghadir el Haj sallied out with the valour of ignorance against us, but the heat-haze blinded them, and we drove them off with loss.

They were on the telegraph, and would notify Maan, which beside, could not fail to hear the repeated thuds of our explosive. It was our aim to bring the enemy down upon us in the night; or rather down here, where they would find no people but many broken bridges, for we worked fast and did great damage. The drainage holes in the spandrils held from three to five pounds of gelatine each. We, firing our mines by short fuses, brought down the arch, shattered the pier, and stripped the side walls, in no more than six minutes' work. So we ruined ten bridges and many rails, and finished our explosive.

After dusk, when our departure could not be seen, we rode five miles westward of the line, to cover. There we made fires and baked bread. Our meal however, was not cooked before three horsemen cantered up to report that a long column of new troops—infantry and guns—had just appeared at Aba el Lissan from Maan. The Dhumaniyeh, disorganized with victory, had had to abandon their ground without fighting. They were at Batra waiting for us. We had lost Aba el Lissan, the blockhouse, the pass, the command of the Akaba road: without a shot being fired.

We learned afterwards that this unwelcome and unwonted vigour on the part of the Turks was accident. A relief battalion had reached Maan that very day. The news of an Arab demonstration against Fuweilah arrived simultaneously; and the battalion, which happened to be formed up ready with its transport in the station yard, to march to barracks, was hurriedly strengthened by a section of pack artillery and some mounted men, and moved straight out as a punitive column to rescue the supposedly-besieged post.

They had left Maan in mid-morning and marched gently along the motor road, the men sweating in the heat of this south country after their native Caucasian snows, and drinking thirstily of every spring. From Aba el Lissan they climbed uphill towards the old blockhouse, which was deserted except for the silent vultures flying above its walls in slow uneasy rings. The battalion commander feared lest the sight be too much for his young troops, and led them back to the roadside spring of Aba el Lissan, in its serpentine narrow valley, where they camped all night in peace about the water.

CHAPTER XI

FIGHTING TO THE SEA

SUCH NEWS shook us into quick life. We threw our baggage across our camels on the instant and set out over the rolling downs of this end of the tableland of Syria. Our hot bread was in our hands, and, as we ate, there mingled with it the taste of the dust of our large force crossing the valley bottoms, and some taint of the strange keen smell of the wormwood which overgrew the slopes. In the breathless air of these evenings in the hills, after the long days of summer, everything struck very acutely on the senses: and when marching in a great column, as we were, the front camels kicked up the aromatic dust-laden branches of the shrubs, whose scent-particles rose into the air and hung in a long mist, making fragrant the road of those behind.

The slopes were clean with the sharpness of wormwood, and the hollows oppressive with the richness of their stronger, more luxuriant growths. Our night-passage might have been through a planted garden, and these varieties part of the unseen beauty of successive banks of flowers. The noises too were very clear. Auda broke out singing, away in front, and the men joined in from time to time, with the greatness, the catch at heart, of an army moving into battle.

We rode all night, and when dawn came were dismounting on the crest of the hills between Batra and Aba el Lissan, with a wonderful view westwards over the green and gold Guweira plain, and beyond it to the ruddy mountains hiding Akaba and the sea. Gasim abu Dumeik, head of the Dhumaniyeh, was waiting anxiously for us, surrounded by his hard-bitten tribesmen, their grey strained faces flecked with the blood of the fighting yesterday. There was a deep greeting for Auda and Nasir. We made hurried plans, and scattered to the work, knowing we could not go forward to Akaba with this battalion in possession of the pass. Unless we dislodged it, our two months' hazard and effort would fail before yielding even first-fruits.

Fortunately the poor handling of the enemy gave us an unearned advantage. They slept on, in the valley, while we crowned the hills in wide circle about them unobserved. We began to snipe them steadily in their positions under the slopes and rock-faces by the water, hoping to provoke them out and up the hill in a charge against us. Meanwhile, Zaal rode away with our horsemen and cut the Maan telegraph and telephone in the plain.

This went on all day. It was terribly hot—hotter than ever before I had felt it in Arabia—and the anxiety and constant moving made it hard for us. Some even of the tough tribesmen broke down under the cruelty of the sun, and crawled or had to be thrown under rocks to recover in their shade. We ran up and down to supply our lack of numbers by mobility, ever looking over the long ranges of hill for a new spot from which to counter this or that Turkish effort. The hill-sides were steep, and exhausted our breath, and the grasses twined like little hands about our ankles as we ran, and plucked us back. The sharp reefs of limestone which cropped out over the ridges tore our feet, and long before evening the more energetic men were leaving a rusty print upon the ground with every stride.

Our rifles grew so hot with sun and shooting that they seared our hands; and we had to be grudging of our rounds, considering every shot, and spending great pains to make it sure. The rocks on

which we flung ourselves for aim were burning, so that they scorched
our breasts and arms, from which later the skin drew off in ragged
sheets. The present smart made us thirst. Yet even water was rare
with us; we could not afford men to fetch enough from Batra, and
if all could not drink, it was better that none should.

We consoled ourselves with knowledge that the enemy's enclosed
valley would be hotter than our open hills: also that they were Turks,
men of white meat, little apt for warm weather. So we clung to them,
and did not let them move or mass or sortie out against us cheap-
ly. They could do nothing valid in return. We were no targets for
their rifles, since we moved with speed, eccentrically. Also, we were
able to laugh at the little mountain guns which they fired up at us.
The shells passed over our heads, to burst behind us in the air; and
yet, of course, for all that they could see from their hollow place,
fairly amongst us above the hostile summits of the hill.

Just after noon I had a heat-stroke, or so pretended, for I was
dead weary of it all, and cared no longer how it went. So I crept
into a hollow where there was a trickle of thick water in a muddy
cup of the hills, to suck some moisture off its dirt through the fil-
ter of my sleeve. Nasir joined me, panting like a winded animal,
with his cracked and bleeding lips shrunk apart in his distress: and
old Auda appeared, striding powerfully, his eyes bloodshot and
staring, his knotty face working with excitement.

He grinned with malice when he saw us lying there, spread out
to find coolness under the bank, and croaked at me harshly, "Well,
how is it with the Howeitat? All talk and no work?" "By God,
indeed," spat I back again, for I was angry with every one and with
myself, "they shoot a lot and hit a little." Auda almost pale with
rage, and trembling, tore his headcloth off and threw it on the
ground beside me. Then he ran back up the hill like a madman,
shouting to the men in his dreadful strained and rustling voice.

They came together to him, and after a moment scattered away
down hill. I feared things were going wrong, and struggled to where
he stood alone on the hill-top, glaring at the enemy: but all he would

EMIR SHAKIR

say to me was, "Get your camel if you want to see the old man's work." Nasir called for his camel and we mounted.

The Arabs passed before us into a little sunken place, which rose to a low crest; and we knew that the hill beyond went down in a facile slope to the main valley of Aba el Lissan, somewhat below the spring. All our four hundred camel men were here tightly collected, just out of sight of the enemy. We rode to their head, and asked the Shimt what it was and where the horsemen had gone.

He pointed over the ridge to the next valley above us, and said, "With Auda there": and as he spoke yells and shots poured up in a sudden torrent from beyond the crest. We kicked our camels furiously to the edge, to see our fifty horsemen coming down the last slope into the main valley like a run-away, at full gallop, shooting from the saddle. As we watched, two or three went down, but the rest thundered forward at marvellous speed, and the Turkish infantry, huddled together under the cliff ready to cut their desperate way out towards Maan in the first dusk, began to sway in and out, and finally broke before the rush, adding their flight to Auda's charge.

Nasir screamed at me, "Come on," with his bloody mouth; and we plunged our camels madly over the hill, and down towards the head of the fleeing enemy. The slope was not too steep for a camel-gallop, but steep enough to make their pace terrific, and their course uncontrollable: yet the Arabs were able to extend to right and left and to shoot into the Turkish brown. The Turks had been too bound up in the terror of Auda's furious charge against their rear to notice us as we came over the eastward slope: so we also took them by surprise and in the flank; and a charge of ridden camels going nearly thirty miles an hour was irresistible.

The Howeitat were very fierce, for the slaughter of their women on the day before had been a new and horrible side of warfare suddenly revealed to them. So there were only a hundred and sixty prisoners, many of them wounded; and three hundred dead and dying were scattered over the open valleys.

A few of the enemy got away, the gunners on their teams, and some mounted men and officers with their Jazi guides. Mohammed el Dheilan chased them for three miles into Mreigha, hurling insults as he rode, that they might know him and keep out of his way. The feud of Auda and his cousins had never applied to Mohammed, the political-minded, who showed friendship to all men of his tribe when he was alone to do so. Among the fugitives was Dhaif-Allah, who had done us the good turn about the King's Well at Jefer.

Auda came swinging up on foot, his eyes glazed over with the rapture of battle, and the words bubbling with incoherent speed from his mouth. "Work, work, where are words, work, bullets, Abu Tayi" . . . and he held up his shattered field-glasses, his pierced pistol-holster, and his leather sword-scabbard cut to ribbons. He had been the target of a volley which had killed his mare under him, but the six bullets through his clothes had left him scathless.

He told me later, in strict confidence, that thirteen years before he had bought an amulet Koran for one hundred and twenty pounds and had not since been wounded. Indeed, Death had avoided his face, and gone scurvily about killing brothers, sons and followers. The book was a Glasgow reproduction, costing eighteenpence; but Auda's deadliness did not let people laugh at his superstition.

He was wildly pleased with the fight, most of all because he had confounded me and shown what his tribe could do. Mohammed was wroth with us for a pair of fools, calling me worse than Auda, since I had insulted him by words like flung stones to provoke the folly which had nearly killed us all: though it had killed only two of us, one Rueili and one Sherari.

It was, of course, a pity to lose any one of our men, but time was of importance to us, and so imperative was the need of dominating Maan, to shock the little Turkish garrisons between us and the sea into surrender, that I would have willingly lost much more than the two. On occasions like this Death justified himself and was cheap.

Meanwhile our Arabs had plundered the Turks, their baggage train, and their camp; and soon after moonrise, Auda came to us and said that we must move. It angered Nasir and myself. To-night there was a dewy west wind blowing, and at Aba el Lissan's four thousand feet, after the heat and burning passion of the day, its damp chill struck very sharply on our wounds and bruises. The spring itself was a thread of silvery water in a runnel of pebbles across delightful turf, green and soft, on which we lay, wrapped in our cloaks, wondering if something to eat were worth preparing: for we were subject at the moment to the physical shame of success, a reaction of victory, when it became clear that nothing was worth doing, and that nothing worthy had been done.

Auda insisted. Partly it was superstition—he feared the newly-dead around us; partly lest the Turks return in force; partly lest other clans of the Howeitat take us, lying there broken and asleep. Some were his blood enemies: others might say they came to help our battle, and in the darkness thought we were Turks and fired blindly. So we roused ourselves, and jogged the sorry prisoners into line.

Most had to walk. Some twenty camels were dead or dying from wounds which they had got in the charge, and others were over weak to take a double burden. The rest were loaded with an Arab and a Turk; but some of the Turkish wounded were too hurt to hold themselves on pillion. In the end we had to leave about twenty on the thick grass beside the rivulet, where at least they would not die of thirst, though there was little hope of life or rescue for them.

Nasir set himself to beg blankets for these abandoned men, who were half-naked; and while the Arabs packed, I went off down the valley where the fight had been, to see if the dead had any clothing they could spare. But the Beduin had been before-hand with me, and had stripped them to the skin. Such was their point of honour.

To an Arab an essential part of the triumph of victory was to wear the clothes of an enemy: and next day we saw our force transformed (as to the upper half) into a Turkish force, each man in a soldier's tunic: for this was a battalion straight from home, very well found and dressed in new uniforms.

In the end our little army was ready, and wound slowly up the height and beyond into a hollow sheltered from the wind; and there, while the tired men slept, we dictated letters to the Sheikhs of the coastal Howeitat, telling them of the victory, that they might invest their nearest Turks, and hold them till we came. We had been kind to one of the captured officers, a policeman despised by his regular colleagues, and him we persuaded to be our Turkish scribe to the commandants of Guweira, Kethera and Hadra, the three posts between us and Akaba, telling them that if our blood was not hot we took prisoners, and that prompt surrender would ensure their good treatment and safe delivery to Egypt.

This lasted till dawn, and then Auda marshalled us for the road, and led us up the last mile of soft heath-clad valley between the rounded hills. It was intimate and home-like till the last green bank; when suddenly we realized it was the last, and beyond lay nothing but clear air. The lovely change this time checked me with amazement; and afterwards, however often we came, there was always a catch of eagerness in the mind, a pricking forward of the camel and straightening up to see again over the crest into openness.

Shtar hill-side swooped away below us for hundreds and hundreds of feet, in curves like bastions, against which summer-morning clouds were breaking: and from its foot opened the new earth of the Guweira plain. Aba el Lissan's rounded limestone breasts were covered with soil and heath, green, well watered. Guweira was a map of pink sand, brushed over with streaks of watercourses, in a mantle of scrub: and, out of this, and bounding this, towered islands and cliffs of glowing sandstone, wind-scarped and rain-furrowed, tinted celestially by the early sun.

After days of travel on the plateau in prison valleys, to meet this brink of freedom was a rewarding vision, like a window in the wall of life. We walked down the whole zigzag pass of Shtar, to feel its excellence, for on our camels we rocked too much with sleep to dare see anything. At the bottom the animals found a matted thorn which gave their jaws pleasure; we in front made a halt, rolled on to sand soft as a couch, and incontinently slept.

Auda came. We pleaded that it was for mercy upon our broken prisoners. He replied that they alone would die of exhaustion if we rode, but if we dallied, both parties might die: for truly there was now little water and no food. However, we could not help it, and stopped that night short of Guweira, after only fifteen miles. At Guweira lay Sheikh ibn Jad, balancing his policy to come down with the stronger: and to-day we were the stronger, and the old fox was ours. He met us with honeyed speeches. The hundred and twenty Turks of the garrison were his prisoners: we agreed with him to carry them at his leisure and their ease to Akaba.

To-day was the fourth of July. Time pressed us, for we were hungry, and Akaba was still far ahead behind two defences. The nearer post, Kethira, stubbornly refused parley with our flags. Their cliff commanded the valley—a strong place which it might be costly to take. We assigned the honour, in irony, to ibn Jad and his unwearied men, advising him to try it after dark. He shrank, made difficulties, pleaded the full moon: but we cut hardly into this excuse, promising that to-night for awhile there should be no moon. By my diary there was an eclipse. Duly it came, and the Arabs forced the post without loss, while the superstitious soldiers were firing rifles and clanging copper pots to rescue their threatened satellite.

Reassured we set out across the strand-like plain. Niazi Bey, the Turkish battalion commander, was Nasir's guest, to spare him the humiliation of Beduin contempt. Now he sidled up by me, and, his swollen eyelids and long nose betraying the moroseness of the man, began to complain that an Arab had insulted him with a gross Turkish word. I apologized, pointing out that it must have been learnt from the mouth of one of his Turkish fellow-governors. The Arab was repaying Cæsar.

Cæsar, not satisfied, pulled from his pocket a wizened hunch of bread to ask if it was fit breakfast for a Turkish officer. My heavenly twins, foraging in Guweira, had bought, found, or stolen a Turkish soldier's ration loaf; and we had quartered it. I said it was not break-fast, but lunch and dinner, and perhaps tomorrow's meals as well. I, a staff officer of the British Army (not less well fed than the Turkish) had eaten mine with the relish of victory. It was defeat, not bread, which stuck in his gullet, and I begged him not to blame me for the issue of a battle imposed on both our honours.

The narrows of Wadi Itm increased in intricate ruggedness as we penetrated deeper. Below Kethira we found Turkish post after Turkish post, empty. Their men had been drawn in to Khadra, the entrenched position (at the mouth of Itm), which covered Akaba so well against a landing from the sea. Unfortunately for them the enemy had never imagined attack from the interior, and of all their great works not one trench or post faced inland. Our advance from so new a direction threw them into panic.

In the afternoon we were in contact with this main position, and heard from the local Arabs that the subsidiary posts about Akaba had been called in or reduced, so that only a last three hundred men barred us from the sea. We dismounted for a council, to hear that the enemy were resisting firmly, in bomb-proof trench-es with a new artesian well. Only it was rumoured that they had little food.

No more had we. It was a deadlock. Our council swayed this way and that. Arguments bickered between the prudent and the bold. Tempers were short and bodies restless in the incandescent gorge whose granite peaks radiated the sun in a myriad shimmer-ing points of light, and into the depths of whose tortuous bed no wind could come to relieve the slow saturation of the air with heat.

Our numbers had swollen double. So thickly did the men crowd in the narrow space, and press about us, that we broke up our coun-cil twice or thrice, partly because it was not good they should overhear us wrangling, partly because in the sweltering confinement our unwashed smells offended us. Through our heads the heavy pulses throbbed like clocks.

JEDDAH

We sent the Turks summonses, first by white flag, and then by
Turkish prisoners, but they shot at both. This inflamed our Beduin,

and while we were yet deliberating a sudden wave of them burst up on to the rocks and sent a hail of bullets spattering against the enemy. Nasir ran out barefoot, to stop them, but after ten steps on the burning ground screeched for sandals; while I crouched in my atom of shadow, too wearied of these men (whose minds all wore my livery) to care who regulated their febrile impulses.

We had a third try to communicate with the Turks, by means of a little conscript, who said that he understood how to do it. We walked down close to the trenches with him, and sent in for an officer to speak with us. After some hesitation this was achieved, and we explained the situation on the road behind us; our growing forces; and our short control over their tempers. The upshot was that they promised to surrender at daylight. So we had another sleep (an event rare enough to chronicle) in spite of our thirst.

Next day at dawn fighting broke out on all sides, for hundreds more hill-men, again doubling our number, had come in the night; and, not knowing the arrangement, began shooting at the Turks, who defended themselves. Nasir went out, with ibn Dgheithir and his Ageyl marching in fours, down the open bed of the valley. Our men ceased fire. The Turks then stopped, for their rank and file had no more fight in them and no more food, and thought we were well supplied. So the surrender went off quietly after all.

As the Arabs rushed in to plunder I noticed an engineer in grey uniform, with red beard and puzzled blue eyes; and spoke to him in German. He was the well-borer, and knew no Turkish. Recent doings had amazed him, and he begged me to explain what we meant. I said that we were a rebellion of the Arabs against the Turks. This, it took him time to appreciate. He wanted to know who was our leader. I said the Sherif of Mecca. He supposed he would be sent to Mecca. I said rather to Egypt. He inquired the price of sugar, and when I replied, "cheap and plentiful," he was glad.

The loss of his belongings he took philosophically, but was sorry for the well, which a little work would have finished as his monument. He showed me where it was, with the pump only half-built.

By pulling on the sludge bucket we drew enough delicious clear water to quench our thirsts. Then we raced through a driving sandstorm down to Akaba, four miles further, and splashed into the sea on July the sixth, just two months after our setting out from Wejh.

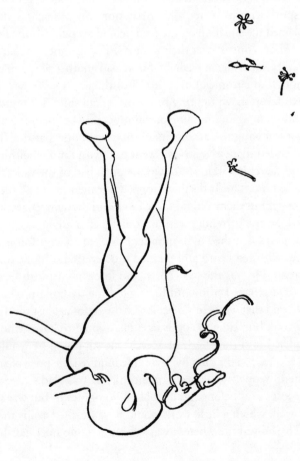

CHAPTER XII

AKABA, SUEZ, ALLENBY

WE SAT down to watch our men streaming past as lines of flushed vacant faces without message for us. For months Akaba had been the horizon of our minds, the goal: we had had no thought, we had refused thought, of anything beside. Now, in achievement, we were a little despising the entities which had spent their extremest effort on an object whose attainment changed nothing radical either in mind or body.

Hunger called us out of our trance. We had now seven hundred prisoners in addition to our own five hundred men and two thousand expectant allies. We had not any money (or, indeed, a market); and the last meal had been two days ago. In our riding camels we possessed meat enough for six weeks, but it was poor diet, and a dear diet, indulgence in which would bring future immobility upon us.

Supper taught us the urgent need to send news over the one hundred and fifty desert miles to the British at Suez for a reliefship. I decided to go across myself with a party of eight, mostly Howeitat, on the best camels in the force—one even was the famous Jedhah, the seven-year-old for whom the Nowasera had fought the beni Sakhr. As we rode round the bay we discussed the manner of our journey. If we went gently, sparing the animals, they might fail with hunger. If we rode hard they might break down with exhaustion or sore feet in mid-desert.

Finally we agreed to keep at a walk, however tempting the surface, for so many hours of the twenty-four as our endurance would allow. On such time tests the man, especially if he were a foreigner, usually collapsed before the beast: in particular, I had ridden fifty miles a day for the last month, and was near my limit of strength. If I held out, we should reach Suez in fifty hours of a march; and, to preclude cooking-halts upon the road, we carried lumps of boiled camel and broiled dates in a rag behind our saddles.

Near midnight we reached Themed, the only wells on our route, in a clean valley-sweep below the deserted guard house of the Sinai police. We let the camels breathe, gave them water and drank ourselves. Then forward again, plodding through a silence of night so intense that continually we turned round in the saddles at fancied noises away there by the cloak of stars. But the activity lay in ourselves, in the crackling of our passage through the undergrowth perfumed like ghost-flowers about us.

We marched into the very slow dawn. At sun-up we were far out in the plain through which sheaves of water-courses gathered towards Arish: and we stopped to give our camels a few minutes mockery of pasture. Then again in the saddle till noon, and past noon, when behind the mirage rose the lonely ruins of Nekhl. These we left on our right. At sunset we halted for an hour.

Camels were sluggish, and ourselves utterly wearied; but Motlog, the one-eyed owner of Jedhah, called us to action. We remounted, and at a mechanical walk climbed the Mitla Hills. The moon came out and their tops, contoured in form-lines of limestone strata, shone as though crystalline with snow.

In the dawn we passed a melon field, sown by some adventurous Arab in this no-man's-land between the armies. We halted another of our precious hours, loosing the disgusted camels to search the sand valleys for food while we cracked the unripe melons and cooled our chapped lips on their pithy flesh. Then again forward, in the heat of the new day; though the canal valley, constantly refreshed by breezes from the Gulf of Suez, was never too oppressive.

By midday we were through the dunes, after a happy switch-back ride up and down their waves, and out on the flatter plain. Suez was to be guessed at, as the frise of indeterminate points mowing and bobbing in the mirage of the canal-hollow far in front.

We reached great trench-lines, with forts and barbed wire, roads and railways, falling to decay. We passed them without challenge. Our aim was the Shatt, a post opposite Suez on the Asiatic bank of the Canal, and we gained it at last near three in the afternoon, forty-nine hours out of Akaba. For a tribal raid this would have been fair time, and we were tired men before ever we started.

Shatt was in unusual disorder, without even a sentry to stop us, plague having appeared there two or three days before. So the old camps had been hurriedly cleared, left standing, while the troops bivouacked out in the clean desert. Of course we knew nothing of this, but hunted in the empty offices till we found a telephone. I rang up Suez headquarters and said I wanted to come across.

They regretted that it was not their business. The Inland Water Transport managed transit across the Canal, after their own methods. There was a sniff of implication that these methods were not those of the General Staff. Undaunted, for I was never a partisan of my nominal branch of the service, I rang up the office of the Water Board, and explained that I had just arrived in Shatt from the desert with urgent news for Headquarters. They were sorry, but had no free boats just then. They would be sure to send first thing in the morning, to carry me to the Quarantine Department: and rang off.

Now I had been four months in Arabia continually on the move. In the last four weeks I had ridden fourteen hundred miles by camel, not sparing myself anything to advance the war; but I refused to spend a single superfluous night with my familiar vermin. I wanted a bath, and something with ice in it to drink: to change these clothes, all sticking to my saddle sores in filthiness: to eat something more tractable than green date and camel sinew. I got through again to the Inland Water Transport and talked like Chrysostom. It had no effect, so I became vivid. Then, once more, they cut me off. I was growing very vivid, when friendly northern accents from the military exchange floated down the line: "It's no bluidy good, sir, talking to them fookin water boogers."

This expressed the apparent truth; and the broad-spoken operator worked me through to the Embarkation Office. Here, Lyttleton, a major of the busiest, had added to his innumerable labours that of catching Red Sea warships one by one as they entered Suez roads and persuading them (how some loved it!) to pile high their decks with stores for Wejh or Yenbo. In this way he ran our thousands of bales and men, free, as a by-play in his routine; and found time as well to smile at the curious games of us curious folk.

He never failed us. As soon as he heard who and where I was, and what was not happening in the Inland Water Transport, the difficulty was over. His launch was ready: would be at the Shatt in half an hour. I was to come straight to his office: and not explain (till perhaps now after the war) that a common harbour launch had entered the sacred canal without permission of the Water Directorate. All fell out as he said. I sent my men and camels north to Kubri; where, by telephone from Suez, I would prepare them rations and shelter in the animal camp on the Asiatic shore. Later, of course, came their reward of hectic and astonishing days in Cairo.

Lyttleton saw my weariness and let me go at once to the hotel. Long ago it had seemed poor, but now was become splendid; and, after conquering its first hostile impression of me and my dress, it produced the hot baths and the cold drinks (six of them) and the dinner and bed of my dreams. A most willing intelligence officer, warned by spies of a disguised European in the Sinai Hotel, charged himself with the care of my men at Kubri and provided tickets and passes for me to Cairo next day.

At Ismailia passengers for Cairo changed, to wait until the express from Port Said was due. In the other train shone an opulent saloon, from which descended Admiral Wemyss and Burmester and Neville, with a very large and superior general. A terrible tension grew along the platform as the party marched up and down it in weighty talk. Officers saluted once: twice: still they marched up and down. Three times was too much. Some withdrew to the fence and stood permanently to attention: these were the mean souls. Some fled: these were the contemptibles. Some turned to the bookstall and studied book-backs avidly: these were shy. Only one was blatant.

Burmester's eye caught my staring. He wondered who it was, for I was burned crimson and very haggard with travel. (Later I found my weight to be less than seven stone.) However, he answered; and I explained the history of our unannounced raid on Akaba. It excited him. I asked that the admiral send a storeship there at once. Burmester said the *Dufferin*, which came in that day, should load all the food in Suez, go straight to Akaba, and bring back the prisoners. (Splendid!) He would order it himself, not to interrupt the Admiral and Allenby.

"Allenby! what's he doing here?" cried I. "Oh, he's in command now." "And Murray?" "Gone home." This was news of the biggest, importantly concerning me: and I climbed back and fell to wondering if this heavy, rubicund man was like ordinary generals, and if we should have trouble for six months teaching him. Murray and Belinda had begun so tiresomely that our thought those first days had been, not to defeat the enemy, but to make our own chiefs let us live. Only by time and performance had we converted Sir Archibald and his Chief of Staff, who in their last months, wrote to the War Office commending the Arab venture, and especially Feisal in it. This was generous of them and our secret triumph, for they were an odd pair in one chariot—Murray all brains and claws, nervous, elastic, changeable; Lynden Bell so solidly built up of layers of professional opinion, glued together after Government testing and approval, and later trimmed and polished to standard pitch.

At Cairo my sandalled feet slip-slapped up the quiet Savoy corridors to Clayton, who habitually cut the lunch hour to cope with his thronging work. As I entered he glanced up from his desk with a muttered "Mush fadi" (Anglo-Egyptian for "engaged") but I spoke and got a surprised welcome. In Suez the night before I had scribbled a short report; so we had to talk only of what needed doing. Before the hour ended, the Admiral rang up to say that the *Dufferin* was loading flour for her emergency trip.

Clayton drew sixteen thousand pounds in gold and got an escort to take it to Suez by the three o'clock train. This was urgent, that Nasir might be able to meet his debts. The notes we had issued at Bair, Jefer and Guweira were pencilled promises, on army telegraph forms, to pay so much to bearer in Akaba. It was a great system, but no one had dared issue notes before in Arabia, because the Beduins had neither pockets in their shirts nor strong-rooms in their tents, and notes could not be buried for safety. So there was an unconquerable prejudice against them, and for our good name it was essential that they be early redeemed.

Afterwards, in the hotel, I tried to find clothes less publicly exciting than my Arab get-up; but the moths had corrupted all my former store, and it was three days before I became normally ill-dressed.

Before I was clothed the Commander-in-Chief sent for me, curiously. In my report, thinking of Saladin and Abu Obeida, I had stressed the strategic importance of the eastern tribes of Syria, and their proper use as a threat to the communications of Jerusalem. This jumped with his ambitions, and he wanted to weigh me.

It was a comic interview, for Allenby was physically large and confident, and morally so great that the comprehension of our littleness came slow to him. He sat in his chair looking at me—not straight, as his custom was, but sideways, puzzled. He was newly from France, where for years he had been a tooth of the great machine grinding the enemy. He was full of Western ideas of gun power and weight—the worst training for our war—but, as a cavalry-man, was already half persuaded to throw up the new school, in this different world of Asia, and accompany Dawnay and Chetwode along the worn road of manoeuvre and movement; yet he was hardly prepared for anything so odd as myself—a little bare-footed silk-skirted man offering to hobble the enemy by his preaching if given stores and arms and a fund of two hundred thousand sovereigns to convince and control his converts.

Allenby could not make out how much was genuine performer and how much charlatan. The problem was working behind his eyes, and I left him unhelped to solve it. He did not ask many questions, nor talk much, but studied the map and listened to my unfolding of Eastern Syria and its inhabitants. At the end he put up his chin and said quite directly, "Well, I will do for you what I can," and that ended it. I was not sure how far I had caught him; but we learned gradually that he meant exactly what he said; and that what General Allenby could do was enough for his very greediest servant.

CHAPTER XIII

REFORMING OURSELVES

UPON CLAYTON I opened myself completely. Akaba had been taken on my plan by my effort. The cost of it had fallen on my brain and nerves. There was much more I felt inclined to do, and capable of doing:—if he thought I had earned the right to be my own master. The Arabs said that each man believed his ticks to be gazelles. I did, fervently.

Clayton agreed they were spirited and profitable ticks; but objected that actual command could not be given to an officer junior to the rest. He suggested Joyce as commanding officer at Akaba: a notion which suited me perfectly. Joyce was a man in whom one could rest against the world: a serene, unchanging, comfortable spirit. His mind, like a pastoral landscape, had four corners to its view: cared-for, friendly, limited, displayed.

The rest was easy. For supply officer we would have Goslett, the London business man who had made chaotic Wejh so prim. The aeroplanes could not yet be moved; but the armoured cars might come straight away, and a guard-ship if the Admiral was generous. We rang up Sir Rosslyn Wemyss, who was very generous: his flagship, the *Euryalus*, should sit there for the first few weeks.

Genius, this was, for in Arabia ships were esteemed by the number of funnels, and the *Euryalus*, with four, was exceptional in ships. Her great reputation assured the mountains that we were indeed the winning side: and her huge crew, by the prompting of Everard Feilding, for fun built us a good pier.

On the Arab side, I asked that the expensive and difficult Wejh be closed down, and Feisal come to Akaba with his full army. Then I showed that Akaba was Allenby's right flank, only one hundred miles from his centre, but eight hundred miles from Mecca. As the Arabs prospered their work would be done more and more in the Palestine sphere. So it was logical that Feisal be transferred from the area of King Hussein to become an army commander of the Allied expedition of Egypt under Allenby.

This idea held difficulties. "Would Feisal accept?" I had talked it over with him in Wejh months ago. "The High Commissioner?" Feisal's army had been the largest and most distinguished of the Hejaz units: its future would not be dull. General Wingate had assumed full responsibility for the Arab Movement in its darkest moment, at great risk in reputation: dare we ask him to relinquish its advance-guard now on the very threshold of success?

Clayton, knowing Wingate very well, was not afraid to broach the idea to him: and Wingate replied promptly that if Allenby could make direct and large use of Feisal, it would be both his duty and his pleasure to give him up for the good of the show.

A third difficulty of the transfer might be King Hussein: an obstinate, narrow-minded, suspicious character, little likely to sacrifice a pet vanity for unity of control. His opposition would endanger the scheme: and I offered to go down to talk him over, calling on the way to get from Feisal such recommendations of the change as should fortify the powerful letters which Wingate was writing to the King. This was accepted. The *Dufferin*, on returning from Akaba, was detailed to take me to Jidda for the new mission.

The King came down from Mecca and talked discursively. Wilson was the royal touchstone by which to try doubtful courses. Thanks

to him, the proposed transfer of Feisal to Allenby was accepted at
once, King Hussein taking the opportunity to stress his complete
loyalty to our alliance. Then, changing his subject, as usual without obvious coherence, he began to expose his religious position,
neither strong Shia nor strong Sunni, aiming rather at a simple pre-
schism interpretation of the faith. In foreign politics he betrayed a
mind as narrow as it had been broad in unworldly things; with much
of that destructive tendency of little men to deny the honesty of
opponents. I grasped something of the fixed jealousy which made

From a portrait by W. Roberts

COLONEL S. F. NEWCOMBE, R. E.

the modern Feisal suspect in his father's court; and realized how easily mischief-makers could corrode the King.

While we played so interestingly at Jidda, two abrupt telegrams from Egypt shattered our peace. The first reported that the Howeitat were in treasonable correspondence with Maan. The second connected Auda with the plot. This dismayed us. Wilson had travelled with Auda, and formed the inevitable judgment of his perfect sincerity: yet Mohammed el Dheilan was capable of double play, and ibn Jad and his friends were still uncertain. We prepared to leave at once for Akaba. Treachery had not been taken into account when Nasir and I had built our plan for the town's defence.

Fortunately the *Hardinge* was in harbour for us. On the third afternoon we were in Akaba, where Nasir had no notion that anything was wrong. I told him only of my wish to greet Auda: he lent me a swift camel and guide; and at dawn we found Auda and Mohammed and Zaal all in a tent at Guweira. They were confused when I dropped in on them, unheralded; but protested that all was well. We fed together as friends.

Others of the Howeitat came in, and there was gay talk about the war. I distributed the King's presents; and told them, to their laughter, that Nasir had got his month's leave to Mecca. The King, an enthusiast for the revolt, believed that his servants should work as manfully. So he would not allow visits to Mecca, and the poor men found continual military service heavy banishment from their wives. We had jested a hundred times that, if he took Akaba, Nasir would deserve a holiday; but he had not really believed in its coming until I gave him Hussein's letter the evening before. In gratitude he sold me Ghazala, the regal camel he won from the Howeitat. As her owner I became of new interest to the Abu Tayi.

After lunch, by pretence of sleep, I got rid of the visitors; and then abruptly asked Auda and Mohammed to walk with me to see the ruined fort and reservoir. When we were alone I touched on their present correspondence with the Turks. Auda began to laugh; Mohammed to look disgusted. At last they explained elaborately that Mohammed had taken Auda's seal and written to the Governor of Maan, offering to desert the Sherif's cause. The Turk had replied gladly, promising great rewards. Mohammed asked for something on account. Auda then heard of it, waited till the messenger with presents was on his way, caught him, robbed him to the skin: and was denying Mohammed a share of the spoils. A farcical story, and we laughed richly over it; but there was more behind.

They were angry that no guns or troops had yet come to their support; and that no rewards had been given them for taking Akaba. They were anxious to know how I had learnt of their secret dealings, and how much more I knew. We were on a slippery ledge. I played on their fear by my unnecessary amusement, quoting in careless laughter, as if they were my own words, actual phrases of the letters they had exchanged. This created the impression desired.

Parenthetically I told them Feisal's entire army was coming up; and how Allenby was sending rifles, guns, high explosive, food and money to Akaba. Finally I suggested that Auda's present expenses in hospitality must be great; would it help if I advanced something of the great gift Feisal would make him, personally, when he arrived? Auda saw that the immediate moment would not be unprofitable: that Feisal would be highly profitable: and that the Turks would be always with him if other resources failed. So he agreed, in a very good temper, to accept my advance; and with it to keep the Howeitat well-fed and cheerful.

It was near sunset. Zaal had killed a sheep and we ate again in real amity. Afterwards I remounted, with Mufaddhi (to draw Auda's allowance), and Abd el Rahman, a servant of Mohammed's who, so he whispered me, would receive any little thing I wished to send him separately. We rode all night towards Akaba, where I roused Nasir from sleep, to run over our last business. Then I paddled out in a derelict canoe from "Euryalus jetty" to the *Hardinge* just as the first dawn crept down the western peaks.

I went below, bathed, and slept till mid-morning. When I came on deck the ship was rushing grandly down the narrow gulf under full steam for Egypt. My appearance caused a sensation, for they had not dreamed I could reach Guweira, assure myself, and get back in less than six or seven days, to catch a later steamer.

We rang up Cairo and announced that the situation at Guweira was thoroughly good, and no treachery abroad. This may have been hardly true; but since Egypt kept us alive by stinting herself, we must reduce impolitic truth to keep her confident and ourselves a legend. The crowd wanted book-heroes, and would not understand how more human old Auda was because, after battle and murder, his heart yearned towards the defeated enemy now subject, at his free choice, to be spared or killed: and therefore never so lovely.

CHAPTER XIV

PRICKING THE ENEMY

VESSELS STEAMED up the Gulf of Akaba. Feisal landed, and with him Jaafar, his staff, and Joyce, the fairy godmother. There came the armoured cars, Goslett, Egyptian labourers and thousands of troops. To repair the six weeks' peace, Falkenhayn had been down to advise the Turks, and his fine intelligence made them worthier our opposition. Maan was a special command, under Behjet, the old G.O.C. Sinai. He had six thousand infantry, a regiment of cavalry and mounted infantry, and had entrenched Maan till it was impregnable according to the standard of manœuvre war. A flight of aeroplanes operated daily thence. Great supply dumps had been collected.

By now the Turkish preparations were complete; they began to move, disclosing that their objective was Guweira, the best road for Akaba. Two thousand infantry pushed out to Aba el Lissan, and fortified it. Cavalry kept the outskirts, to contain a possible Arab counter-stroke from the Wadi Musa side.

This nervousness was our cue. We would play with them and provoke them to go for us in Wadi Musa, where the natural obstacles were so tremendous that the human defending factor might behave as badly as it liked, and yet hold the place against attack.

To bait the hook, the men of neighbouring Delagha were set busy. The Turks, full of spirit, put in a counter-stroke, and suffered sharply. We rubbed in to the peasantry of Wadi Musa the rich booty now enjoyed by their rivals of Delagha. Maulud, the old war-horse, went up with his mule-mounted regiment, and quartered himself among the famous ruins of Petra. The encouraged Liathena, under their one-eyed sheikh, Khalil, began to foray out across the plateau, and to snap up by twos and threes Turkish riding or transport animals, together with the rifles of their occasional guards. This went on for weeks, while the irritated Turks grew hotter and hotter.

We could also prick the Turks into discomfort by asking General Salmond for his promised long-distance air raid on Maan. As it was difficult, Salmond had chosen Stent, with other tried pilots of Rabegh or Wejh, and told them to do their best. They had experience of forced landing on desert surfaces, and could pick out an unknown destination across unmapped hills: Stent spoke Arabic perfectly. The flight had to be air-contained, but its commander was full of resource and display, like other bundles of nerves, who, to punish themselves, did outrageous things. On this occasion he ordered low flying, to make sure the aim; and profited by reaching Maan, and dropping thirty-two bombs in and about the unprepared station. Two bombs into the barracks killed thirty-five men and wounded fifty. Eight struck the engine-shed, heavily damaging the plant and stock. A bomb in the General's kitchen finished his cook and his breakfast. Four fell on the aerodrome. Despite the shrapnel our pilots and engines returned safely to their temporary landing ground at Kuntilla above Akaba.

That afternoon they patched the machines, and after dark slept under their wings. In the following dawn they were off once more, three of them this time, to Aba el Lissan, where the sight of the great camp had made Stent's mouth water. They bombed the horse lines and stampeded the animals, visited the tents and scattered the Turks. As on the day before, they flew low and were much hit, but not fatally. Long before noon they were back in Kuntilla.

Stent looked over the remaining petrol and bombs, and decided they were enough for one more effort. So he gave directions to every one to look for the battery which had troubled them in the morning. They started in the midday heat. Their loads were so heavy they could get no height, and therefore came blundering over the crest behind Aba el Lissan, and down the valley at about three hundred feet. The Turks, always somnolent at noon, were taken completely by surprise. Thirty bombs were dropped: one silenced the battery, the others killed dozens of men and animals. Then the lightened machines soared up and home to El Arish. The Arabs rejoiced: the Turks were seriously alarmed. Behjet Pasha set his men to digging shelters, and when his aeroplanes had been repaired, he disposed them innocuously about the plateau for camp defence.

By air we had perturbed the Turks: by irritative raids we were luring them towards a wrong objective. Our third resource to ruin their offensive was to hinder the railway, whose need would make them split up the striking force on defensive duties. Accordingly we arranged many demolitions for mid-September.

I decided also to revive the old idea of mining a train. Something more vigorous and certain than automatic mines was indicated, and I had imagined a direct firing, by electricity, of a charge under the locomotive. The British sappers encouraged me to try, especially General Wright, the chief engineer in Egypt, whose experience took a sporting interest in my irregularities. He sent me the recommended tools: an exploder and some insulated cable. With them I went on board H.M.S. *Humber*, our new guardship, and introduced myself to Captain Snagge, in command.

Snagge was fortunate in his ship, which had been built for Brazil, and was much more comfortably furnished than British monitors; and we were doubly fortunate in him and in this, for he was the spirit of hospitality. His inquiring nature took interest in the shore, and saw the comic side even of our petty disasters. To tell him the story of a failure was to laugh at it, and always for a good story he gave me a hot bath, and tea with civilized trappings, free from every suspicion of blown sand. His kindness and help served us in lieu of visits to Egypt for repairs, and enabled us to hammer on against the Turks through month after month of feckless disappointment.

The exploder was in a formidable locked white box, very heavy. We split it open, found a ratchet handle, and pushed it down without harming the ship. The wire was heavy rubber-insulated cable. We cut it in half, fastened the ends to screw terminals on the box, and transmitted shocks to one another convincingly. It worked.

I fetched detonators. We stuffed the free ends of the cable into one and pumped the handle: nothing followed. We tried again and again ineffectually, grieving over it. At last Snagge rang his bell for the gunner warrant officer who knew all about circuits. He suggested special electric detonators. The ship carried six, and gave me three of them. We joined one up with our box, and when the handle was crashed down it popped off beautifully. So I felt that I knew all about it and turned to arrange the details of the raid.

Of targets, the most promising and easiest-reached seemed Mudowwara, a water station eighty miles south of Maan. A smashed train there would embarrass the enemy. For men, I would have the tried Howeitat; and, at the same time, the expedition would test the three Haurani peasants whom I had added to my personal followers. In view of the new importance of the Hauran, there was need for us to learn its dialect, the construction and jealousies of its clan-framework, and its names and roads. These three fellows, Rahail, Assaf and Hemeid, would teach me their home-affairs imperceptibly, as we rode on business, chatting.

To make sure of the arrested train required guns and machine-guns. For the first, why not trench-mortars? for the second, Lewis guns? Accordingly, Egypt chose two forceful sergeant-instructors from the Army School at Zeitun, to teach squads of Arabs in Akaba how to use such things. Snagge gave them quarters in his ship, since we had, as yet, no convenient English camp ashore.

Their names may have been Yells and Brooke, but became Lewis and Stokes, after their jealously-loved tools. Lewis was an Australian, long, thin and sinuous, his supple body lounging in unmilitary curves. His hard face, arched eyebrows, and predatory nose set off the peculiarly Australian air of reckless willingness and capacity to do something very soon. Stokes was a stocky English yeoman, work-man-like and silent; always watching for an order to obey.

Lewis, full of suggestion, emerged bursting with delight at what had been well done whenever a thing happened. Stokes never offered opinion until after action, when he would stir his cap reflectively, and painstakingly recount the mistakes he must next time avoid. Both were admirable men. In a month, without common language or interpreter, they got on terms with their classes and taught them their weapons with reasonable precision. More was not required for an empirical habit appeared to agree with the spirit of our haphaz-ard raids better than complete scientific knowledge.

As we worked at the organization of the raid, our appetites rose. Mudowwara station sounded vulnerable. Three hundred men might rush it suddenly. That would be an achievement, for its deep well was the only one in the dry sector below Maan. Without its water, the train-service across the gap would become uneconomic in load.

Lewis, the Australian, at such an ambitious moment, said that he and Stokes would like to be of my party. A new, attractive idea. With them we should feel sure of our technical detachments, whilst attacking a garrisoned place. Also, the sergeants wanted to go very much, and their good work deserved reward. They were warned that their experiences might not at the moment seem altogether joy-ful. There were no rules; and there could be no mitigation of the marching, feeding, and fighting, inland. If they went they would lose their British Army comfort and privilege, to share and share with the Arabs (except in booty!) and suffer exactly their hap in food and discipline. If anything went wrong with me, they, not speak-ing Arabic, would be in a tender position.

Lewis replied that he was looking for just this strangeness of life. Stokes supposed that if we did it, he could. So they were lent two of my best camels (their saddle-bags tight with bully-beef and biscuits) and on the seventh of September, 1917, we went together up Wadi Itm, to collect our Howeitat from Auda in Guweira.

For the sergeants' sake, to harden them gently, things were made better than my word. We marched very easily for to-day, while we were our own masters. Neither had been on a camel before, and there was risk that the fearful heat of the naked granite walls of Itm might knock them out before the trip had properly begun. September was a bad month. A few days before, in the shade of the palm-gardens of Akaba beach, the thermometer had shown a hundred and twenty degrees. So we halted for midday under a cliff, and in the evening rode only ten miles to camp for the night.

Next day, in the early heat, we were near Guweira, comfortably crossing the sanded plain of restful pink with its grey-green undergrowth, when there came a droning through the air. Quickly we drove the camels off the open road into the bush-speckled ground, where their irregular colouring would not be marked by the enemy airmen; for the loads of blasting gelatine, my favourite and most powerful explosive, and the many ammonal-filled shells of the Stokes' gun would be ill neighbours in a bombing raid. We waited there, soberly, in the saddle, while our camels grazed the little which was worth eating in the scrub, until the aeroplane had circled twice about the rock of Guweira in front of us, and planted three loud bombs.

The aeroplane was the quaint regulator of public business in the Guweira camp. The Arabs, up as ever before dawn, waited for it: Mastur set a slave on the crag's peak to sound the first warning. When its constant hour drew near the Arabs would saunter, chatting in parade of carelessness, towards the rock. Arrived beneath it, each man climbed to the ledge he favoured. After Mastur would climb the bevy of his slaves, with his coffee on the brazier, and his carpet. In a shaded nook he and Auda would sit and talk till the little shiver of excitement tightened up and down the crowded ledges when first was heard the song of the engine over the pass of Shtar.

Every one pressed back against the wall and waited stilly while the enemy circled vainly above the strange spectacle of this crimson rock banded with thousands of gaily-dressed Arabs, nesting like ibises in every cranny of its face. The aeroplane dropped three bombs, or four bombs, or five bombs, according to the day of the week. Their bursts of dense smoke sat on the sage-green plain compactly like cream-puffs; writhing for minutes in the windless air before they slowly spread and faded. Though we knew there was no menace in it, yet we could not but catch our breath when the sharp-growing cry of the falling bombs came through the loud engine overhead.

Gladly we left the noise and heart-burning of Guweira. So soon as we had lost our escort of flies we halted: indeed there was no need of haste, and the two unfortunate fellows with me were tasting of such heat as they had never known; for the stifling air was like a metal mask over our faces. It was admirable to see them struggle not to speak of it, that they might keep the spirit of the Akaba undertaking to endure as firmly as the Arabs; but by this silence the sergeants went far past their bond. It was ignorance of Arabic which made them so superfluously brave, for the Arabs themselves were loud against the tyrannous sun and the breathlessness; but the test-effort was wholesome; and, for effect, I played about, seeming to enjoy myself.

In the late afternoon we marched farther and stopped for the night under a thick screen of tamarisk trees. The camp was very beautiful, for behind us rose a cliff, perhaps four hundred feet in height, a deep red in the level sunset. Under our feet was spread a floor of buff-coloured mud, as hard and muffled as wood-paving, flat like a lake for half a mile each way: and on a low ridge to one side of it stood the grove of tamarisk stems of brown wood, edged with a sparse and dusty fringe of green, which had been faded by drought and sunshine till it was nearly of the silvered grey below the olive leaves about Les Baux, when a wind from the river-mouth rustled up the valley-grass and made the trees turn pale.

We were riding for Rumm, the northern water of the Beni Atiyeh: a place which stirred my thought, as even the unsentimental Howeitat had told me it was lovely. The morrow would be new with our entry to it: but very early, while the stars were yet shining, I was roused by Aid, the humble Harithi Sherif accompanying us. He crept to me, and said in a chilled voice, "Lord, I am gone blind." I made him lie down, and felt that he shivered as if cold; but all he could tell me was that in the night, waking up, there had been no sight, only pain in his eyes. The sun-blink had burned them out.

Day was still young as we rode between two great pikes of sandstone to the foot of a long, soft slope poured down from the domed hills in front of us. It was tamarisk-covered: the beginning of the Valley of Rumm, they said. We looked up on the left to a long wall of rock, sheering in like a thousand-foot wave towards the middle of the valley; whose other arc, to the right, was an opposing line of steep, red broken hills. We rode up the slope, crashing our way through the brittle undergrowth.

As we went, the brushwood grouped itself into thickets whose massed leaves took on a stronger tint of green, the purer for their contrasted setting in plots of open sand of a cheerful delicate pink. The ascent became gentle, till the valley was a confined tilted plain. The hills on the right grew taller and sharper, a fair counterpart of the other side which straightened itself to one massive rampart of redness. They drew together until only two miles divided them: and then, towering gradually till their parallel parapets must have been a thousand feet above us, ran forward in an avenue for miles.

They were not unbroken walls of rock, but were built sectionally, in crags like gigantic buildings, along the two sides of their street. Deep alleys, fifty feet across, divided the crags, whose planes were smoothed by the weather into huge apses and bays, and enriched with surface fretting and fracture, like design. Caverns high up on the precipice were round like windows: others near the foot gaped like doors. Dark stains ran down the shadowed front for hundreds of feet, like accidents of use. The cliffs were striated vertically, in their granular rock; whose main order stood on two hundred feet of broken stone deeper in colour and harder in texture. This plinth did not, like the sandstone, hang in folds like cloth; but chipped itself into loose courses of scree, horizontal as the footings of a wall.

The crags were capped in nests of domes, less hotly red than the body of the hill; rather grey and shallow. They gave the finishing semblance of Byzantine architecture to this irresistible place: this processional way greater than imagination. The Arab armies would have been lost in the length and breadth of it, and within the walls a squadron of aeroplanes could have wheeled in formation. Our little caravan grew self-conscious, and fell dead quiet, afraid and ashamed to flaunt its smallness in the presence of the stupendous hills.

For hours the perspectives grew greater and more magnificent in ordered design, till a gap in the cliff-face opened on our right to a new wonder. The gap, perhaps three hundred yards across, was a crevice in such a wall; and led to an amphitheatre, oval in shape, shallow in front, and long-lobed right and left. The walls were precipices, like all the walls of Rumm; but appeared greater, for the pit lay in the very heart of a ruling hill, and its smallness made the besetting heights seem overpowering.

The sun had sunk behind the western wall, leaving the pit in shadow; but its dying glare flooded with startling red the wings each side of the entry, and the fiery bulk of the farther wall across the great valley. The pit-floor was of damp sand, darkly wooded with shrubs; while about the feet of all the cliffs lay boulders greater than houses, sometimes, indeed, like fortresses which had crashed down from the sheer heights above. In front of us a path, pale with use, zigzagged up the cliff-plinth to the point from which the main face rose, and there it turned precariously southward along a shallow ledge outlined by occasional leafy trees. From between these trees, in hidden crannies of the rock, issued strange cries; the echoes, turned into music, of the voices of the Arabs watering camels at the springs which there flowed out three hundred feet above ground.

Mohammed turned into the amphitheatre's left-hand lobe. At its far end Arab ingenuity had cleared a space under an overhanging rock: there we unloaded and settled down. The dark came upon us quickly in this high prisoned place; and we felt the water-laden air cold against our sunburnt skin. The Howeitat who had looked after the loads of explosives collected their camel drove, and led them with echo-testing shouts up the hill path to water against their early return to Guweira. We lit fires and cooked rice to add to the sergeants' bully-beef, while my coffee men prepared for the visitors who would come to us.

The Arabs in the tents outside the hollow of the springs had seen us enter, and were not slow to learn our news. In an hour we had the head men of the Darausha, Zelebani, Zuweida and Togatga clans about us; and there mounted great talk, none too happy. Aid, the Sherif, was too cast down in heart by his blindness to lift the burden of entertainment from my shoulders; and a work of such special requirements was not to be well done by me alone.

CHAPTER XV

MINES IN THE RAILWAY

AT DAWN on the sixteenth of September 1917 we rode out from Rumm. Aid, the blind Sherif, insisted on coming, despite his lost sight; saying he could ride, if he could not shoot, and that if God prospered us he would take leave from Feisal in the flush of the success, and go home, not too sorry, to the blank life which would be left. Zaal led his twenty-five Nowasera, a clan of Auda's Arabs who called themselves my men, and were famous the desert over for their saddle-camels. My hard riding tempted them to my company.

Old Motlog el Awar, owner of el Jedha, the finest she-camel in North Arabia, rode her in our van. We looked at her with proud or greedy eyes, according to our relationship with him. My Ghazala was taller and more grand, with a faster trot, but too old to be galloped. However she was the only other animal in the party, or, indeed, in this desert, to be matched with the Jedha, and my honour was increased by her dignity.

The rest of our party strayed like a broken necklace. No one group would ride or speak with another, and I passed back and forth all day like a shuttle, talking first to one lowering sheikh, and then to another, striving to draw them together, so that before a cry to action came there might be solidarity. As yet they agreed only in not hearing any word from Zaal as to the order of our march; though he was admitted the most intelligent warrior, and the most experienced. For my private part he was the only one to be trusted farther than eyesight. Of the others, it seemed to me that neither their words nor their counsels, perhaps not their rifles, were sure.

We put our mid-day halt in a fertile place, where the late spring rain, falling on a sandy talus, had brought up a thick tufting of silvery grass which our camels loved. The weather was mild, perfect as an August in England; and we lingered in great content, recovered at last from the bickering appetites of the days before the start, and from that slight rending of nerve inevitable when leaving even a temporary settlement. Man, in our circumstances, took root so soon.

Late in the day we rode again, winding downhill in a narrow valley between moderate sandstone walls: till before sunset we were out on another flat of laid yellow mud, like that which had been so wonderful a prelude to Rumm's glory. By its edge we camped. My care had borne fruit, for we settled in only three parties, by bright fires of crackling, flaring tamarisk. At one supped my men; at the second Zaal; at the third the other Howeitat; and late at night, when all the chiefs had been well adjusted with gazelle meat and hot bread, it became possible to bring them to my neutral fire, and discuss sensibly our course for the morrow.

It seemed that about sunset we should water at Mudowwara well, two or three miles this side of the station, in a covered valley. Then, in the early night, we might go forward to examine the station and see if, in our weakness, we might yet attempt some stroke against it. I held strongly to this (against the common taste) for it was by so much the most critical point of the line. The Arabs could not see it, since their minds did not hold a picture of the long, linked Turkish front with its necessitous demands. However, we had reached internal harmony, and scattered confidently to sleep.

In the morning we delayed to eat again, having only six hours of march before us; and then pushed across the mud-flat to a plain of firm limestone rag, carpeted with brown, weather-blunted flint. This was succeeded by low hills, with occasional soft beds of sand, under the steeper slopes where eddying winds had dropped their dust. Through these we rode up shallow valleys to a crest; and then by like valleys down the far side, whence we issued abruptly, from dark, tossed stone-heaps into the sun-steeped wideness of a plain. Across it an occasional low dune stretched a drifting line.

We had made our noon halt at the first entering of the broken country; and, rightly, in the late afternoon came to the well. It was an open pool, a few yards square, in a hollow valley of large stone-slabs and flint and sand. The stagnant water looked uninviting. Over its face lay a thick mantle of green slime, from which swelled curious bladder-islands of floating fatty pink. The Arabs explained that the Turks had thrown dead camels into the pool to make the water foul; but that time had passed and the effect was grown faint. It would have been fainter had the criterion of their effort been my taste.

Yet it was all the drink we should get up here unless we took Mudowwara, so we set to and filled our waterskins. One of the Howeitat, while helping in this, slipped off the wet edge into the water. Its green carpet closed oilily over his head and hid him for an instant: then he came up, gasping vigorously, and scrambled out amid our laughter, leaving behind him a black hole in the scum from which a stench of old meat rose like a visible pillar, and hung about us and him and the valley, disconcertingly.

At dusk, Zaal and I, with the sergeants and others, crept forward quietly. In half an hour we were at the last crest, in a place where the Turks had dug trenches, and stoned up an elaborate outpost of engrailed sangars, which on this black newmoon night of our raid were empty. In front and below lay the station, its doors, and windows sharply marked by the yellow cooking fires and lights of the garrison. It seemed close under our observation; but the Stokes gun would carry only three hundred yards. Accordingly we went nearer, hearing the enemy noises, and attentively afraid lest their barking dogs uncover us. Sergeant Stokes made casts out to left and right, in search of gun-positions, but found nothing that was satisfactory.

Meanwhile, Zaal and I crawled across the last flat, till we could count the unlighted tents and hear the men talking. One came out a few steps in our direction, then hesitated. He struck a match to light a cigarette, and the bold light flooded his face, so that we saw him plainly, a young, hollow-faced sickly officer. He squatted, busy for a moment, and returned to his men, who hushed as he passed.

We moved back to our hill and consulted in whispers. The station was very long, of stone buildings, so solid that they might be proof against our time-fused shell. The garrison seemed about two hundred. We were one hundred and sixteen rifles and not a happy family. Surprise was the only benefit we could be sure of.

So, in the end, I voted that we leave it, unalarmed, for a future occasion, which might be soon. But, actually, one accident after another saved Mudowwara; and it was not until August, 1918, that Buxton's Camel Corps at last measured to it the fate so long overdue.

Quietly we regained our camels and slept. Next morning we returned on our tracks to let a fold of the plain hide us from the railway, and then marched south across the sandy flat; seeing tracks of gazelle, oryx and ostrich; with, in one spot, stale padmarks of leopard. We were making for the low hills bounding the far side, intending to blow up a train; for Zaal said that where these touched the railway was such a curve as we needed for minelaying, and that the spurs commanding it would give us ambush and a field of fire for our machine-guns.

So we turned east in the southern ridges till within half a mile of the line. There the party halted in a thirty-foot valley, while a few of us walked down to the line, which bent a little eastward to avoid the point of higher ground under our feet. The point ended in a flat table fifty feet above the track, facing north across the valley.

The metals crossed the hollow on a high bank, pierced by a two-arched bridge for the passage of rain-water. This seemed an ideal spot to lay the charge. It was our first try at electric mining and we had no idea what would happen; but it stood to our reason that the job would be more sure with an arch under the explosive because, whatever the effect on the locomotive, the bridge would go, and the succeeding coaches be inevitably derailed.

Back with our camels, we dumped the loads, and sent the animals to safe pasture near some undercut rocks from which the Arabs scraped salt. The freedmen carried down the Stokes gun with its shells; the Lewis guns; and the gelatine with its insulated wire, magneto and tools to the chosen place. The sergeants set up their toys on a terrace, while we went down to the bridge to dig a bed between the ends of two steel sleepers, wherein to hide my fifty pounds of gelatine. We had stripped off the paper wrapping of the individual explosive plugs and kneaded them together by help of the sun heat into a shaking jelly in a sandbag.

The burying of it was not easy. The embankment was steep, and in the sheltered pocket between it and the hill-side was a wind-laid bank of sand. No one crossed this but myself, stepping carefully; yet I left unavoidable great prints over its smoothness. The ballast dug out from the track I had to gather in my cloak for carriage in repeated journeys to the culvert, whence it could be tipped naturally over the shingle bed of the watercourse.

It took me nearly two hours to dig in and cover the charge: then came the difficult job of unrolling the heavy wires from the detonator to the hills whence we would fire the mine. The top sand was crusted and had to be broken through in burying the wires. They were stiff wires, which scarred the wind-rippled surface with long lines like the belly marks of preposterously narrow and heavy snakes. When pressed down in one place they rose into the air in another. At last they had to be weighted down with rocks which, in turn, had to be buried at the cost of great disturbance of the ground.

Afterwards it was necessary, with a sandbag, to stipple the marks into a wavy surface; and, finally, with a bellows and long fanning sweeps of my cloak, to simulate the smooth laying of the wind. The whole job took five hours to finish; but then it was well finished: neither myself nor any of us could see where the charge lay, or that double wires led out underground from it to the firing-point two hundred yards off, behind the ridge marked for our rifle-men.

The wires were just long enough to cross from this ridge into a depression. There we brought up the two ends and connected them with the electric exploder. It was an ideal place both for it and for the men who fired it, except that the bridge was not visible thence.

However, this only meant that some one would have to press the handle at a signal from a point fifty yards ahead, commanding the bridge and the ends of the wires alike. Salem, Feisal's best slave, asked for this task of honour, and was yielded it by acclamation. The end of the afternoon was spent in showing him (on the disconnected exploder) what to do, till he was act-perfect and banged down the ratchet precisely as I raised my hand with an imaginary engine on the bridge.

We walked back to camp, leaving one man on watch by the line. Our baggage was deserted, and we stared about in a puzzle for the rest, till we saw them suddenly sitting against the golden light of sunset along a high ridge. We yelled to them to lie down or come down, but they persisted up there on their perch like a school of hooded crows, in full view of north and south.

At last we ran up and threw them off the skyline, too late. The Turks in a little hillpost by Hallat Ammar, four miles south of us, had seen them, and opened fire in their alarm upon the long shadows which the declining sun was pushing gradually up the slopes towards the post. Beduin were past-masters in the art of using country, but in their abiding contempt for the stupidity of the Turks they would take no care to fight them. This ridge was visible at once from Mudowwara and Hallat Ammar, and they had frightened both places by their sudden ominous expectant watch.

However, the dark closed on us, and we knew we must sleep away the night patiently in hope of the morrow. Perhaps the Turks would reckon us gone if our place looked desert in the morning. So we lit fires in a deep hollow, baked bread and were comfortable. The common tasks had made us one party, and the hill-top folly shamed every one into agreement that Zaal should be our leader.

CHAPTER XVI

VICTORY AND LOOT

DAY BROKE quietly, and for hours we watched the empty railway with its peaceful camps. The constant care of Zaal and of his lame cousin, Howeimil, kept us hidden, though with difficulty, because of the insatiate restlessness of the Beduin, who would never sit down for ten minutes, but must fidget and do or say something. This defect made them very inferior to the stolid English for the long, tedious strain of a waiting war. Also it partly accounted for their uncertain stomachs in defence. Today they made us very angry.

Perhaps, after all, the Turks saw us, for at nine o'clock some forty men came out of the tents on the hill-top by Hallat Ammar to the south and advanced in open order. If we left them alone, they would turn us off our mine in an hour; if we opposed them with our superior strength and drove them back, the railway would take notice, and traffic be held up. It was a quandary, which eventually we tried to solve by sending thirty men to check the enemy patrol gradually; and, if possible, to draw them lightly aside into the broken hills. This might hide our main position and reassure them as to our insignificant strength and purpose.

For some hours it worked as we had hoped; the firing grew desultory and distant. A permanent patrol came confidently up from the south and walked past our hill, over our mine and on towards Mudowwara without noticing us. There were eight soldiers and a stout corporal, who mopped his brow against the heat, for it was now after eleven o'clock and really warm. When he had passed us by a mile or two the fatigue of the tramp became too much for him. He marched his party into the shade of a long culvert, under whose arches a cool draught from the east was gently flowing, and there in comfort they lay on the soft sand, drank water from their bottles, smoked, and at last slept. We presumed that this was the noon-day rest which every solid Turk in the hot summer of Arabia took as a matter of principle, and that their allowing themselves the pause showed that we were disproved or ignored. However, we were in error.

Noon brought a fresh care. Through my powerful glasses we saw a hundred Turkish soldiers issue from Mudowwara Station and make straight across the sandy plain towards our place. They were coming very slowly, and no doubt unwillingly, for sorrow at losing their beloved midday sleep: but at their very worst marching and temper they could hardly take more than two hours before they reached us.

We began to pack up, preparatory to moving off, having decided to leave the mine and its leads in place on chance that the Turks might not find them, and we be able to return and take advantage of all the careful work. We sent a messenger to our covering party on the south, that they should meet us farther up, near those scarred rocks which served as screen for our pasturing camels.

Just as he had gone, the watchman cried out that smoke in clouds was rising from Hallat Ammar. Zaal and I rushed uphill and saw by its shape and volume that indeed there must be a train waiting in that station. As we were trying to see it over the hill, suddenly it moved out in our direction. We yelled to the Arabs to get into position as quick as possible, and there came a wild scramble over sand

and rock. Stokes and Lewis, being booted, could not win the race; but they came well up, their pains and dysentery forgotten.

The men with rifles posted themselves in a long line behind the spur running from the guns past the exploder to the mouth of the valley. From it they would fire directly into the derailed carriages at less than one hundred and fifty yards, whereas the ranges for the Stokes and Lewis guns were about three hundred yards. An Arab stood up on high behind the guns and shouted to us what the train was doing—a necessary precaution, for if it carried troops and detrained them behind our ridge we should have to face about like a flash and retire fighting up the valley for our lives. Fortunately it held on at all the speed the two locomotives could make on wood fuel.

It drew near where we had been reported, and opened random fire into the desert. I could hear the racket coming, as I sat on my hillock by the bridge to give the signal to Salem, who danced round the exploder on his knees, crying with excitement, and calling urgently on God to make him fruitful. The Turkish fire sounded heavy, and I wondered with how many men we were going to have affair, and if the mine would be advantage enough for our eighty fellows to equal them. It would have been better if the first electrical experiment had been simpler.

However, at that moment the engines, looking very big, rocked with screaming whistles into view around the bend. Behind them followed ten box-wagons, crowded with rifle-muzzles at the windows and doors; and in little sandbag nests on the roofs Turks precariously held on, to shoot at us. I had not thought of two engines, and on the moment decided to fire the charge under the second, so that however little the mine's effect, the uninjured engine should not be able to uncouple and drag the carriages away.

Accordingly, when the front "driver" of the second engine was on the bridge, I raised my hand to Salem. There followed a terrific roar, and the line vanished from sight behind a spouting column of black dust and smoke a hundred feet high and wide. Out of the darkness came shattering crashes and long, loud metallic clangings of ripped steel, with many lumps of iron and plate; while one entire wheel of a locomotive whirled up suddenly black out of the cloud against the sky, and sailed musically over our heads to fall slowly and heavily into the desert behind. Except for the flight of these, there succeeded a deathly silence, with no cry of men or rifle-shot, as the now-grey mist of the explosion drifted from the line towards us, and over our ridge until it was lost in the hills.

In the lull, I ran southward to join the sergeants. Salem picked up his rifle and charged out into the murk. Before I had climbed to the guns the hollow was alive with shots, and with the brown figures of the Beduin leaping forward to grips with the enemy. I looked round to see what was happening so quickly, and saw the train stationary and dismembered along the track, with its wagon sides jumping under the bullets which riddled them, while Turks were falling out from the far doors to gain the shelter of the rail-way embankment.

As I watched, our machine-guns chattered out over my head, and the long rows of Turks on the carriage roofs rolled over, and were swept off the top like bales of cotton before the furious shower of bullets which stormed along the roofs and splashed clouds of yel-low chips from the planking. The dominant position of the guns had been an advantage to us so far.

When I reached Stokes and Lewis the engagement had taken another turn. The remaining Turks had got behind the bank, here about eleven feet high, and from cover of the wheels were firing point-blank at the Beduin twenty yards away across the sand-filled dip. The enemy in the crescent of the curving line were secure from the machine-guns; but Stokes slipped in his first shell, and after a few seconds there came a crash as it burst beyond the train in the desert.

He touched the elevating screw, and his second shot fell just by the trucks in the deep hollow below the bridge where the Turks were taking refuge. It made a shambles of the place. The survivors of the group broke out in a panic across the desert, throwing away their rifles and equipment as they ran. This was the opportunity of the

Lewis gunners. The sergeant grimly traversed with drum after drum, till the open sand was littered with bodies. Mushagraf, the Sherari boy behind the second gun, saw the battle over, threw aside his weapon with a yell, and dashed down at speed with his rifle to join the others who were beginning, like wild beasts, to tear open the carriages and fall to plunder. It had taken nearly ten minutes.

I ran down to the ruins to see what the mine had done. The bridge was gone; and into its gap was fallen the front wagon, which had been filled with sick. The smash had killed all but three or four and had rolled dead and dying into a bleeding heap against the splintered end. One of those yet alive deliriously cried out the word typhus. So I wedged shut the door, and left them there, alone.

Succeeding wagons were derailed and smashed: some had frames irreparably buckled. The second engine was a blanched pile of smoking iron. Its driving wheels had been blown upward, taking away the side of the fire-box. Cab and tender were twisted into strips, among the piled stones of the bridge abutment. It would never run again. The front engine had got off better: though heavily derailed and lying half-over, with the cab burst, yet its steam was at pressure, and driving-gear intact.

The valley was a weird sight. The Arabs, gone raving mad, were rushing about at top speed bareheaded and half-naked, screaming, shooting into the air, clawing one another nail and fist, while they burst open trucks and staggered back and forward with immense bales, which they ripped by the rail-side, and tossed through, smashing what they did not want.

There were scores of carpets spread about; dozens of mattresses and flowered quilts; blankets in heaps; clothes for men and women in full variety; clocks, cooking-pots, food, ornaments and weapons. To one side stood thirty or forty hysterical women, unveiled, tearing their clothes and hair; shrieking themselves distracted. The Arabs without regard to them went on wrecking the household goods; looting their absolute fill. Camels had become common property. Each man frantically loaded the nearest with what it could carry and shooed it westward into the void, while he turned to his next fancy.

Seeing me tolerably unemployed, the women rushed, and caught at me with howls for mercy. I assured them that all was going well: but they would not get away till some husbands delivered me. These knocked their wives off and seized my feet in a very agony of terror of instant death. A Turk so broken down was a nasty spectacle: I kicked them off as well as I could with bare feet, and finally broke free.

Lewis and Stokes had come down to help me. I was a little anxious about them; for the Arabs, having lost their wits, were as ready to assault friend as foe. Three times I had had to defend myself when they pretended not to know me and snatched at my things. However, the sergeants' war-stained khaki presented few attractions. Lewis went out east of the railway to count the thirty men he had slain; and, incidentally, to find Turkish gold and trophies in their haversacks. Stokes strolled through the wrecked bridge, saw there the bodies of twenty Turks torn to pieces by his second shell, and retired hurriedly.

Ahmed came up to me with his arms full of booty and shouted (no Arab could speak normally in the thrill of victory) that an old woman in the last wagon but one wished to see me. I sent him at once, empty handed, for my camel and some baggage camels to remove the guns; for the enemy's fire was now plainly audible, and the Arabs, sated with spoils, were escaping one by one towards the hills, driving tottering camels before them into safety. It was bad tactics to leave the guns until the end: but the confusion of a first, overwhelmingly successful, experiment had dulled our judgment.

Ahmed never brought the camels. My men, possessed by greed, had dispersed over the land with the Beduins. The sergeants and I were alone by the wreck, which had a strange silence now. We began to fear that we must abandon the guns and run for it, but just then saw two camels dashing back. Zaal and Howeimil had missed me and had returned in search.

We were rolling up the insulated cable, our only piece. Zaal dropped from his camel and would have me mount and ride; but, instead, we loaded it with the wire and the exploder. Zaal found time to laugh at our quaint booty, after all the gold and silver in the train. Howeimil was dead lame from an old wound in the knee and could not walk, but we made him couch his camel, and hoisted the Lewis guns, tied butt to butt like scissors, behind his saddle. There remained the trench mortars; but Stokes reappeared, unskilfully leading by the nose a baggage camel he had found straying. We packed the mortars in haste; put Stokes (who was still weak with his dysentery) on Zaal's saddle, with the Lewis guns, and sent off the three camels in charge of Howeimil, at their best pace.

Meanwhile, Lewis and Zaal, in a sheltered and invisible hollow behind the old gun-position, made a fire of cartridge boxes, petrol and waste, banked round it the Lewis drums and the spare small-arms ammunition; and, gingerly, on the top, laid some loose Stokes' shells. Then we ran. As the flames reached the cordite and ammonal there was a colossal and continuing noise. The thousands of cartridges exploded in series like massed machine-guns, and the shells roared off in thick columns of dust and smoke. The outflanking Turks, impressed by the tremendous defence, felt that we were in strength and strongly posted. They halted their rush, took cover, and began carefully to surround our position and reconnoitre it according to rule, while we sped panting into concealment among the ridges.

It seemed a happy ending to the affair, and we were glad to get off with no more loss than my camels and baggage; though this included the sergeants' cherished kits. However, there was food at Rumm, and Zaal thought perhaps we should find our property with the others, who were waiting ahead. We did. My men were loaded with booty, and had with them all our camels, whose saddles were being suddenly delivered of spoils to look ready for our mounting.

We asked if any one were hurt, and a voice said that the Shimt's boy—a very dashing fellow—had been killed in the first rush forward at the train. This rush was a mistake, made without instructions,

JEDDA

as the Lewis and Stokes guns were sure to end the business if the mine
worked properly. So I felt that his loss was not directly my reproach.

Three men had been slightly wounded. Then one of Feisal's
slaves vouchsafed that Salem was missing. We called every one
together and questioned them. At last an Arab said that he had
seen him lying hit, just beyond the engine. This reminded Lewis,
who, ignorant that he was one of us, had seen a negro on the
ground there, badly hurt. I had not been told and was angry, for
half the Howeitat must have known of it, and that Salem was in
my charge. By their default now, for the second time, I had left a
friend behind.

I asked for volunteers to come back and find him. After a little
Zaal agreed, and then twelve of the Nowasera. We trotted fast across
the plain towards the line. As we topped the last ridge but one we
saw the train-wreck with Turks swarming over it. There must have
been one hundred and fifty of them, and our attempt was hopeless.
Salem would have been dead, for the Turks did not take Arab prisoners. Indeed, they used to kill them horribly; so, in mercy, we were
finishing those of our badly wounded who would have to be left
helpless on abandoned ground.

We gave up Salem: and prepared, heavily, to march away. Of
our ninety prisoners, ten were friendly Medina women electing to
go to Mecca by way of Feisal. There had been twenty-two riderless
camels. The women had climbed on to five pack saddles, and the
wounded were in pairs on the residue. It was late in the afternoon.
We were exhausted, the prisoners had drunk all our water. We must
refill from the old well at Mudowwara that night to sustain ourselves so far as Rumm.

As the well was close to the station, it was highly desirable that
we get to it and away, lest the Turks divine our course and find us
there defenceless. We broke up into little parties and struggled north.
Victory always undid an Arab force, so we were no longer a raiding
party, but a stumbling baggage caravan, loaded to breaking-point
with enough household goods to make rich an Arab tribe for years.

My sergeants asked me for a sword each, as souvenir of their first private battle. As I went down the column to look out something, suddenly I met Feisal's freedmen; and to my astonishment on the crupper behind one of them, strapped to him, soaked with blood, unconscious, was the missing Salem.

I trotted up to Ferhan and asked wherever he had found him. He told me that when the Stokes gun fired its first shell, Salem rushed past the locomotive, and one of the Turks shot him in the back. The bullet had come out near his spine, without, in their judgment, hurting him mortally. After the train was taken, the Howeitat had stripped him of cloak, dagger, rifle and headgear. Mijbil, one of the freedmen, had found him, lifted him straight to his camel, and trekked off homeward without telling us. Ferhan, overtaking him on the road, had relieved him of Salem; who, when he recovered as later he did, perfectly, bore me always a little grudge for having left him behind, when he was of my company and wounded. I had failed in staunchness. My habit of hiding behind a Sherif was to avoid measuring myself against the pitiless Arab standard, with its no-mercy for foreigners who wore its clothes, and aped its manners. Not often was I caught with so poor a shield as blind Sherif Aid.

We reached the well in three hours and watered without mishap. Afterwards we moved off another ten miles or so, beyond fear of pursuit. There we lay down and slept, and in the morning found ourselves happily tired. Stokes had had his dysentery heavy upon him the night before, but sleep and the ending of anxiety made him well. He and I and Lewis, the only unburdened ones, went on in front across one huge mud flat after another till just before sunset we were at the bottom of Wadi Rumm.

This new route was important for our armoured cars, because its twenty miles of hard mud might enable them to reach Mudowwara easily. If so, we should be able to hold up the circulation of trains when we pleased. Thinking of this, we wheeled into the avenue of Rumm, still gorgeous in sunset colour; the cliffs as red as the clouds in the west, like them in scale and in the level bar they raised against the sky. Again we felt how Rumm inhibited excitement by its serene beauty. Such whelming greatness dwarfed us, stripped off the cloak of laughter in which we had ridden over the jocund flats.

Two days later we were at Akaba; entering in glory, laden with precious things, and boasting that the trains were at our mercy. From Akaba the two sergeants took hurried ship to Egypt. Cairo had remembered them and gone peevish because of their non-return. However, they could pay the penalty of this cheerfully. They had won a battle single handed; had had dysentery; lived on camel-milk; and learned to ride a camel fifty miles a day without pain. Also Allenby gave them a medal each.

CHAPTER XVII

MAKING UP OUR MINDS

OCTOBER, 1917, was a month of anticipation for us, in the knowledge that Allenby, with Bols and Dawnay, was planning to attack the Gaza-Beersheba line.

Gaza had been entrenched on a European scale with line after line of defences in reserve. It was so obviously the enemy's strongest point, that the British higher command had twice chosen it for frontal attack. Allenby, fresh from France, insisted that any further assault must be delivered by overwhelming numbers of men and guns, and their thrust maintained by enormous quantities of all kinds of transport.

Dawnay sought to destroy the enemy's strength with the least fuss. He advised a drive at the far end of the Turkish line, near Beersheba. To make his victory cheap he wanted the enemy main force behind Gaza, which would be best secured if the British concentration was hidden so that the Turks would believe the flank attack to be a shallow feint.

We on the Arab front were very intimate with the enemy. Our Arab officers had been Turkish officers, and knew every leader on the other side personally. Relation between us and them was universal, for the civil population of the enemy area was wholly ours without pay or persuasion. In consequence our intelligence service was the widest, fullest and most certain imaginable.

We knew, better than Allenby, the enemy hollowness, and the magnitude of the British resources. We under-estimated the crippling effect of Allenby's too plentiful artillery, and the cumbrous intricacy of his infantry and cavalry, which moved only with rheumatic slowness. We hoped Allenby would be given a month's fine weather; and, in that case, expected to see him take, not merely Jerusalem, but Haifa too, sweeping the Turks in ruin through the hills.

Such would be our moment, and we needed to be ready for it in the spot where our weight and tactics would be least expected and most damaging. For my eyes, the centre of attraction was Deraa, the junction of the Jerusalem-Haifa-Damascus-Medina railways, the navel of the Turkish Armies in Syria, the common point of all their fronts; and, by chance, an area in which lay great untouched reserves of Arab fighting men, educated and armed by Feisal from Akaba.

I pondered for a while whether we should not call up all these adherents and tackle the Turkish communications in force. We were certain, with any management, of twelve thousand men: enough to rush Deraa, to smash all the railway lines, even to take Damascus by surprise. Any one of these things would make the position of the Beersheba army critical: and my temptation to stake our capital instantly upon the issue was very sore.

The local people were imploring us to come. Sheikh Talal el Hareidhin, leader of the hollow country about Deraa, sent repeated messages that, with a few of our riders as proof of Arab support, he would give us Deraa. Such an exploit would have done the Allenby business, but was not one which Feisal could scrupulously afford unless he had a fair hope of then establishing himself there. Deraa's sudden capture, followed by a retreat, would have involved the massacre, or the ruin, of all the splendid peasantry of the district.

They could only rise once, and their effort on that occasion must be decisive. To call them out now was to risk the best asset Feisal held for eventual success, on the speculation that Allenby's first attack would sweep the enemy before it, and that the month of November would be rainless, favourable to a rapid advance.

I weighed the English army in my mind, and could not honestly assure myself of them. The men were often gallant fighters, but their generals as often gave away in stupidity what they had gained in ignorance. Allenby was quite untried, and his troops had broken down in and been broken by the Murray period. Of course, we were fighting for an Allied victory, and since the English were the leading partners, the Arabs would have, in the last resort, to be sacrificed for them. But was it the last resort? The war generally was going neither well nor very ill, and it seemed as though there might be time for another try next year. So I decided to postpone the hazard for the Arabs' sake.

However, the Arab Movement lived on Allenby's good pleasure, so it was needful to undertake some operation, less than a general revolt, in the enemy rear: an operation which could be achieved by a raiding party without involving the settled peoples; and yet one which would please him by being of material help to the British pursuit of the enemy. These conditions and qualifications pointed, upon consideration, to an attempted cutting of one of the great bridges in the Yarmuk Valley.

It was by the narrow and precipitous gorge of the river Yarmuk that the railway from Palestine climbed to Hauran, on its way to Damascus. The depth of the Jordan depression, and the abruptness of the eastern plateau-face made this section of the line most difficult to build. The engineers had to lay it in the very course of the winding river valley: and to gain its development the line had to cross and recross the stream continually by a series of bridges, the farthest west and the farthest east of which were hardest to replace.

To cut either of these bridges would isolate the Turkish army in Palestine, for one fortnight, from its base in Damascus, and destroy its power of escaping from Allenby's advance. To reach the Yarmuk we should need to ride from Akaba, by way of Azrak, some four hundred and twenty miles. The Turks thought the danger from us so remote that they guarded the bridges insufficiently.

Accordingly we suggested the scheme to Allenby, who asked that it be done on November the fifth, or one of the three following days.

Nasir, our usual pioneer, was absent: but out with the Beni Sakhr was Ali ibn el Hussein, the youthful and attractive Harith Sherif, who had distinguished himself in Feisal's early desperate days about Medina, and later had outnewcombed Newcombe about el Ula.

Ali, having been Jemal's guest in Damascus, had learned something of Syria: so I begged a loan of him from Feisal. His courage, his resource, and his energy were proven. There had never been any adventure, since our beginning, too dangerous for Ali to attempt, nor a disaster too deep for him to face with his high yell of a laugh.

He was physically splendid: not tall nor heavy, but so strong that he would kneel down, resting his forearms palm-up on the ground, and rise to his feet with a man on each hand. In addition, Ali could outstrip a trotting camel on his bare feet, keep his speed over half a mile and then leap into the saddle. He was impertinent, headstrong, conceited; as reckless in word as in deed; impressive (if he pleased) on public occasions, and fairly educated for a person whose native ambition was to excel the nomads of the desert in war and sport.

My detailed plan was to rush from Azrak under guidance of Rafa (that most gallant sheikh who had convoyed me in June), to Um Keis, in one or two huge marches with a handful of, perhaps, fifty men. Um Keis was Gadara, very precious with its memories of Menippus and of Meleager, the immortal Greek-Syrian whose self-expression marked the highest point of Syrian letters. It stood just over the westernmost of the Yarmuk bridges, a steel masterpiece whose destruction would fairly enrol me in the Gadarene school. Only half a dozen sentries were stationed actually on the girders and abutments. Reliefs for them were supplied from a garrison of sixty, in the station buildings of Hemme, where the hot springs of Gadara yet gushed out to the advantage of local sick. My hope was to persuade some of the Abu Tayi under Zaal to come with me. These men-wolves would make certain the actual storming of the bridge. To prevent enemy reinforcements coming up we would sweep the approaches with machine-guns, handled by Captain Bray's Indian volunteers from the cavalry division in France, under Jemadar Hassan Shah.

The demolition of great underslung girders with limited weights of explosive was a precise operation, difficult to do under fire. Wood, the base engineer at Akaba, was invited to come along and double me. He immediately agreed, though condemned medically for active service as the result of a bullet through the head in France. George Lloyd, who was spending a last few days in Akaba before going to Versailles on a regretted inter-Allied Commission, said that he would ride up with us to Jefer.

We were making our last preparations when an unexpected ally arrived in Emir Abd el Kader el Jezairi, grandson of the chivalrous defender of Algiers against the French.

To Feisal he offered the bodies and souls of his villagers, sturdy, hard-smiting Algerian exiles living compactly along the north bank of the Yarmuk. We seized at the chance this would give us to control for a little time the middle section of the Valley railway, including two or three main bridges, without the disability of raising the countryside; since the Algerians were hated strangers and the Arab peasantry would not join them. Accordingly, we put off calling Rafa to meet us at Azrak, and said not a word to Zaal, concentrating our thoughts instead on Wadi Khalid and its bridges.

While we were in this train of mind arrived a telegram from Colonel Brémond, warning us that Abd el Kader was a spy in pay of the Turks. It was disconcerting.

Feisal said to me, "I know he is mad. I think he is honest. Guard your heads and use him." We carried on, showing him our complete confidence, on the principle that a crook would not credit our honesty, and that an honest man was made a crook soonest by suspicion. As a matter of fact, he was an Islamic fanatic, half-insane with religious enthusiasm and a most violent belief in himself. His Moslem susceptibilities were outraged by my undisguised Christianity. His pride was hurt by our companionship; for the tribes greeted Ali as greater, and treated me as better, than himself. His bullet-headed stupidity broke down Ali's self-control twice or thrice into painful scenes: while his final effort was to leave us in the lurch at a desperate moment, after hindering our march and upsetting ourselves and our plans as far as he could.

GENERAL SIR REGINALD WINGATE, *Sirdar and High Commissioner in Egypt*

CHAPTER XVIII

ACROSS THE LINE AGAIN

WE HAD an immense final meal in the luxury of camp, and started in the evening of October the twenty-fourth 1917. For four hours we marched slowly: a first march was always slow, and both camels and men hated the setting out on a new hazard. Loads slipped, saddles had to be re-girthed, and riders changed. In addition to my own camels (Ghazala, the old grandmother, now far gone in foal, and Rima, a full-pointed Sherari camel which the Sukhur had stolen from the Rualla) and those of the bodyguard, I had mounted the Indians, and lent one to Wood (who was delicate in the saddle and rode a fresh animal nearly every day), and one to Thorne, Lloyd's yeomanry trooper, who sat his saddle like an Arab and looked workmanlike in a headcloth, with a striped cloak over his khaki. Lloyd himself was on a thoroughbred Dheraiyeh which Feisal had lent him: a fine, fast-looking animal, but clipped after mange and thin.

Our party straggled. Wood fell behind, and my men, being fresh, and having much work to keep the Indians together, lost touch with him. So he found himself alone with Thorne, and missed our turn to the east, in the blackness which always filled the depths of the Itm gorge by night, except when the moon was directly overhead.

They went on up the main track towards Guweira, riding for hours; but at last decided to wait for day in a side valley. Both were new to the country, and not sure of the Arabs, so they took turns to keep watch. We guessed what had happened when they failed to appear at our midnight halt, and before dawn Ahmed, Aziz and Abd el Rahman went back, with orders to scatter up the three or four practicable roads and bring the missing pair to Rumm.

I stayed with Lloyd and the main body as their guide across the curved slopes of pink sandstone and tamarisk-green valleys to Rumm, which we entered at last, while the crimson sunset burned on its stupendous cliffs and slanted ladders of hazy fire down the walled avenue. Wood and Thorne were there already, in the sandstone amphitheatre of the springs. Wood was ill, and lying on the platform of my old camp.

He had begun to believe that he would never see us again, and was ungrateful when we proved too overcome with the awe that Rumm compelled on her visitors to sympathize deeply with his sufferings. In fact, we stared and said "Yes," and left him lying there while we wandered whispering about the wonder of the place. Fortunately Ahmed and Thorne thought more of food: and with supper friendly relations were restored.

Next day, while we were saddling, Ali and Abd el Kader appeared. Lloyd and I had a second lunch with them, for they were quarrelling, and to have guests held them in check. Lloyd was the rare sort of traveller who could eat anything with anybody, anyhow and at any time. Then, making pace, we pushed across the flat, matching our camels in a burst over its velvet surface, until we overtook the main body, and scattered them with the excitement of our gallop. The Indians' soberly laden camels danced like ironmongery till they had shed their burdens. Then we calmed ourselves, and plodded together gently up Wadi Hafira, a gash like a sword-cut into the plateau. At its head lay a stiff pass to the height of Batra; but to-day we fell short of this, and out of laziness and craving for comfort stopped in the sheltered bottom of the valley. We lit great fires, which were cheerful in the cool evening. Farraj prepared rice in his manner for me as usual. Lloyd and Wood and Thorne had brought with them bully beef in tins and British army biscuits. So we joined ranks and feasted.

Next day we climbed the zigzag broken pass, the grassy street of Hafira below us framing a cone-hill in its centre, with, as background, the fantastic grey domes and glowing pyramids of the mountains of Rumm, prolonged to-day into wider fantasies by the cloud-masses brooding over them. We watched our long train wind upwards, till before noon the camels, Arabs, Indians and baggage had reached the top without accident. Contentedly we plumped ourselves down in the first green valley over the crest, sheltered from the wind, and warmed by the faint sunshine which tempered the autumn chill of this high tableland. Some one began to talk again about food.

I went away north, scouting with Awad, a Sherari camel-boy, engaged in Rumm without investigation. There were so many baggage camels in our party, and the Indians proved such novices at loading and leading them, that my bodyguard were being diverted from their proper duty of riding with me. So when Showakh introduced his cousin, a Khayal Sherari who would serve with me on any conditions, I accepted him at the glance: and now set out to measure his worth in a predicament.

We circled round Aba el Lissan to make sure that the Turks were in seemly idleness, for they had a habit of rushing a mounted patrol over the Batra sites at sudden notice, and I had no mind to put our party into unnecessary action yet. Awad was a ragged, brown-skinned lad of perhaps eighteen, splendidly built, with the muscles and sinews of an athlete, active as a cat, alive in the saddle (he rode magnificently) and not ill-looking, though with an air of constant and rather suspicious expectancy, as though he looked any moment for something new from life, and that something not of his seeking or ordering, nor wholly grateful.

Awad before me showed himself confused and self-conscious, though with his fellows he could be merry and full of japes. His engagement was a sudden fortune beyond dreams, and he was pitifully determined to suit my mind. For the moment this was to wander across the Maan highroad in order to draw the Turks' notice. When we had succeeded, and they trotted out in chase, we returned back, doubled again, and so tricked their mule-riders away northward out of the direction of danger. Awad took gleeful concern in the game, and handled his new rifle well.

Afterwards I climbed with him to the top of a hill overlooking Batra, and the valleys which sloped to Aba el Lissan, and we lay there lazily till we saw Ali's cavalcade beginning to lip over the head of the pass. Then we ran down the slopes to meet them, and heard how he had lost four camels on the pass. Also, he had fallen out again with Abd el Kader, from whose deafness and conceit and boorish manners he prayed God to deliver him.

We left them to follow us after dark, and as they had no guide, I loaned them Awad. We would meet again in Auda's tents. Then we moved forward over shallow valleys and cross-ridges till the sun set behind the last high bank, from whose top we saw the square box of the station at Ghadir el Haj breaking artificially out of the level, miles and miles away.

Lloyd and I marked the bearing of the railway where we purposed to cross just below Shedia. As the stars rose we agreed that we must march upon Orion. So we started and marched on Orion for hour after hour, with effect that Orion seemed no nearer, and there were no signs of anything between us and him. We had debouched from the ridges upon the plain, and the plain was neverending, and monotonously striped by shallow wadi-beds, with low, flat, straight banks, which in the milky star-light looked always like the earthwork of the expected railway. The going underfoot was firm, and the cool air of the desert in our faces made the camels swing out freely.

Lloyd and I went in front to spy out the line, that the main body might not be involved if chance put us against a Turkish blockhouse or night-patrol. Our fine camels, lightly ridden, set too long a stride;

so that, without knowing, we drew more and more ahead of the laden Indians. Hassan Shah the Jemadar threw out a man to keep us in sight, and then another, and after that a third, till his party was a hurrying string of connecting files. Then he sent up an urgent whisper to go slowly, but the message which reached us after its passage through three languages was unintelligible.

We halted and so knew that the quiet night was full of sounds, while the scents of withering grass ebbed and flowed about us with the dying wind. Afterwards we marched again more slowly, as it seemed for hours, and the plain was still barred with deceitful dykes, which kept our attention at unprofitable stretch. We felt the stars were shifting and that we were steering wrong. Lloyd had a compass somewhere. We halted and groped in his deep saddle-bags. Thorne rode up and found it. We stood around calculating on its luminous arrow-head, and deserted Orion for a more auspicious northern star. Then again interminably forward till, as we climbed a larger bank, Lloyd reined up with a gasp and pointed. Fair in our track on the horizon were two cubes blacker than the sky, and by them a pointed roof. We were bearing straight for Shedia station, nearly into it.

We swung to the right, and jogged hastily across an open space, a little nervous lest some of the caravan strung out behind us should miss the abrupt change of course: but all was well, and a few minutes later in the next hollow we exchanged our thrill in English and Turkish, Arabic and Urdu. Behind us broke out a faint pulse-quickening clamour of dogs in the Turkish camp.

We now knew our place, and took a fresh bearing to avoid the first blockhouse below Shedia. We led off confidently, expecting in a little to cross the line. Yet again time dragged and nothing showed itself. It was midnight, we had marched for six hours, and Lloyd began to speak bitterly of reaching Bagdad in the morning. There could be no railway here. Thorne saw a row of trees, and saw them move; the bolts of our rifles clicked, but they were only trees.

We gave up hope, and rode carelessly, nodding in our saddles, letting our tired eyes lid themselves. Again the Indians lagged far behind our hasty selves; but after an hour the last bank of to-night loomed differently in front of us. It took straight shape, and over its length grew darker patches which might be the shadowed mouths of culverts. When we were nearer, the bank put up a fencing of sharp spikes along its edge. These were the telegraph poles.

Quickly we halted our party and rode to one side and then straight in, to challenge what lay behind the quiet of the place, expecting the darkness to spout fire at us suddenly, and the silence to volley out in rifle shots. But there was no alarm. We reached the bank and found it deserted. We dismounted and ran up and down each way two hundred yards: nobody. There was room for our passage.

We ordered the others immediately over into the empty, friendly desert on the east, and sat ourselves on the metals under the singing wires, while the long line of shadowy bulks wavered up out of the dark, shuffled a little on the bank and its ballast, and passed down behind us into the dark in that strained noiselessness which was a night march of camels. The last one crossed. Another hour, and we ordered a rest till dawn. Next day we found Auda camped unobtrusively in the broken, bushy expanse south-west of the wells. He received us with constraint. His large tents, with the women, had been sent away beyond reach of the Turkish aeroplanes. There were few Toweiha present: and those in violent dispute over the distribution of tribal wages. The old man was sad we should find him in such weakness.

I did my best tactfully to smooth the troubles by giving their minds a new direction and countervailing interests. Successfully too, for they smiled, which with Arabs was often half the battle. Enough advantage for the time; we adjourned to eat with Mohammed el Dheilan. He was a better diplomat, because less open than Auda. So we were made very welcome to his platter of rice and meat and dried tomatoes. Mohammed, a villager at heart, fed too well.

After the meal, as we were wandering back over the grey dry ditches, like mammoth-wallows, which floods had hacked deeply into the fibrous mud, I broached to Zaal my plans for an expedition to the Yarmuk bridges. He disliked the idea very much. Zaal in October was not the Zaal of August. Success was changing the hard-riding gallant of spring into a prudent man, whose new wealth made life precious to him. In the spring he would have led me anywhere; but the last raid had tried his nerve, and now he said he would mount only if I made a personal point of it.

I asked what party we could make up; and he named three of the men in the camp as good fellows for so desperate a hope. The rest of the tribe were away, dissatisfied. To take three Toweiha would be worse than useless, for their just conceit would inflame the other men, while they themselves were too few to suffice alone: so I said I would try elsewhere. Zaal showed his relief.

Lloyd was to go back from here to Versailles. It was a sorry thing. He was understanding, helped wisely, and wished our cause well. Also he was the one fully-taught man with us in Arabia, and in these few days together our minds had ranged abroad, discussing any book or thing in heaven or earth which crossed our fancy. When he left we were given over again to war and tribes and camels without end.

The night began with a surfeit of such work. The matter of the Howeitat must be put right. After dark we gathered round Auda's hearth, and for hours I was reaching out to this circle of fire-lit faces, playing on them with all the tortuous arts I knew, now catching one, now another (it was easy to see the flash in their eyes when a word got home); or again, taking a false line, and wasting minutes of precious time without response. The Abu Tayi were as hard-minded as they were hard-bodied, and the heat of conviction had burned out of them long since in stress of work.

Gradually I won my points, but the argument was yet marching near midnight when Auda held up his stick and called silence. We listened, wondering what the danger was, and after a while we felt a creeping reverberation, a cadence of blows too dull, too wide, too slow easily to find response in our ears. It was like the mutter of a distant, very lowly thunderstorm. Auda raised his haggard eyes towards the west, and said, "The English guns." Allenby was leading off in preparation, and his helpful sounds closed my case for me beyond dispute.

CHAPTER XIX

SERVICES AND SERMONS

NEXT MORNING the atmosphere of the camp was serene and cordial. Old Auda, his difficulties over for this time, embraced me warmly, invoking peace upon us. At the last, whilst I was standing with my hand on my couched camel, he ran out, took me in his arms again, and strained me to him. I felt his harsh beard brush my ear as he whispered to me windily, "Beware of Abd el Kader." There were too many about us to say more.

We camped for lunch and for a midday rest—the soldiers had to have three meals a day. Suddenly there was an alarm. Men on horses and camels appeared from the west and north, and closed quickly on us. We snatched our rifles. The Indians, getting used to short notices, now carried their Vickers' and Lewis mounted for action. After thirty seconds we were in complete posture of defence.

It was a picture that the party made. I was admiring ourselves and Sherif Ali was exhorting us to hold our fire till the attack became real, when Awad, with a merry laugh ran out towards the enemy, waving his full sleeve over his head in sign of friendliness. They fired at, or over him, ineffectually. He lay down and shot back, one shot, aimed just above the head of the foremost rider. That, and our ready silence perplexed them. They pulled off in a hesitant group, and after a minute's discussion, flagged back their cloaks in half-hearted reply to our signal.

One of them rode towards us at a foot's pace. Awad, protected by our rifles, went two hundred yards to meet him, and saw that he was a Sukhurri, who, when he heard our names, feigned shock. They were a raiding party from the Zebn Sukhur, who were camped, as we had expected, in front at Bair.

Ali, furious with them for their treacherous attack on us, threatened all sorts of pains. They accepted his tirade sullenly, saying that it was a Beni Sakhr manner to shoot over strangers. Ali accepted this as their habit, and a good habit in the desert, but protested that their unheralded appearance against us from three sides showed a premeditated ambush. The Beni Sakhr were a dangerous gang, not pure enough nomads to hold the nomadic code of honour or to obey the desert law in spirit, and not villagers enough to have abjured the business of rapine and raid.

Our late assailants went into Bair to report our coming. Mifleh, chief of their clan, thought it best to efface the ill-reception by a public show in which all men and horses in the place turned out to welcome us with wild cheers and gallopings and curvettings, and much firing of shots and shouting. They whirled round and round us in desperate chase, clattering over rocks with reckless horsemanship and small regard for our staidness, as they broke in and out of the ranks and let off their rifles under our camels' necks continually. Clouds of parching chalk dust arose, so that men's voices croaked.

Eventually the parade eased off, but then Abd el Kader, thinking the opinion even of fools desirable, felt it upon him to assert his virtue. They were shouting to Ali ibn el Hussein, "God give victory to our Sherif," and were reining back on their haunches beside me with "Welcome, Aurans, harbinger of action." So he climbed up his mare, into her high Moorish saddle, and with his seven Algerian servants behind him in stiff file, began to prance delicately in slow curves, crying out "Houp, Houp," in his throaty voice, and firing a pistol unsteadily in the air.

The Bedu, astonished at this performance, gaped silently; till Mifleh came to us, and said, in his wheedling way, "Lords, pray call off your servant, for he can neither shoot nor ride, and if he hits some one he will destroy our good fortune of to-day."

We off-loaded by the ruins. Beyond us the black tents of the Beni Sakhr were like a herd of goats spotting the valley. A messenger bade us to Mifleh's tent. My men whispered excitedly that sheep had been seen to die behind it, high on the knoll above the graves.

Howeitat feasts had been wet with butter; the Beni Sakhr were overflowing. Our clothes were splashed, our mouths running over, the tips of our fingers scalded with its heat. As the sharpness of hunger was appeased the hands dipped more slowly; but the meal was still far from its just end when Abd el Kader grunted, rose suddenly to his feet, wiped his hands on a handkerchief, and sat back on the carpets by the tent wall. We hesitated, but Ali muttered "The fellah" and the work continued until all the men of our sitting were full, and the more frugal of us had begun to lick the stiff fat from our smarting fingers.

Ali cleared his throat, and we returned to our carpets while the second and third relays round the pans were satisfied. One little thing, of five or six, in a filthy smock, sat there stuffing solemnly with both hands from first to last, and, at the end, with swollen belly and face glistening with grease, staggered off speechlessly hugging a huge unpicked rib in triumph to its breast.

In front of the tent the dogs cracked the dry bones loudly, and Mifleh's slave in the corner split the sheep's skull and sucked out the brains. Meanwhile, Abd el Kader sat spitting and belching and picking his teeth. Finally, he sent one of his servants for his medicine chest, and poured himself out a draught, grumbling that tough meat was bad for his digestion. He had meant by such unmannerliness to make himself a reputation for grandeur. His own villagers could no doubt be browbeaten so, but the Zebn were too near the desert to be measured by a purely peasant-measure. Also to-day they had before their eyes the contrary example of Sherif Ali ibn el Hussein, a born desert-lord. So poor Abd el Kader was not understood.

He took himself off, and we sat in the tent mouth, above the dark hollow, now set out in little constellations of tent-fires, seeming to mimic or reflect the sky above. It was a clam night, except when the dogs provoked one another to choral howlings, and as these grew rarer we heard again the quiet, steady thudding of the heavy guns preparing assault in Palestine.

To this artillery accompaniment we told Mifleh that we were about to raid the Deraa district, and would be glad to have him and some fifteen of his tribesmen with us, all on camels. After our failure with the Howeitat, we had decided not to announce our plain object, lest its forlorn character dissuade our partisans. However, Mifleh agreed at once, apparently with haste and pleasure, promising to bring with him the fifteen best men in the tribe and his own son, Turki.

Dark had fallen long before our caravan left Bair, after watering. We chiefs waited longer still while the Zebn got ready. Mifleh's preparations included a visit to Essad, the supposed ancestor of the clan, in his bedecked tomb near Annad's grave. The Sheikh thought the occasion warranted his adding another head-cord to the ragged collection looped round Essad's headstone, and characteristically asked us to provide the offering. I handed over one of my rich red-silk-and-silver Mecca ornaments, remarking that the virtue lay with the donor. The thrifty Mifleh pressed upon me one halfpenny in exchange, that he might plead purchase; and when I came past a few weeks later and saw that the gaud was gone, he cursed loudly in my hearing the sacrilege of some godless Sherari, who had robbed his ancestor. Turki would have told me more.

A steep old pathway took us out of Wadi Bair. Near the crest of a ridge we found the others camped for the night round a fire, but there passed no talk or coffee-making for this time. We lay close together, hushed and straining the ears to catch the throbbing of

Allenby's guns. They spoke eloquently: and sheet lightning in the west made gun-flashes for them.

Next day we passed to the left of the Thlaithukhwat, the "Three sisters" whose clean white peaks were landmarks on their lofty watershed for a day's journey all about; and went down the soft rolling slopes beyond them. The exquisite November morning had a softness in it like an English summer; but its beauty had to be fought off. I was spending the halts, and riding the stages, in the ranks of the Beni Sakhr; teaching my ear their dialect, and storing in my memory the tribal, family or personal notes they let drop.

At nightfall we camped in an affluent of Wadi Jesha, by some bushes of faint grey-green foliage, which pleased our camels and gave us firewood. That night the guns were very clear and loud, perhaps because the intervening hollow of the Dead Sea drummed the echoes up and over our high plateau. The Arabs whispered, "They are nearer; the English are advancing; God deliver the men under that rain." They were thinking compassionately of the passing Turks, so long their weak oppressors; whom, for their weakness, though oppressors, they loved more than the strong foreigner with his blind indiscriminate justice.

We were up early, meaning to push the long way to Ammari by sunset. About noon a party of trotting camels appeared over the ridge, moving fast and openly towards us. Little Turki cantered out on his old she-camel, with cocked carbine across his thighs, to find what they meant. "Ha," cried Mifleh to me while they were still a mile off, "that is Fahad, on his Shaara, in the front. These are our kinsmen," and sure enough they were. Fahad and Adhub, chief warleaders of the Zebn, had been camped west of the railway by Ziza, when a Gomani came in with news of our march. They had saddled at once, and by hard riding caught us, only half-way on the road. Fahad, in courteous fashion, chided me gently for presuming to ride their district on an adventure while his father's sons lay in their tent.

Fahad was a melancholy, soft-voiced, little-spoken man of perhaps thirty, with a white face, trim beard and tragic eyes. His young brother Adhub was taller and stronger, yet not above middle height. Unlike Fahad, he was active, noisy, uncouth-looking; with a snub nose, hairless boy's face and gleaming green eyes flickering hungrily from object to object. His commonness was pointed by his dishevelled hair and dirty clothes. Fahad was neater, but still very plainly dressed, and the pair, on their shaggy home-bred camels, looked as little like sheikhs of their reputation as can be conceived. However, they were famous fighters.

At Ammari a high cold night wind was stirring the ashen dust of the salt-ground about the wells into a haze, which gritted in our teeth like the stale breath of an eruption; and we were ungrateful for the water. It was on the surface, like so much of Sirhan, but most of the pools were too bitter to drink. One notable one, however, called Bir el Emir was thought very good by contrast. It lay in a little floor of bare limestone among sand-hummocks.

The water (opaque and tasting of mixed brine and ammonia) was just below the level of the rock-slab, in a stone bath with ragged undercut lips. Its depth Daud proved by hurling Farraj fully dressed into it. He sank out of view in its yellowness, and afterwards rose quietly to the surface under the rock-edge where he could not be seen in the dusk. Daud waited a strained minute; but when his victim did not appear tore off his cloak and plunged after—to find him smiling under the overhanging ledge.

They were dragged out, and then had a wild struggle in the sand beside the water-hole. Each sustained hurt, and they returned to my fire dripping wet, in rags, bleeding, with their hair and faces, legs, arms and bodies covered with mud and thorns, more like the devils of a whirlwind than their usual suave delicate presences. They said they had been dancing, and had tripped over a bush; it would be like my generosity to make them a gift of new clothes. I blasted their hopes, and sent them off to repair damages.

The wind became faint at dawn, and we moved forward for Azrak, half a march ahead. Hardly, however, were we clear of the drifts beside the wells when there was an alarm. Mounted men had been seen in the brushwood. This country was a tomtiddler's ground of raiding parties. We drew together in the best place and halted. The Indian section chose a tiny ridge hacked about with narrow ruts of water-channels. They couched camels in the hollow behind, and had their guns mounted in due order in a moment. Ali and Abd el Kader threw out their great crimson banners in the intermittent breeze. Our skirmishers, headed by Ahmed and Awad, ran out to right and left, and long shots were exchanged. All of it ended suddenly. The enemy broke cover, and marched in line towards us, waving their cloaks and sleeves in the air, and chanting their war-march of welcome. They were the fighting men of the Serhan tribe on their way to swear allegiance to Feisal. When they heard our news they turned back with us, rejoicing to be spared the road, for this tribe was not ordinarily warlike or nomadic. They made some little pomp over our joint entry to their tents at Ain el Beidha, a few miles east of Azrak, where the whole tribe was gathered; and our reception was loud, because there had been fear and lamentation among the women that morning when they saw their men march away.

The chief men distributed our party among their tents for the privilege of entertainment. Ali, Abd el Kader, Wood and myself were taken in by Mteir, the paramount sheikh of the tribe, an old, toothless, friendly thing, whose loose jaw sagged in his supporting hand all the while he talked. He gave us a fussy greeting and abundant hospitality of seethed sheep and bread. Wood and Abd el Kader were, perhaps, a little squeamish, for the Serahin seemed primitive in food-discipline, and at the common bowl there was more splashing and spluttering than was proper in the best tents. Afterwards, by constraint of Mteir's urgency, we lay on his rugs for the one night. Round our fresh bodies, for the change of food, collected all such local ticks, fleas and lice as were sick of a diet of unmitigated Serhan. Their delight made them so ravenous that with the best will in the world I could not go on feasting them. Nor apparently could Ali; for he, too, sat up and said that he felt wakeful. So we roused

Sheikh Mteir, and sent for Mifleh ibn Bani, a young, active man, accustomed to command their battles. To them we explained Feisal's needs, and our plan to relieve him.

Gravely they heard us. The western bridge, they said, was quite impossible. The Turks had just filled its country with hundreds of military wood-cutters. No hostile party could slip through undetected. They professed great suspicion of the Moorish villages, and of Abd el Kader. Nothing would persuade them to visit the one under the guidance of the other. For Tell el Shehab, the nearest bridge, they feared lest the villagers, their inveterate enemies, attack them in the rear. Also if it rained the camels would be unable to trot back across the muddy plains by Remthe, and the whole party would be cut off and killed.

We were now in deep trouble. The Serahin were our last resource, and if they refused to come with us we should be unable to carry out Allenby's project by the appointed time. Accordingly Ali collected about our little fire more of the better men of the tribe, and fortified the part of courage by bringing in Fahad, and Mifleh, and Adhub. Before them we began to combat in words this crude prudence of the Serahin, which seemed all the more shameful to us after our long sojourn in the clarifying wilderness.

We put it to them, not abstractedly, but concretely, for their case, how life in mass was sensual only, to be lived and loved in its extremity. There could be no rest-houses for revolt, no dividend of joy paid out. Its spirit was accretive, to endure as far as the senses would endure, and to use each advance as base for further adventure, deeper privation, sharper pain.

To be of the desert was, as they knew, a doom to wage unending battle with an enemy who was not of the world, nor life, nor anything, but hope itself; and failure seemed God's freedom to mankind.

There could be no honour in a sure success, but much might be wrested from a sure defeat. Omnipotence and the Infinite were our two worthiest foemen, indeed the only ones for a full man to meet, they being monsters of his own spirit's making; and the stoutest enemies were always of the household. In fighting Omnipotence, honour was proudly to throw away the poor resources that we had, and dare Him empty-handed; to be beaten, not merely by more mind, but by its advantage of better tools.

This was a halting, half-coherent speech, struck out desperately, moment by moment, in our extreme need, upon the anvil of those white minds round the dying fire; and hardly its sense remained with me afterwards; for once my picture-making memory forgot its trade and only felt the slow humbling of the Serahin, the night-quiet in which their worldliness faded, and at last their flashing eagerness to ride with us whatever the bourne. Before daylight we called old Abd el Kader, and, taking him aside among the sandy thickets, screamed into his dense ear that the Serahin would start with us, under his auspices, for Wadi Khalid, after sunrise. He grunted that it was well: and we said to one another that never, if life and opportunity were prolonged for us, would we take a deaf man for a conspirator again.

CHAPTER XX

RACING TO THE BRIDGE

EXHAUSTED, WE lay down a moment, but were astir again very early to review the camel-men of the Sirhan. They made a wild and ragged show, dashing past, but we thought them loose riders, and they blustered too much to be quite convincing. However, they were the force we had so there was an end to it, and at three in the afternoon we mounted for Azrak. Abd el Kader and his servants mounted their mares, as sign that the fighting-line was near. They rode just behind us.

It was to be Ali's first view of Azrak, and we hurried up the stony ridge in high excitement, talking of the wars and songs and passions of the early shepherd kings, with names like music, who had loved this place; and of the Roman legionaries who languished here as garrison in yet earlier times. Then the blue fort on its rock above the rustling palms, with the fresh meadows and shining springs of water broke on our sight, and halted us.

At last Ali shook his rein, and his camel picked her careful way down the lava flow to the rich turf behind the springs. Our puckered eyes opened wide with relief that the bitterness of many weeks was gone out of the reflected sunlight. Ali screamed "Grass," and flung himself off the saddle to the ground on hands and feet, his face bowed down among the harsh stems which seemed so kindly in the desert.

When we turned again to business, there was no Abd el Kader. We looked for him in the castle, in the palm-garden, over by the spring. Eventually we sent our men away to search, and they came back with Arabs, who told us that from just after the start he had ridden off northward through the flaky hillocks, towards Jebel Druse. The rank and file did not know our plans, hated him, and had been glad to see him go: but it was bad news for us.

Of our three alternatives, Um Keis had been abandoned: without Abd el Kader, Wadi Khalid was impossible: this meant that we must necessarily attempt the bridge at Tell el Shehab. To reach it we had to cross the open land between Remthe and Deraa. Abd el Kader was gone up to the enemy, with information of our plans and strength. The Turks, if they took the most reasonable precautions, would trap us at the bridge. We took council with Fahad and decided to push on none the less, trusting to the usual incompetence of our enemy. It was not a confident decision. While we took it the sunshine seemed less lambent, and Azrak not so aloof from fear.

Next morning we pushed on for miles over perfect going, through rich country for the camels, till at Abu Sawana we found a flinty hollow, brimful of deliciously clear rain-water in a narrow channel two feet deep, and perhaps ten feet wide, but half a mile long. This would serve as starting-point for our bridge-raid. To be sure of its safety, we rode a few yards further, to the top of a stony knoll and there found ourselves looking down upon a retreating party of Circassian horsemen, sent out by the Turks to report if the waters were occupied. They had missed us, to our mutual benefit, by five minutes.

At dawn we marched leisurely until the desert ended in a three-foot depression at the edge of a clean plain, which extended flatly to the metals of the railway some miles off. We halted for dusk to make its crossing possible. Our plan was to slip over secretly, and hide in the further foothills, below Deraa.

STOKES GUN CLASS AT AKABA

We made our halt another opportunity of food, for we were recklessly eating all we could as often as we had the chance. It lightened our stores, and kept us from thinking: but even with this help the day was very long. At last sunset came. The plain shivered once, as the darkness, which for an hour had been gathering among the facing hills, flowed slowly out and drowned it. We mounted. Two hours later after a quick march over gravel, we came to the railway; and without difficulty found a stony place where our caravan would make no signs of passage. The Turkish rail-guards were clearly at their ease, which meant that Abd el Kader had not yet caused a panic by his news.

We rode the other side of the line for half an hour, and then dipped into a very slight rocky depression full of succulent plants. This was Ghadir el Abyadh, recommended by Mifleh as our ambush. We took his surprising word that we were in cover, and lay down among our loaded beasts for a short sleep. Dawn would show us how far we were safe and hidden.

As day was breaking, Fahad led me to the edge of our pit, some fifteen feet above, and from it we looked straight across a slowly-dropping meadow to the railway, which seemed nearly within shot. It was most inconveniently close, but the Sukhur knew no better place. We had to stand-to all the day. Each time something was reported, our men ran to look at it, and the low bank would grow a serried frieze of human heads. Also, the grazing camels required many guards to keep them from straying into view. Whenever a patrol passed we had to be very gentle in controlling the beasts, since if one of them had roared or ruckled it would have drawn the enemy. Yesterday had been long: to-day was longer: we could not feed, as our water had to be husbanded with jealous care against the scarcity of to-morrow. The very knowledge made us thirsty.

Ali and I worked at the last arrangements for our ride. We were penned here until sunset; and must reach Tell el Shehab, blow up the bridge, and get back east of the railway by dawn. This meant a ride of at least eighty miles in the thirteen hours of darkness, with an elaborate demolition thrown in. Such a performance was beyond the capacity of most of the Indians. They were not good riders, and had broken up their camels in the march from Akaba.

An Arab by saving his beast, could bring it home in fair condition after hard work. The Indians had done their best; but the discipline of their cavalry training had tired out them and the animals in our easy stages.

So we picked out the six best riders and put them on the six best camels, with Hassan Shah their officer and greatest-hearted man, to lead them. He decided that this little party would be fittest armed with just one Vickers gun. It was a very serious reduction of our offensive power. The more I looked at it, the less fortunate seemed the development of this Yarmuk plan of ours.

The Beni Sakhr were fighting men; but we distrusted the Serahin. So Ali and I decided to make the Beni Sakhr, under Fahad, our storming party. We would leave some Serahin to guard the camels while the others carried the blasting gelatine in our dismounted charge upon the bridge.

Ali ibn el Hussein took six of his servants, and the party was completed by twenty Beni Sakhr and forty Serahin. We left the lame and weak camels behind at Abyadh in charge of the balance of our men, with instructions to get back to Abu Sawana before dawn tomorrow and wait there for our news.

Just at sunset we said good-bye to them, and went off up our valley, feeling miserably disinclined to go on at all. Darkness gathered as we rode over the first ridge and turned west, for the abandoned pilgrim road, whose ruts would be our best guide. We were stumbling down the irregular hillside, when the men in front suddenly dashed forward. We followed and found them surrounding a terrified pedlar, with two wives and two donkeys laden with raisins, flour and cloaks. They had been going to Mafrak, the station just behind us. This was awkward; and in the end we told them to camp, and left a Sirhani, to see they did not stir: he was to release them at dawn, and escape over the line to Abu Sawana.

We went plodding across country in the now absolute dark till we saw the gleam of the white furrows of the pilgrim road. It was the same road along which the Arabs had ridden with me on my first night in Arabia out by Rabegh. Since then in twelve months we had fought up it for some twelve hundred kilometres, past Medina and Hedia, Dizad, Mudowwara and Maan.

Some shepherd or other scattered these calculations by firing his rifle at our caravan, seen by him approaching silently and indistinctly in the dark. He missed widely, but began to cry out in extremity of terror and, as he fled, to pour shot after shot into the brown of us.

Mifleh el Gomaan, who was guiding, swerved violently, and in a blind trot carried our plunging line down a slope, over a break-neck bottom, and round the shoulder of a hill. There we had peaceful unbroken night once more, and swung forward in fair order under the stars. The next alarm was a barking dog on the left and then a camel unexpectedly loomed up in our track. It was, however, a stray, and riderless. We moved on again.

Mifleh made me ride with him, calling me "Arab" that my known name might not betray me to strangers in the blackness. We were coming down into a very thick hollow when we smelt ashes, and the dusky figure of a woman leaped from a bush beside the track and rushed shrieking out of sight. She may have been a gipsy, for nothing followed. We came to a hill. At the top was a village which blazed at us while we were yet distant. Mifleh bore off to the right over a broad stretch of plough; we climbed it slowly, with creaking saddles. At the edge of the crest we halted.

Away to the north below our level were some brilliant clusters of lights. These were the flares of Deraa station, lit for army traffic: and we felt something reassuring perhaps, but also a little blatant in this Turkish disregard for us. [It was our revenge to make it their last illumination: Deraa was obscured from the morrow for a whole year until it fell.] In a close group we rode to the left along the summit and down a long valley into the plain of Remthe, from which village an occasional red spark glowed out, in the darkness to the north-west. The going became flat; but it was land half-ploughed, and very soft with a labyrinth of cony-burrows, so that our plunging camels sank fetlock-in and laboured. None the less, we had to put on speed, for the incidents and roughness of the way had made us late. Mifleh urged his reluctant camel into a trot.

I was better mounted than most, on a red camel I had bought from the Adham. She was a long, raking beast, with a huge piston-stride very hard to suffer: pounding, yet not fully mechanical, because there was courage in the persistent effort which carried her sailing to the head of the line. There, all competitors out-stripped, her ambition died into a solid step, longer than normal by some inch-es, but like any other animal's, except that it gave a confident feeling of immense reserves in strength and endurance. I rode back down the ranks and told them to press forward faster. The Indians, rid-ing wooden, like horsemen, did their best, as did most of our number; but the ground was so bad that the greatest efforts were not very fruitful, and as hours went on first one and then another rider dropped behind. There-upon I chose the rear position, with Ali ibn el Hussein who was riding a rare old racing camel. She may have been fourteen years old, but never flagged nor jogged the whole night. With her head low she shuffled along in the quick, hang-kneed Nejd pace which was so easy for the rider. Our speed and camel-sticks made life miserable for the last men and camels.

Soon after nine o'clock we left the plough. The going should have improved: but it began to drizzle, and the rich surface of the land grew slippery. A Sirhani camel fell. Its rider had it up in a moment and trotted forward. One of the Beni Sakhr came down. He also was unhurt, and remounted hastily. Then we found one of Ali's servants standing by his halted camel. Ali hissed him on, and when the fellow mumbled an excuse cut him savagely across the head with his cane. The terrified camel plunged forward, and the slave, snatching at the hinder girth, was able to swing himself into the saddle. Ali pursued him with a rain of blows. Mustafa, my man, an inexperienced rider, fell off twice. Awad, his rank-man, each time caught his halter, and had helped him up before we over-took them.

The rain stopped, and we went faster. Down-hill, now. Suddenly Mifleh, rising in his saddle, slashed at the air overhead. A sharp metallic contact from the night showed we were under the telegraph line to Mezerib. Then the grey horizon before us went more distant. We seemed to be riding on the camber of an arc of land, with a growing darkness at each side and in front. There came to our ears a faint sighing, like wind among trees very far away, but continuous and slowly increasing. This must be from the great waterfall below Tell el Shehab, and we pressed forward confidently.

A few minutes later Mifleh pulled up his camel and beat her neck very gently till she sank silently on her knees. He threw himself off, while we reined up beside him on this grassy platform by a tumbled cairn. Before us from a lip of blackness rose very loudly the rushing of the river which had been long dinning our ears. It was the edge of the Yarmuk gorge, and the bridge lay just under us to the right.

We helped down the Indians from their burdened camels, that no sound betray us to listening ears; then mustered, whispering, on the clammy grass. The moon was not yet over Hermon, but the night was only half-dark in the promise of its dawn, with wild rags of tattered clouds driving across a livid sky. I served out the explosives to the fifteen porters, and we started. The Beni Sakhr under Adhub sank into the dark slopes before us to scout the way. The rainstorm had made the steep hill treacherous, and only by driving our bare toes sharply into the soil could we keep a sure foot-hold. Two or three men fell heavily.

A little farther; and at last, below our feet, we saw a something blacker in the precipitous blackness of the valley, and at its other end a speck of flickering light. It was the bridge, seen from this height in plan, with a guard tent pitched under the shadowy village-crested wall of the opposite bank. Everything was quiet, except the river; everything was motionless, except the dancing flame outside the tent.

Wood, who was only to come down if I were hit, got the Indians ready to spray the guard tent if affairs became general; while Ali, Fahad, Mifleh and the rest of us, with Beni Sakhr and explosive porters, crept on till we found the old construction path to the near abutment. We stole along this in single file, our brown cloaks and soiled clothes blending perfectly with the limestone above us, and the depths below, until we reached the metals just before they curved to the bridge. There the crowd halted, and I crawled on with Fahad.

We reached the naked abutment, and drew ourselves forward on our faces in the shadow of its rails till we could nearly touch the grey skeleton of underhung girders, and see the single sentry leaning against the other abutment, sixty yards across the gulf. Whilst we watched, he began to move slowly up and down, up and down, before his fire, without ever setting foot on the dizzy bridge.

I crept away to bring the gelatine bearers. Before I reached them there was the loud clatter of a dropped rifle, and a scrambling fall from up the bank. The sentry started and stared up at the noise. He saw, high up, in the zone of light with which the rising moon slowly made beautiful the gorge, the machine-gunners climbing down to a new position in the receding shadow. He challenged loudly, then lifted his rifle and fired, while yelling the guard out.

Instantly all was complete confusion. The invisible Beni Sakhr, crouched along the narrow path above our heads, blazed back at random. The guard rushed into trenches, and opened rapid fire at our flashes. The Indians, caught moving, could not get their Vickers in action to riddle the tent before it was empty. Firing became general. The volleys of the Turkish rifles, echoing in the narrow place, were doubled by the impact of their bullets against the rocks behind our party. The Serahin porters had learned from my body-guard that gelatine would go off if hit. So when shots spattered about them they dumped the sacks over the edge and fled. Ali leaped down to Fahad and me, where we stood on the obscure abutment unperceived, but with empty hands, and told us that the explosives were now somewhere in the deep bed of the ravine.

It was hopeless to think of recovering them, with such hell let loose, so we scampered, without accident, up the hill path through the Turkish fire, breathlessly to the top. There we met the disgusted

Wood and the Indians, and told them it was all over. We hastened back to the cairn, where the Serahin were scrambling on their camels. We copied them as soon as might be, and trotted off at speed, while the Turks were yet rattling away in the bottom of the valley. Turra, the nearest village, heard the clamour and joined in. Other villages awoke, and lights began to sparkle everywhere across the plain.

Our rush over-ran a party of peasants returning from Deraa. The Serahin, sore at the part they had played (or at what I said in the heat of running away) were looking for trouble, and robbed them bare. The victims dashed off through the moonlight with their women, raising the ear-piercing Arab call for help. Remthe heard them. Its massed shrieks alarmed every sleeper in the neighbourhood. Their mounted men turned out to charge our flank, while settlements for miles about manned their roofs and fired volleys.

We left the Serahin offenders with their encumbering loot, and drove on in grim silence, keeping together in what order we could, while my trained men did marvellous service helping those who fell, or mounting behind them those whose camels got up too hurt to canter on. The ground was still muddy, and the ploughed strips more laborious than ever; but behind us was the riot, spurring us and our camels to exertion, like a pack hunting us into the refuge of the hills. At length we entered these, and cut through by a better road towards peace, yet riding our jaded animals as hard as we could, for dawn was near. Gradually the noise behind us died away, and the last stragglers fell into place, driven together, as on the advance, by the flail of Ali ibn el Hussein and myself in the rear.

The day broke just as we rode down to the railway, and Wood, Ali and the chiefs, now in front to test the passage, were amused by cutting the telegraph in many places while the procession marched over. We had crossed the line the night before to blow up the bridge at Tell el Shehab, and so cut Palestine off from Damascus, and we were actually cutting the telegraph to Medina after all our pains and risks! Allenby's guns, still shaking the air away there on our right, were bitter recorders of the failure we had been.

The grey dawn drew on with gentleness in it, foreboding the grey drizzle of rain which followed, a drizzle so soft and hopeless that it seemed to mock our broken-footed plodding towards Abu Sawana. At sunset we reached the long water-pool; and there the rejects of our party were curious after the detail of our mistakes. We were fools, all of us equal fools, and so our rage was aimless. Ahmed and Awad had another fight; young Mustafa refused to cook rice; Farraj and Daud knocked him about until he cried; Ali had two of his servants beaten; and none of us or of them cared a little bit. Our minds were sick with failure, and our bodies tired after nearly a hundred strained miles over bad country in bad conditions, between sunset and sunset, without halt or food.

CHAPTER XXI

TO CATCH A TRAIN

FOOD WAS going to be our next preoccupation, and we held a council in the cold driving rain to consider what we might do. For lightness' sake we had carried from Azrak three days' rations, which made us complete until to-night; but we could not go back empty-handed. The Beni Sakhr wanted honour, and the Serahin were too lately disgraced not to clamour for more adventure. We had still a reserve bag of thirty pounds of gelatine, and Ali ibn el Hussein, who had heard of the performances below Maan, and was as Arab as any Arab, said, "Let's blow up a train." The word was hailed with universal joy, and they looked at me: but I was not able to share their hopes, all at once.

Blowing up trains was an exact science when done deliberately, by a sufficient party, with machine-guns in position. If scrambled at it might become dangerous. The difficulty this time was that the available gunners were Indians; who, though good men fed, were only half-men in cold and hunger. I did not propose to drag them off without rations on an adventure which might take a week. There was no cruelty in starving Arabs; they would not die of a few days' fasting, and would fight as well as ever on empty stomachs; while, if things got too difficult, there were the riding camels to kill and eat: but the Indians, though Moslems, refused camel-flesh on principle.

I explained these delicacies of diet. Ali at once said that it would be enough for me to blow up the train, leaving him and the Arabs with him to do their best to carry its wreck without machine-gun support. As, in this unsuspecting district, we might well happen on a supply train, with civilians or only a small guard of reservists aboard, I agreed to risk it. The decision having been applauded, we sat down in a cloaked circle, to finish our remaining food in a very late and cold supper (the rain had sodden the fuel and made fire not possible), our hearts somewhat comforted by chance of another effort.

At dawn, the remnant of us, some sixty men, turned back towards the railway. I led them to Minifir, whose re-curved hill-top was an excellent observation post camp, grazing-ground and way of retreat, and we sat there till sunset, shivering and staring out over the immense plain which stretched map-like to the clouded peaks of Jebel Druse, with Um el Jemal and her sister-villages like ink-smudges on it through the rain.

In the first dusk we walked down to lay the mine. A culvert at Kilometre 172 seemed the fittest place. While we stood by it there came a rumbling, and through the gathering darkness and mist a train suddenly appeared round the northern curve, only two hundred yards away. We scurried under the long arch and heard it roll overhead. This was annoying; but when the course was clear again, we fell to burying the charge. The evening was bitterly cold, with drifts of rain blowing down the valley.

The arch was solid masonry, of four metres span, and stood over a shingle water-bed which took its rise on our hill-top. The winter rains had cut this into a channel four feet deep, narrow and winding, which served us as an admirable approach till within three hundred yards of the line. There the gully widened out and ran straight towards the culvert, open to the sight of any one upon the rails.

We hid the explosive carefully on the crown of the arch, deeper than usual, beneath a tie, so that the patrols would not feel its jelly softness under their feet. The wires were taken down the bank into the shingle bed of the water-course, where concealment was quick; and up it as far as they would reach. Unfortunately, this was only sixty yards; however, the ends happened to coincide with a little bush about ten inches high, on the edge of the water-course, and we buried them beside this very convenient mark. It was impossible to leave them joined up to the exploder in the proper way, since the spot was evident to the permanent-way patrols as they made their rounds.

Owing to the mud the job took longer than usual, and it was very nearly dawn before we finished. I waited under the draughty arch till day broke, wet and dismal, and then I went over the whole area of disturbance, spending another half-hour in effacing its every mark, scattering leaves and dead grass over it, and watering down the broken mud from a shallow rain-pool near. Then they waved to me that the first patrol was coming, and I went up to join the others.

Before I had reached them they came tearing down into their prearranged places, lining the watercourse and spurs each side. A train was coming from the north. Hamud, Feisal's long slave, had the exploder; but before he reached me a short train of closed box-wagons rushed by at speed. The rain-storms on the plain, and the thick morning had hidden it from the eyes of our watchman until too late. This second failure saddened us further, and Ali began to say that nothing would come right this trip. Such a statement held risk as prelude of the discovery of an evil eye present; so, to divert attention, I suggested new watching posts be sent far out, one to the ruins on the north, one to the great cairn of the southern crest.

The rest, having no breakfast, were to pretend not to be hungry. They all enjoyed doing this, and for a while we sat cheerfully in the rain, huddling against one another for warmth behind a breastwork of our streaming camels. The moisture made the animals' hair curl up like a fleece, so that they looked queerly dishevelled. When the rain paused, which it did frequently, a cold moaning wind searched out the unprotected parts of us very thoroughly. After a time we found our wetted shirts clammy and comfortless things. We had nothing to eat, nothing to do, and nowhere to sit except on wet rock, wet grass or mud. However, this persistent weather kept reminding me that it would delay Allenby's advance on Jerusalem, and rob him of his great possibility. So large a misfortune to our lion was a half-encouragement for the mice. We would be partners into next year.

In the best circumstances, waiting for action was hard. To-day it was beastly. Even enemy patrols stumbled along without care, perfunctorily, against the rain. At last, near noon, in a snatch of fine weather, the watchmen on the south peak flagged their cloaks wildly in signal of a train. We reached our positions in an instant, for we had squatted the late hours on our heels in a streaming ditch near the line, so as not to miss another chance. The Arabs took cover properly. I looked back at their ambush from my firing point, and saw nothing but the grey hill-sides.

I could not hear the train coming, but trusted, and knelt ready for perhaps half an hour, when the suspense became intolerable, and I signalled to know what was up. They sent down to say it was coming very slowly, and was an enormously long train. Our appetites stiffened. The longer it was the more would be the loot. Then came word that it had stopped. It moved again.

Finally, near one o'clock, I heard it panting. The locomotive was evidently defective (all these wood-fired trains were bad), and the heavy load on the up-gradient was proving too much for its capacity. I crouched behind my bush, while it crawled slowly into view past the south cutting, and along the bank above my head towards the culvert. The first ten trucks were open trucks, crowded with troops. However, once again it was too late to choose, so when the engine was squarely over the mine I pushed down the handle of the exploder. Nothing happened. I sawed it up and down four times.

Still nothing happened, and I realized that it had gone out of order, and that I was kneeling on a naked bank, with a Turkish troop train crawling past fifty yards away. The bush, which had seemed a foot high, shrank smaller than a fig-leaf; and I felt myself the most distinct object in the countryside. Behind me was an open valley for two hundred yards to the cover where my Arabs were waiting and wondering what I was at. It was impossible to make a bolt for it, or the Turks would step off the train and finish us.

So there I sat, counting for sheer life, while eighteen open trucks, three box-wagons, and three officers' coaches dragged by. The engine panted slower and slower, and I thought every moment that it would break down, but at last the end of the brake van slowly disappeared into the cutting on the north. As it went, I jumped up, buried my wires, snatched hold of the wretched exploder, and went like a rabbit up hill into safety.

Mifleh was past tears, thinking I had intentionally let the train through; and when the Serahin had been told the real cause they said, "Bad luck is with us." Historically they were right; but they meant it for a prophecy, so I made sarcastic reference to their courage at the bridge the week before, hinting that it might be a tribal preference to sit on camel-guard. At once there was uproar, the Serahin attacking me furiously, the Beni Sakhr defending. Ali heard the trouble, and came running.

When we had made it up the original despondency was half forgotten. Ali backed me nobly, though the wretched boy was blue with cold and shivering in an attack of fever. He gasped that their ancestor the Prophet had given to Sherifs the faculty of "sight," and by it he knew that our luck was turning. This was comfort for them: my first instalment of good fortune came when in the wet, without other tool than my dagger, I got the box of the exploder opened and persuaded its electrical gear to work properly once more.

We returned to our vigil by the wires, but nothing happened, and evening drew down with more squalls and beastliness, everybody full of grumbles. There was no train; it was too wet to light a cooking

JIDDAH

fire; our only potential food was camel. Raw meat did not tempt any
one that night; and so our beasts survived to the morrow.

Ali lay down on his belly, which position lessened the hungerache, trying to sleep off his fever. Khazen, Ali's servant, lent him his cloak for extra covering. I went down hill to connect up the exploder, and afterwards spent the night there alone by the singing telegraph wires, hardly wishing to sleep, so painful was the cold. Nothing came all the long hours, and dawn, which broke wet, looked even uglier than usual. We were sick to death of railways and wrecking by now. I climbed up to the main body while the early patrol searched the railway. Then the day cleared a little. Ali awoke, much refreshed, and his new spirit cheered us. Hamud, the slave, produced some sticks which he had kept under his clothes by his skin all night. They were nearly dry. We shaved down some blasting gelatine, and with its hot flame got a fire going, while the Sukhur hurriedly killed a mangy camel, the best spared of our riding-beasts, and began with entrenching tools to hack it into handy joints.

Just at that moment the watchman on the north cried a train. We left the fire and made a breathless race of the six hundred yards down hill to our old position. Round the bend, whistling its loudest, came the train, a splendid two-engined thing of twelve passenger coaches, travelling at top speed on the favouring grade. I touched off under the first driving wheel of the first locomotive, and the explosion was terrific. The ground spouted blackly into my face and I was sent spinning helplessly. Recovering myself, I hobbled towards the upper valley, whence the Arabs were now shooting fast into the crowded coaches.

When the enemy began to return our fire, I found myself much between the two. Ali saw me fall, and thinking that I was hard hit, ran out, with Turki and about twenty men of his servants and the Beni Sakhr, to help me.

The train was badly derailed, with the listing coaches butted end to end at all angles, zigzagged along the track. One of them was a saloon, decorated with flags. In it had been Mehmed Jemal Pasha, commanding the Eighth Army Corps, hurrying down to defend Jerusalem against Allenby.

We could see that our chances of carrying the wreck were slight. There had been some four hundred men on board, and the survivors, now recovered from the shock, were under shelter and shooting hard at us.

Mifleh and Adhub rejoined us on the hill, and asked after Fahad. One of the Serahin told how he had led the first rush, while I lay knocked out beside the exploder, and had been killed near it. They showed his belt and rifle as proof that he was dead and that they had tried to save him. Adhub said not a word, but leaped out of the gully, and raced downhill. We caught our breaths till our lungs hurt us, watching him; but the Turks seemed not to see. A minute later he was dragging a body behind the left-hand bank.

Mifleh went back to his mare, mounted, and took her down behind a spur. Together they lifted the inert figure on to the pommel, and returned. A bullet had passed through Fahad's face, knocking out four teeth, and gashing the tongue. He had fallen unconscious, but had revived just before Adhub reached him, and was trying on hands and knees, blinded with blood, to crawl away. He now recovered poise enough to cling to a saddle. So they changed him to the first camel they found, and led him off at once.

The Turks, seeing us so quiet, began to advance up the slope. We let them come half-way, and then poured in volleys which killed some twenty and drove the others back. The ground about the train was strewn with dead, and the broken coaches had been crowded: but they were fighting under eye of their Corps-Commander, and undaunted began to work round the spurs to outflank us.

We were now only about forty left, and obviously could do no good against them. So we ran in batches up the little streambed, to the hill-top. Each man there jumped on the nearest camel, and made away at full speed eastward into the desert, for an hour. Then in safety we sorted our animals. The excellent Rahail, despite the ruling excitement, had brought off with him, tied to his saddle-girth, a huge haunch of the camel slaughtered just as the train arrived. He gave us the motive for a proper halt, five miles farther on, in Wadi

Dhuleil, where was a barren fig tree. I bought another mangy camel for extra meat, paid rewards, compensated the relatives of the killed, and gave prize-money for the sixty or seventy rifles we had taken. It was small booty, but not to be despised. Some Serahin, who had gone into the action without rifles, able only to throw unavailing stones, had now two guns apiece. Next day we moved into Azrak, having a great welcome, and boasting—God forgive us—that we were victors.

The Druse Emir of Salkhad reached our old castle just before we did. He told us the rest of the history of the Emir Abd el Kader, the Algerian. After stealing away from us he had ridden straight to their village, and entered in triumph, the Arab flag displayed, and his seven horsemen cantering about him, firing joyshots. The people were astonished, and the Turkish Governor protested that such doings were an insult to him. He was introduced to Abd el Kader, who, sitting in pomp on the divan, made a bombastic speech, stating that the Sherif now took over Jebel Druse through his agency, and all existing officials were confirmed in their appointments.

Next morning he made a second progress through the district. The suffering Governor complained again. Emir Abd el Kader drew his gold-mounted Meccan sword, and swore that with it he would cut off Jemal Pasha's head. The Druses reproved him, vowing that such things should not be said in their house before his Excellency the Governor. Abd el Kader called them whoresons, ingle's accidents, sons of a bitch, profiteering cuckolds and pimps, jetting his insults broadcast to the room-full. The Druses got angry. Abd el Kader flung raging out of the house and mounted, shouting that when he stamped his foot all Jebel Druse would rise on his side.

With his seven servants, he spurred down the road to Deraa Station, which he entered as he had entered Salkhad. The Turks, who knew his madness of old, left him to play. They disbelieved even his yarn that Ali and I would try the Yarmuk bridge that night. When, however, we did, they took a graver view, and sent him under custody

to Damascus. Jemal's brutal humour was amused, and he enlarged
him as a butt.

CHAPTER XXII

RETURN TO THE WORLD

THE WEATHER was now dreadful, with sleet and snow and storms continually; it was obvious that at Azrak there would be nothing but teaching and preaching in the next months. For this I was not eager. When necessary, I had done my share of proselytizing fatigues, converting as best I could; conscious all the time of my strangeness, and of the incongruity of an alien's advocating national liberty. The war for me held a struggle to side-track thought, to get into the people's attitude of accepting the revolt naturally and trustingly. I had to persuade myself that the British Government could really keep the spirit of its promises. Especially was this difficult when I was tired and ill, when the delirious activity of my brain tore to shreds my patience. And then, after the blunt Beduin, who would thrust in, hailing me "Ya Auruns," and put their need without compliments, these smooth townspeople were maddening as they crawled for the favour of an audience with their Prince and Bey and Lord and Deliverer. So I flung away from them in a rage, determined to go south and see if anything active could be done, in the cold weather, about the Dead Sea, which the enemy held as a trench dividing us from Palestine.

My remaining money was handed over to Sherif Ali, and the Indians commended to his care. He and I took affectionate leave of one another. Ali gave me half his wardrobe: shirts, headcloths, belts, tunics. I gave him an equivalent half of mine, and we kissed like David and Jonathan, each wearing the other's clothes. Afterwards, with Rahail only, on my two best camels, I struck away southward.

We left Azrak one evening, riding into a glowing west, while over our heads schools of cranes flew into the sunset like the outdrawn barbs of arrows. It was toilsome from the start. Night was deep by Wadi Butum, where the conditions became even worse. All the plain was wet, and our poor camels slithered and fell time and again. We fell as often as they did, but at least our part of sitting still, between falls, was easier than their part of movement. By midnight we had crossed the Ghadaf and the quag felt too awful for further progress.

We slept where we were, in the mud; rose up plated with it at dawn; and smiled crackily at one another. The wind blew, and the ground began to dry. Until noon we made poor travelling, for the camels still broke through the loose crust of flints, and foundered in the red under-clay. After noon, on the higher ground, we did better, and began rapidly to close the white sky-tents which were the Thlaithakhwat peaks.

From the ridge at sunset we looked back for an instant upon the northern plain, as it sank away from us greyly, save that here and there glowed specks or great splashes of crimson fire, the reflection of the dying sun in shallow pools of rain-water on the flats. These eyes of a dripping bloody redness were so much more visible than the plain that they carried our sight miles into the haze, and seemed to hang detached in the distant sky, tilted up, like mirage.

We passed Bair long after dark, when only its latest tent-fires still shone. As we went we saw the stars mirrored in a valley-bottom, and were able to water our breathless camels in a pool of yesterday's rain. After their drink we eased them for half an hour. This night journeying was hard on both men and animals. By day the camels saw the irregularities of their path, and undulated over them; and the rider could swing his body to miss the jerk of a long or short stride: but by night everything was blinded, and the march racked with shocks. I had a heavy bout of fever on me, which made me angry, so that I paid no attention to Rahail's appeals for rest. That young man had maddened all of us for months by his abundant vigour, and by laughing at our weaknesses; so this time I was determined to ride him out, showing no mercy. Before dawn he was blubbering with self-pity; but softly, lest I hear him.

Dawn in Jefer came imperceptibly through the mist like a ghost of sunlight, which left the earth untouched, and demonstrated itself as a glittering blink against the eyes alone. Our shadows had no edge: we doubted if that faint stain upon the soil below was cast by us or not. In the forenoon we reached Auda's camp; and stopped for a greeting, and a few Jauf dates. Auda could not provide us a relay of camels. We mounted again to get over the railway in the early night. Rahail was past protest now. He rode beside me white-faced, bleak and silent, wrought up only to outstay me, beginning to take a half pride in his pains.

Even had we started fair, he had the advantage anyhow over me in strength, and now I was nearly finished. Step by step I was yielding myself to a slow ache which conspired with my abating fever and the numb monotony of riding to close up the gate of my senses. I seemed at last approaching the insensibility which had always been beyond my reach: but a delectable land for one born so slug-tissued that nothing this side fainting would let his spirit free. Now I found myself dividing into parts. There was one which went on riding wisely, sparing or helping every pace of the wearied camel. Another hovering above and to the right bent down curiously, and asked what the flesh was doing. The flesh gave no answer, for, indeed, it was conscious only of a ruling impulse to keep on and on; but a third garrulous one talked and wondered, critical of the body's self-inflicted labour, and contemptuous of the reason for effort.

The night passed in these mutual conversations. My unseeing eyes saw the dawn-goal in front; the head of the pass, below which

that other world of Rumm lay out like a sunlit map; and my parts
debated that the struggle might be worthy, but the end foolishness
and a re-birth of trouble. This spent body toiled on doggedly and
took no heed, quite rightly, for the divided selves said nothing which
I was not capable of thinking in cold blood; they were all my natives.
Telesio, taught by some such experience, split up the soul. Had he
gone on, to the furthest limit of exhaustion, he would have seen his
conceived regiment of thoughts and acts and feelings ranked around
him as separate creatures; eyeing, like vultures, the passing in their
midst of the common thing which gave them life.

Rahail collected me out of my death-sleep by jerking the headstall and striking me, while he shouted that we had lost our direction,
and were wandering toward the Turkish lines at Aba el Lissan. He
was right, and we had to make a long cut back to reach Batra safely. The incident broke the tension between us; and, chatting, we
rode out upon the Gaa. There under the tamarisk we passed the
middle hour of the day in sleep, since by our slowness in the march
over Batra we had lost the possibility of reaching Akaba within the
three days from Azrak.

We rode in the early afternoon; easier now and exchanging jests
with one another, as the long winter evening crept down. When we
got past the Khuzail in the ascent we found the sun veiled behind
level banks of low clouds in the west, and enjoyed a rich twilight of
the English sort. In Itm the mist steamed up gently from the soil,
and collected into wool-white masses in each hollow. We reached
Akaba at midnight, and slept outside the camp till breakfast, when
I called on Joyce.

Later came urgent orders for me to go up at once to Palestine
by air. Croil flew me to Suez. Thence I went up to Allenby's headquarters beyond Gaza. He was so full of victories that my short
statement that we had failed to carry a Yarmuk bridge was sufficient, and the miserable details of failure could remain concealed.

While I was still with him, word came from Chetwode that
Jerusalem had fallen; and Allenby made ready to enter in the official

manner which the catholic imagination of Mark Sykes had devised. He was good enough, although I had done nothing for the success, to let Clayton take me along as his Staff-Officer for the day. The personal Staff tricked me out in their spare clothes till I looked like a major in the British Army. Dalmeny lent me red tabs, Evans his brass hat; so that I had the gauds of my appointment in the ceremony of the Jaffa Gate, which for me was the supreme moment of the war.

Shamefaced with triumph—which was not so much a triumph as homage by Allenby to the mastering spirit of the place—we drove back to Shea's headquarters. It was the moment to ask Allenby what he would do next. He thought he was immobilized till the middle of February, when he would push down to Jericho. Much enemy food was being lightered up the Dead Sea, and he asked me to note this traffic as a second objective if the effort to Tafileh prevailed.

I, hoping to improve on this, replied that, should the Turks be continually shaken, we might join him at the north end of the Dead Sea. If he could put Feisal's fifty tons a day of supplies, stores and ammunition into Jericho, we would abandon Akaba and transfer our head-quarters to Jordan Valley.

This idea commended itself to Allenby and Dawnay. Accordingly we agreed. The Arabs were to reach the Dead Sea as soon as possible; to stop the transport of food up it to Jericho before the middle of February; and to arrive at the Jordan before the end of March.

On our return to Akaba domestic affairs engaged the remaining free days. My part mostly concerned the bodyguard which I formed for private protection, as rumour gradually magnified my importance. On our first going up country from Rabegh and Yenbo, the Turks had been curious: afterwards they were annoyed; to the point of ascribing to the English the direction and motive force of the Arab Revolt, much as we used to flatter ourselves by attributing the Turkish efficiency to German influence.

However, the Turks said it often enough to make it an article of faith, and began to offer a reward of one hundred pounds for a

British officer alive or dead. As time went on they not only increased the general figure, but made a special bid for me. After the capture of Akaba the price became respectable; while after we blew up Jemal Pasha they put Ali and me at the head of their list; worth twenty thousand pounds alive or ten thousand dead.

Of course, the offer was rhetorical; with no certainty whether in gold or paper, or that the money would be paid at all. Still, perhaps, it might justify some care. I began to increase my people to a troop, adding such lawless men as I found, fellows whose dash had got them into trouble elsewhere. I needed hard riders and hard livers; men proud of themselves, and without family. By good fortune three or four of this sort joined me at the first, setting a tone and standard.

One afternoon, I was quietly reading in Marshall's tent at Akaba (I lodged with Marshall, our Scottish doctor, as often as I was in camp), when there entered over the noiseless sand an Ageyly, thin, dark, and short, but most gorgeously dressed. He carried on his shoulder the richest Hasa saddle-bag I had ever seen. Its woollen tapestry of green and scarlet, white, orange and blue, had tassels woven over its sides in five rows, and from the middle and bottom hung five-foot streamers, of geometric pattern, tasselled and fringed.

Respectfully greeting me, the young man threw the saddle-bag on my carpet, saying "Yours" and disappeared suddenly, as he had come. Next day, he returned with a camel-saddle of equal beauty, the long brass horns of its cantles adorned with exquisite old Yemeni engraving. On the third day he reappeared empty-handed, in a poor cotton shirt, and sank down in a heap before me, saying he wished to enter my service. He looked odd without his silk robes; for his face, shrivelled and torn with smallpox, and hairless, might have been of any age; while he had a lad's supple body, and something of a lad's recklessness in his carriage.

His long black hair was carefully braided into three shining plaits down each cheek. His eyes were weak, closed up to slits. His mouth was sensual, loose, wet; and gave him a good-humoured, half cynical expression. I asked him his name; he replied Abdulla, surnamed el Nahabi, or the Robber; the nickname, he said, was an inheritance from his respected father. His own adventures had been unprofitable. He was born in Boreida, and while young had suffered from the civil power for his impiety. When half-grown, a misfortune in a married woman's house had made him leave his native town, in a hurry, and take service with ibn Saud, Emir of Nejd.

In this service his hard swearing earned lashes and imprisonment. Consequently he deserted to Kuweit, where again he had been amorous. On his release he had moved to Hail, and enrolled himself among the retainers of ibn Rashid, the Emir. Unfortunately there he had disliked his officer to the point of striking him in public with a camel stick. Return was made in kind; and, after a slow recovery in prison, he had once more been thrust friendless on the world.

The Hejaz Railway was being built, and to its works he had come in search of fortune: but a contractor docked his wages for sleeping at noonday. He retorted by docking the contractor of his head. The Turkish Government interfered, and he found life very hard in the prison at Medina. However, through a window, he came to Mecca, and for his proved integrity and camelmanship was made post-carrier between Mecca and Jidda. To this employ he settled down, laying aside his young extravagances, bringing to Mecca his father and mother and setting them up in a shop to work for him, with the capital provided by commission from merchants and robbers.

After a year's prosperity he was waylaid, losing his camel and its consignment. They seized his shop in compensation. From the wreck he saved enough to fit himself out as a man-at-arms in the Sherifian camel-police. Merit made him a petty officer, but too much attention was drawn to his section by a habit of fighting with daggers, and by his foul mouth; a maw of depravity which had eaten filth in the stews of every capital in Arabia. Once too often his lips trembled with humour, sardonic, salacious, lying; and when reduced, he charged his downfall to a jealous Ateibi, whom he stabbed in Court before the eyes of the outraged Sherif Sharraf.

Sharraf's stern sense of public decency punished Abdulla by the severest of his chastisements, from which he very nearly died. When well enough, he entered Sharraf's service. On the outbreak of war he became orderly to ibn Dakhil, captain of the Ageyl with Feisal. His reputation grew; but the mutiny at Wejh turned ibn Dakhil into an ambassador. Abdulla missed the comradeship of the ranks, and ibn Dakhil had given him a written character to enter my service.

The letter said that for two years he had been faithful, but disrespectful; the wont of sons of shame. He was the most experienced Ageyli, having served every Arabian prince and having been dismissed each employment, after stripes and prison, for offences of too great individuality. Ibn Dakhil said that the Nahabi rode second to himself, was a master-judge of camels, and as brave as any son of Adam; easily, since he was too blind-eyed to see danger. In fact, he was the perfect retainer, and I engaged him instantly.

In my service only once did he taste cells. That was at Allenby's head-quarters, when a despairing provost-marshal rang up to say that a wild man, with weapons, found sitting on the Commander-in-Chief's doorstep, had been led without riot to the guard-room, where he was eating oranges as though for a wager, and proclaiming himself my son, one of Feisal's dogs. Oranges were running short.

So Abdulla experienced his first telephone conversation. He told the A.P.M. that such a fitting would be a comfort in all prisons, and took a ceremonious leave. He scouted absolutely the notion that he might walk about Ramleh unarmed, and was given a pass to make lawful his sword, dagger, pistol, and rifle. His first use of this pass was to revisit the guard-room with cigarettes for the military police.

He examined the applicants for my service, and, thanks to him and to the Zaagi, my other commander (a stiff man of normal officer cut), a wonderful gang of experts grew about me. The British at Akaba called them cut-throats but they cut throats only to my order. Perhaps in others' eyes it was a fault that they would recognize no authority but mine. Yet when I was away they were kind to Major Marshall, and would hold him in incomprehensible talk

about points of camels, their breeds and ailments from dawn till
night time. Marshall was very patient; and two or three of them
would sit attentive by his bedside, from the first daylight, waiting
to continue his education as soon as he became conscious.

A good half (nearly fifty of the ninety) were Ageyl, the nervous
limber Nejdi villagers who made the colour and the parade in Feisal's
army, and whose care for their riding-camels was such a feature of
their service. They would call them by name, from a hundred yards
away, and leave them in charge of the kit when they dismounted.
The Ageyl, being mercenaries, would not do well unless well paid,
and for lack of that condition had fallen into disrepute: yet the
bravest single effort of the Arab war belonged to that one of them
who twice swam down the subterranean water-conduit into
Medina, and returned with a full report of the invested town.

I paid my men six pounds a month, the standard army wage for
a man and camel, but mounted them on my own animals, so that
the money was clear income: this made the service enviable, and
put the eager spirits of the camp at my disposal. For my timetable's
sake, since I was more busy than most, my rides were long, hard
and sudden. The ordinary Arab, whose camel represented half his
wealth, could not afford to founder it by travelling my speed: also
such riding was painful for the man.

Consequently, I had to have with me picked riders, on my own
beasts. We bought at long prices the fastest and strongest camels to
be obtained. We chose them for speed and power, no matter how
hard and exhausting they might be under the saddle: indeed, often
we chose the hard-paced as the more enduring. They were changed
or rested in our own camel-hospital when they became thin: and their
riders were treated likewise. The Zaagi held each man bodily responsible for his mount's condition, and for the fitness of his saddlery.

Fellows were very proud of being in my bodyguard, which developed a professionalism almost flamboyant. They dressed like a bed
of tulips, in every colour but white; for that was my constant wear,
and they did not wish to seem to presume. In half an hour they

would make ready for a ride of six weeks, that being the limit for which food could be carried at the saddle-bow. Baggage-camels they shrank from as a disgrace. They would travel day and night at my whim, and made it a point of honour never to mention fatigue. If a new man grumbled, the others would silence him, or change the current of his complaint, brutally.

They fought like devils, when I wanted, and sometimes when I did not, especially with Turks or with outsiders. For one guardsman to strike another was the last offence. They expected extravagant reward and extravagant punishment. They made boast throughout the army of their pains and gains.

However, for the time the Arabs were possessed, and cruelty of governance answered their need. Besides, my men were blood-enemies of thirty tribes, and only for my hand over them would have murdered in the ranks each day. Their feuds prevented them combining against me; while their unlikeness gave me sponsors and spies wherever I went or sent, between Akaba and Damascus, between Beersheba and Bagdad. In my service nearly sixty of them died.

CHAPTER XXIII

FIGHTING FOR TAFILEH

WE WAITED in Guweira for news of the opening of our operation against Tafileh, the knot of villages commanding the south end of the Dead Sea. We planned to tackle it from west, south, and east, at once; the east opening the ball by attacking Jurf, its nearest station on the Hejaz line. Conduct of this attack had been trusted to Sherif Nasir, the Fortunate. With him went Nuri Said, Jaafar's chief of staff, commanding some regulars, a gun, and some machine guns. They were working from Jefer. After three days their post came in. As usual Nasir had directed his raid with skill and deliberation. Jurf, the objective, was a strong station of three stone buildings with outer-works and trenches. Behind the station was a low mound, trenched and walled, on which the Turks had set two machine-guns and a mountain-gun. Beyond the mound lay a high, sharp ridge, the last spur of the hills which divided Jefer from Bair.

The weakness of the defence lay in this ridge, for the Turks were too few to hold both it and the knoll or station, and its crest overlooked the railway. Nasir one night occupied the whole top of the hill without alarm, and then cut the line above and below the station. A few minutes later, when it was light enough to see, Nuri

Said brought his mountain-gun to the edge of the ridge; and, with a third lucky shot, a direct hit, silenced the Turkish gun beneath his view.

Nasir grew greatly excited: the Beni Sakhr mounted their camels, swearing they would charge in forthwith. Nuri thought it madness while Turkish machine-guns were still in action from trenches: but his words had no effect upon the Bedu. In desperation he opened a rattling fire with all he had against the Turkish position, and the Beni Sakhr swept round the foot of the main ridge and up over the knoll in a flash. When they saw this camel-horde racing at them, the Turks flung away their rifles and fled into the station. Only two Arabs were fatally hurt.

Nuri ran down to the knoll. The Turkish gun was undamaged. He slewed it round and discharged it point blank into the ticket office. The Beni Sakhr mob yelled with joy to see the wood and stones flying, jumped again on their camels and loped into the station just as the enemy surrendered. Nearly two hundred Turks, including seven officers, survived as our prisoners.

After the looting, the engineers fired charges under the two engines, against the water-tower, in the pump, and between the points of the sidings. They burned the captured trucks and damaged a bridge; but perfunctorily, for, as usual after victory, every one was too loaded and too hot to care for altruistic labour.

Then the weather once more broke. For three successive days came falls of snow. Nasir's force with difficulty regained the tents at Jefer. This plateau about Maan lay between three and five thousand feet above sea level, open to all winds from north and east. They blew from Central Asia, or from Caucasus, terribly over the great desert to these low hills of Edom, against which their first fury broke. The surplus bitterness lipped the crest and made a winter, quite severe of its degree, below, in Judæa and Sinai.

Outside Beersheba and Jerusalem the British found it cold; but our Arabs fled there to get warm. Unhappily the British supply staff realized too late that we were fighting in a little Alp. They would not give us tents for one-quarter of our troops, nor serge clothing, nor boots, nor blankets enough to issue two to each man of the mountain garrisons. Our soldiers, if they neither deserted nor died, existed in an aching misery which froze the hope out of them.

According to our plan the good news of Jurf was to send the Arabs of Petra, under Sherif Abd el Mayin, at once up their hills into the forest towards Shobek. It was an uncanny march in the hoar mist, that of these frozen-footed peasants in their sheep-skins, up and down sharp valleys and dangerous hill-sides, out of whose snow-drifts the heavy trunks of junipers, grudging in leaves, jutted like castings in grey iron. The ice and frost broke down the animals, and many of the men; yet these hardy high-landers, used to being too cold throughout their winter, persisted in the advance.

The Turks heard of them as they struggled slowly nearer, and fled from the caves and shelters among the trees to the branch rail-head, littering the roads of their panic with cast baggage and equipment.

However, the advantage lay with Nasir, who leaped in one day from Jefer, and after a whirlwind night appeared at dawn on the rocky brink of the ravine in which Tafileh hid, and summoned it to surrender on pain of bombardment: an idle threat, for Nuri Said with the guns had gone back to Guweira. There were only one hundred and eighty Turks in the village, but they had supporters in the Muhaisin, a clan of the peasantry; not for love so much as because Dhiab, the vulgar head-man of another faction, had declared for Feisal. So they shot up at Nasir a stream of ill-directed bullets.

The Howeitat spread out along the cliffs to return the peasants' fire. This manner of going displeased Auda, the old lion, who raged that a mercenary village folk should dare to resist their secular masters, the Abu Tayi. So he jerked his halter, cantered his mare down the path, and rode out plain to view beneath the easternmost houses of the village. There he reined in, and shook a hand at them, booming in his wonderful voice: "Dogs, do you not know Auda?" When they realized it was that implacable son of war their hearts failed them, and an hour later Sherif Nasir in the town-house was sipping tea with his guest the Turkish Governor, trying to console him for the sudden change of fortune.

At dark Mastur rode in. His Motalga looked blackly at their blood-enemies the Abu Tayi, lolling in the best houses. The two Sherifs divided up the place, to keep their unruly followers apart.

Feisal had delegated command of this push towards the Dead Sea to his young half-brother Zeid. It was Zeid's first office in the north, and he set out eager with hope. As adviser he had Jaafar Pasha, our general. His infantry, gunners and machine-gunners stuck, for lack of food, at Petra; but Zeid himself and Jaafar rode on to Tafileh.

Things were almost at a break. Auda affected a magnanimity very galling to the Motalga boys, Metaab and Annad, sons of Abtan, whom Auda's son had killed. They, lithe, definite, self-conscious figures, began to talk about revenge—tom-tits threatening a hawk. Auda declared he would whip them in the Market-place if they were rude. This was very well, but their followers were two to every man of his, and we should have the village in a blaze. The young fellows, with Rahail, my ruffler, went flaunting in every street.

Zeid thanked and paid Auda, and sent him back to his desert. The enlightened heads of the Muhaisin had to go as forced guests to Feisal's tent. Dhiab, their enemy, was our friend: we remembered regretfully the adage that the best allies of a violently-successful new régime were not its partisans, but its opponents. By Zeid's plenty of gold the economic situation improved. We appointed an officer-governor and organized our five villages for further attack.

Notwithstanding, these plans quickly went adrift. Before they had been agreed upon we were astonished by a sudden try of the Turks to dislodge us. We had never dreamed of this, for it seemed out of the question that they should hope to keep Tafileh, or want to keep it. Allenby was just in Jerusalem, and for the Turks the issue of the war might depend on their successful defence of the Jordan against him. Unless Jericho fell, or until it fell, Tafileh was an obscure village of no interest. Nor did we value it as a possession; our desire was to get past it towards the enemy. For men so critically placed as the Turks to waste one single casualty on its recapture appeared the rankest folly.

Hamid Fakhri Pasha, commanding the 48th Division and the Amman sector, thought otherwise, or had his orders. He collected about nine hundred infantry, made up of three battalions (in January 1918 a Turkish battalion was a poor thing) with a hundred cavalry, two mountain howitzers, and twenty-seven machine guns, and sent them by rail and road to Kerak. There he impressed all the local transport, drew a complete set of civil officials to staff his new administration in Tafileh, and marched southward to surprise us.

Surprise us he did. We first heard of him when his cavalry feelers fell on our pickets in Wadi Hesa, the gorge of great width and depth and difficulty which cut off Kerak from Tafileh, Moab from Edom. By dusk he had driven them back, and was upon us.

Jaafar Pasha had sketched a defence position on the south bank of the great ravine of Tafileh; proposing, if the Turks attacked, to give them the village, and defend the heights which overhung it, behind. This seemed to me doubly unsound. The slopes were dead, and their defence as difficult as their attack. They could be turned from the east; and by quitting the village we threw away the local people, whose votes and hands would be for the occupiers of their houses.

However, it was the ruling idea—all Zeid had—and so about midnight he gave the order, and servants and retainers loaded up their stuff. The men-at-arms proceeded to the southern crest, while the baggage train was sent off by the lower road to safety. This move created panic in the town. The peasants thought we were running away (I think we were) and rushed to save their goods and lives. It was freezing hard, and the ground was crusted with noisy ice. In the blustering dark the confusion and crying through the narrow streets were terrible.

Dhiab the Sheikh had told us harrowing tales of the disaffection of the townspeople, to increase the splendour of his own loyalty; but my impression was that they were stout fellows of great potential use. To prove it I sat out on my roof, or walked in the dark up

and down the steep alleys, cloaked against recognition, with my
guards unobtrusively about me within call. So we heard what passed.
The people were in a very passion of fear, nearly dangerous, abus-
ing everybody and everything: but there was nothing pro-Turkish
abroad. They were in horror of the Turks returning, ready to do all
in their physical capacity to support against them a leader with fighting intention. This was satisfactory, for it chimed with my hankering
to stand where we were and fight stiffly.

Finally, I met the young Jazi sheikhs Metaab and Annad, beautiful in silks and gleaming silver arms, and sent them to find their
uncle, Hamd el Arar. Him I asked to ride away north of the ravine,
to tell the peasantry, who, by the noise, were still fighting the Turks,
that we were on our way up to help them. Hamd, a melancholy,
courtly, gallant cavalier, galloped off at once with twenty of his relations, all that he could gather in the distracted moment.

Their passage at speed through the streets added the last touch
required to perfect the terror. The housewives bundled their goods
pell-mell out of doors and windows, though no men were waiting
to receive them. Children were trampled on, and yelled, while their
mothers were yelling anyhow. The Motalga during their gallop fired
shot after shot into the air to encourage themselves, and, as though
to answer them, the flashes of the enemy rifles became visible, out-
lining the northern cliffs in that last blackness of sky before the
dawn. I walked up the opposite heights to consult with Sherif Zeid.

Zeid sat gravely on a rock, sweeping the country with field-glasses for the enemy. As crises deepened, Zeid grew detached, nonchalant.
I was in a furious rage. The Turks should never, by the rules of sane
generalship, have ventured back to Tafileh at all. It was simple greed,
a dog-in-the-manger attitude unworthy of a serious enemy, just the
sort of hopeless thing a Turk would do. How could they expect a
proper war when they gave us no chance to honour them? Our
morale was continually being ruined by their follies, for neither
could our men respect their courage, nor our officers respect their
brains. Also, it was an icy morning, and I had been up all night and

was Teutonic enough to decide that they should pay for my changed mind and plan.

First I suggested that Abdulla go forward with two Hotchkiss guns to test the strength and disposition of the enemy. Then we talked of what next; very usefully, for Zeid was a cool and gallant little fighter, with the temperament of a professional officer. We saw Abdulla climb the other bank. The shooting became intense for a time, and then faded into distance. His coming had stimulated the Motalga horsemen and the villagers, who fell on the Turkish cavalry and drove them over a first ridge, across a plain two miles wide, and over a ridge beyond it down the first step of the great Hesa depression.

Behind this lay the Turkish main body, just getting on the road again after a severe night which had stiffened them in their places. They came properly into action, and Abdulla was checked at once. We heard the distant rolling of machine-gun fire, growing up in huge bursts, laced by a desultory shelling. Our ears told us what was happening as well as if we saw it, and the news was excellent. I wanted Zeid to come forward at once on that authority: but his caution stepped in and he insisted that we wait exact word from his advance-guard, Abdulla.

This was not necessary, according to book, but they knew I was a sham soldier, and took licence to hesitate over my advice when it came peremptorily. However, I held a hand worth two of that, and went off myself for the front to prejudge their decision. On the way I saw my body-guard, turning over the goods exposed for removal in the streets, and finding much of interest to themselves. I told them to recover our camels and to bring their Hotchkiss automatic to the north bank of the gorge in a hurry.

The road dipped into a grove of fig-trees, knots of blue snaky boughs; bare, as they would be long after the rest of nature was grown green. Thence it turned eastward, to wind lengthily in the valley to the crest. I left it, climbing straight up the cliffs. An advantage of going barefoot was a new and incredible sureness upon rock when the soles had got hard by painful insistence, or were too chilled to feel jags and scrapes. The new way, while warming me, also shortened my time appreciably, and very soon, at the top, I found a level bit, and then a last ridge overlooking the plateau.

This last straight bank, with Byzantine foundations in it, seemed very proper for a reserve or ultimate line of defence for Tafileh. To be sure, we had no reserve as yet—no one had the least notion who or what we would have anywhere—but, if we did have anybody, here was their place; and at that precise moment Zeid's personal Ageyl became visible, hiding coyly in a hollow. To make them move required words of a strength to unravel their plaited hair: but at last I had them sitting along the skyline of Reserve Ridge. They were about twenty, and from a distance looked beautiful, like "points" of a considerable army. I gave them my signet as a token, with orders to collect there all newcomers, especially my fellows with their gun.

As I walked northward towards the fighting, Abdulla met me, on his way to Zeid with news. He had finished his ammunition, lost five men from shell-fire, and had one automatic gun destroyed. Two guns, he thought the Turks had. His idea was to get up Zeid with all his men and fight: so nothing remained for me to add to his message; and there was no subtlety in leaving alone my happy masters to cross and dot their own right decision.

He gave me leisure in which to study the coming battlefield. The tiny plain was about two miles across, bounded by low green ridges, and roughly triangular, with my reserve ridge as base. Through it ran the road to Kerak, dipping into the Hesa valley. The Turks were fighting their way up this road. Abdulla's charge had taken the western or left-hand ridge, which was now our firing-line.

Shells were falling in the plain as I walked across it, with harsh stalks of wormwood stabbing into my wounded feet. The enemy fuzing was too long, so that the shells grazed the ridge and burst away behind. One fell near me, and I learned its calibre from the hot cap. As I went they began to shorten range, and by the time I

LORD LLOYD, *High Commissioner in Egypt*

got to the ridge it was being freely sprinkled with shrapnel. Obviously the Turks had got observation somehow, and looking round I saw them climbing along the eastern side beyond the gap of the Kerak road. They would soon outflank us at our end of the western ridge.

"Us" proved to be about sixty men, clustered behind the ridge in two bunches, one near the bottom, one by the top. The lower was made up of peasants, on foot, blown, miserable, and yet the only warm things I had seen that day. They said their ammunition was finished, and it was all over. I assured them it was just beginning and pointed to my populous reserve ridge, saying that all arms were there in support. I told them to hurry back, refill their belts and hold on to it for good. Meanwhile we would cover their retreat by sticking here for the few minutes yet possible.

They ran off, cheered, and I walked about among the upper group quoting how one should not quit firing from one position till ready to fire from the next. In command was young Metaab, stripped to his skimp riding-drawers for hard work, with his black love-curls awry, his face stained and haggard. He was beating his hands together and crying hoarsely with baffled vexation, for he had meant to do so well in this, his first fight for us.

My presence at the last moment, when the Turks were breaking through, was bitter; and he got angrier when I said that I only wanted to study the landscape. He thought it flippancy, and screamed something about a Christian going into battle unarmed. I retorted with a quip from Clausewitz, about a rear-guard effecting its purpose more by being than by doing: but he was past laughter, and perhaps with justice, for the little flinty bank behind which we sheltered was crackling with fire. The Turks, knowing we were there, had turned twenty machine-guns upon it. It was four feet high and fifty feet long, of bare flinty ribs, off which the bullets slapped deafeningly: while the air above so hummed or whistled with ricochets and chips that it felt like death to look over. Clearly we must leave very soon, and as I had no horse I went off first, with Metaab's promise that he would wait where he was, if he dared, for another ten minutes.

The run warmed me. I counted my paces, to help in ranging the Turks when they ousted us; since there was only that one position for them, and it was poorly protected against the south. In losing this Motalga ridge we would probably win the battle. The horsemen held on for almost their ten minutes, and then galloped off without hurt. Metaab lent me his stirrup to hurry me along, till we found ourselves breathless among the Ageyl. It was just noon, and we had leisure and quiet in which to think.

Our new ridge was about forty feet up, and a nice shape for defence. We had eighty men on it, and more were constantly arriving. My guards were in place with their gun; Lutfi, an engine destroyer, rushed up hotly with his two, and after him came another hundred Ageyl. The thing was becoming a picnic, and by saying "excellent" and looking overjoyed, we puzzled the men, and made them consider the position dispassionately. The automatics were put on the skyline, with orders to fire occasional shots, short, to disturb the Turks a little, but not too much, after the expedient of Massena in delaying enemy deployment. Otherwise a lull fell; I lay down in a sheltered place which caught a little sun, and no wind, and slept a blessed hour, while the Turks occupied the old ridge, extending over it like a school of geese, and about as wisely. Our men left them alone, being contented with a free exhibition of themselves.

In the middle of the afternoon Zeid arrived, with Mastur, Rasim and Abdulla. They brought our main body, comprising twenty mounted infantry on mules, thirty Motalga horsemen, two hundred villagers, five automatic rifles, four machine-guns and the Egyptian Army mountain-gun which had fought about Medina, Petra and Jurf. This was magnificent, and I woke up to welcome them.

The Turks saw us crowding, and opened with shrapnel and machine-gun fire: but they had not the range and fumbled it. We reminded one another that movement was the law of strategy, and started moving. Rasim became a cavalry officer, and mounted with all our eighty riders of animals to make a circuit about the eastern ridge and envelop the enemy's left wing, since the books advised attack not upon a line, but upon a point, and by going far enough along any finite wing it would be found eventually reduced to a point of one single man. Rasim liked this, my conception of his target.

He promised, grinningly, to bring us that last man: but Hamd el Arar took the occasion more fittingly. Before riding off he devoted himself to the death for the Arab cause, drew his sword ceremoniously, and made to it, by name, a heroic speech. Rasim took five automatic guns with him; which was good.

We in the centre paraded about, so that their departure might be unseen of the enemy, who were bringing up an apparently endless procession of machine-guns and dressing them by the left at intervals along the ridge, as though in a museum. It was lunatic tactics. The ridge was flint, without cover for a lizard. We had seen how, when a bullet struck the ground, it and the ground spattered up in a shower of deadly chips. Also we knew the range, and elevated our Vickers' guns carefully, blessing their long, old-fashioned sights; our mountain-gun was propped into place ready to let go a sudden burst of shrapnel over the enemy when Rasim was at grips.

As we waited, a reinforcement was announced of one hundred men from Aima. They had fallen out with Zeid over war-wages the day previous, but had grandly decided to sink old scores in the crisis. Their arrival convinced us to abandon Marshal Foch and to attack from, at any rate, three sides at once. So we sent the Aima men, with three automatic guns, to outflank the right, or western wing. Then we opened against the Turks from our central position, and bothered their exposed lines with hits and ricochets.

The enemy felt the day no longer favourable. It was passing, and sunset often gave victory to defenders yet in place. Old General Hamid Fakhri collected his Staff and Headquarters, and told each man to take a rifle. "I have been forty years a soldier, but never saw rebels fight like these. Enter the ranks" . . . but he was too late. Rasim pushed forward an attack of his five automatic guns, each with its two-man crew. They went in rapidly, unseen till they were in position, and crumpled the Turkish left.

The Aima men, who knew every blade of grass on these, their own village pastures, crept, unharmed, within three hundred yards of the Turkish machine-guns. The enemy, held by our frontal threat, first knew of the Aima men when they, by a sudden burst of fire, wiped out the gun-teams and flung the right wing into disorder. We saw it, and cried advance to the camel men and levies about us.

Mohammed el Ghasib, comptroller of Zeid's household, led them on his camel, in shining wind-billowed robes, with the crimson banner of the Ageyl over his head. All who had remained in the centre with us, our servants, gunners and machine-gunners, rushed after him in a wide, vivid line.

The day had been too long for me, and I was now only shaking with desire to see the end: but Zeid beside me clapped his hands with joy at the beautiful order of our plan unrolling in the frosty redness of the setting sun. On the one hand Rasim's cavalry were sweeping a broken left wing into the pit beyond the ridge: on the other the men of Aima were bloodily cutting down fugitives. The enemy centre was pouring back in disorder through the gap, with our men after them on foot, on horse, on camel. The Armenians, crouching behind us all day anxiously, now drew their knives and howled to one another in Turkish as they leaped forward.

I thought of the depths between here and Kerak, the ravine of Hesa, with its broken, precipitous paths, the undergrowth, the narrows and defiles of the way. It was going to be a massacre and I should have been crying-sorry for the enemy; but after the angers and exertions of the battle my mind was too tired to care to go down into that awful place and spend the night saving them. By my decision to fight, I had killed twenty or thirty of our six hundred men, and the wounded would be perhaps three times as many. It was one-sixth of our force gone on a verbal triumph, for the destruction of this thousand poor Turks would not affect the issue of the war.

In the end we had taken their two mountain howitzers (Skoda guns, very useful to us), twenty-seven machine guns, two hundred horses and mules, two hundred and fifty prisoners. Men said only

fifty got back, exhausted fugitives, to the railway. The Arabs on their
track rose against them and shot them ignobly as they ran. Our own
men gave up the pursuit quickly, for they were tired and sore and
hungry, and it was pitifully cold.

As we turned back it began to snow; and only very late, and by
a last effort did we get our hurt men in. The Turkish wounded lay
out, and were dead next day.

CHAPTER XXIV

WINTER SHUTS US DOWN

NEXT DAY and the next it snowed yet harder. We were weather-bound, and as the days passed in monotony we lost the hope of doing. We should have pushed past Kerak on the heels of victory, frighting the Turks to Amman with our rumour: as it was, nothing came of all the loss and effort.

The winter's potency drove leaders and men into the village and huddled them in a lack-lustre idleness against which counsels of movement availed little. Indeed, Reason also, was within doors. Twice I ventured up to taste the snow-laden plateau, upon whose even face the Turkish dead, poor brown pats of stiffened clothes, were littered: but life there was not tolerable. In the day it thawed a little and in the night it froze. The wind cut open the skin: fingers lost power, and sense of feel: cheeks shivered like dead leaves till they could shiver no more, and then bound up their muscles in a witless ache.

To launch out across the snow on camels, beasts singularly inept on slippery ground, would be to put ourselves in the power of however few horsemen wished to oppose us; and, as the days dragged on, even this last possibility was withdrawn. Barley ran short in

Tafileh, and our camels, already cut off by the weather from natural grazing, were now also cut off from artificial food. We had to
drive them down into the happier Ghor, a day's journey from our
vital garrison.

My private party were more fortunate than most, as the Zaagi
had found us an empty unfinished house, of two sound rooms and
a court. My money provided fuel, and even grain for our camels,
which we kept sheltered in a corner of the yard, where Abdulla, the
animal lover, could curry them and teach every one by name to take
a gift of bread, like a kiss, from his mouth, gently, with her loose
lips, when he called her. Still, they were unhappy days, since to have
a fire was to be stifled with green smoke, and in the window-spaces
were only makeshift shutters of our own joinery. The mud roof
dripped water all the day long, and the fleas on the stone floor sang
together nightly, for praise of the new meats given them. We were
twenty-eight in the two tiny rooms, which reeked with the sour
smell of our crowd.

In my saddle-bags was a *Morte d'Arthur*. It relieved my disgust.
The men had only physical resources; and in the confined misery
their tempers roughened. Their oddnesses, which ordinary time
packed with a saving film of distance, now jostled me angrily; while
a grazed wound in my hip had frozen, and irritated me with painful
throbbing. Day by day, the tension among us grew, as our state
became more sordid, more animal.

January 1918 dragged into February, and such nervous sharpening ourselves on each other's faults became so revolting that I
decided to scatter the party, and go off myself in search of the extra
money we should need when fine weather came. Zeid had spent
the first part of the sum set aside for Tafileh and the Dead Sea; partly on wages, partly on supplies and in rewards to the victors of Seil
Hesa. Wherever we next put our front line, we should have to enlist
and pay fresh forces, for only local men knew the qualities of their
ground instinctively; and they fought best, defending their homes
and crops against the enemy.

Joyce might have arranged to send me money: but not easily in this season. It was surer to go down myself: and more virtuous than continued fœtor and promiscuity in Tafileh. So five of us started off on a day which promised to be a little more open than usual. We made good time to Reshidiya and as we climbed the saddle, beyond, found ourselves momentarily above the clouds in a faint sunshine.

In the afternoon the weather drew down again and the wind hardened from the north and east, and made us sorry to be out on the bare plain. When we had forded the running river of Shobek, rain began to fall, first in wild gusts, but then more steadily, reeding down over our left shoulders and seeming to cloak us from the main bleakness of wind. Where the rainstreaks hit the ground they furred out whitely like a spray. We pushed on without halting and till long after sunset urged our trembling camels, with many slips and falls across the greasy valleys. We made nearly two miles an hour, despite our difficulties; and progress was becoming so exciting and unexpected that its mere exercise kept us warm.

It had been my intention to ride all night: but, near Odroh, mist came down about us in a low ring curtain, over which the clouds, like tatters of a veil, spun and danced high up across the calmness of the sky. The perspective seemed to change, so that far hills looked small, and near hillocks great. We bore too much to the right.

This open country, though appearing hard, broke rottenly beneath their weight and let our camels in, four or five inches deep, at every stride. The poor beasts had been chilled all day, and had bumped down so often that they were stiff with bruises. Consequently, they made unwilling work of the new difficulties. They hurried for a few steps, stopped abruptly, looked round, or tried to dart off sideways.

We prevented their wishes, and drove them forward till our blind way met rocky valleys, with a broken skyline; dark to right and left, and in front apparent hills where no hills should be. It froze again, and the slabby stones of the valley became iced. To push farther, on the wrong road, through such a night was folly. We found a larger outcrop of rock. Behind it, where there should have been shelter, we couched our camels in a compact group, tails to wind: facing it, they might die of cold. We snuggled down beside them, hoping for warmth and sleep.

The warmth I, at least, never got, and hardly the sleep. I dozed once only to wake with a start when slow fingers seemed to stroke my face. I stared out into a night livid with large, soft snowflakes. They lasted a minute or two; but then followed rain, and after it more frost, while I squatted in a tight ball, aching every way but too miserable to move, till dawn. It was a hesitant dawn, but enough: I rolled over in the mud to see my men, knotted in their cloaks, cowering abandoned against the beasts' flanks. On each man's face weighed the most dolorous expression of resigned despair.

With daylight the horizon had grown very close, and we saw that our proper road was a quarter of a mile to our left. Along it we struggled afoot. The camels were too done to carry our weight (all but my own died later of this march) and it was so muddy in the clay bottoms that we ourselves slid and fell like them.

The air seemed cold enough to freeze anything, but did not: the wind, which had changed during the night, swept into us from the west in hindering blizzards. Our cloaks bellied out and dragged like sails, against us. At last we skinned them off, and went easier, our bare shirts wrapped tightly about us to restrain their slapping tails. The whirling direction of the squalls was shown to our eyes by the white mist they carried across hill and dale. Our hands were numbed into insensibility, so that we knew the cut on them only by red stains in their plastered mud: but our bodies were not so chill, and for hours quivered under the hailstones of each storm. We twisted ourselves to get the sharpness on an unhurt side, and held our shirts free from the skin, to shield us momentarily.

By late afternoon we had covered the ten miles to Aba el Lissan. Maulud's men were gone to ground, and no one hailed us; which was well, for we were filthy and miserable: stringy like shaven cats. Afterwards the going was easier, the last two miles to the head of Shtar being frozen like iron. We remounted our camels, whose breath escaped whitely through their protesting nostrils, and raced up to the first wonderful glimpse of the Guweira plain, warm, red and comfortable, as seen through the cloud-gaps. The clouds had ceiled the hollow strangely, cutting the mid-sky in a flat layer of curds at the level of the hill-top on which we stood: we gazed on them contentedly for minutes. Every little while a wisp of their fleecy sea-foam stuff would be torn away and thrown at us. We on the wall of bluffs would feel it slash across our faces; and, turning would see a white hem draw over the rough crest, tear to shreds, and vanish in a powdering of hoar grains or a trickle of water across the peaty soil.

After having wondered at the sky we slid and ran gaily down the pass to dry sand in a calm mild air. Yet the pleasure was not vivid, as we had hoped. The pains of the blood fraying its passage once more about our frozen limbs and faces were much faster than the pain of its driving out: and we grew sensible that our feet had been torn and bruised nearly to pulp among the stones. We had not felt them tender while in the icy mud; but this warm, salty sand scoured the cuts. In desperation we climbed up our sad camels, and beat them woodenly towards Guweira. However, the change had made them happier, and they brought us home there sedately, but with success.

Thirty thousand pounds in gold came up from Akaba for me, and my cream camel, Wodheiha, the best of my remaining stud. She was Ateiba-bred and had won many races for her old owner: also, she was in splendid condition, fat but not too fat, her pads hardened by much practice over the northern flints, and her coat thick and matted. She was not tall, and looked heavy, but was docile and smooth to ride, turning left or right if the saddle horn were tapped on the required side. So I rode her without a stick, comfortably reading a book when the march permitted.

As my proper men were at Tafileh or Azrak, or out on mission, I asked Feisal for temporary followers. He lent me his two Ateiba horsemen, Serj and Rameid; and, to help carry my gold, added to the party Sheikh Motlog, whose worth we had discovered when our armoured cars explored the plains below Mudowwara for Tebuk.

Motlog had gone as sponsor, pointing out the country from a perch high on the piled baggage of a box-Ford. They were dashing in and out of sand-hills at speed, the Fords swaying like launches in a swell. At one bad bend they skidded half-round on two wheels crazily. Motlog was tossed out on his head. Marshall stopped the car and ran back contrite, with ready excuses for the driving; but the Sheikh, ruefully rubbing his head, said gently, "Don't be angry with me. I have not learnt to ride these things."

The gold was in thousand-pound bags. I gave two bags each to fourteen of Motlog's twenty-men, and took the last two myself. A bag weighed twenty-two pounds, and in the awful road-conditions two were weight enough for a camel, and swung fairly on either side in the saddle-bags. We started at noon, hoping to make a good first stage before getting into the trouble of the hills: but unfortunately it turned wet after half an hour, and a steady rain soaked us through and through, and made our camels' hair curl like a wet dog's.

Motlog at that precise stage saw a tent, Sherif Fahad's, in the corner of a sandstone pike. Despite my urging, he voted to spend the night there, and see what it looked like on the hills tomorrow. I knew this would be a fatal course, wasting days in indecision, so I said farewell to him and rode on with my two men, and with six Shobek-bound Howeitat, who had joined our caravan.

The argument had delayed us, and consequently we only reached the foot of the pass at dark. By the sad, soft rain we were made rather sorry for our virtue, inclined to envy Motlog his hospitality with Fahad, when suddenly a red spark to our left drew us across to find Saleh ibn Shefia camped there in a tent and three caves, with a hundred of his freed-men fighters from Yenbo.

He welcomed me, in spite of my drenched condition, to his own carpet in his tent and gave me a new garment of his mother's sewing, while waiting for the hot stew of meat and rice. Then we lay down and slept a full night of great satisfaction, hearing the patter of rain on the double canvas of his Meccan tent.

In the morning we were off at dawn, munching a handful of Saleh's bread. As we set foot on the ascent, Serj looked up and said, "The mountain wears his skull-cap." There was a white dome of snow on every crest; and the Ateiba pushed quickly and curiously up the pass to feel this new wonder with their hands. The camels, too, were ignorant, and stretched their slow necks down to sniff its whiteness twice or thrice in tired inquiry; but then drew their heads away and looked forward without life interest, once more.

Our inactivity lasted only another moment; for, as we put our heads over the last ridge, a wind from the north-east took us in the teeth, with a cold so swift and biting that we gasped for breath and turned hurriedly back into shelter. It seemed as if it would be fatal to face it; but that we knew was silly: so we pulled ourselves together and rode hard through its first extreme to the half-shelter of the valley. Serj and Rameid, terrified by these new pains in their lungs, thought they were strangling; and to spare them the mental struggle of passing a friendly camp, I led our little party aside behind Maulud's hill, so that we saw nothing of his weather-beaten force.

These men of Maulud's had been camped in this place, four thousand feet above the sea, for two months without relief. They had to live in shallow dug-outs on the hill-side. They had no fuel except the sparse, wet wormwood, over which they were just able to bake their necessary bread every other day. They had no clothes, but khaki drill uniform of the British summer sort. They slept in their rain-sodden verminous pits on empty or half-empty flour-sacks, six or eight of them together in a knotted bunch, that enough of the worn blankets might be pooled for warmth.

Rather more than half of them died or were injured by the cold and wet; yet the others maintained their watch, exchanging shots daily with the Turkish outposts, and protected only by the inclement weather from crushing counter-attack. We owed much to them, and more to Maulud, whose fortitude stiffened them in their duty.

We, for our one day, had a fill of hardship. Just on the ridge about Aba el Lissan the ground was crusted with frost, and only the smart of the wind in our eyes hindered us: but then our troubles began. The camels came to a standstill in the slush at the bottom of a twenty-foot bank of slippery mud, and lowed at it helplessly, as if to say that they could not carry us up that. We jumped off to help them, and slid back ourselves just as badly. At last we took off our new, cherished boots, donned to armour us against the winter; and hauled the camels up the glacis barefoot, as on the journey down.

That was the end of our comfort, and we must have been off twenty times before sunset. Some of the dismounts were involuntary, when our camels side-slipped under us, and came down with the jingle of coin ringing through the hollow rumble of their cask-like bellies. While they were strong, this falling made them as angry as she-camels could be: afterwards they grew plaintive, and finally afraid. We also grew short with one another, for the foul wind gave us no rest. Nothing in Arabia could be more cutting than a north wind at Maan, and to-day's was of the sharpest and strongest. It blew through our clothes as if we had none, fixed our fingers in claws not able to hold either halter or riding-stick, and cramped our legs so that we had no grip of our saddle-pin. Consequently, when thrown from our falling beasts we pitched off, to crash stiffly on the ground, still frozen-brittle in the cross-legged attitude of riding.

However, there was no rain, and the wind felt like a drying one, so we held on steadily to the north. By evening we had almost made the rivulet of Basta. This meant that we were travelling more than a mile an hour; and for fear lest on the morrow we and our camels would both be too tired to do so well, I pushed on in the dark across the little stream. It was swollen and the beasts jibbed at it, so that we had to lead the way on foot, through three feet of chilly water.

Over the high ground, beyond, the wind buffeted us like an enemy: at about nine o'clock, the others flung themselves crying down on the ground and refused to go further. I too, was very near crying; sustained, indeed, only by my annoyance with their open lamentations; and therefore reluctantly glad at heart to yield to their example. We built up the nine camels in a phalanx, and lay between them in fair comfort, listening to the driving wrack clashing about us as loud as the surges by night round a ship at sea. The visible stars were brilliant, seeming to change groups and places wayward-ly between the clouds which scudded over our heads. We had each two army blankets, and a packet of cooked bread; so we were armed against evil and could sleep securely in the mud and cold.

At dawn we went forward refreshed: but the weather had turned soft, with a greyness through which loomed the sad wormwood-covered hills. Upon their slopes the limestone ribs of this very old earth stood wearily exposed. In their hollows our difficulties increased with the mud. The misty valleys were sluggish streams of melting snow: and at last new thick showers of wet flakes began to fall. We reached the desolate ruins of Odroh in a midday like twilight: a wind was blowing and dying intermittently, and slow-moving banks of cloud and drizzle closed us about.

I bore right, to avoid the Beduin between us and Shobek: but our Howeitat companions led us straight upon their camp. We had ridden six miles in seven hours, and they were exhausted. The two Ateiba were not only exhausted, but demoralized, and swore muti-nously that nothing in the world should keep us from the tribal tents. We wrangled by the roadside under the soft drift.

For myself I felt quite fresh and happy, averse from the delay of needless tribal hospitality. Zeid's penniless state was excellent pre-text for a trial of strength with the Edomite winter. Shobek was only ten miles further, and daylight had yet five hours to run. So I decid-ed to go on alone. It would be quite safe, for in such weather neither Turk nor Arab was abroad, and the roads were mine. I took their four thousand pounds from Serj and Rameid, and cursed them into the valley for cowards: which really they were not. Rameid was catch-ing his breath in great sobs, and Serj's nervous pain marked each lurch of his camel with a running moan. They raved with miserable rage when I dismissed them and turned away.

The truth was that I had the best camel. The excellent Wodheiha struggled gamely forward under the weight of the extra gold. In flat places I rode her: at ascents and descents we used to slide together side by side with comic accidents, which she seemed rather to enjoy.

By sunset the snow-fall ceased; we were coming down to the river of Shobek, and could see a brown track straggling over the opposite hill towards the village. I tried a short cut, but the frozen crust of the mud banks deceived me, and I crashed through the cat-ice (which was sharp, like knives) and bogged myself so deeply that I feared I was going to pass the night there, half in and half out of the sludge: or wholly in, which would be a tidier death.

Wodheiha, sensible beast, had refused to enter the morass: but she stood at a loss on the hard margin, and looked soberly at my mudlarking. However, I managed, with the still-held headstall, to persuade her a little nearer. Then I flung my body suddenly back-ward against the squelching quag, and, grabbing wildly behind my head, laid hold of her fetlock. She was frightened, and started back: and her purchase dragged me clear. We crawled farther down the bed to a safe place, and there crossed: after I had hesitatingly sat in the stream and washed off the weight of stinking clay.

Shiveringly I mounted again. We went over the ridge and down to the base of the shapely cone, whose mural crown was the ring-wall of the old castle of Monreale, very noble against the night-sky. The chalk was hard, and it was freezing; snow drifts lay a foot deep each side of the spiral path which wound up the hill. The white ice crackled desolately under my naked feet as we neared the gate, where, to make a stage entry, I climbed up by Wodheiha's patient shoulder into the saddle. Then I repented, since only by throwing myself sideways along her neck did I avoid the voussoirs of the arch as she crashed underneath in half-terror of this strange place.

I knew that Sherif Abd el Main should be still at Shobek, so rode boldly up the silent street in the reeded starlight, which played with the white icicles and their underlying shadows among the walls and snowy roofs and ground. The camel stumbled doubtfully over steps hidden beneath a thick covering of snow: but I had no care of that, having reached my night's goal, and having so powdery a blanket to fall on. At the crossways I called out the salutation of a fair night: and after a minute, a husky voice protested to God through the thick sacking which stuffed a loophole of the mean house on my right. I asked for Abd el Mayein, and was told "in the Government house" which lay at the further end of the old castle's enceinte.

Arrived there, I called again. A door was flung open, and a cloud of smoky light streamed recklessly across, whirling with motes, through which black faces peered to know who I was. I hailed them friendly, by name, saying that I was come to eat a sheep with the master: upon which these slaves ran out, noisy with astonishment, and relieved me of Wodheiha, whom they led into the reeking stable where themselves lived. One lit me with a flaming spar up the stone outside-stairs to the house door, and between more servants, down a winding passage dripping with water from the broken roof, into a tiny room. There lay Abd el Muein upon a carpet, face down, breathing the least smoky level of air.

My legs were shaky, so I dropped beside him, and gladly copied his position to avoid the choking fumes of a brass brazier of flaming wood which crackled in a recessed shot-window of the mighty outer wall. He searched out for me a waistcloth, while I stripped off my things and hung them to steam before the fire, which became less smarting to the eyes and throat as it burned down into red coals. Meanwhile, Abd el Mayin clapped his hands for supper to be hastened and served "Fauzan" (tea in Harith slang, so named from his cousin, governor of their village) hot and spiced and often, till the mutton, boiled with raisins in butter, was carried in.

He explained, with his blessings on the dish, that next day they would starve or rob, since he had here two hundred men, and no food or money, and his messengers to Feisal were held up in the snow. Whereat I, too, clapped hands, commanding my saddle-bags, and presented him with five hundred pounds on account, till his subsidy came. This was good payment for the food, and we were very merry

over my oddness of riding alone, in winter, with a hundredweight
and more of gold for baggage. I repeated that Zeid, like himself,
was straitened; and told of Serj and Rameid with the Arabs. The
Sherif's eyes darkened, and he made passes in the air with his riding stick. I explained, in extenuation of their failure, that the cold
did not trouble me, since the English climate was of this sort most
of the year. "God forbid it," said Abd el Muyein.

After an hour he excused himself, because he had just married
a Shobek wife. I rolled up in the rugs and slept warmly. The fleas
were serried, but my nakedness, the Arab defence against a verminous bed, lessened their plague: and the bruises did not prevail
because I was too tired.

In the morning I rose with a splitting headache, and said I must
go on. Two men were found to ride with me, though all said we
should not reach Tafileh that night. However, I thought it could
not be worse than yesterday; so we skated timorously down the rapid
path to the plain across which still stretched the Roman road with
its groups of fallen milestones, inscribed by famous emperors.

From this plain the two faint-hearts with me slipped back to
their fellows on the castle-hill. I proceeded, alternately on and off
my camel, like the day before, though now the way was all too slippery, except on the ancient paving, the last footprint of Imperial
Rome which had once so much more preciously, played the Turk
to the desert dwellers. On it I could ride: but I had to walk and
wade the dips where the floods of fourteen centuries had washed
the road's foundations out. Rain came on, and soaked me, and then
it blew fine and freezing till I crackled in armour of white silk, like
a theatre knight: or like a bridal cake, hard iced.

The camel and I were over the plain in three hours; wonderful
going: but our troubles were not ended. The snow was indeed as my
guides had said, and completely hid the path, which wound up hill
between walls and ditches, and confused piles of stone. It cost me an
infinity of pain to turn the first two corners. Wodheiha, tired of wad-
ing to her bony knees in useless white stuff, began perceptibly to flag.

ABDULLA EL ZAAGI, *Captain of the author's bodyguard*

However, she got up one more steep bit, only to miss the edge of the path in a banked place. We fell together some eighteen feet down the

hill-side into a yard-deep drift of frozen snow. After the fall she rose
to her feet whimpering, and stood still, in a tremble.

When he-camels so baulked, they would die on their spot, after
days; and I feared that now I had found the limit of effort in she-
camels. I plunged to my neck in front of her, and tried to tow her
out, vainly. Then I spent a long time hitting her behind. I mounted, and she sat down. I jumped off, heaved her up, and wondered
if, perhaps, it was that the drift was too thick. So I carved her a beautiful little road, a foot wide, three deep, and eighteen paces long,
using my bare feet and hands as tools. The snow was so frozen on
the surface that it took all my weight first to break it down, and
then to scoop it out. The crust was sharp, and cut my wrists and
ankles till they bled freely, and the roadside became lined with pink
crystals looking like pale, very pale, watermelon flesh.

Afterwards I went back to Wodheiha, patiently standing there,
and climbed into the saddle. She started easily. We went running
at it, and such was her speed that the rush carried her right over
the shallow stuff, back to the proper road. Up this we went cautiously, with me, afoot, sounding the path in front with my stick,
or digging new passes when the drifts were deep. In three hours
we were on the summit, and found it wind-swept on the western side. So we left the track, and scrambled unsteadily along the
very broken crest, looking down across the chess-board houses of
Dana village, into sunny Arabah, fresh and green, thousands of
feet below.

When the ridge served no more we did further heavy work, and
at last Wodheiha baulked again. It was getting serious, for the evening
was near; suddenly I realized the loneliness, and that if the night
found us yet beyond help on this hill-top, Wodheiha would die,
and she was a very noble beast. There was also the solid weight of
gold, and I felt not sure how far, even in Arabia, I could safely put
six thousand sovereigns by the roadside with a signet as mark of
ownership, and leave them for a night. So I took her back a hundred yards along our beaten track, mounted, and charged her at the

bank. She responded. We burst through and over the northern lip which looked down on the Senussi village of Rasheidiya.

This face of the hill, sheltered from the wind and open to the sun all afternoon, had thawed. Underneath the superficial snow lay wet and muddy ground; and when Wodheiha ran upon this at speed her feet went from under her and she sprawled, with her four legs locked.

So on her tail, with me yet in the saddle, we went sliding round and down a hundred feet. Perhaps it hurt the tail (there were stones under the snow) for on the level she sprang up unsteadily, grunting, and lashed it about like a scorpion's. Then she began to run at ten miles an hour down the greasy path towards Rasheidiya, sliding and plunging wildly: with me, in terror of a fall and broken bones, clinging to the horns of the saddle.

A crowd of Arabs, Zeid's men, weather-bound here on their way to Feisal, ran out when they heard her trumpeting approach, and shouted with joy at so distinguished an entry to the village. I asked them the news; they told me all was well. Then I remounted, for the last eight miles into Tafileh, where I gave Zeid his letters and some money, and went gladly to bed . . . flea-proof for another night.

CHAPTER XXV

THE SIEGE OF MAAN

ZEID WAS yet weather-bound. While I chafed at this, an accidental circumstance constrained me to leave him and return to Palestine for urgent consultation with Allenby, who told me that the War Cabinet were leaning heavily on him to repair the stalemate of the West. He was to take at least Damascus; and, if possible, Aleppo, as soon as he could. Turkey was to be put out of the war once and for all. His difficulty lay with his eastern flank, the right, which to-day rested on Jordan. He had called me to consider if the Arabs could relieve him of its burden.

I pointed out that this was the Jordan scheme seen from the British angle. Allenby assented, and asked if we could still do it. I said: Not at present, unless new factors were first discounted.

The first was Maan. We should have to take it before we could afford a second sphere. If more transport gave a longer range to the units of the Arab Regular Army, they could take position some miles north of Maan and cut the railway permanently, so forcing the Maan garrison to come out and fight them; and in the field the Arabs would easily defeat the Turks. We would require seven hundred baggage camels; more guns and machine-guns; and, lastly, assurance against flank attack from Amman, while we dealt with Maan.

On this basis a scheme was worked out. Allenby ordered down to Akaba two units of the Camel Transport Corps, an organization of Egyptians under British officers, which had proved highly successful in the Beersheba campaign. It was a great gift, for its carrying capacity ensured that we should now be able to keep our four thousand regulars eighty miles in advance of their base. The guns and machine-guns were also promised. As for shielding us against attack from Amman, Allenby said that was easily arranged. He intended, for his own flank's security, shortly to take Salt, beyond Jordan, and hold it with an Indian Brigade. A Corps Conference was due next day and I was to stay for it.

At this Conference it was determined that the Arab army move instantly to the Maan Plateau, to take Maan. That the British cross the Jordan, occupy Salt, and destroy south of Amman as much of the railway as possible; especially the great tunnel. It was debated what share the Amman Arabs should take in the British operation. Bols thought we should join in the advance. I opposed this, since the later retirement to Salt would cause rumour and reaction, and it would be easier if we did not enter till this had spent itself.

Chetwode, who was to direct the advance, asked how his men were to distinguish friendly from hostile Arabs, since their tendency was a prejudice against all wearing skirts. I was sitting skirted in their midst and replied, naturally, that skirt-wearers disliked men in uniform. The laugh clinched the question, and it was agreed that we support the British retention of Salt only after they came to rest there. As soon as Maan fell the Arab Regulars would move up and draw supplies from Jericho. The seven hundred camels would come along, still giving them eighty miles radius of action. This would be enough to let them work above Amman in Allenby's grand attack along the line from the Mediterranean to the Dead Sea, the second phase of the operation, directed to the capture of Damascus.

I pledged Feisal's warm co-operation in every detail of this scheme: and as soon as the conference was finished, hurried down to Akaba by air to make him partner in my convictions. I gave him the good news that Allenby, as thanks for the Dead Sea and Aba el Lissan, had put three hundred thousand pounds into my independent credit, and given us a train of seven hundred pack camels complete with personnel and equipment.

This raised great joy in all the army, for the baggage columns would enable us to prove the value in the field of the Arab regular troops on whose training and organization Joyce, Jaafar, and so many Arab and English officers had worked for months. We arranged rough time-tables and schemes: then I shipped busily back to Egypt.

In Cairo, where I spent four days, our affairs were now far from haphazard. Allenby's smile had given us Staff. We had supply officers, a shipping expert, an ordnance expert, an intelligence branch: under Alan Dawnay, brother of the maker of the Beersheba plan, who had now gone to France. Dawnay was Allenby's greatest gift to us—greater than thousands of baggage camels. As a professional officer, he had the class-touch: so that even the reddest hearer recognized an authentic redness. His was an understanding mind, feeling instinctively the special qualities of rebellion: at the same time, his war-training enriched his treatment of this antithetic subject. He married war and rebellion in himself; as, of old in Yenbo, it had been my dream every regular officer would. Yet, in three years' practice, only Dawnay succeeded.

The Arab Movement had lived as a wild-man show, with its means as small as its duties and prospects. Henceforward Allenby counted it as a sensible part of his scheme; and the responsibility upon us of doing better than we wished, knowing that forfeit for our failure would necessarily be part-paid in his soldiers' lives, removed it terrifyingly farther from the sphere of joyous adventure.

With Joyce we laid our triple plan to support Allenby's first stroke. In our centre the Arab regulars, under Jaafar, would attack

Maan. Joyce with our armoured cars would slip down to Mudowwara, and destroy the railway—permanently this time, for now we were ready to cut off Medina.

Mirzuk would ride north with me, to effect the junction with the British. After Joyce and Dawnay had gone, I rode off on April the third, 1918, from Aba el Lissan, with Mirzuk. Our starting day promised to crown the spring-freshness of this lofty table-land. A week before there had been a furious blizzard, and some of the whiteness of the snow seemed to have passed into the light. The ground was vivid with new grass; and the sunlight, which slanted across us, pale like straw, mellowed the fluttering wind.

With us journeyed two thousand Sirhan camels, carrying our ammunition and food. For the convoy's sake we marched easily, to reach the railway after dark. A few of us rode forward, to search the line by daylight, and be sure of peace during the hours these scattered numbers would consume in crossing.

Near sunset the line became visible, curving spaciously across the disclosed land, among low tufts of grass and bushes. Seeing everything was peaceful I pushed on, meaning to halt beyond and watch the others over. There was always a little thrill in touching the rails, which were the target of so many of our efforts.

As I rode up the bank my camel's feet scrambled in the loose ballast, and out of the long shadow of a culvert to my left, where, no doubt, he had slept all day, rose a Turkish soldier. He glanced wildly at me and at the pistol in my hand, and then with sadness at his rifle against the abutment, yards beyond. He was a young man; stout, but sulky-looking. I stared at him, and said, softly, "God is merciful." He knew the sound and sense of the Arabic phrase, and raised his eyes like a flash to mine, while his heavy sleep-ridden face began slowly to change into incredulous joy.

However, he said not a word. I pressed my camel's hairy shoulder with my foot, she picked her delicate stride across the metals and down the further slope, and the little Turk was man enough not to shoot me in the back, as I rode away, feeling warm towards

him, as ever towards a life one has saved. At a safe distance I glanced
back. He put thumb to nose, and twinkled his fingers at me.

We lit a coffee fire as beacon for the rest, and waited till their
dark lines passed by. Next day we marched to Wadi el Jinz; to flood-
pools, shallow eyes of water set in wrinkles of the clay, their rims
lashed about with scrubby stems of brushwood. The water was grey,
like the marly valley-bed, but sweet. There we rested for the night,
since the Zaagi had shot a bustard, and Xenophon did rightly call
its white meat good. While we feasted the camels feasted. By the
bounty of spring they were knee-deep in succulent green-stuff.

A fourth easy march took us to the Atara, our goal, where our
allies, Mifleh, Fahad and Adhub, were camped. Fahad was still strick-
en, but Mifleh, with honeyed words, came out to welcome us, his
face eaten up by greed, and his voice wheezy with it.

Our plan, thanks to Allenby's lion-share, promised simply. We
would, when ready, cross the line to Themed, the main Beni Sakhr
watering. Thence under cover of a screen of their cavalry we would
move to Madeba, and fit it as our headquarters, while Allenby put
the Jericho-Salt road in condition. We ought to link up with the
British comfortably without firing a shot.

Meanwhile we had only to wait in the Atatir, which to our joy
were really green, with every hollow a standing pool, and the val-
ley-beds of tall grass prinked with flowers. The chalky ridges, sterile
with salt, framed the water-channels delightfully. From their tallest
point we could look north and south, and see how the rain, running down, had painted the valleys across the white in broad stripes
of green, sharp and firm like brush-strokes. Everything was growing, and daily the picture was fuller and brighter till the desert
became like a rank water-meadow. Playful packs of winds came
crossing and tumbling over one another, their wide, brief gusts surg-
ing through the grass, to lay it momentarily in swathes of dark and
light satin, like young corn after the roller. On the hill we sat and
shivered before these sweeping shadows, expecting a heavy blast—
and there would come into our faces a warm and perfumed breath,

very gentle, which passed away behind us as a silver-grey light down
the plain of green. Our fastidious camels grazed an hour or so, and
then lay down to digest, bringing up stomach-load after stomach-
load of butter-smelling green cud, and chewing weightily.

At last news came that the English had taken Amman. In half
an hour we were making for Themed, across the deserted line. Later
messages told us that the English were falling back, and though we
had forewarned the Arabs of it, yet they were troubled. A further
messenger reported how the English had just fled from Salt. This
was plainly contrary to Allenby's intention, and I swore straight out
that it was not true. A man galloped in to say that the English had
broken only a few rails south of Amman, after two days of vain
assaults against the town. I grew seriously disturbed in the conflict
of rumour, and sent Adhub, who might be trusted not to lose his
head, to Salt with a letter for Chetwode or Shea, asking for a note
on the real situation. For the intervening hours we tramped restlessly over the fields of young barley, our minds working out plan
after plan with feverish activity.

Very late at night Adhub's racing horse-hooves echoed across the
valley and he came in to tell us that Jemal Pasha was now in Salt,
victorious, hanging those local Arabs who had welcomed the English. The Turks were still chasing Allenby far down the Jordan Valley.
It was thought that Jerusalem would be recovered. I knew enough
of my countrymen to reject that possibility; but clearly things were
very wrong. We slipped off, bemused, to the Atatir again.

This reverse, being unawares, hurt me the more. Allenby's plan
had seemed modest, and that we should so fall down before the
Arabs was deplorable. They had never trusted us to do the great
things which I foretold; and now their independent thoughts set
out to enjoy the springtide here.

I determined to order the Indians from Azrak back to Feisal, and
to return myself. We started on one of those clean dawns which
woke up the senses with the sun, while the intellect, tired after the
long thinking of the night, was yet abed. For an hour or two on

such a morning the sounds, scents and colours of the world struck man individually and directly, not filtered through or made typical by thought; they seemed to exist sufficiently by themselves, and the lack of design and of carefulness in creation no longer irritated.

In the morning, near Wadi el Jinz, we met the Indians, halted by a solitary tree. It was like old times, like our gentle and memorable ride to the bridges the year before, to be going again across country with Hassan Shah, hearing the Vickers' guns still clinking in the carriers, and helping the troopers re-tie their slipping loads, or saddles. They seemed just as unhandy with camels as at first; so not till dusk did we cross the railway.

There I left the Indians, because I felt restless, and movement fast in the night might cure my mind. So we pressed forward all the chill darkness, riding for Odroh. When we topped its rise we noticed gleams of fire to our left: bright flashes went up constantly, it might be from about Jerdun. We drew rein and heard the low boom of explosions: a steady flame appeared, grew greater and divided into two. Perhaps the station was burning. We rode quick, to ask Mastur.

However, his place was deserted, with only a jackal on the old camping ground. I decided to push ahead to Feisal. We trotted our fastest, as the sun grew higher in the heavens. The road was bestial with locusts—though from a little distance they looked beautiful, silvering the air with the shimmer of their wings. April the twelfth: summer had come upon us unawares; my seventh consecutive summer in this East.

As we approached, we heard firing in front, on Semna, the crescent mound which covered Maan. Parties of troops walked gently up its face to halt below the crest. Evidently we had taken the Semna, so we rode towards the new position. On the flat, this side of it, we met a camel with litters. The man leading it said, "Maulud Pasha," pointing to his load. I ran up, crying, "Is Maulud hit?" for he was one of the best officers in the army, a man also most honest towards us; not, indeed, that admiration could anyhow have been refused so sturdy and uncompromising a patriot. The old man replied out of his litter in a weak voice, saying, "Yes, indeed, Lurens Bey, I am hurt: but, thanks be to God, it is nothing. We have taken Semna." I replied that I was going there. Maulud craned himself feverishly over the edge of the litter, hardly able to see or speak (his thighbone was splintered above the knee), showing me point after point, for organizing the hillside defensively.

We arrived as the Turks were beginning to throw half-hearted shells at it. Nuri Said was commanding in Maulud's place. He stood coolly on the hill-top. Most men talked faster under fire, and acted a betraying ease and joviality. Nuri grew calmer, and Zeid bored.

I asked where Jaafar was. Nuri said that at midnight he was due to have attacked Jerdun. I told him of the night-flares, which must have marked his success. While we were glad together his messengers arrived, reporting prisoners and machine-guns; also the station and three thousand rails destroyed. So splendid an effort would settle the northern line for weeks. Then Nuri told me that the preceding dawn he had rushed Ghadir el Haj station and wrecked it, with five bridges and a thousand rails. So the southern line was also settled.

Late in the afternoon it grew deadly quiet. Both sides stopped their aimless shelling. They said that Feisal had moved to Uheida. We crossed the little flooded stream, by a temporary hospital where Maulud lay. Mahmud, the red-bearded, defiant doctor, thought that he would recover without amputation. Feisal was on the hill-top, on the very edge, black against the sun, whose light threw a queer haze about the slender figure, and suffused his head with gold, through the floss-silk of his headcloth. I made my camel kneel. Feisal stretched out his hands, crying, "Please God, good?" I replied, "The praise and the victory be to God." And he swept me into his tent that we might exchange the news.

Feisal had heard from Dawnay more than I knew of the British failure before Amman; of the bad weather and confusion, and how Allenby had telephoned to Shea, and made one of his lightning decisions to cut the loss; a wise decision, though it hurt us sorely. Joyce

was in hospital, but mending well; and Dawnay lay ready at Guweira
to start for Mudowwara with all the cars.

Feisal asked me about Semna and Jaafar, and I told him what I
knew, and Nuri's opinion, and the prospects. Nuri had complained
that the Abu Tayi had done nothing for him all day. Auda denied
it; and I recalled the story of our first taking the plateau, and the
gibe by which I had shamed them into the charge at Aba el Lissan.
The tale was new to Feisal. Its raking-up hurt old Auda deeply. He
swore vehemently that he had done his best to-day, only conditions
were not favourable for tribal work: and, when I withstood him further, he went out of the tent, very bitter.

Maynard and I spent the next days watching operations. The
Abu Tayi captured two outposts east of the station, while Saleh ibn
Shefia took a breast-work with a machine-gun and twenty prisoners. These gains gave us liberty of movement round Maan; and on
the third day Jaafar massed his artillery on the southern ridge, while
Nuri Said led a storming party into the sheds of the railway station.
As he reached their cover the French guns ceased fire. We were wandering in a Ford car, trying to keep up with the successive advances,
when Nuri, perfectly dressed and gloved, smoking his briar pipe,
met us and sent us back to Captain Pisani, artillery commander,
with an urgent appeal for support. We found Pisani wringing his
hands in despair, every round expended. He said he had implored
Nuri not to attack at this moment of his penury.

There was nothing to do but see our men volleyed out of the
railway station again. The road was littered with crumpled khaki
figures, and the eyes of the wounded, gone rich with pain, stared
accusingly at us. The control had gone from their broken bodies
and their torn flesh shook them helplessly. We could see everything
and think dispassionately, but it was soundless: our hearing had
been taken away by the knowledge that we had failed.

Afterwards we understood that we had never expected such excellent spirit from our infantry, who fought cheerfully under machine-gun
fire, and made clever use of ground. So little leading was required

that only three officers were lost. Maan showed us that the Arabs were good enough without British stiffening. This made us more free to plan: so the failure was not unredeemed.

On the morning of the eighteenth of April, Jaafar wisely decided that he could not afford more loss, and drew back to the Semna positions while the troops rested. Being an old college friend of the Turkish Commandant, he sent him a white-flagged letter, inviting surrender. The reply said that they would love it, but had orders to hold out to the last cartridge. Jaafar offered a respite, in which they could fire off their reserves: but the Turks hesitated till Jemal Pasha was able to collect troops from Amman, re-occupy Jerdun, and pass a pack-convoy of food and ammunition into the beleaguered town. The railway remained broken for weeks.

CHAPTER XXVI

DAWNAY ATTACKS SHAHM

FORTHWITH I took car to join Dawnay. I was uneasy at a regular fighting his first guerilla battle with that most involved and intricate weapon, the armoured car. Also Dawnay was no Arabist, and neither Peake, his camel-expert, nor Marshall, his doctor, was fluent. His troops were mixed, British, Egyptian and Bedouin. The last two were antipathetic. So I drove into his camp above Tell Shahm after midnight, and offered myself, delicately, as an interpreter.

Fortunately he received me well, and took me round his lines. A wonderful show. The cars were parked geometrically here; armoured cars there; sentries and pickets were out, with machine-guns ready. Even the Arabs were in a tactical place behind a hill, in support, but out of sight and hearing: by some magic Sherif Hazaa and himself had kept them where they were put. My tongue coiled into my cheek with the wish to say that the only thing lacking was an enemy.

His conversation as he unfolded his plan deepened my admiration to unplumbed depths. He had prepared operation orders; orthodox-sounding things with zero times and a sequence of movements. Each unit had its appointed duty. We would attack the "plain post" at dawn (armoured cars) from the vantage of the hillock on which Joyce and myself had sat and laughed ruefully the last abortive time. The cars, with closed cut-outs, would "take station" before daylight, and carry the trenches by surprise. Tenders 1 and 3 would then demolish bridges A and B on the operations' plan (scale 1/250,000) at zero 1.30 hours while the cars moved to Rock Post, and with the support of Hazaa and the Arabs, rushed it (zero 2.15).

Hornby and the explosives in Talbots No. 40531 and 41226, would move after them, and demolish bridges D, E and F, while the force lunched. After lunch, when the low sun permitted sight through the mirage, at zero 8 hours to be exact, the united mass would attack South Post; the Egyptians from the East, the Arabs from the North, covered by long range machine-gun fire from the cars, and by Brodie's ten-pounder guns, sited on Observation Hill. The post would fall and the force transport itself to the station of Tell Shahm, which would be shelled by Brodie from the North-West, bombed by aeroplanes flying from the mud-flats of Rum, (at zero 10 hours), and approached by armoured cars from the west. The Arabs would follow the cars, while Peake with his Camel Corps descended from South Post. "The station will be taken at zero 11.30," said the scheme, breaking into humour at the last. But there it failed, for the Turks ignorantly and in haste, surrendered ten minutes too soon, and made the only blot on a bloodless day.

In a liquid voice I inquired if Hazaa understood. I was informed that as he had no watch to synchronize (by the way, would I please put mine right now?) he would make his first move when the cars turned northward, and time his later actions by express order. I crept away and hid myself for an hour's sleep.

At dawn we saw the cars roll silently on top of the sleeping sandy trenches, and the astonished Turks walk out with their hands up. It was like picking a ripe peach. Hornby dashed up in his two Rolls tenders, put a hundred-weight of guncotton under bridge A and blew it up convincingly. The roar nearly lifted Dawnay and myself out of our third tender, in which we sat grandly overseeing all: and we ran in, to show Hornby the cheaper way of the drainage holes as mine-chambers. Subsequent bridges came down for ten slabs apiece.

While we were at bridge B the cars concentrated their machine-guns on the parapet of "rock-post," a circle of thick stone walls (very visible from their long early shadows) on a knoll too steep for wheels. Hazaa was ready, willing and excited, and the Turks so frightened by the splashing and splattering of the four machine-guns that the Arabs took them almost in their stride. That was peach the second.

Then it was interval for the others, but activity for Hornby, and for myself, now assistant-engineer. We ran down the line in our Rolls-Royces, carrying two tons of guncotton; bridges and rails roared up wherever fancy dictated. The crews of the cars covered us; and sometimes covered themselves, under their cars, when fragments came sailing musically through the smoky air. One twenty-pound flint clanged plumb on a turret-head and made a harmless dint. At intervals everybody took photographs of the happy bursts. It was fighting de luxe, and demolition de luxe: we enjoyed ourselves. After the peripatetic lunch-hour we went off to see the fall of "south post." It fell to its minute, but not properly. Hazaa and his Amran were too wound up to advance soberly in alternate rushes like Peake and the Egyptians. Instead they thought it was a steeplechase, and did a camel-charge up the mound over breastwork and trenches. The war-weary Turks gave it up in disgust.

Then came the central act of the day, the assault upon the station. Peake drew down towards it from the north, moving his men by repeated exposure of himself; hardly, for they were not fierce for honour. Brodie opened on it with his usual nicety, while the aeroplanes circled round in their cold-blooded way, to drop whistling bombs into its trenches. The armoured cars went forward snuffling smoke, and through this haze a file of Turks waving white things rose out of their main trench in a dejected fashion.

We cranked up our Rolls tenders; the Arabs leaped on to their camels; Peake's now-bold men broke into a run, and the force converged wildly upon the station. Our car won; and I gained the station bell, a dignified piece of Damascus brass-work. The next man took the ticket punch and the third the office stamp, while the bewildered Turks stared at us, with a growing indignation that their importance should be merely secondary.

A minute later, with a howl, the Beduin were upon the maddest looting of their history. Two hundred rifles, eighty thousand rounds of ammunition, many bombs, much food and clothing were in the station, and everybody smashed and profited. An unlucky camel increased the confusion by firing one of the many Turkish trip-mines as it entered the yard. The explosion blew it arse over tip, and caused a panic. They thought Brodie was opening up again.

In the pause the Egyptian officer found an unbroken storehouse, and put a guard of soldiers over it, because they were short of food. Hazaa's wolves, not yet sated, did not recognize the Egyptians' right to share equally. Shooting began: but by mediation we obtained that the Egyptians pick first what rations they needed: afterwards there followed a general scramble, which burst the storeroom walls.

The profit of Shahm was so great that eight out of every ten of the Arabs were contented with it. In the morning only Hazaa and a handful of men remained with us for further operations. Dawnay's programme said Ramleh station; but his orders were inchoate, since the position had not been examined. So we sent down Wade in his armoured car, with a second car in support. He drove on, cautiously, stage by stage, in dead silence. At last, without a shot fired, he entered the station yard, carefully, for fear of the mines, whose trip and trigger wires diapered the ground.

The station was closed up. He put half a belt through the door and shutters, and, getting no reply, slipped out of his car, searched the building, and found it empty of men, though full enough of desirable goods to make Hazaa and the faithful remnant prize their virtue aloud. We spent the day destroying miles more of the unoccupied line, till we judged that we had done damage to occupy the largest possible repair party for a fortnight.

The third day was to be Mudowwara, but we had no great hope or force left. The Arabs were gone, Peake's men too little warlike. However, Mudowwara might panic like Ramleh, so we slept the night by our latest capture. The unwearied Dawnay set out sentries, who, emulous of their smart commanding officer, did a Buckingham Palace stunt up and down beside our would-be sleeping heads, till I got up, and instructed them in the arts of desert-watching.

In the morning we set off to look at Mudowwara, driving like kings splendidly in our roaring cars over the smooth plains of sand and flint, with the low sun pale behind us in the East. The light hid us till we were close in and saw that a long train stood in the station. Reinforcement or evacuation? A moment afterwards they let fly at us with four guns, of which two were active and accurate little Austrian mountain howitzers. At seven thousand yards they did admirable shooting, while we made off in undignified haste to some distant hollows. Thence we made a wide circuit to where, with Zaal, we had mined our first train. We blew up the long bridge under which the Turkish patrol had slept out that tense midday. Afterwards we returned to Ramleh, and persevered in destroying line and bridges, to make our break permanent, a demolition too serious for Fakhri ever to restore: while Feisal sent Mohammed el Dheilan against the yet intact stations between our break and Maan. Dawnay joined up with them, geographically, below the escarpment, a day later; and so this eighty miles from Maan to Mudowwara, with its seven stations, fell wholly into our hands. The active defence of Medina ended with this operation.

CHAPTER XXVII

TRANSPORT AND SUPPLY

A NEW officer, Young, came from Mesopotamia, to reinforce our staff. He was a regular of exceptional quality, with long and wide experience of war, and perfect fluency in Arabic. His intended rôle was to double mine, with the tribes, that our activity against the enemy might be broader and better directed. To let him play himself in to our fresh conditions, I handed him over the possibility of combining Zeid, Nasir and Mirzuk into an eighty-mile long interruption of the railway from Maan northward, while I went down to Akaba, and took ship for Suez, to discuss futures with Allenby.

Dawnay met me, and we talked over our brief before going up to Allenby's camp. There General Bols smiled happily at us, and said, "Well, we're in Salt all right." To our amazed stares he went on that the chiefs of the Beni Sakhr had come into Jericho one morning, to offer the immediate co-operation of their twenty thousand tribesmen at Themed; and in his bath next day he had thought out a scheme, and fixed it all right.

I asked who the chief of the Beni Sakhr was, and he said "Fahad": triumphing in his efficient inroad into what had been my province.

It sounded madder and madder. I knew that Fahad could not raise four hundred men; and that at the moment there was not a tent on Themed: they had moved south, to Young.

We hurried to the office for the real story, and learned that it was, unfortunately, as Bols had said. The British cavalry had gone impromptu up the hills of Moab on some airy promise of the Zebn sheikhs; greedy fellows who had ridden into Jerusalem only to taste Allenby's bounty, but had there been taken at their mouth-value.

Of course, this raid miscarried, while I was still in Jerusalem, solacing myself against the inadequacy of Bols with Storrs, now the urbane and artful Governor of the place. The Beni Sakhr were supine in their tents or away with Young. General Chauvel, without the help of one of them, saw the Turks reopen the Jordan fords behind his back and seize the road by which he had advanced. We escaped heavy disaster only because Allenby's instinct for a situation showed him his danger just in time. Yet we suffered painfully.

Our movement, clean-cut while alone with a simple enemy, was now bogged in its partner's contingencies. We had to take our tune from Allenby, and he was not happy. The German offensive in France was stripping him of troops. He would retain Jerusalem, but could not afford a casualty, much less an attack, for months. The War Office promised him Indian divisions from Mesopotamia, and Indian drafts. With these he would rebuild his army on the Indian model; perhaps, after the summer, he might be again in fighting trim: but for the moment, we must both just hold on.

At tea-time, Allenby mentioned the Imperial Camel Brigade in Sinai, regretting that in the new stringency he must abolish it and use its men as mounted reinforcements. I asked, "What are you going to do with their camels?" He laughed, and said, "Ask 'Q.'"

Obediently, I went across the dusty garden, broke in upon the Quartermaster-General, Sir Walter Campbell—very Scotch—and repeated my question. He answered firmly that they were ear-marked as divisional transport for the second of the new Indian divisions. I explained that I wanted two thousand of them. His first reply was irrelevant; his second conveyed that I might go on wanting. I argued, but he seemed unable to see my side at all. Of course, it was of the nature of a "Q" to be costive.

I returned to Allenby and said aloud, before his party, that there were for disposal two thousand two hundred riding camels, and thirteen hundred baggage camels. All were provisionally allotted to transport; but of course, riding camels were riding camels. The staff whistled, and looked wise; as though they, too, doubted whether riding camels could carry baggage. A technicality, even a sham one, might be helpful. Every British officer understood animals, as a point of honour. So I was not astonished when Sir Walter Campbell was asked to dine with the Commander-in-Chief that night.

We sat on the right hand and on the left, and with the soup Allenby began to talk about camels. Sir Walter broke out that the providential dispersing of the camel brigade brought the transport of the —th Division up to strength; a godsend, for the Orient had been vainly ransacked for camels. He over-acted. Allenby, a reader of Milton, had an acute sense of style: and the line was a weak one. He cared nothing for strengths, the fetish of administrative branches.

He looked at me with a twinkle. "And what do you want them for?" I replied hotly, "To put a thousand men into Deraa any day you please." He smiled and shook his head at Sir Walter Campbell, saying sadly, "Q, you lose." The goat became giddy and the sheep sheepish. It was an immense, a regal gift; the gift of unlimited mobility. The Arabs could now win their war when and where they liked.

Next morning I was off to join Feisal in his cool eyrie at Aba el Lissan. We discussed histories, tribes, migration, sentiments, the spring rains, pasture, at length. Finally, I remarked that Allenby had given us two thousand camels. Feisal gasped and caught my knee, saying, "How?" I told him all the story. He leaped up and kissed me; then he clapped his hands loudly. Hejris' black shape appeared at the tent door. "Hurry," cried Feisal, "call them." Hejris asked whom. "Oh, Fahad, Abdulla el Feir, Auda, Motlog, Zaal. . . ." "And

From a drawing by W. Roberts

NIGHT BOMBING

not Mirzuk?" queried Hejris mildly. Feisal shouted at him for a fool, and the black ran off; while I said, "It is nearly finished. Soon you can let me go." He protested, saying that I must remain with them always, and not just till Damascus, as I had promised in Um Lejj. I, who wanted so to get away.

Feet came pattering to the tent door, and paused, while the chiefs recovered their grave faces and set straight their headcloths for the entry. One by one they sat down stilly on the rugs, each saying unconcernedly, "Please God, good?" To each Feisal replied, "Praise God!" and they stared in wonder at his dancing eyes.

When the last had rustled in, Feisal told them that God had sent the means of victory—two thousand riding camels. Our war was to march unchecked to freedom, its triumphant end. They murmured in astonishment; doing their best, as great men, to be calm; eyeing me to guess my share in the event. I said, "The bounty of Allenby. . . ." Zaal cut in swiftly for them all, "God keep his life and yours." I replied, "We have been made victorious," stood up, with a "By your leave" to Feisal, and slipped away to tell Joyce. Behind my back they burst out into wild words of their coming wilder deeds: childish, perhaps, but it would be a pretty war in which each man did not feel that he was winning it.

Joyce also was gladdened and made smooth by the news of the two thousand camels. We dreamed of the stroke to which they should be put: of their march from Beersheba to Akaba: and where for two months we could find grazing for this vast multitude of animals; they must be broken from barley if they were to be of use to us.

These were not pressing thoughts. We had, meanwhile, the need to maintain ourselves all summer on the plateau, besieging Maan, and keeping the railways cut. The task was difficult.

First, about supply. I had just thrown the existing arrangements out of gear. The Egyptian Camel Transport companies had been carrying steadily between Akaba and Aba el Lissan, but carrying less and marching less than our least sanguine estimate. We urged them to increase weights and speeds, but found ourselves up against cast-iron corps regulations, framed to keep down the figures of animal wastage. By increasing them slightly, we could double the carrying capacity of the column; consequently, I had offered to take over the animals and send back the Egyptian camel-men.

The British, being short of labour, jumped at my idea; almost too quickly. We had a terrible scramble to improvise drivers upon the moment. Young took over transport and quartermaster work, in which his drive and ability would be better employed. Using his full power, he grappled with the chaos. He had no stores for his columns, no saddles, no clerks, no veterinaries, no drugs and few drivers, so that to run a harmonious and orderly train was impossible; but Young very nearly did it, in his curious ungrateful way. Thanks to him, the supply problem of the Arab regulars on the plateau was solved.

All this time the face of our Revolt was growing. Feisal, veiled in his tent, maintained incessantly the teaching and preaching of his Arab movement. Akaba boomed: even our field work was going well. The Arab regulars had just had their third success against Jerdun, the battered station which they made it almost a habit to take and lose. Our armoured cars happened on a Turkish sortie from Maan and smashed it in such style that the opportunity never recurred. Zeid, in command of half the army posted north of Uheida, was showing great vigour. His gaiety of spirit appealed more to the professional officers than did Feisal's poetry and lean earnestness; so this happy association of the two brothers gave every sort of man a sympathy with one or other of the leaders of the revolt.

For six weeks we marked time. Zeid and Jaaffar, with their regulars, continued a profitable battering upon the Maan sector. Sherif Nasir accompanied by Peake and Hornby moved to Hesa, forty miles northward, and occupied eight miles of railway in one happy thrust. By intensive demolition the very foundations of the line thereabout were destroyed and the Turkish contemplated offensive against Feisal in Aba el Lissan was brought to nought. Dawnay and myself took advantage of the lull to go up again to Allenby.

At G.H.Q. we felt a remarkable difference in the air. The place was, as always, throbbing with energy and hope, but now logic and co-ordination were manifest in an uncommon degree. The new army was arriving to time from Mesopotamia and India; prodigious advances in grouping and training were being made. On June the

fifteenth it had been the considered opinion of a private conference
that the army would be capable of a general and sustained offensive in September.

The sky was, indeed, opening over us; and we went in to
Allenby, who said outright that late in September he would make
a grand attack to fulfil the Smuts' plan even to Damascus and
Aleppo. Our rôle would be as laid down in the spring; we must
make the Deraa raid on the two thousand new camels. Times and
details would be fixed as the weeks went on.

On July the eleventh, 1918, Dawnay and I were again talking to Allenby and Bartholomew, his new staff officer, and, of
their generosity and confidence, seeing the undress working of a
general's mind. It was an experience: technical, reassuring, and
very valuable to me, who was mildly a general too, in my own
odd show.

Allenby's confidence was like a wall. Before the attack he went
to see his troops massed in secrecy, waiting the signal, and told
them he was sure, with their good help, of thirty thousand prisoners; this, when the whole game turned on a chance! Bartholomew
was most anxious. He said it would be desperate work to have the
whole army re-formed by September, and, even if they were ready
(actually some brigades existed as such for the first time when
they went over) we must not assume that the attack would follow
as planned. It could be delivered only in the coastal sector, opposite Ramleh, the railhead, where only could a necessary reserve of
stores be gathered. This seemed so obvious that he could not dream
of the Turk staying blind, though momently their dispositions
ignored it.

Allenby's plan was to collect the bulk of his infantry and all
his cavalry under the orange and olive groves of Ramleh just
before the nineteenth of September. Simultaneously he hoped to
make in the Jordan Valley such demonstrations as should persuade the Turks of a concentration there in progress. The two
raids to Salt had fixed the Turks' eyes exclusively beyond Jordan.

Every move there, whether of British or Arabs, was accompanied by counter-precautions on the Turks' part, showing how fearful they were. In the coast sector, the area of real danger, the enemy had absurdly few men. Success hung on maintaining them in this fatal misappreciation.

Deceptions, which for the ordinary general were just witty *hors d'œuvres* before battle, had become for Allenby a main point of strategy. Bartholomew would accordingly erect (near Jericho) all condemned tents in Egypt; would transfer veterinary camps and sick lines there; would put dummy camps, dummy horses and dummy troops wherever there was plausible room; would throw more bridges across the river; would collect and open against enemy country all captured guns; and on the right days would ensure the movement of non-combatant bodies along the dusty roads, to give the impression of eleventh-hour concentrations for an assault. At the same time the Royal Air Force was going to fill the air with husbanded formations of the latest fighting machines. The preponderance of these would deprive the enemy for days of the advantage of air reconnaissance.

Bartholomew wished us to supplement his efforts with all vigour and ingenuity, from our side of Amman. Yet he warned us that even with this, success would hang on a thread, since the Turks could save themselves and their army, and give us our concentration to do over again, by simply retiring their coast sector seven or eight miles. The British Army would then be like a fish flapping on dry land, with its railways, its heavy artillery, its dumps, its stores, its camps all misplaced; and without olive groves in which to hide its concentration next time. So, while he guaranteed that the British were doing their utmost, he implored us not to engage the Arabs, on his behalf, in a position from which they could not escape.

The noble prospect sent Dawnay and myself back to Cairo in great fettle and cogitation. News from Akaba had raised again the question of defending the plateau against the Turks, who had just turned Nasir out of Hesa and were contemplating a stroke against

Aba el Lissan about the end of August, when our Deraa detachment should start. Unless we could delay the Turks another fortnight, their threat might cripple us. A new factor was urgently required.

At this juncture Dawnay was inspired to think of the surviving battalion of the Imperial Camel Corps. Perhaps G.H.Q. might lend it us to confuse the Turks' reckoning. We telephoned Bartholomew, who understood, and backed our request to Bols in Alexandria, and to Allenby. After an active telegraphing, we got our way. Colonel Buxton, with three hundred men, was lent to us for a month on two conditions: first, that we should forth-with furnish their scheme of operations; second, that they should have no casualties. Bartholomew felt it necessary to apologize for the last magnificent, heart-warming condition, which he thought unsoldierly!

Dawnay and I sat down with a map and measured that Buxton should march from the Canal to Akaba; thence, by Rum, to carry Mudowwara by night attack; thence by Bair, to destroy the bridge and tunnel near Amman; and back to Palestine on August thirty. Their activity would give us a peaceful month, in which our two thousand new camels could learn to graze, while carrying the extra dumps of forage and food which Buxton's force would expect.

As regards the main scheme Allenby meant to attack on the nineteenth of September, and wanted us to lead off not more than four nor less than two days before he did. His words to me were that three men and a boy with pistols in front of Deraa on September the sixteenth would fill his conception; would be better than thousands a week before or a week after. The truth was, he cared nothing for our fighting power, and did not reckon us part of his tactical strength. Our purpose, to him, was moral, to keep the enemy command intent upon the trans-Jordan front. In my English capacity I shared this view, but on my Arab side both agitation and battle seemed equally important, the one to serve the joint success, the other to establish Arab self-respect, without which victory would not be wholesome.

Accordingly I planned to march five hundred regular mounted infantry, the battery of French quick-firing .65 mountain guns, proportionate machine-guns, two armoured cars, sappers, camel scouts, and two aeroplanes to Azrak where their concentration must be complete on September the thirteenth. On the sixteenth we would envelop Deraa, and cut its railways. Two days later we would fall back east of the Hejaz railway and wait events with Allenby. As reserve against accident we would purchase barley in Jebel Druse, and store it at Azrak.

Nuri Shaalan would accompany us with a contingent of Rualla: also the Serdiyeh; the Serahin; and Haurani peasants of the "Hollow Land," under Talal el Hareidhin. Dawnay helped the organizing side by getting us from G.H.Q. the loan of Stirling, a skilled staff officer, tactful and wise. Stirling's passion for horses was a passport to intimacy with Feisal and the chiefs.

Among the Arab officers were distributed some British military decorations, tokens of their gallantry about Maan. Jaafar Pasha's deserved C.M.G. was pointed by Allenby's wit. Jaafar came up to Palestine to receive it, and the Staff took the opportunity to stage a formal little ceremony of presentation, as token of respect for their erstwhile captive. The guard of honour was furnished by the Dorset Yeomanry, who had galloped the Pasha down, and hacked him with their sabres in the Senussi Desert less than three years before. Jaafar laughed with delight at an incident so much in his own hearty vein. These marks of Allenby's esteem heartened the Arab Army. Nuri Pasha Said offered to command the Deraa expedition, for which his courage, authority and coolness marked him as the ideal leader. He began to pick for it the best four hundred men in the army.

Pisani, the French commandant, fortified by a Military Cross, and in urgent pursuit of a D.S.O., took bodily possession of the four Schneider mountain guns which Cousse had sent down to us after Brémond left; and spent agonized hours with Young, trying to put the scheduled ammunition, and mule-forage, with his men and his own private kitchen, on to one-half the requisite camels. The camps buzzed with eagerness and preparation, and all promised well.

CHAPTER XXVIII

BUXTON AND THE I.C.C.

IT WAS now the end of July, and by the end of August the Deraa expedition must be on the road. In the meantime Buxton's Camel Corps had to be guided through their programme, Nuri Shaalan warned, the armoured cars taught their road to Azrak, and landing grounds found for aeroplanes. A busy month. Nuri Shaalan, the furthest, was tackled first. He was called to meet Feisal at Jefer about the seventh of August. Buxton's force seemed the second need. I told Feisal, under seal, of their coming. To ensure their having no casualties, they must strike Mudowwara with absolute surprise. I would guide them myself to Rumm, in the first critical march through the fag-ends of Howeitat about Akaba.

Accordingly I went down to Akaba, where Buxton let me explain to each company their march, and the impatient nature of the Allies whom they, unasked, had come to help; begging them to turn the other cheek if there was a row; partly because they were better educated than the Arabs, and therefore less prejudiced; partly because they were very few. After such solemnities came the ride up the oppressive gorge of Itm, under the red cliffs of Nejed and over the breast-like curves of Imram—that slow preparation for Rumm's greatness—till we passed through the gap before the rock Khuzail, and into the inner shrine of the springs, with its worship-compelling coolness. There the landscape refused to be accessory, but took the skies, and we chattering humans became dust at its feet.

In Rumm the men had their first experience of watering in equality with Arabs, and found it troublesome. However, they were wonderfully mild, and Buxton was an old Sudan official, speaking Arabic, and understanding nomadic ways; very patient, good-humoured, sympathetic. Hazaa was helpful in admonishing the Arabs, and Stirling and Marshall, who accompanied the column, were familiars of the Beni Atiyeh. Thanks to their diplomacy, and to the care of the British rank and file, nothing untoward happened.

Later I rode for Akaba, through the high-walled Itm, alone now with six silent, unquestioning guards, who followed after me like shadows, harmonious and submerged in their natural sand and bush and hill; and a home-sickness came over me, stressing vividly my outcast life among these Arabs, while I exploited their highest ideals and made their love of freedom one more tool to help England win.

In Akaba the rest of my bodyguard were assembled, prepared for victory, for I had promised the Hauran men that they should pass this great feast in their freed villages: and its date was near. So for the last time we mustered on the windy beach by the sea's edge, the sun on its brilliant waves glinting in rivalry with my flashing and changing men. They were sixty. Seldom had the Zaagi brought so many of his troop together, and as we rode into the brown hills for Guweira he was busy sorting them in Ageyl fashion, centre and wings, with poets and singers on the right and left. So our ride was musical. It hurt him I would not have a banner, like a prince.

I was on my Ghazala, the old grandmother camel, now again magnificently fit. Her foal had lately died, and Abdulla, who rode next me, had skinned the little carcass, and carried the dry pelt behind his saddle, like a crupper piece. We started well, thanks to the Zaagi's chanting, but after an hour Ghazala lifted her head high, and began to pace uneasily, picking up her feet like a sword-dancer.

I tried to urge her: but Abdulla dashed alongside me, swept his cloak about him, and sprang from his saddle, calf's skin in hand. He lighted with a splash of gravel in front of Ghazala, who had come to a standstill, gently moaning. On the ground before her he spread the little hide, and drew her head down to it. She stopped crying, snuffled its dryness thrice with her lips; then again lifted her head and, with a whimper, strode forward. Several times in the day this happened; but afterwards she seemed to forget.

At Guweira, Siddons had an aeroplane waiting. Nuri Shaalan and Feisal wanted me at once in Jefer, where they met us in the smoothest spirits. It seemed incredible that this old man had freely joined our youth. For he was very old; livid, and worn, with a grey sorrow and remorse about him, and a bitter smile the only mobility of his face. Upon his coarse eyelashes the eyelids sagged down in tired folds, through which, from the overhead sun, a red light glittered into his eye-sockets and made them look like fiery pits in which the man was slowly burning. Only the dead black of his dyed hair, only the dead skin of the face, with its net of lines, betrayed his seventy years.

There was ceremonial talk about this little-spoken leader, for with him were the head men of his tribe, famous sheikhs so bodied out with silks of their own wearing, or of Feisal's gift, that they rustled like women while moving in slow state like oxen. First of them was Faris: like Hamlet, not forgiving Nuri his murdered father, Sottam: a lean man with drooping moustache, and white, unnatural face, who met the hidden censure of the world with a soft manner and luscious, deprecating voice. "Yifham," he squeaked of me in astonishment, "He understands our Arabic." Trad and Sultan were there, round-eyed, grave, and direct-spoken; honourable figures of men, and great leaders of cavalry. Also Mijhem, the rebellious, had been brought in by Feisal and reconciled with his unwilling uncle, who seemed only half to tolerate his small-featured bleak presence beside him, though Mijhem's manner was eagerly friendly.

Mijhem was a great leader too, Trad's rival in the conduct of raids, but weak and cruel at heart. He sat next Khalid, Trad's brother, another healthy, cheerful rider, like Trad in face, but not so full a man. Durzi ibn Dughmi swelled in and welcomed me, reminding me ungratefully of his greediness at Nebk: a one-eyed, sinister, hook-nosed man: heavy, menacing and mean, but brave. There was the Khaffaji, the spoilt child of Nuri's age, who looked for equality of friendliness from me, because of his father, and not for any prom-ise in himself: he was young enough to be glad of the looming adventure of war and proud of his new bristling weapons.

Bender, the laughing boy, fellow in years and play with the Khaffaji, tripped me before them all by begging for a place in my bodyguard. He had heard from my Rahail, his foster-brother, of their immoderate griefs and joys, and servitude called to him with its unwholesome glamour. I fenced, and when he pleaded further, turned it by muttering that I was not a King to have Shaalan ser-vants. Nuri's sombre look met mine for a moment, in approval.

Behind me sat Rahail, peacocking his lusty self in strident clothes. Under cover of the conversation he whispered me the name of each chief. They had not to ask who I was, for my clothes and appear-ance were peculiar in the desert. It was notoriety to be the only clean-shaven one, and I doubled it by wearing always the suspect pure silk, of the whitest (at least outside), with a gold and crimson Meccan headrope, and gold dagger. By so dressing I staked a claim, which Feisal's public consideration of me confirmed.

Many times in such councils had Feisal won over and set aflame new tribes, many times had the work fallen to me; but never until to-day had we been actively together in one company, reinforcing and relaying one another, from our opposite poles: and the work went like child's play; the Rualla melted in our double heat. We could move them with a touch and a word. There was tenseness, a hold-ing of breath, the glitter of belief in their thin eyes so fixed on us.

Feisal brought nationality to their minds in a phrase, which set them thinking of Arab history and language; then he dropped into silence for a moment: for with these illiterate masters of the tongue words were lively, and they liked to savour each, unmingled, on the palate. Another phrase showed them the spirit of Feisal, their fellow and leader, sacrificing everything for the national freedom; and then silence again, while they imagined him day and night in his tent, teaching, preaching, ordering and making friends: and they felt something of the idea behind this pictured man sitting there iconically, drained of desires, ambitions, weakness, faults; so rich a personality enslaved by an abstraction, made one-eyed, one-armed, with the one sense and purpose, to live or die in its service.

Of course it was a picture-man; not flesh and blood, but nevertheless true, for his individuality had yielded its third dimension to the idea, had surrendered the world's wealth and artifices. Feisal was hidden in his tent, veiled to remain our leader: while in reality he was nationality's best servant, its tool, not its owner. Yet in the tented twilight nothing seemed more noble.

Our conversation was cunningly directed to light trains of their buried thoughts; that the excitement might be their own and the conclusions native, not inserted by us. Soon we felt them kindle: we leaned back, watching them move and speak, and vivify each other with mutual heat, till the air was vibrant, and in stammered phrases they experienced the first heave and thrust of notions which ran up beyond their sight. They turned to hurry us, themselves the begetters, and we laggard strangers: strove to make us comprehend the full intensity of their belief; forgot us; flashed out the means and end of our desire. A new tribe was added to our comity: though Nuri's plain "Yes" at the end carried more than all had said.

Siddons flew me back to Guweira that evening, and in the night at Akaba I told Dawnay, just arrived, that life was full, but slipping smoothly. Next morning we heard by aeroplane how Buxton's force had fared at Mudowwara. They decided to assault it before dawn mainly by means of bombers, in three parties, one to enter the station, the other two for the main redoubts.

Accordingly, before midnight white tapes were laid as guides to the zero point. The opening had been timed for a quarter to four, but the way proved difficult to find, so that daylight was almost upon them before things began against the southern redoubt. After a number of bombs had burst in and about it, the men rushed up and took it easily—to find that the station party had achieved their end a moment before. These alarms roused the middle redoubt, but only for defeat. Its men surrendered twenty minutes later.

The northern redoubt, which had a gun, seemed better-hearted and splashed its shot freely into the station yard, and at our troops. Buxton, under cover of the southern redoubt, directed the fire of Brodie's guns which, with their usual deliberate accuracy, sent in shell after shell. Siddons came over in his machines and bombed it, while the Camel Corps from north and east and west subjected the breastworks to severe Lewis gun fire. At seven in the morning the last of the enemy surrendered quietly. We had lost four killed and ten wounded. The Turks lost twenty-one killed, and one hundred and fifty prisoners, with two field-guns and three machine-guns.

Buxton at once set the Turks to getting steam on the pumping engine, so that he could water his camels, while men blew in the wells, and smashed the engine-pumps, with two thousand yards of rail. At dusk, charges at the foot of the great water-tower spattered it in single stones across the plain: Buxton a moment later called "Walk-march!" to his men, and the four hundred camels, rising like one and roaring like the day of judgment, started off for Jefer. Thence we had news of them. They rested a day, revictualled, and marched for Bair where Joyce and myself had agreed to join them.

Accordingly on the evening of August fifteenth, 1918, we sat down with Buxton in a council of war. Young had duly sent to Bair fourteen days' rations for man and beast. Of this there remained eight days for the men, ten for the animals. The camel-drivers of the supply column, driven forward only by Young's strong will, had left Jefer half-mutinous with fear of the desert. They had lost, stolen or sold the rest of Buxton's stores upon their way.

We had to adjust the plan to its new conditions. Buxton purged his column of every inessential, while I cut down the two armoured cars to one, and changed the route.

Buxton and his men started in the mid-afternoon while I delayed till evening, seeing my men load our six thousand pounds of gun-cotton on the thirty Egyptian pack-camels. My disgusted bodyguard were for this ride to lead or drive the explosives' train.

We had judged that Buxton would sleep just short of the Hadi, so we rode thither: but saw no camp-fire, nor was the track trodden. We looked over the crest of the ridge, into a bitter north wind coming off Hermon into our flustered faces. The slopes beyond were black and silent, and to our town-dwellers, accustomed to the reek of smoke, or sweat, or the ferment of soil freshly dug, there was something searching, disquieting, almost dangerous, in the steely desert wind. So we turned back a few paces, and hid under the lip of the ridge to sleep comfortably in its cloistered air.

In the morning we looked out across fifty miles of blank country, and wondered at this missing our companions: but Daher shouted suddenly from the Hadi side, seeing their column winding up from the south-east. They had early lost the track and camped till dawn. My men jested with humour against Sheikh Saleh, their guide, as one who could lose his road between the Thlaithukhwat and Bair: just like one might say between the Marble Arch and Oxford Circus.

However, it was a perfect morning, with the sun hot on our backs, and the wind fresh in our faces. The Camel Corps strode splendidly past the frosted tips of the three peaks into the green depths of Dhirwa. They looked different from the stiff, respectful companies which had reached Akaba, for Buxton's supple brain and friendly observation had taken in the experience of irregular fighting, and revised their training rules for the new needs.

He had changed their column formation, breaking its formal sub-division of two hard companies: he had changed the order of march, so that, instead of their old immaculate lines, they came clotted, in groups which split up or drew together without delay upon each variation of road or ground surface. He had reduced the loads and re-hung them, thereby lengthening the camels' pace and daily mileage. He had cut into their infantry system of clockwork halts every so often (to let the camels stale!) and grooming was less honoured. In the old days, they had prinked their animals, cosseting them like Pekinese and each halt had been lightened by a noisy, flapping massage of the beasts' stripped humps with the saddle blanket; whereas now the spare time was spent in grazing.

Consequently, our Imperial Camel Corps had become rapid, elastic, enduring, silent; except when they mounted by numbers, for then the three hundred he-camels would roar in concert, giving out a wave of sound audible miles across the night. Each march saw them more workman-like, more at home on the animals, tougher, leaner, faster. They behaved like boys on holiday, and the easy mixing of officers and men made their atmosphere delightful.

My camels were brought up to walk in Arab fashion, that bent-kneed gait with much swinging of the fetlock, the stride a little longer and a little quicker than the normal. Buxton's camels strolled along at their native pace, unaffected by the men on their backs, who were kept from direct contact with them by iron-shod boots and by their wood and steel Manchester-made saddles.

Consequently, though I started each stage alongside Buxton in the van, I forged steadily in front with my five attendants; especially when I rode my Baha, the immensely tall, large-boned, upstanding beast, who got her name from the bleat-voice forced on her by a bullet through the chin. She was very finely bred, but bad-tempered, half a wild camel, and had never patience for an ordinary walk. Instead, with high nose and wind-stirred hair, she would jig along in an uneasy dance, hateful to my Ageyl, for it strained their tender loins, but to me not unamusing.

In this fashion we would gain three miles on the British, look for a plot of grass or juicy thorns, lie in the warm freshness of air, and let our beasts graze while we were overtaken; and a beautiful sight the Camel Corps would be as it came up.

Through the mirage of heat which flickered over the shining flint-stones of the ridge we would see, at first, only the knotted brown

From a portrait by Eric Kennington

SERJ EL ATEIBI

mass of the column, swaying in the haze. As it grew nearer the masses used to divide into little groups, which swung, parting and breaking into one another. At last, when close to us, we would distinguish the individual riders, like great water-birds breast-deep in the silver mirage, with Buxton's athletic, splendidly-mounted figure leading his sunburnt, laughing, khaki men.

It was odd to see how diversely they rode. Some sat naturally, despite the clumsy saddle; some pushed out their hinder-parts, and leaned forward like Arab villagers; others lolled in the saddle as if they were Australians riding horses. My men, judging by the look, were inclined to scoff. I told them how from that three-hundred I would pick forty fellows who would out-ride, out-fight and out-suffer any forty men in Feisal's army.

At noon, by Ras Muheiwer, we halted an hour or two, for though the heat to-day was less than in Egypt in August, Buxton did not wish to drive his men through it without a break. The camels were loosed out, while we lay and lunched and tried to sleep, defying the multitude of flies which had marched with us from Bair in colonies on our sweaty backs. Meanwhile, my bodyguard passed through, grumbling at their indignity of baggage driving, making believe never to have been so shamed before, and praying profanely that the world would not hear of my tyranny to them.

Their sorrow was doubled since the baggage animals were Somali camels, whose greatest speed was about three miles an hour. Buxton's force marched nearly four, myself more than five, so that the marches were for the Zaagi and his forty thieves a torment of slowness, modified only by baulking camels, or displaced loads.

We abused their clumsiness, calling them drovers and coolies, offering to buy their goods when they came to market; till perforce they laughed at their plight. After the first day they kept up with us by lengthening the march into the night (only a little, for these ophthalmia-stricken brutes were blind in the dark) and by stealing from the breakfast and midday halts. They brought their caravan through without losing one of all of their charges; a fine performance for such gilded gentlemen; only possible because under their gilt they were the best camel-masters for hire in Arabia.

That night we slept in Ghadaf. The armoured car overtook us as we halted, its delighted Sherari guide grinning in triumph on the turret lid. An hour or two later the Zaagi arrived, reporting all up and well. He begged that Buxton should not kill, directly in the road, such camels as broke down on the march; for his men made each successive carcass excuse for a feast and a delay.

Abdulla was troubled to understand why the British shot their abandoned beasts. I pointed out how we Arabs shot one another if badly wounded in battle; but Abdulla retorted it was to save us from being so tortured that we might do ourselves shame. He believed there was hardly a man alive who would not choose a gradual death of weakness in the desert, rather than a sudden cutting off; indeed, in his judgment, the slowest death was the most merciful of all, since absence of hope would prevent the bitterness of a losing fight, and leave the man's nature untrammelled to compose itself and him into the mercy of God. Our English argument, that it was kinder to kill quickly anything except a man, he would not take seriously.

Our morrow was like the day before, a steady grind of forty miles. Next day was the last before the bridge-effort. I took half of my men from the baggage-train, and threw them forward on our line of march, to crown each hill-top. This was well done, but did not profit us, for in mid-morning, with Muaggar, our ambush, in full sight, we were marching strongly and hopefully when a Turkish aeroplane came from the south, flew the length of our column, and went down, before us, into Amman.

We plodded heavily into Muaggar by noon, and hid in the sub-structures of the Roman temple-platform. Our watchers took post on the crest, looking out over the harvested plains to the Hejaz Rail-way. Over these hill-slopes, as we stared through our glasses, the grey stones seemed to line out like flocks of grazing sheep.

We sent my peasants into the villages below us, to get news, and warn the people to keep within doors. They returned to say that chance was fighting against us. Round the winnowed corn upon the threshing floors stood Turkish soldiers, for the tax-gatherers were measuring the heaps under guard of sections of mounted infantry. Three such troops, forty men, lay for this night in the three villages nearest the great bridge—villages through whose precincts we must necessarily go and come.

We held a hurried council. The aeroplane had or had not seen us. It would cause, at worst, the strengthening of the bridge-guard, but I had little fear of its effect. The Turks would believe we were the advance-guard of a third raid on Amman, and were more likely to concentrate than to detach troops. Buxton's men were great fighters, he had laid admirable plans. Success was certain.

The doubt was about the bridge's cost, or rather as to its value in British life, having regard to Bartholomew's prohibition of casualties. The presence of these mule-riders meant that our retreat would not be unencumbered. The camel corps were to dismount nearly a mile from the bridge of Kissir (their noisy camels!) and advance on foot. The noise of their assault, not to speak of the firing of three tons of guncotton against the bridge-piers, would wake up the district. The Turkish patrols in the villages might stumble on our camel-park—a disaster for us—or, at least, would hamper us in the broken ground, as we retired.

Buxton's men could not scatter like a swarm of birds, after the bridge explosion, to find their own way back to the Muaggar. In any night-fighting some would be cut off and lost. We should have to wait for them, possibly losing more in the business. The whole cost might be fifty men, and I put the worth of the bridge at less than five. Its destruction was so to frighten and disturb the Turks, that they would leave us alone till August the thirtieth when our long column set out for Azrak. To-day was the twentieth. The danger had seemed pressing in July, but was now nearly over.

Buxton agreed. We decided to cry off, and move back at once. At the moment more Turkish machines got up from Amman and quartered the rough hills northward from Muaggar, looking for us.

The men groaned in disappointment when they heard the change. They had set pride on this long raid, and were burning to tell incredulous Egypt that their programme had been literally fulfilled.

To gain what we could, I sent Saleh and the other chiefs down to spruce their people with tall rumours of our numbers, and our coming as the reconnaissance of Feisal's army, to carry Amman by assault in the new moon. This was the story the Turks feared to learn: the operation they imagined: the stroke they dreaded. They pushed cavalry cautiously into Muaggar, and found confirmation of the wild tales of the villagers, for the hill-top was littered with empty meat-tins, and the valley slopes cut up by the deep tracks of enormous cars. Very many tracks there were! This alarm checked them, and, at a bloodless price for us, kept them hovering a week. The destruction of the bridge would have gained us a fortnight.

We waited till dusk was thick, and then rode off for Azrak, fifty miles away. We pretended that the raid was become a tour, and talked of Roman remains and of Ghassanide hunting-palaces. The Camel Corps had practice, almost a habit, of night journeys, so that their pace was as by day, and units never strayed nor lost touch. There was a brilliant moon and we marched till it was pale in the morning, passing the lone palace of Kharaneh about midnight, too careless to turn aside and see its strangeness. Part-blame for this lay on the moon, whose whiteness made our minds as frozen and shadowless as itself, so that we sat still in our saddles, just sitting still.

In the afternoon, tired, we came to Kusair el Amra, the little hunting lodge of Harith, the Shepherd King, a patron of poets; it stood beautifully against its background of bosky rustling trees. Buxton put headquarters in the cool dusk of its hall, and we lay there puzzling out the worn frescoes of the wall, with more laughter than moral profit. Of the men, some sheltered themselves in other rooms, most, with the camels, stretched themselves beneath the trees, for a slumberous afternoon and evening. The aeroplanes had not found us—could not find us here. To-morrow there was

Azrak, and fresh water to replace this stuff of Bair which, with the passing days, was getting too tasty for our liking.

Next day we walked gently to Azrak. When we were over the last ridge of lava-pebbles and saw the ring of the Mejaber graves, that most beautifully put of cemeteries, I trotted forward with my men, to be sure against accident in the place, and to feel again its remoteness before the others came.

We rested there two days, the refreshment of the pools being so great. Buxton rode with me to the fort, to examine the altar of Diocletian and Maximian, meaning to add a word in favour of King George the Fifth; but our stay was poisoned by the grey flies, and then ruined by a tragic accident. An Arab, shooting fish in the fort pool, dropped his rifle, which exploded and killed instantly Lieutenant Rowan, of the Scottish Horse. We buried him in the little Mejaber graveyard, whose spotless quiet had long been my envy.

On the third day we marched past Ammari, across Jesha to near the Thlaithukhwat, the old country whose almost imperceptible variations I had come to know. By the Hadi we felt at home, and made a night march, the men's strident yells of "Are we well fed? No." "Do we see life? Yes," thundering up the long slopes after me. When they tired of telling the truth I could hear the rattle of their accoutrements hitched over the wooden saddles—eleven or fifteen hitchings they had, each time they loaded up, in place of the Arab's all-embracing saddle bag thrown on in one movement.

I was so bound up in their dark body and tail behind me, that I, too, lost my way between the Hadi and Bair. However, till dawn we steered by the stars (the men's next meal was in Bair, for yesterday their iron ration was exhausted), and day broke on us in a wooded valley which was certainly Wadi Bair; but for my life I could not tell if we were above or below the wells. I confessed my fault to Buxton and Marshall, and we tettered for awhile, till, by chance, Sagr ibn Shaalan, one of our old allies of the distant days of Wejh, rode down the track, and put us on the road. An hour later the Camel Corps had new rations and their old tents by the wells, and found that Salama, the provident Egyptian doctor, calculating their return to-day, had already filled the drinking cisterns with enough water to slake the half of their thirsty beasts.

I determined to go into Aba el Lissan with the armoured cars, for Buxton was now on proved ground among friends, and could do without my help. Joyce, Dawnay and Young reported all going marvellously. In fact, preparations were complete, and they were breaking up, Joyce for Cairo to see a dentist, Dawnay for G.H.Q. to tell Allenby we were prosperous and obedient.

CHAPTER XXIX

WASHING OUR LINEN

JOYCE'S SHIP had come up from Jidda, with the Meccan mail. Feisal opened his Kibla (King Hussein's Gazette), to find staring at him a Royal Proclamation, saying that fools were calling Jaafar Pasha the General Officer Commanding the Arab Northern Army, whereas there was no such rank, indeed no rank higher than captain in the Arab Army, wherein Sheikh Jaafar, like another, was doing his duty!

This had been published by King Hussein (after reading that Allenby had decorated Jaafar) without warning Feisal; to spite the northern town-Arabs, the Syrian and Mesopotamian officers, whom the King at once despised for their laxity and feared for their accomplishments. He knew that they were fighting, not to give him dominion, but to set free their own countries for their own governing, and the lust for power had grown uncontrollable in the old man.

Jaafar came in and proffered his resignation to Feisal. There followed him our divisional officers and their staffs, with the regimental and battalion commanders. I begged them to pay no heed to the humours of an old man of seventy, out of the world in Mecca, whose greatness they themselves had made; and Feisal refused to accept their resignations, pointing out that the commissions (since his father had not approved their service) were issued by himself, and he alone was discredited by the proclamation.

On this assumption he telegraphed to Mecca, and received a return telegram which called him traitor and outlaw. He replied laying down his command of the Akaba front. Hussein appointed Zeid to succeed him. Zeid promptly refused. Hussein's cipher messages became corrupt with rage, and the military life of Aba el Lissan came to a sudden stop. Dawnay, from Akaba, before the ship sailed, rang me up, and asked dolefully if all hope were over. I answered that things hung on chance, but perhaps we should get through.

Three courses lay before us. The first, to get pressure put on King Hussein to withdraw his statement. The second, to carry on, ignoring it. The third, to set up Feisal in formal independence of his father. There were advocates of each course, amongst the English, as amongst the Arabs. We wired to Allenby asking him to smooth out the incident. Hussein was obstinate and crafty, and it might take weeks to force him out of his obstacles to an apology. Normally, we could have afforded these weeks; but to-day we were in the unhappy position that after three days, if at all, our expedition to Deraa must start. We must find some means of carrying on the war, while Egypt sought for a solution.

My first duty was to send express to Nuri Shaalan that I could not meet him at the gathering of his tribes in Kaf, but would be in Azrak from the first day of the new moon, at his service. This was a sad expedient, for Nuri might take suspicion of my change and fail at the tryst; and without the Rualla half our efficiency and importance at Deraa on September the sixteenth would disappear. However, we had to risk this smaller loss, since without Feisal and the regulars and Pisani's guns there would be no expedition, and for the sake of reforming their tempers I must wait in Aba el Lissan.

The second duty was to start off the caravans for Azrak—the baggage, the food, the petrol, the ammunition. Young prepared these, rising, as ever, to any occasion not of his own seeking. He was his own first obstacle, but would have no man hinder him. Never could I forget the radiant face of Nuri Said, after a joint conference, encountering a group of Arab officers with the cheerful words, "Never mind, you fellows; he talks to the English just as he does to us!" Now he saw that each echelon started—not, indeed, to time but only a day late—under its appointed officers, according to programme. It had been our principle to issue orders to the Arabs only through their own chiefs, so they had no precedent either for obedience or for disobedience: and off they went like lambs.

Our next duty was to start off the troops for Azrak on the right day. To effect this, their confidence in the confidence of the officers had to be restored. Stirling's tact was called upon. Nuri Said was ambitious as any soldier would have been, to make much of the opportunity before him, and readily agreed to move as far as Azrak, pending Hussein's apology. If this was unsatisfactory they could return, or throw off allegiance; if it was adequate, as I assured him it would be, the interim and unmerited services of the Northern Army should bring a blush to the old man's cheek.

The ranks responded to bluffer arguments. We made plain that such gross questions as food and pay depended entirely on the maintenance of organization. They yielded, and the separate columns, of mounted infantry, of machine-gunners, of Egyptian sappers, of Ghurkas, of Pisani's gunners, moved off in their courses, according to the routine of Stirling and Young, only two days late.

The last obligation was to restore Feisal's supremacy. To attempt anything serious between Deraa and Damascus without him would be vain. We could put in the attack on Deraa, which was what Allenby expected from us; but the capture of Damascus—which was what I expected from the Arabs, the reason why I had joined with them in the field, taken ten thousand pains, and spent my wit and strength— that depended on Feisal's being present with us in the fighting line undistracted by military duties, but ready to take over and exploit the political value of what our bodies conquered for him. Eventually he offered to come up under my orders.

As for the apology from Mecca, Allenby and Wilson were doing their best, engrossing the cables. If they failed, my course would be to promise Feisal the direct support of the British Government, and drive him into Damascus as sovereign prince. It was possible: but I wanted to avoid it except as a last necessity. The Arabs hitherto in their revolt had made clean history, and I did not wish our adventure to come to the pitiable state of scission before the common victory and its peace.

King Hussein behaved truly to type, protesting fluently, with endless circumlocution, showing no understanding of the grave effect of his incursion into Northern Army affairs. To clear his mind we sent him plain statements, which drew abusive but involved returns. His telegrams came through Egypt and by wireless to our operators in Akaba, and were sent up to me by car, for delivery to Feisal. The Arabic ciphers were simple, and I had undesirable passages mutilated by rearranging their figures into nonsense, before handing them in code to Feisal. By this easy expedient the temper of his entourage was not needlessly complicated.

The play went on for several days, Mecca never repeating a message notified corrupt, but telegraphing in its place a fresh version toned down at each re-editing from the previous harshness. Finally, there came a long message, the first half a lame apology and withdrawal of the mischievous proclamation, the second half a repetition of the offence in a new form. I suppressed the tail, and took the head marked "very urgent" to Feisal's tent, where he sat in the full circle of his staff-officers.

His secretary worked out the dispatch, and handed the decipher to Feisal. My hints had roused expectation, and all eyes were on him as he read it. He was astonished, and gazed wonderingly at me, for the meek words were unlike his Father's querulous obstinacy. Then he pulled himself together, read the apology aloud, and at the end said thrillingly, "The telegraph has saved all our honour."

A chorus of delight burst out, during which he bent aside to whisper in my ear, "I mean the honor of nearly all of us." It was done so delightfully that I laughed, and said demurely, "I cannot understand what you mean." He replied, "I offered to serve for this last march under your orders: why was that not enough?" "Because it would not go with your honour." He murmured, "You prefer mine always before your own," and then sprang energetically to his feet, saying, "Now, Sirs, praise God and work."

In three hours we had settled time-tables, and arranged for our successors here in Aba el Lissan, with their spheres and duties. I took my leave. Joyce had just returned to us from Egypt, and Feisal promised that he would come, with him and Marshall, to Azrak to join me on the twelfth at latest. All the camp was happy as I got into a Rolls tender and set off northward, hoping, though already it was the fourth of September, yet to rally the Rualla under Nuri Shaalan in time for our attack on Deraa.

CHAPTER XXX

IN THE ADVANCE GUARD

It was an inexpressible pleasure to have left the mists behind. We caught at each other with thankfulness as we drove along, Winterton, Nasir and myself. Lord Winterton was our last-found recruit; an experienced officer from Buxton's Camel Corps. Sherif Nasir, who had been the spear-point of the Arab army since the first days of Medina, had been chosen by us for the field-work on this last occasion also. He deserved the honour of Damascus, for his had been the honours of Medina, of Wejh, of Akaba, and of Tafileh; and of many barren days beside.

We were never out of sight of men; of tenuous camel-columns of troops and tribesmen and baggage moving slowly northward over the interminable Jefer flat. Past this activity (of good omen for our punctual concentration at Azrak) we roared, my excellent driver, Green, once achieving sixty-seven miles an hour. The half-stifled Nasir who sat in the box-body could only wave his hand across a furlong to each friend we overtook.

At Bair we heard from the alarmed Beni Sakhr that the Turks, on the preceding day, had launched suddenly westward from Hesa into Tafileh. Mifleh thought I was mad, or most untimely merry,

when I laughed outright at the news which four days sooner would
have held up the Azrak expedition: but, now we were started, the
enemy might take Aba el Lissan, Guweira, Akaba itself—and welcome! Our formidable talk of advance by Amman had pulled
their leg nearly out of socket, and the innocents were out to counter our feint. Each man they sent south was a man, or rather ten
men, lost.

In Azrak we found a few servants of Nuri Shaalan, and the
Crossley car with a flying officer, an airman, some spares, and a canvas hangar for the two machines protecting our concentration. We
spent our first night on their aerodrome and suffered for it. A reckless armoured-plated camel fly, biting like a hornet, occupied our
exposed parts till sunset. Then came a blessed relief as the itch grew
milder in the evening cool—but the wind changed and hot showers of blinding salty dust swept us for three hours. We lay down and
drew covers over our heads, but could not sleep. Each half-hour we
had to throw off the sand which threatened to bury us. At midnight
the wind ceased. We issued from our sweaty nests and restfully prepared to sleep—when, singing, a cloud of mosquitoes rolled over
us: them we fought till dawn.

Consequently, at dawn we changed camp to the height of the
Mejaber ridge, a mile west of the water and a hundred feet above
the marshes, open to all winds that blew. We rested awhile, then
put up the hangar, and afterwards went off to bathe in the silver
water. We undressed beside the sparkling pools whose pearl-white
sides and floor reflected the sky with a moony radiance. "Delicious," I yelled as I splashed in and swam about. "But why do you
keep on bobbing under water?" asked Winterton a moment later.
Then a camel-fly bit him behind, and he understood and leapt in
after me. We swam about, desperately keeping our heads wet, to
dissuade the grey swarms: but they were too bold with hunger to
be afraid of water, and after five minutes we struggled out, and
frantically into our clothes, the blood running from twenty of
their daggerbites.

Nasir stood and laughed at us: and later we journeyed together to the fort, to rest midday there. Ali ibn el Hussein's old corner tower, this only roof in the desert, was cool and peaceful. The wind stirred the palm-fronds outside to a frosty rustling: neglected palms, too northerly for their red date-crop to be good; but the stems were thick with low branches, and threw a pleasant shade. Under them, on his carpet, sat Nasir in the quietness. The grey smoke of his thrown-away cigarette undulated out on the warm air, flickering and fading through the sun-spots which shone between the leaves. "I am happy," said he. We were all happy.

In the afternoon an armoured car came up, completing our necessary defence, though the risk of enemy was minute. Three tribes covered the country between us and the railway. There were only forty horsemen in Deraa, none in Amman: also, as yet the Turks had no news of us. One of their aeroplanes flew over on the morning of the ninth, made a perfunctory circle, and went off, probably without seeing us. Our camp, on its airy summit, gave us splendid observation of the Deraa and Amman roads. By day we twelve English, with Nasir and his slave, lazed, roaming, bathing at sunset, sight-seeing, thinking; and slept comfortably at night: or rather I did: enjoying the precious interval between the conquered friends of Aba el Lissan and the enemy of next month.

The preciousness would seem to have been partly in myself, for on this march to Damascus (and such it was already in our imagination) my normal balance had changed. I could feel the taut power of Arab excitement behind me. The climax of the preaching of years had come, and a united country was straining towards its historic capital. In confidence that this weapon, tempered by myself, was enough for the utmost of my purpose, I seemed to forget the English companions who stood outside my idea in the shadow of ordinary war. I failed to make them partners of my certainty.

Long after, I heard that Winterton rose each dawn and examined the horizon, lest my carelessness subject us to surprise: and at Umtaiye and Sheikh Saad the British for days thought we were a

forlorn hope. Actually I knew (and surely said?) that we were as safe
as any one in the world at war. Because of the pride they had, I never
saw their doubt of my plans.

These plans were a feint against Amman and a real cutting of
the Deraa railways: further than this we hardly went, for it was ever
my habit, while studying alternatives, to keep the stages in solution.

By our establishment at Azrak the first part of our plan, the feint,
was accomplished. We had sent our "horsemen of St. George," gold
sovereigns, by the thousand to the Beni Sakhr, purchasing all the
barley on their threshing floors: begging them not to mention it,
but we would require it for our animals and for our British allies,
in a fortnight. Dhiab of Tafileh—that jerky, incomplete hobblede-
hoy—gossiped the news instantly through to Kerak.

In addition, Feisal warned the Zebn to Bair, for service; and
Hornby, now (perhaps a little prematurely) wearing Arab clothes,
was active in preparations for a great assault on Madeba. His plan
was to move about the nineteenth, when he heard that Allenby was
started; his hope being to tie on to Jericho, so that if we failed by
Deraa our force could return and reinforce his movement: which
would then be not a feint, but the second string to our bow. However, the Turks knocked this rather crooked by their advance to
Tafileh, and Hornby had to defend Shobek against them.

For our second part, the Deraa business, we had to plan an attack
proper. As preliminary we determined to cut the line near Amman,
thus preventing Amman's reinforcement of Deraa, and maintaining its conviction that our feint against it was real. It seemed to me
that (with Egyptians to do the actual destruction) this preliminary
could be undertaken by the Ghurkas, whose detachment would not
distract our main body from the main purpose.

This main purpose was to cut the railways in the Hauran and
keep them cut for at least a week; and there seemed to be three ways
of doing it. The first was to march north of Deraa to the Damascus
railway, as on my ride with Tallal in the winter, cut it; and then cross
to the Yarmuk railway. The second was to march south of Deraa to

the Yarmuk, as with Ali ibn el Hussein in November, 1917. The third was to rush straight at Deraa town.

The third scheme could be undertaken only if the Air Force would promise so heavy a daylight bombing of Deraa station that the effect would be tantamount to artillery bombardment, enabling us to risk an assault against it with our few men. Salmond hoped to do this; but it depended on how many heavy machines he received or assembled in time. Dawnay would fly over to us here with his last word on September the eleventh. Till then we would hold the schemes equal in our judgment.

Of our supports, my bodyguard were the first to arrive, prancing up Wadi Sirhan on the ninth of September: happy, fatter than their fat camels, rested, and amused after their month of feasting with the Rualla. They reported Nuri nearly ready, and determined to join us. The contagion of the new tribe's first vigour had quickened in them a life and spirit which made us jolly.

On the tenth the two aeroplanes came through from Akaba. Murphy and Junor, the pilots, settled down to the horse-flies which gambolled in the air about their juiciness. On the eleventh, the other armoured cars and Joyce drove in, with Stirling, but without Feisal. Marshall had remained to squire him up next day; and things were always safe to go well where Marshall, the capable soul, directed them with a cultivated humour, which was not so much riotous as persistent. Young, Peake, Scott-Higgins and the baggage arrived. Azrak became many-peopled and its lakes were again resonant with voices and the plunge of brown and lean, brown and strong, copper-coloured, or white bodies into the transparent water.

On the eleventh the aeroplane from Palestine arrived. Unfortunately, Dawnay was again ill, and the staff officer who took his place (being raw) had suffered severely from the roughness of the air.

So he forgot his most important news, how on September the sixth Allenby, with a new inspiration, had said to Bartholomew, "Why bother about Messudieh? Let the cavalry go straight to Afuleh, and Nazareth": and so the whole plan had been changed,

and an enormous indefinite advance substituted for the fixed
objective. We got no notion of this; but by cross-questioning the
pilot, whom Salmond had informed, we got a clear statement of
the resources in bombing machines. They fell short of our minimum for Deraa; so we asked for just a hamper-bombing of it while
we went round it by the north, to make sure of destroying the
Damascus line.

The next day Feisal arrived with, behind him, the army of troops,
Nuri Said the spick and span, Jemil the gunner, Pisani's coster-like
Algerians, and the other items of our "three men and a boy" effort.
The grey flies had now two thousand camels to fatten upon, and in
their weariness gave up Junor and his half-drained mechanics.

In the afternoon Nuri Shaalan appeared, with Trad and Khalid,
Faris, Durzi, and the Khaffaji. Auda abu Tayi arrived, with Mohammed
el Dheilan; also Fahad and Adhub, the Zebn leaders, with ibn Bani,
the chief of the Serahin, and ibn Genj of the Serdiyeh. Majid ibn
Sultan, of the Adwan near Salt, rode across to learn the truth of our
attack on Amman. Later in the evening there was a rattle of rifle
fire in the north, and Talal el Hareidhin, my old companion, come
ruffling at the gallop, with forty or fifty mounted peasants behind
him. His sanguine face beamed with joy at our long-hoped-for
arrival. Druses and town-Syrians, Isawiyeh and Hawarneh swelled
the company. Even the barley for our return if the venture failed (a
possibility we seldom entertained) began to arrive in steady loads.
Every one was stout and in health.

Except myself. The crowd had destroyed my pleasure in Azrak,
and I went off down the valley to our remote Ain el Essad and lay
there all day in my old lair among the tamarisk, where the wind in
the dusty green branches played with such sounds as it made in
English trees. It told me I was tired to death of these Arabs; petty
incarnate Semites who attained heights and depths beyond our
reach, though not beyond our sight. They realized our absolute in
their unrestrained capacity for good and evil; and for two years I
had profitably shammed to be their companion!

Joyce meanwhile shouldered the responsibility which my defection endangered. By his orders Peake, with the Egyptian Camel Corps, now a sapper party, Scott-Higgins, with his fighting Ghurkas, and two armoured cars as insurance, went off to cut the railway by Ifdein.

The scheme was for Scott-Higgins to rush a blockhouse after dark with his nimble Indians—nimble on foot that was to say, for they were like sacks, on camels. Peake was then to demolish until dawn. The cars would cover their retreat eastward in the morning, over the plain, upon which we, the main body, would be marching north from Azrak for Umtaiye, a great pit of rain-water fifteen miles below Deraa, and our advanced base. We gave them Rualla guides and saw them off, hopefully, for this important preliminary.

Just at dawn our column marched. Of them one thousand were the Aba el Lissan contingent: three hundred were Nuri Shaalan's nomad horse. He had also two thousand Rualla camel-riders: these we asked him to keep in Wadi Sirhan. It seemed not wise, before the supreme day, to launch so many disturbing Beduin among the villages of Hauran. The horsemen were sheikhs, or sheikhs' servants, men of substance, under control.

Affairs with Nuri and Feisal held me the whole day in Azrak: but Joyce had left me a tender, the Blue Mist, by which on the following morning I overtook the army, and found them breakfasting among the grass-filled roughness of the Giaan el Khunna. The camels, joying to be out of the barren circle of Azrak, were packing their stomachs hastily with this best of food.

Joyce had bad news. Peake had rejoined, reporting failure to reach the line, because of trouble with Arab encampments in the neighbourhood of his proposed demolition. We had set store on breaking the Amman railway, and the check was an offence. I left the car, took a load of guncotton, and mounted my camel, to push in advance of the force. The others made a detour to avoid harsh tongues of lava which ran down westwards towards the railway; but

JAAFAR PASHA, *C.-in-C. Arab Northern Army, later Prime Minister, Irak*

we, Ageyl and others of the well-mounted, cut straight across by a thieves' path to the open plain about the ruined Um el Jemal.

I was thinking hard about the Amman demolition, puzzled as to what expedient would be quickest and best; and the puzzle of these ruins added to my care. There seemed evidence of bluntness of mind in these Roman frontier cities, Um el Jemal, Um el Surab, Umtaiye. Such incongruous buildings, in what was then and now a desert cockpit, accused their builders of insensitiveness; almost of a vulgar assertion of man's right (Roman right) to live unchanged in all his estate. Italianate buildings—only to be paid for by taxing more docile provinces—on these fringes of the world disclosed a prosaic blindness to the transience of politics. A house which so survived the purpose of its builder was a pride too trivial to confer honour upon the mind responsible for its conception.

Um el Jemal seemed aggressive and impudent, and the railway beyond it so tiresomely intact, that they blinded me to an air-battle between Murphy in our Bristol Fighter and an enemy two-seater. The Bristol was badly shot about before the Turk went down in flames. Our army were delighted spectators, but Murphy, finding the damage too great for his few materials at Azrak, went for repair to Palestine in the morning. So our tiny Air Force was reduced to the B.E. 12, a type so out of date that it was impossible for fighting, and little use for reconnaissance. This we discovered on the day: meanwhile we were as glad as the army at our man's win.

Umtaiye was reached, just before sunset. The troops were five or six miles behind, so as soon as our beasts had had a drink we struck off to the railway, four miles downhill to the westward, thinking to do a snatch-demolition. The dusk let us get close without alarm, and, to our joy, we found that the going was possible for armoured cars: while just before us were two good bridges.

These points decided me to return in the morning, with cars and more guncotton, to abolish the larger, four-arched bridge. Its destruction would give the Turks some days' hard mending, and set us free of Amman all the time of our first Deraa raid; thus the purpose of Peake's frustrated demolition would be filled. It was a happy discovery, and we rode back, quartering the ground while the darkness gathered, to pick the best car road.

As we climbed the last ridge, a high unbroken watershed which hid Umtaiye completely from the railway and its possible watchmen, the fresh north-east wind blew into our faces the warm smell and dust of ten thousand feet; and from the crest the ruins appeared so startlingly unlike themselves three hours before that we pulled up to gasp. The hollow ground was festively spangled with a galaxy of little evening fires, fresh-lighted, still twinkling with the flame reflections in their smoke. About them men were making bread or coffee, while others drove their noisy camels to and from the water.

In the morning, while the army breakfasted, and thawed the dawn-chill from its muscles in the sun, we explained to the Arab leaders in council the fitness of the line for a car-raid; and it was determined that two armoured cars should run down to the bridge and attack it, while the main body continued their march to Tell Arar on the Damascus Railway, four miles north of Deraa. They would take post there, possessing the line, at dawn to-morrow, the seventeenth of September; and we with the cars would have finished this bridge and rejoined them before that.

About two in the afternoon, as we drove towards the railway, we had the great sight of a swarm of our bombing planes droning steadily up towards Deraa on their first raid. The place had hitherto been carefully reserved from air attack; so the damage among the unaccustomed, unprotected, unarmed garrison was heavy. The *morale* of the men suffered as much as the railway traffic: and till our onslaught from the north forced them to see us, all their efforts went into digging bomb-proof shelters.

We lurched across plots of grass, between bars and fields of rough stone, in our two tenders and two armoured cars; but arrived all well behind a last ridge, just this side of our target. On the rise south of the bridge stood a stone blockhouse.

We settled to leave the tenders here, under cover. I transferred myself, with one hundred and fifty pounds of guncotton, fused and ready, to one armoured car; intending to drive passively down the valley towards the bridge, till its arches, sheltering us from the fire of the post, enabled me to lay and light the demolition charges. Meanwhile the other, the active fighting car, would engage the block-house at short range to cover my operation.

The two cars set out simultaneously. When they saw us the aston-ished garrison of seven or eight Turks got out of their trenches, and, rifles in hand, advanced upon us in open order: moved either by panic, by misunderstanding, or by an inhuman unmixed courage.

In a few minutes the second car came into action against them: while four other Turks appeared beside the bridge and shot at us. Our machine-gunners ranged, and fired a short burst. One man fell, another was hit: the rest ran a little way, thought better of it, and returned, making friendly signs. We took their rifles, and sent them up valley to the tenders, whose drivers were watching us keen-ly from their ridge. The blockhouse surrendered at the same moment. We were very content to have taken the bridge, and its section of track, in five minutes without loss.

Joyce rushed down in his tender with more guncotton, and hasti-ly we set about the bridge, a pleasant little work, eighty feet long and fifteen feet high, honoured with a shining slab of white mar-ble, bearing the name and titles of Sultan Abd el Hamid. In the drainage holes of the spandrils six small charges were inserted zigzag, and with their explosion all the arches were scientifically shattered; the demolition being a fine example of that finest sort which left the skeleton of its bridge intact indeed, but tottering, so that the repairing enemy had a first labour to destroy the wreck, before they could attempt to rebuild.

When we had finished, enemy patrols were near enough to give us fair excuse for quitting. The few prisoners, whom we valued for Intelligence reasons, were given place on our loads; and we bumped off. Unfortunately we bumped too carelessly in our satisfaction, and at the first water-course there was a crash beneath my tender. One side of its box body tipped downward till the weight came on the tyre of the back wheel, and we stuck.

The front bracket of the near back spring had crystallized through by the chassis, in a sheer break which nothing but a workshop could mend. We gazed in despair, for we were only three hundred yards from the railway, and stood to lose the car, when the enemy came along in ten minutes. A Rolls in the desert was above rubies; and though we had been driving in these for eighteen months, not upon the polished roads of their makers' intention, but across country of the vilest, at speed, day or night, carrying a ton of goods and four or five men up, yet this was our first structural accident in the team of nine.

Rolls, the driver, our strongest and most resourceful man, the ready mechanic, whose skill and advice largely kept our cars in running order, was nearly in tears over the mishap. The knot of us, officers and men, English, Arabs and Turks, crowded round him and watched his face anxiously. As he realized that he, a private, commanded in this emergency, even the stubble on his jaw seemed to harden in sullen determination. At last he said there was just one chance. We might jack up the fallen end of the spring, and wedge it, by baulks upon the running board, in nearly its old position. With the help of ropes the thin angle-irons of the running boards might carry the additional weight.

We had on each car a length of scantling to place between the double tyres if ever the car stuck in sand or mud. Three blocks of this would make the needful height. We had no saw, but drove bullets through it cross-wise till we could snap it off. The Turks heard us firing, and halted cautiously. Joyce heard us and ran back to help. Into his car we piled our load, jacked up the spring and the chassis, lashed in the wooden baulks, let her down on them (they bore splendidly) cranked up, and drove off. Rolls eased her to walking speed at every stone and ditch, while we, prisoners and all, ran beside with cries of encouragement, clearing the track.

In camp we stitched the blocks with captured telegraph wire, and bound them together and to the chassis, and the spring to the chassis; till it looked as strong as possible, and we put back the load. So enduring was the running board that we did the ordinary work with the car for the next three weeks, and took her so into Damascus at the end. Great was Rolls, and great was Royce! They were worth hundreds of men to us in these deserts.

This darning the car delayed us for hours, and at its end we slept in Umtaiye, confident that, by starting before dawn, we should not be much late in meeting Nuri Said on the Damascus line to-morrow: and we could tell him that, for a week, the Amman line was sealed, by loss of a main bridge. This was the side of quickest reinforcement for Deraa, and its death made our rear safe. Even we had helped poor Zeid, behind there in Aba el Lissan: for the Turks massed in Tafileh would hold up that attack till their communications were again open. Our last campaign was beginning auspiciously.

CHAPTER XXXI

WE CUT THE MAIN LINES

DULY, BEFORE dawn, we drove upon the track of Stirling's cars, eager to be with them before their fight. Unfortunately the going was not helpful. At first we had a bad descent, and then difficult flats of jagged dolerite, across which we crawled painfully. Later we ran over ploughed slopes. The soil was heavy for the cars, for with summer drought this red earth cracked a yard deep and two or three inches wide. The five-ton armoured cars were reduced to first speed, and nearly stuck.

We overtook the Arab army about eight in the morning, on the crest of the slope to the railway, as it was deploying to attack the little bridge-guarding redoubt between us and the mound of Tell Arar whose head overlooked the countryside to Deraa.

Rualla horsemen, led by Trad, dashed down the long slope and over the liquorice-grown bed of the watercourse to the line. Young bounced after them in his Ford. From the ridge we thought the railway taken without a shot, but while we gazed, suddenly from the neglected Turkish post came a vicious spitting fire, and our braves who had been standing in splendid attitudes on the coveted line (wondering privately what on earth to do next) disappeared.

Nuri Said moved down Pisani's guns and fired a few shots. Then the Rualla and troops rushed the redoubt easily, with only one killed. So the southern ten miles of the Damascus line was freely ours by nine in the morning. It was the only railway to Palestine and Hejaz and I could hardly realize our fortune; hardly believe that our word to Allenby was fulfilled so simply and so soon.

The Arabs streamed down from the ridge in rivers of men, and swarmed upon the round head of Tell Arar, to look over their plain, whose rimmed flatness the early sun speciously relieved, by yet throwing more shadow than light. Our soldiers could see Deraa, Mezerib and Ghazale, the three key-stations, with their naked eyes.

I was seeing farther than this: northward to Damascus, the Turkish base, their only link with Constantinople and Germany, now cut off: southward to Amman and Maan and Medina, all cut off: westward to Liman von Sandars isolated in Nazareth: to Nablus: to the Jordan Valley. To-day was September the seventeenth, the promised day, forty-eight hours before Allenby would throw forward his full power. In forty-eight hours the Turks might decide to change their dispositions to meet our new danger; but they could not change them before Allenby struck. Bartholomew had said, "Tell me if he will be in his Auja line the day before we start, and I will tell you if we will win." Well, he was; so we would win. The question was by how much.

I wanted the whole line destroyed in a moment: but things seemed to have stopped. The army had done its share: Nuri Said was posting machine-guns about the Arar mound to keep back any sortie from Deraa: but why was there no demolition going on? I rushed down, to find Peake's Egyptians making breakfast. It was like Drake's game of bowls, and I fell dumb with admiration.

However, in an hour they were mustered for their rhythmic demolition by numbers; and already the French gunners, who also carried guncotton, had descended with intention upon the near bridge. They were not very good, but at the second try did it some hurt.

From the head of Tell Arar, before the mirage had begun to dance, we examined Deraa carefully through my strong glass, wanting to

see what the Turks had in store for us this day. The first discovery was
disturbing. Their aerodrome was alive with gangs pulling machine
after machine into the open. I could count eight or nine lined up. Otherwise things were as we expected. Some few infantry were doubling
out into the defence-position, and their guns were being fired towards
us: but we were four miles off. Locomotives were getting up steam:
but the trains were unarmoured. Behind us, towards Damascus, the
country lay still as a map. From Mezerib on our right there was no
movement. We held the initiative.

Our hope was to fire six hundred charges, tulip fashion, putting
out of commission six kilometres of rail. Tulips had been invented
by Peake and myself for this occasion. Thirty ounces of guncotton
were planted beneath the centre of the central sleeper of each ten-
metre section of the track. The sleepers were steel, and their box-shape
left an air-chamber which the gas expansion filled, to blow the middle of the sleeper upward. If the charge was properly laid, the metal
did not snap, but humped itself, bud-like, two feet in the air. The
lift of it pulled the rails three inches up; the drag of it pulled them
six inches together; and, as the chairs gripped the bottom flanges,
warped them inward seriously. The triple distortion put them beyond
repair. Three or five sleepers would be likewise ruined, and a trench
driven across the earthwork: all this with one charge, fired by a fuse
so short that the first, blowing off while the third was being lighted, cast its debris safely overhead.

Six hundred such charges would take the Turks a fair week to
mend. This would be a generous reading of Allenby's "three men
and a boy with pistols." I turned to go back to the troops, and at
that moment two things happened. Peake fired his first charge, like
a poplar-tree of black smoke, with a low following report; and the
first Turkish machine got up and came for us. Nuri Said and I fitted admirably under an outcrop of rock, fissured into deep natural
trenches, on the hill's southern face. There we waited coolly for the
bomb: but it was only a reconnaissance machine, a Pfalz, which
studied us, and returned to Deraa with its news.

Bad news it must have been, for three two-seaters, and four scouts and an old yellow-bellied Albatross got up in quick succession, and circled over us, dropping bombs, or diving at us with machine-gun fire. Nuri put his Hotchkiss gunners in the rock cracks, and rattled back at them. Pisani cocked up his four mountain guns, and let fly some optimistic shrapnel. This disturbed the enemy, who circled off, and came back much higher. Their aim became uncertain.

We scattered out the troops and camels, while the irregulars scattered themselves. To open into the thinnest target was our only hope of safety, as the plain had not overhead cover for a rabbit; and our hearts misgave us when we saw what thousands of men we had, dotted out below. It was strange to stand on the hill-top looking at these two rolling square miles, liberally spread with men and animals, and bursting out irregularly with lazy silent bulbs of smoke where bombs dropped (seemingly quite apart from their thunder) or with sprays of dust where machine-gun groups lashed down.

Things looked and sounded hot, but the Egyptians went on working as methodically as they had eaten. Four parties dug in tulips, while Peake and one of his officers lit each series as it was laid. The two slabs of guncotton in a tulip-charge were not enough to make a showy explosion, and the aeroplanes seemed not to see what was going on: at least they did not wash them particularly with bombs; and as the demolition proceeded, the party drew gradually out of the danger-area into the quiet landscape to the north. We traced their progress by the degradation of the telegraph. In virgin parts its poles stood trimly, drilled by the taut wire: but behind Peake they leaned and tottered anyhow, or fell.

Nuri Said, Joyce and myself met in council, and pondered how to get at the Yarmuk section of the Palestine line to top off our cutting of the Damascus and Hejaz Railways. In view of the reported opposition there we must take nearly all our men, which seemed hardly wise under such constant air observation. For one thing, the bombs might hurt us badly on the march across the open plain; and, for another Peake's demolition party would be at the mercy of

Deraa if the Turks plucked up the courage to sally. For the moment they were fearful: but time might make them brave.

While we hesitated, things were marvellously solved. Junor, the pilot of the B.E. 12 machine, now alone at Azrak, had heard from the disabled Murphy of the enemy machines about Deraa, and in his own mind decided to take the Bristol Fighter's place, and carry out the air programme. So when things were at their thickest with us he suddenly sailed into the circus.

We watched with mixed feelings, for his hopelessly old-fashioned machine made him cold meat for any one of the enemy scouts or two-seaters: but at first he astonished them, as he rattled in with his two guns. They scattered for a careful look at this unexpected opponent. He flew westward across the line, and they went after in pursuit, with that amiable weakness of aircraft for a hostile machine, however important the ground target.

We were left in perfect peace. Nuri caught at the lull to collect three hundred and fifty regulars, with two of Pisani's guns; and hurried them over the saddle behind Tell Arar, on the first stage of their march to Mezerib. If the aeroplanes gave us a half-hour's law they would probably notice neither the lessened numbers by the mound, nor the scattered groups making along every slope and hollow across the stubble westward. This cultivated land had a quilt-work appearance from the air: also the ground was tall with maize stalks, and thistles grew saddle-high about it in great fields.

We sent the peasantry after the soldiers, and half an hour later I was calling up my bodyguard that we might get to Mezerib before the others, when again we heard the drone of engines; and, to our astonishment, Junor reappeared, still alive, though attended on three sides by enemy machines, spitting bullets. He was twisting and slipping splendidly, firing back. Their very numbers hindered them, but of course the affair could have only one ending.

In the faint hope that he might get down intact we rushed towards the railway where was a strip of ground, not too boulder-strewn. Every one helped to clear it at speed, while Junor was being driven lower. He threw us a message to say his petrol was finished. We worked feverishly for five minutes, and then put out a landing signal. He dived at it, but as he did so the wind flawed and blew across at a sharp angle. The cleared strip was too little in any case. He took ground beautifully, but the wind puffed across once more. His undercarriage went, and the plane turned over in the rough.

We rushed up to rescue, but Junor was out, with no more hurt than a cut on the chin. He took off his Lewis gun, and the Vickers, and the drums of tracer ammunition for them. We threw everything into Young's Ford, and fled, as one of the Turkish two-seaters dived viciously and dropped a bomb by the wreck.

Junor five minutes later was asking for another job. Joyce gave him a Ford for himself, and he ran boldly down the line till near Deraa, and blew a gap in the rails there, before the Turks saw him. They found such zeal excessive, and opened on him with their guns: but he rattled away again in his Ford, unhurt for the third time.

My bodyguard waited in two long lines on the hillside. Joyce was staying at Tell Arar as covering force, with a hundred of Nuri Said's men, the Rualla, the Ghurkas and the cars; while we slipped across to break the Palestine Railway. My party would look like Beduins, so I determined to move openly to Mezerib by the quickest course, for we were very late. Unfortunately we drew enemy attention. An aeroplane crawled over us, dropping bombs: one, two, three, misses: the fourth into our midst. Two of my men went down. Their camels, in bleeding masses, struggled on the ground. The men had not a scratch, and leaped up behind two of their friends.

We opened out and rode greatly, knowing the ground by heart; checking only to tell the young peasants we met that the work was now at Mezerib. The field paths were full of these fellows, pouring out afoot from every village to help us. They were very willing: but our eyes had rested so long on the brown leanness of desert men that these gay village lads with their flushed faces, clustering hair, and plump pale arms and legs seemed like girls. They had kilted up their gowns above the knee for fast work: and the more active raced beside us through the fields, chaffing back my veterans.

As we reached Mezerib, Durzi ibn Dughmi met us, with news that Nuri Said's soldiers were only two miles back. We watered our camels, and drank deeply ourselves, for it had been a long, hot day and was not ended. Then from behind the old fort we looked over the lake, and saw movement in the French railway station.

Some of the white-legged fellows told us that the Turks held it in force. However, the approaches were too tempting. Abdulla led our charge; for my days of adventure were ended, with the sluggard excuse that my skin must be kept for a justifying emergency. Otherwise, I wanted to enter Damascus. This job was too easy. Abdulla found grain: also flour; and some little booty of weapons, horses, ornaments. These excited my hangers-on. New adherents came running across the grass, like flies to honey. Tallal arrived at his constant gallop. We passed the stream, and walked together up the far bank knee-deep in weeds till we saw the Turkish station three hundred yards in front. We might capture this before attacking the great bridge below Tell el Shehab. Tallal advanced carelessly. Turks showed themselves to right and left. "It's all right," said he, "I know the stationmaster": but when we were two hundred yards away, twenty rifles fired a shocking volley at us. We dropped unhurt into the weeds (nearly all of them thistles), and crawled gingerly back, Tallal swearing.

My men heard him, or the shots, and came streaming up from the river: but we returned them, fearing a machine-gun in the station buildings. Nuri Said was due. He arrived with Nasir, and we considered the business. Nuri pointed out that delay at Mezerib might lose us the bridge, a greater objective. I agreed, but thought this bird in hand might suffice, since Peake's main line demolition would stand for a week, and the week's end bring a new situation.

So Pisani unfolded his willing guns and smashed in a few rounds of point-blank high explosive. Under their cover, with our twenty machine-guns making a roof overhead, Nuri walked forward, gloved and sworded, to receive the surrender of the forty soldiers left alive.

EL SAKHARA

Upon this most rich station hundreds of Haurani peasants hurled themselves in frenzy, plundering. Men, women and children fought like dogs over every object. Doors and windows, door-frames and window-frames, even steps of the stairs, were carried off. One hopeful blew in the safe and found postage stamps inside. Others smashed open the long range of wagons in the siding, to find all manner of goods. Tons were carried off. Yet more were strewn in wreckage on the ground.

Young and I cut the telegraph, here an important network of trunk and local lines, indeed the Palestine army's main link with their homeland. It was pleasant to imagine Liman von Sandars' fresh curse, in Nazareth, as each severed wire tanged back from the clippers. We did them slowly, with ceremony, to draw out the indignation. The Turks' hopeless lack of initiative made their army a "directed" one, so that by destroying the telegraphs we went far towards turning them into a leaderless mob. After the telegraph we blew in the points, and planted tulips: not very many, but enough to annoy. While we worked a light engine came down the line from Deraa on patrol. The bang and dust clouds of our tulips perturbed it. It withdrew discreetly. Later an aeroplane visited us.

Among the captured rolling-stock, on platform trucks, were two lorries crammed with delicacies for some German canteen. The Arabs, distrusting tins and bottles, had spoiled nearly everything: but we got some soups and meat, and later Nuri Said gave us bottled asparagus. He had found an Arab prizing open the case and had cried "pigs' bones" at him in horror when the contents came to light. The peasant spat and dropped it, and Nuri quickly stuffed all he could into his saddle-bags.

The lorries had huge petrol tanks. Beyond them were some trucks of firewood. We set the whole afire at sunset, when the plundering was finished, and the troops and tribesmen had fallen back to the soft grass by the outlet from the lake.

The splendid blaze spreading along the line of wagons illuminated our evening meal. The wood burned with a solid glare, and the fiery tongues and bursts of the petrol went towering up, higher than the water-tanks. We let the men make bread and sup and rest, before a night attempt on the Shehab bridge, which lay three miles to the westward. We had meant to attack at dark, but the wish for food stopped us, and then we had swarms of visitors, for our beacon-light advertised us over half Hauran.

Visitors were our eyes, and had to be welcomed. My business was to see every one with news, and let him talk himself out to me, afterwards arranging and combining the truth of these points into a complete picture in my mind. Complete, because it gave me certainty of judgment: but it was not conscious nor logical, for my informants were so many that they informed me to distraction, and my single mind bent under all its claims.

Men came pouring down from the north on horse, on camel, and on foot, hundreds and hundreds of them in a terrible grandeur of enthusiasm, thinking this was the final occupation of the country, and that Nasir would seal his victory by taking Deraa in the night. Even the magistrates of Deraa came to open us their town. By acceding we should hold the water supply of the railway station, which must inevitably yield: yet later, if the ruin of the Turkish army came but slowly, we might be forced out again, and lose the plainsmen between Deraa and Damascus, in whose hands our final victory lay. A nice calculation, if hardly a fresh one, but on the whole the arguments were still against taking Deraa. Again we had to put off our friends with excuses within their comprehension.

Slow work; and when at last we were ready a new visitor appeared, the boy-chief of Tell el Shehab. His village was the key to the bridge. He described the position; the large guard; how it was placed. Obviously the problem was harder than we had believed, if his tale was true. We doubted it, for his just-dead father had been hostile, and the son sounded too suddenly devoted to our cause. However, he finished by suggesting that he return after an hour with the officer commanding the garrison, a friend of his. We sent him off to bring his Turk, telling our waiting men to lie down for another brief rest.

Soon the boy was back with a captain, an Armenian, anxious to harm his government in any way he could. Also he was very nervous.

We had hard work to assure him of our enlightenment. His subalterns, he said, were loyal Turks, and some of the non-commissioned officers. He proposed we move close to the village, and lie there secretly, while three or four of our lustiest men hid in his room. He would call his subordinates one by one to see him; and, as each entered, our ambush might pinion him.

This sounded in the proper descent from books of adventure, and we agreed enthusiastically. It was nine at night. At eleven precisely we would line up round the village and wait for the Sheikh to show our strong men to the Commandant's house. The two conspirators departed, content, while we woke up our army, asleep with the sleep of exhaustion beside their loaded camels. It was pitchy dark.

My bodyguard prepared bridge-cutting charges of gelatine. I filled my pockets with detonators. Nasir sent men to each section of the Camel Corps to tell them of the coming adventure, that they might work themselves up to the height of it; and to ensure their mounting quietly, without the disaster of a roaring camel. They played up. In a long double line our force crept down a winding path beside an irrigation ditch, on the crest of the dividing ridge. If there was treachery before us, this bare road would be a death-trap, without issue to right or left, narrow, tortuous, and slippery with the ditch-water. So Nasir and I went first with our men, their trained ears attentive to every sound, their eyes keeping constant guard. In front of us was the waterfall, whose burdening roar had given its character to that unforgettable night with Ali ibn el Hussein when we had attempted this bridge from the other wall of the ravine. Only to-night we were nearer, so that the noise flooded up oppressively and filled our ears.

We crept very slowly and carefully now, soundless on our bare feet, while behind us the heavier soldiery snaked along, holding their breath. They also were soundless, for camels moved always stilly at night, and we had packed the equipment not to tap, the saddles not to creak. Their quietness made the dark darker, and

deepened the menace of those whispering valleys either side. Waves
of dank air from the river met us, chilly in our faces; and then Rahail
came down swiftly from the left and caught my arm, pointing to a
slow column of white smoke rising from the valley.

We ran to the edge of the descent, and peered over: but the depth
was grey with mist risen off the water, and we saw only dimness and
this pale vapour spiring from the level fog bank. Somewhere down
there was the railway, and we stopped the march, afraid lest this be
the suspected trap. Three of us went foot by foot down the slippery
hill-side till we could hear voices. Then suddenly the smoke broke
and shifted, with the panting of an opened throttle, and afterwards
the squealing of brakes as an engine came again to a standstill. There
must be a long train waiting beneath; reassured, we marched again
to the very spur below the village.

We extended in line across its neck, and waited five minutes,
ten minutes. They passed slowly. The murk night before moonrise
was hushing in its solidity, and would have compelled patience on
our restless fellows, without the added warnings of the dogs, and
the intermittent ringing challenge of sentries about the bridge. At
length we let the men slip quietly from their camels to the ground,
and sat wondering at the delay, and the Turk's watchfulness, and
the meaning of that silent train standing below us in the valley. Our
woollen cloaks got stiff and heavy with the mist, and we shivered.

After a long while a lighter speck came through the dark. It was
the boy sheikh, holding his brown cloak open to show us his white
shirt like a flag. He whispered that his plan had failed. A train (this
one in the ravine) had just arrived with a German colonel and the
German and Turk reserves from Afuleh, sent up by Liman von
Sandars, to rescue panic-stricken Deraa.

They had put the little Armenian under arrest for being absent
from his post. There were machine-guns galore, and sentries patrolling
the approaches with ceaseless energy. In fact, there was a strong
picket on the path, not a hundred yards from where we sat: the odd-
ity of our joint state made me laugh, though quietly.

Nuri Said offered to take the place by main force. We had bombs enough, and pistol flares; numbers and preparedness would be on our side. It was a fair chance: but I was at the game of reckoning the value of the objective in terms of life, and as usual finding it too dear. Of course most things done in war were too dear, and we should have followed good example by going in and going through with it. But I was secretly and disclaimedly proud of the planning of our campaigns: so I told Nuri that I voted against it. We had to-day twice cut the Damascus-Palestine railway; and the bringing here of the Afuleh garrison was a third benefit to Allenby. Our bond had been most heavily honoured.

Nuri, after a moment's thought agreed. We said good-night to the lad who had honestly tried to do so much for us. We passed down the lines, whispering to each man to lead back in silence. Then we sat in a group with our rifles (mine Enver's gold inscribed Lee-Enfield trophy from the Dardanelles, given by him to Feisal years ago) waiting till our men should be beyond the danger zone.

Oddly enough this was the hardest moment of the night. Now the work was over we could scarcely resist the temptation to rouse the spoil-sport Germans out. It would have been so easy to have cracked off a Very light into their bivouac; and the solemn men would have turned out in ludicrous hurry, and shot hard into the bare, misty hill-side silent at their feet. The identical notion came independently to Nasir, Nuri Said, and myself. We blurted it out together, and each promptly felt ashamed that the others had been as childish. By mutual cautions we managed to keep our respectability.

CHAPTER XXXII

FIGHTING UP AND DOWN

BEFORE DAWN Pisani's other guns and the rest of Nuri Said's troops arrived from Tell Arar. We had written to Joyce that on the morrow we would return southward, by Nisib, to complete the circle of Deraa. I suggested that he move straight back to Umtaiye and there wait for us: for it, with its abundant water, splendid pasture, and equidistance from Deraa and Jebel Druse and the Rualla Desert, seemed an ideal place in which we might rally and wait news of Allenby's fortune. By holding Umtaiye we as good as cut off the Turkish fourth army of beyond Jordan (our special bird) from Damascus: and were in place quickly to renew our main-line demolitions, whenever the enemy had nearly set them right.

Reluctantly we pulled ourselves together for another day of effort, called up the army and moved in a huge straggle through Mezerib station. Our fires had burned out, and the place stood dishevelled. Young and myself leisurely laid tulips, while the troops melted into broken ground towards Remthe, to be out of sight of both Deraa and Shehab. Turkish aeroplanes were humming overhead, looking for us, so we sent our peasants back through Mezerib for their villages. Consequently, the airmen reported that we were very numerous, possibly eight or nine thousand strong, and that our centrifugal movements seemed to be directed towards every direction at once.

To increase their wonderment, the French gunners' long-fused charge blew up the water-tower at Mezerib loudly, hours after we had passed. The Germans were marching out of Shehab, for Deraa, at the moment, and the inexplicable shock sent these humourless ones back there on guard till late afternoon.

Meanwhile we were far away, plodding steadily towards Nisib, whose hill-top we reached about four in the afternoon. We gave the mounted infantry a short rest, while we moved our gunners and machine-guns to the crest of the first ridge, from which the ground fell away hollowly to the Railway Station.

We posted the guns there in shelter, and asked them to open deliberately upon the station buildings at two thousand yards. Pisani's sections worked in emulation so that, before long, ragged holes appeared in the roofs and sheds. At the same time we pushed our machine-gunners forward on the left, to fire long bursts against the trenches, which returned a hot obstinate fire. However, our troops had natural shelter and the advantage of the afternoon sun behind their backs. So we suffered no hurt. Nor did the enemy. Of course, all this was just a game, and the capture of the station not in our plan. Our real objective was the great bridge north of the village. The ridge below our feet curved out in a long horn to this work, serving as one bank of the valley which it was built to span. The village stood on the other bank. The Turks held the bridge by means of a small redoubt, and maintained touch with it by riflemen posted in the village under cover of its walls.

We turned two of Pisani's guns and six machine-guns on the small but deeply-dug bridge-post, hoping to force its defenders out. Five machine-guns directed their fire on the village. In fifteen minutes its elders were out with us, very much perturbed. Nuri put, as the condition of cease-fire, their instant ejectment of the Turks from the houses. They promised. So station and bridge were divided.

We redoubled against these. The firing from the four wings became violent, thanks to our twenty-five machine-guns, the Turks also being plentifully supplied. At last we put all four of Pisani's guns against the redoubt; and, after a few salvos, thought we saw its guard slipping from their battered trenches through the bridge into cover of the railway embankment.

This embankment was twenty feet high. If the bridge-guard chose to defend their bridge through its arches they would be in a costly position. However, we reckoned that the attraction of their fellows in the station would draw them away. I told off the half of my bodyguard, carrying explosives, to move along the machine-gun crest till within a stone's throw of the redoubt.

It was a noble evening, yellow, mild and indescribably peaceful; a foil to our incessant cannonade. The declining light shone down the angle of the ridges, its soft rays modelling them and their least contour in a delicate complexity of planes. Then the sun sank another second, and the surface became shadow, out of which for a moment there rose, starkly, the innumerable flints strewing it; each western (reflecting) facet tipped like a black diamond with flame.

The redoubt was indeed abandoned: so we dismounted, and signalled Nuri to cease fire. In the silence we crept discreetly through the bridge-arches, and found them also evacuated.

Hurriedly we piled guncotton against the piers, which were about five feet thick and twenty-five feet high; a good bridge, my seventy-ninth, and strategically most critical, since we were going to live opposite it at Umtaiye until Allenby came forward and relieved us. So I had determined to leave not a stone of it in place.

Nuri meanwhile was hurrying the infantry, gunners and machine-gunners down in the thickening night, towards the line, with orders to get a mile beyond into the desert, form up into column, and wait.

Yet the passing of so many camels over the track must take tediously long. We sat and chafed under the bridge, matches in hand, to light at once (despite the troops) if there was an alarm. Fortunately everything went well, and after an hour Nuri gave me my signal. Half a minute later (my preference for six-inch fuses!) just as I tumbled into the Turkish redoubt, the eight hundred pounds of stuff exploded in one burst, and the black air became sibilant with flying stones. The explosion was numbing from my twenty yards, and must have been heard half-way to Damascus.

Nuri, in great distress, sought me out. He had given the "all clear" signal before learning that one company of mounted infantry was missing. Fortunately my guards were aching for service. Talal el Hareidhin took them with him up the hills, while Nuri and I stood by the yawning pit which had been the bridge, and flashed an electric torch, to give them a fixed point for their return.

Mahmud came back in half an hour triumphantly leading the lost unit. We fired shots to recall the other searchers, and then rode two or three miles into the open towards Umtaiye. The going became very broken, over moraines of slipping dolerite: so we gladly called a halt, and lay down in our ranks for an earned sleep.

However, it seemed that Nasir and I were to lose the habit of sleeping. Our noise at Nisib had proclaimed us as widely as the flames of Mezerib. Hardly were we still when visitors came streaming in from three sides to discuss the latest events. It was being rumoured that we were raiding, and not occupying; that later we would run away, as had the British from Salt, leaving our local friends to pay the bills.

The night, for hour after hour, was broken by these newcomers challenging round our bivouacs, crying their way to us like lost souls; and, peasant-fashion, slobbering over our hands with protestations that we were their highest lords and they our deepest servants. Perhaps the reception of them fell short of our usual standard; but, in revenge, they were applying the torture of keeping us awake, uneasily awake. We had been at strain for three days and nights; thinking, ordering and executing; and now, on our road to rest, it was bitter to play away this fourth night also, at the old lack-lustre, dubious game of making friends.

And their shaken *morale* impressed us worse and worse, till Nasir drew me aside and whispered that clearly there existed a focus of discontent in some centre near. I loosed out my peasant bodyguards to mix with the villagers and find the truth; and from their reports it seemed that the cause of distrust lay in the first settlement, at Taiyibe, which had been shaken by the return of Joyce's armoured cars yesterday, by some chance incidents, and by a just fear that they were the spot most exposed in our retreat.

I called Aziz, and we rode straight to Taiyibe, over rough stretches of lava, trackless, and piled across with walls of broken stone. In the head-man's hut sat the conclave which infected our visitors. They were debating whom to send to implore mercy from the Turks; when we walked in unannounced. Our single coming abashed them, in its assumption of supreme security. We talked irrelevantly an hour, of crops and farmyard prices, and drank some coffee: then rose to go. Behind us the babble broke out again; but now their inconstant spirits had veered to what seemed our stronger wind, and they sent no word to the enemy; though next day they were bombed and shelled for such stubborn complicity with us.

We got back before dawn, and stretched out to sleep: when there came a loud boom from the railway, and a shell shattered beyond our sleeping host. The Turks had sent down an armoured train mounting a field gun. By myself I would have chanced its aim, for my sleep had been just long enough to make me rage for more: but the army had slept six hours and was moving.

We hurried across horrible going. An aeroplane came over, and circled round to help the gunners. Shells began to keep accurate pace with our line of march. We doubled our speed, and broke into a ragged procession of very open order. The directing aeroplane faltered suddenly, swerved aside towards the line, and seemed to land. The gun put in one more lucky shot, which killed two camels; but for the rest it lost accuracy, and after about fifty shots we drew out of range. It began to punish Taiyibe.

Joyce, at Umtaiye, had been roused by the shooting, and came out to welcome us. Behind his tall figure the ruins were crested by a motley band, samples from every village and tribe in the Hauran, come to do homage and offer at least lip-service. To Nasir's tired disgust I left these to him, while I went off with Joyce and Winterton, telling them of the landed aeroplane, and suggesting that an armoured car beat it up at home. Just then two more enemy machines appeared and landed in about the same place.

However, breakfast, our first for some while, was getting ready. So we sat down and Joyce related how the men of Taiyibe had fired at him as he passed by, presumably to show their opinion of strangers who stirred up a hornet's nest of Turks, and then hopped it!

Breakfast ended. We called for a volunteer car to investigate the enemy aerodrome. Everybody came forward with a silent goodwill and readiness which caught me by the throat. Finally Joyce chose two cars—one for Junor and one for me—and we drove for five miles to the valley in whose mouth the planes had seemed to land.

We silenced the cars and crept down its course. When about two thousand yards from the railway, it bent round into a flat meadow, by whose further side stood three machines. This was magnificent, and we leaped forward, to meet a deep ditch with straight banks of cracking earth, quite impassable.

We raced frantically along it, by a diagonal route, till we were within twelve hundred yards. As we stopped two of the aeroplanes started. We opened fire, searching the range by dust spurts, but already they had run their distance and were off, swaying and clattering up across the sky over our heads.

The third engine was sulky. Its pilot and observer savagely pulled the propeller round, while we ranged nearer. Finally they leaped into the railway ditch as we put bullet after bullet into the fuselage till it danced under the rain. We fired fifteen hundred bullets at our target (they burned it in the afternoon) and then turned home.

Unfortunately the two escaped machines had had time to go to Deraa, and return, feeling spiteful. One was not clever and dropped his four bombs from a height, missing us widely. The other swooped low, placing one bomb each time with the utmost care. We crept on defencelessly, slowly, among the stones, feeling like sardines in a doomed tin, as the bombs fell closer. One sent a shower of small stuff through the driving slit of the car, but only cut our knuckles. One tore off a front tyre and nearly lurched the car over.

Of all danger give me the solitary sort. However, we reached Umtaiye well and reported success to Joyce. We had proved to the Turks that that aerodrome was not fit for use; and Deraa lay equally open to car attack. Later I lay in the shadow of a car and slept; all the Arabs in the desert, and the Turkish aeroplanes which came and bombed us, having no effect upon my peace. In the clash of events men became feverishly tireless: but to-day we had finished our first round fortunately; and it was necessary that I rest, to clear my mind about our next moves. As usual when I lay down I dropped asleep, and slept till afternoon.

CHAPTER XXXIII

ROYAL AIR FORCE HELP

STRATEGICALLY, OUR business was to hold on to Umtaiye, which gave us command at will of Deraa's three railways. If we held it another week we should strangle the Turkish armies, however little Allenby did. Yet tactically Umtaiye was a dangerous place. An inferior force composed exclusively of regulars, without a guerilla screen, could not safely hold it: yet to that we should shortly be reduced, if our air helplessness continued patent.

The Turks had at least nine machines. We were camped twelve miles from their aerodrome, in the open desert, about the only possible water-supply, with great herds of camels and many horses necessarily grazing round us. The Turks' beginning of bombing had been enough to disquiet the irregulars who were our eyes and ears. Soon they would break up and go home, and our usefulness be ended: Taiyibe, too, that first village which covered us from Deraa— it lay defenceless and quivering under repeated attack. If we were to remain in Umtaiye, Taiyibe must be content with us.

Clearly our first duty was to get air reinforcement from Allenby, who had arranged to send a news machine to Azrak on the day after to-morrow. I judged it would be profitable for me to go across and talk with him. I could be back on the twenty-second. Umtaiye would hold out so long, for we might always fox the aeroplanes a while by moving to Um el Surab, the next Roman village.

Whether at Umtaiye or Um el Surab, to be safe we must keep the initiative. The Deraa side was temporarily closed by the suspicion of the peasants: there remained the Hejaz line. The bridge at Kilo. 149 was nearly mended. We must smash it again, and smash another to the south, to deny the repair trains access to it. An effort by Winterton yesterday showed that the first was a matter for troops and guns. The second was objective for a raid.

So I suggested to Joyce that the Egyptians and Ghurkas return to Akaba; proposing further that he lend me an armoured car, to go down with them to the railway, their first stage, and do what could be done. We went up to Nasir and Nuri Said, and told them I would be back on the twenty-second with fighting machines, to deliver us from air scouts and bombing. Meanwhile we would salve Taiyibe with money for the Turkish damage, and Joyce would make landing grounds, here and at Um el Surab, against my return with our air reinforcements.

The demolition of that night was a fantastic muddle. We moved at sunset to an open valley, three easy miles from the railway. Trouble might threaten from Mafrak station. My armoured car, with Junor attendant in his Ford, would guard that side against hostile advance. The Egyptians would move direct to the line, and fire their charges.

My guiding fell through. We wandered for three hours in a maze of valleys, not able to find the railway, nor the Egyptians, nor our starting-point. At last we saw a light and drove for it, to find ourselves in front of Mafrak. We turned back to get into place, and heard the clank of an engine running northward out of the station. We chased its intermittent flame, hoping to catch it between us and the broken bridge: but before we overtook it there came flashes and explosions far up, as Peake fired his thirty charges.

Some mounted men galloped headlong past us, southward. We fired at them, and then the patrolling train returned, backing at its best speed from Peake's danger. We ran alongside, and opened on the trucks with our Vickers, while Junor sent a green shower of tracer bullets from his Lewis across the dark. Above our shooting and the noise of the engine we heard the Turks howling with terror of this luminous attack. They fired back raggedly, but as they did so the big car suddenly sneezed and stood still. A bullet had pierced the unarmoured end of the petrol tank, the only unarmoured spot of all our team of cars. It took us an hour to plug the leak.

Then we drove along the silent line to the twisted rails and gaping culverts, but could not find our friends. So we drew a mile back, and there at last I had my sleep out, three perfect hours of it before the dawn. I awoke fresh, and recognized our place. Probably it was only the fifth sleepless night which had made my wits woolly. We pushed forward, passing the Egyptians with the Ghurkas, and reached Azrak in the early afternoon. There were Feisal and Nuri Shaalan, eager to hear our news. We explained particularly; and then I went over to Marshall, in the temporary hospital. He had all our badly-wounded in his quiet care: but they were fewer than he had expected, so he was able to spare me a stretcher for my bed.

At dawn Joyce unexpectedly arrived. He had made up his mind that in this lull it was his duty to go down to Aba el Lissan to help Zeid and Jaafar before Maan, and to press forward Hornby among the Beni Sakhr. Then the plane from Palestine arrived, and we heard the amazing first chronicle of Allenby's victory. He had smashed and burst through and driven the Turks inconceivably. The face of our war was changed, and we gave hurried word of it to Feisal, with counsels of the general revolt to take profit of the situation. An hour later I was safely in Palestine.

From Ramleh the Air Force gave me a car up to Headquarters; and there I found the great man unmoved, except for the light in his eye as Bols bustled in every fifteen minutes, with news of some wider success. Allenby had been so sure, before he started, that to him the result was almost boredom: but no general, however scientific, could see his intricate plan carried out over an enormous

From a pencil sketch by Eric Kennington

STRATA

field in every particular with complete success, and not know an inward gladness: especially when he felt it (as he must have felt it) a reward of the breadth and judgment which made him conceive such unorthodox movements; and break up the proper book of his administrative services to suit them; and support them by every moral and material asset, military or political, within his grasp.

He sketched to me his next intentions. Historic Palestine was his, and the broken Turks, in the hills, expected a slackening of the pursuit. Not at all! Bartholomew and Evans were prepared to provision three more thrusts: one across Jordan to Amman, to be done by Chaytor's New Zealanders; one across Jordan to Deraa, to be done by Barrow and his Indians; one across Jordan to Kuneitra, to be done by Chauvel's Australians. Chaytor would rest at Amman; Barrow and Chauvel on attaining the first objectives would converge on Damascus. We were to assist the three: and I was not to carry out my saucy threat to take Damascus, till we were all together.

I explained our prospects, and how everything was being wrecked by air-impotence. He pressed a bell and in a few minutes Salmond and Borton were conferring with us. Their machines had taken an indispensable part in Allenby's scheme: (the perfection of this man who could use infantry and cavalry, artillery and Air Force, Navy and armoured cars, deceptions and irregulars, each in its best fashion!): and had fulfilled it. There were no more Turks in the sky—except on our side, as I hurriedly interpolated. So much the better, said Salmond; they would send two Bristol fighters over to Umtaiye to sit with us while we needed them. Had we spares? Petrol? Not a drop? How was it to be got there? Only by air? An air-contained fighting unit? Unheard of!

However, Salmond and Borton were men avid of novelty. They worked out loads for D.H.9. and Handley-Page, while Allenby sat by, listening and smiling, sure it would be done. The co-operation of the air with his unfolding scheme had been so ready and elastic, the liaison so complete and informed and quick. It was the R.A.F. which had converted the Turkish retreat into rout, which had abolished their telephone and telegraph connections, had blocked their lorry-columns, scattered their infantry units. Salmond and Borton shared, so to speak, not merely in Allenby's tactical work, but in his very strategy. Tul Keram, Messudieh, Jenin and Afuleh in turn were air-contained so drastically that their use was denied the enemy for hours before any of our ground troops drew near.

But the climax of air attack, and the holocaust of the miserable Turks, fell in the valley by which Esdraelon drained to the Jordan by Beisan. The modern motor road, the only way of escape for the Turkish divisions, was scalloped between cliff and precipice in a murderous defile. For four hours our aeroplanes replaced one another in series above the doomed columns: nine tons of small bombs or grenades and fifty thousand rounds of S.A.A. were rained upon them. When the smoke had cleared it was seen that the organization of the enemy had melted away. They were a dispersed horde of trembling individuals, hiding for their lives in every fold of the vast hills. Nor did their commanders ever rally them again. When our cavalry entered the silent valley next day they could count ninety guns, fifty lorries, nearly a thousand carts abandoned with all their belongings. The R.A.F. lost four killed. The Turks lost a corps.

The Air chiefs turned on me and asked if our landing grounds were good enough for a Handley-Page with full load. I had seen the big machine once in its shed, but unhesitatingly said "Yes," though they had better send an expert over with me in the Bristols to-morrow and make sure. He might be back by noon, and the Handley come at three o'clock. Salmond got up: "That's all right, Sir, we'll do the necessary." I went out and breakfasted.

Allenby's headquarters was a perfect place: a cool, airy, white-washed house, proofed against flies, and made musical by the moving of the wind in the trees outside. I felt immoral, enjoying white table-cloths, and coffee, and soldier servants, while our people at Umtaiye lay like lizards among the stones, eating unleavened bread, and waiting for the next plane to bomb them. I felt restless as the dusty sunlight which splashed a diaper over the paths, through chinks in the leaves; because, after a long spell of the restrained desert, flowers and grass seemed to fidget, and the everywhere-burgeoning green of tilth became vulgar, in its fecundity.

However, Clayton and Deedes and Dawnay were friendliness itself, and also the Air Force staff; while the good cheer and conscious strength of the Commander-in-Chief was a bath of comfort to a weary person after long strained days. Bartholomew moved maps about, explaining what they would do. I added to his knowledge of the enemy, for I was his best served intelligence officer: and in return his perspective showed me the victory sure, whatever happened to our strained little stop-block over there. Yet it seemed to me that in the Arab hands lay an option, whether to let this victory be just one more victory, or, by risking themselves once more, to make it final. Not that, so stated, it was a real option: but, when body and spirit were as wearily sick as mine, they almost instinctively sought a plausible avoidance of the way of danger.

Before dawn, on the Australian aerodrome, stood two Bristols and a D.H.9. In one was Ross Smith, my old pilot, who had been picked out to fly the new Handley-Page, the single machine of its class in Egypt, the apple of Salmond's eye. His lending it to fly over the enemy line on so low an errand as baggage carrying, was a measure of the good-will toward us.

We reached Umtaiye in an hour, and saw that the army had gone: so I waved ourselves back to Um el Surab; and there they were, the defensive group of cars, and Arabs hiding from our suspect noise here, there and everywhere; the cute camels dispersed singly over the plain, filling themselves with the wonderful grazing. Young, when he saw our markings, put a landing signal and smoke bombs on the turf which his care and Nuri Said's had swept clear of stones.

Ross Smith anxiously paced the length and breadth of the prepared space, and studied its imperfections: but rejoined us, where the drivers were making breakfast, with a clear face. The ground was O.K. for the Handley-Page. Young told us of repeated bombings yesterday and the day before, which had killed some regulars and some of Pisani's gunners, and tired the life out of every one, so that they moved in the night to Um el Surab. The idiot Turks were still bombing Umtaiye though men went to it only in the neutral noons and nights to draw water.

Also I heard of Winterton's last blowing up of the railway: an amusing night, in which he had met an unknown soldier and explained to him in broken Arabic how well they were getting on. The soldier had thanked God for His mercies, and disappeared in the dark; whence, a moment later, machine-gun fire opened from left and right! Nevertheless Winterton had fired all his charges, and withdrawn in good order without loss. Nasir came to us, and reported this man hurt, and that killed, this clan getting ready, those already joined, but others gone home—all the gossip of the country. The three shining aeroplanes had much restored the Arabs, who lauded the British, and their own bravery and endurance, while I told them the scarce-credible epic of Allenby's success:—Nablus taken, Afuleh taken, Beisan and Semakh and Haifa. My hearers' minds drew after me like flames. Tallal took fire, boasting; while the Rualla shouted for instant march upon Damascus. A shiver of self-assertion and confidence ran across the camp. I determined to bring up Feisal and Nuri Shaalan for the final effort.

Meanwhile it was breakfast time with a smell of sausage in the air. We sat round, very ready: but the watcher on the broken tower yelled, "Aeroplane up," seeing one coming over from Deraa. Our Australians, scrambling wildly to their yet-hot machines, started them in a moment. Ross Smith, with his observer, leaped into one, and climbed like a cat up the sky. After him went Peters, while the third pilot stood beside the D.H.9. and looked hard at me.

I seemed not to understand him. Lewis guns, scarfe mountings, sights, rings which turned, vanes, knobs which rose and fell on swinging parallel bars; to shoot, one aimed with this side of the ring or with that, according to the varied speed and direction of oneself and the enemy. I had been told the theory, could repeat some of it:

but it was in my head, and rules of action were only snares of action till they had run out of the empty head into the hands, by use. No: I was not going up to air-fight, no matter what caste I lost with the pilot. He was an Australian, of a race delighting in additional risks, not an Arab to whose gallery I must play.

He was too respectful to speak: only he looked reproach at me while we watched the battle in the air. There were one enemy two-seater and three scouts. Ross Smith fastened on the big one, and, after five minutes of sharp machine-gun rattle, the German dived suddenly towards the railway line. As it flashed behind the low ridge, there broke out a pennon of smoke, and from its falling place a soft, dark cloud. An "Ah!" came from the Arabs about us. Five minutes later Ross Smith was back, and jumped gaily out of his machine, swearing that the Arab front was the place.

Our sausages were still hot; we ate them, and drank tea (our last English stores, broached for the visitors), but were hardly at the grapes from Jebel Druse when again the watchman tossed up his cloak and screamed, "A plane!" This time Peters won the race, Ross Smith second, with Traill, disconsolate, in reserve: but the shy enemy turned back so soon that Peters did not catch them till near Arar: there he drove down his quarry, fighting. Later, when the wave of war rolled thither, we found the hopeless crash and two charred German bodies.

Ross Smith wished he might stay for ever on this Arab front with an enemy every half-hour; and deeply envied Peters his coming days. However, he must go back for the Handley-Page with petrol, food and spares. The third plane was for Azrak, to get the observer marooned there yesterday; and I went in it so far, to see Feisal.

Time became spacious to those who flew: we were in Azrak thirty hours after leaving it. Ghurkas and Egyptians I turned back to rejoin the army, for new demolitions in the north. Then, with Feisal and Nuri Shaalan, I packed into the green Vauxhall, and off we went for Um el Surab to see the Handley-Page alight.

We ran at speed over the smooth flint or mud-flat, letting the strong car throb itself fully: but luck was hostile. A dispute was reported us, and we had to turn aside to a local Serahin camp. However, we made profit of our loss, by ordering their fighting men to Umtaiye: and we had them send word of victory across the railway, that the roads through the Ajlun hills might be closed to the broken Turkish armies, trying to escape into safety.

Then our car flashed northward again. Twenty miles short of Um el Surab we perceived a single Badawi, running southward all in a flutter, his grey hair and grey beard flying in the wind, and his shirt (tucked up in his belly-cord) puffing out behind him. He altered course to pass near us, and, raising his bony arms, yelled, "The biggest aeroplane in the world," before he flapped on into the south, to spread his great news among the tents.

At Um el Surab the Handley stood majestic on the grass, with the Bristols like tiny fledglings beneath its spread of wings. Round it admired the Arabs, saying, "Indeed and at last they have sent us THE aeroplane, of which these things were foals." Before night rumour of Feisal's resource went over Jebel Druse and the hollow of Hauran, telling people that the balance was weighted on our side.

Borton himself had come over in the machine, to concert help. We talked with him while our men drew from her bomb-racks and fuselage a ton of petrol; oil and spare parts for Bristol fighters; tea and sugar and rations for our men; letters, Reuter telegrams and medicines for us. Then the great machine rose into the early dusk, for Ramleh, with an agreed programme of night bombing against Deraa and Mafrak, to complete that ruin of the railway traffic which our guncotton had begun.

We, for our share, would keep up the guncotton pressure. Allenby had assigned us the Turkish Fourth Army, to harass and contain till Chaytor forced them out of Amman; and afterwards to cut up, on their retreat. This retreat was only an affair of days, and it was as certain as things could be in war that we should raise the plains between us and Damascus next week. So Feisal decided to add to our column Nuri Shaalan's Rualla camel-men from Azrak. It would increase us to about four thousand strong, more than three-fourths irregular;

but reliably so, for Nuri, the hard, silent, cynical old man, held the tribe between his fingers like a tool.

He was that rarity in the desert, a man without sense of argument. He would or would not, and there was no more to it. When others finished talking, he would announce his will in a few flat phrases, and wait calmly for obedience; which came, for he was feared. He was old and wise, which meant tired and disappointed: so old that it was my abiding wonder he should link himself to our enthusiasm.

CHAPTER XXXIV

THE TURKS CRUMPLE UP

I RESTED next day in Nasir's tent, among his peasant visitors; sorting out the too-abundant news furnished by their quick wit and good will. During my rest-day, Nuri Said, with Pisani and two guns, Stirling, Winterton, Young, their armoured cars, and a considerable force, went openly to the railway, cleared it by approved military means, destroyed a kilometre of rail, and burnt the tentative wooden structure with which the Turks were mending the bridge blown up by Joyce and myself before our first attack on Deraa. Nuri Shaalan, in black broadcloth cloak, personally led his Rualla horsemen, galloping with the best of them. Under his eye the tribe showed a valour which drew praise even from Nuri Said.

Nuri's operation of to-day was the Turks' final blow, after which they gave up trying to restore the line between Amman and Deraa. We did not know this, but still had its bogy set over us, and were urgent to put out of action a yet longer stretch. Accordingly, next dawn, Winterton, Jemil and I went out on cars to examine the line south of Mafrak station. We were received with machine-gun fire of a vigour, direction and intensity beyond any of our experience. Later we captured the experts and found they were a German machine-gun unit. For the moment we drew out, puzzled, and went further to a tempting bridge. My plan was to run under it in the car till the vault enabled us to lay the charge against the pier in shelter. So I transferred myself to an armoured car, put sixty pounds of guncotton on the backboard, and told the driver to push in under the arch.

Winterton and Jemil came behind in the supporting car. "It's very hot," groaned Jemil. "It's going to be still hotter where we're going," replied Winterton, as we drew in slowly over indifferent ground with aimless shells falling about. We were picking our way forward, about fifty yards from the bank, with enough machine-gun bullets for a week's fighting rattling off our armour, when some one from behind the line bowled a hand grenade at us.

This new condition made impossible my plan of getting under the bridge. For one thing, a hit on the back of the car would have set off our guncotton and blown us to blazes; for another, the car was helpless against a lobbed grenade. So we drew off, perplexed to understand this defence lavished on a bit of railway, and much interested, indeed amused, at worthy opposition after so long ease. In our imaginations, Check was a short, compact, furious man, darting glances every way from beneath tangled eyebrows, for an end to his troubles; beside him Victory seemed a lanky, white-skinned, rather languid woman. We must try again after dark.

At Um el Surab we found that Nasir wished to fix camp once more at Umtaiye. It was a first stage of our journey to Damascus, so his wish delighted me, and we moved; winning thereby good excuse for doing nothing this night to the line. Instead, we sat and told stories of experience and waited for midnight, when the Handley-Page was to bomb Mafrak station. It came, and hundred-pound bomb after hundred-pound bomb crashed into the packed sidings till they caught fire, and the Turks' shooting stopped.

All night, and next day, the fire among the trucks burned greater and greater. It was proof of the breakdown of the Turks, which the Arabs had been rumouring since yesterday. They said the Fourth Army was streaming up from Amman in a loose mob. The Beni

H. M. KING FEISAL OF IRAK

Hassan, who were cutting off stragglers and weak detachments, compared them to gipsies on the march.

We held a council. Our work against the Fourth Army was finished. Such remnants as avoided out of the hands of the Arabs would reach Deraa as unarmed stragglers. Our new endeavour should be to force the quick evacuation of Deraa, in order to prevent the Turks there reforming the fugitives into a rearguard. So I proposed that we march north, past Tell Arar, and over the railway at dawn to-morrow, into Sheikh Saad village. It lay in familiar country with abundant water, perfect observation, and a secure retreat west or north, or even south-west, if we were directly attacked. It cut off Deraa from Damascus; and Mezerib also.

Tallal seconded me with fervour. Nuri Shaalan gave his nod: Nasir and Nuri Said. So we prepared to strike camp. The armoured cars could not come with us. They had better stay in Azrak, till Deraa fell and we wanted them to help us into Damascus. The Bristol Fighters, likewise, had done their work, clearing the air of Turkish aeroplanes. They might return to Palestine with news of our move to Sheikh Saad.

Off they circled. We, watching their line of flight, noticed a great cloud of dust added to the slow smoke from ruined Mafrak. One machine turned back and dropped a scribble that a large body of hostile cavalry were heading out from the railway towards us.

This was unwelcome news, for we were not in trim for a fight. The cars had gone, the aeroplanes had gone, one company of the mounted infantry had marched, Pisani's mules were packed and drawn up in column. I went off to Nuri Said, standing with Nasir on an ash heap at the head of the hill, and we wavered whether to run or stand. At last it seemed wiser to run, since Sheikh Saad was a more profitable stop-block. So we hurried the regulars away.

Yet things could hardly be left like that. Accordingly Nuri Shaalan and Tallal led the Rualla horse and the Hauran horse back to delay the pursuit. They had an unexpected ally, for our cars, on their way to Azrak, had seen the enemy. After all, the Turks were not cavalry coming to attack us, but deluded elements seeking a shorter way home. We took some hundreds of thirsty prisoners and much transport;

causing such panic that the main rout in the plain cut the traces of their limbers and rode off on the bare horses. The infection of terror spread down the line, and troops miles from any Arab interference threw away all they had, even to their rifles, and made a mad rush towards supposed safety in Deraa.

However, this interruption delayed us; for we could hardly march a khaki-clad body of regular camel corps across Hauran at night without enough local cavalry to go bail to the suspicious villagers that we were not Turks. So late in the afternoon we halted for Tallal and Nasir and Nuri Shaalan to catch up.

They had overshot us in the dark. Our joined forces marched, with a heady breeze in the teeth, northward across the ploughlands' fat, happy villages. Over the harvested fields, whose straw had been rather plucked than reaped, grew thistles, tall as a child, but now yellow and dried and dead. The wind snapped them off at the hollow root, and pitch-polled their branchy tops along the level ground, thistle blowing against thistle and interlocking spines, till in huge balls they careered like run-away haycocks across the fallow.

Arab women, out with their donkeys to fetch water, ran to us, crying that an aeroplane had landed a while since, near-by. It bore the round rings of the Sherifian camel brand upon its body. Peake rode across, to find two Australians whose Bristol had been hit in the radiator, over Deraa. They were glad, though astonished, to meet friends. After the leak had been plugged, we levied water from the women to fill them up, and they flew home safely.

Men rode up every minute and joined us, while from each village the adventurous young ran out afoot to enter our ranks. As we moved on, so closely knit in the golden sunlight, we were able, in rare chance, to see ourselves as a whole: quickly we became a character, an organism, in whose pride each of us was uplifted. We cracked bawdy jokes to set off the encompassing beauty.

At noon we entered water-melon fields. The army ran upon them, while we spied out the line, which lay desertedly quivering in the sunlight ahead. As we watched a train passed down. Only last night had the railway been mended: and this was the third train. We moved without opposition upon the line in a horde two miles across, and began hastily to blow up things, any one who had explosive using it as he fancied. Our hundreds of novices were full of zeal and the demolitions, albeit uninstructed, were wide.

Clearly our return had surprised the dazed enemy: we must extend and improve this chance. So we went to Nuri Shaalan, Auda, and Talal, and asked what local effort each would undertake. Talal, the energetic, would attack Ezraa, the big grain depot to the north. Auda was for Khirbet el Ghazale the corresponding station southward: Nuri would sweep his men down the main road, towards Deraa, on chance of Turkish parties.

These were three good ideas. The chiefs went to put them into being, while we, pulling our column to its shape again, pursued our road past the ruined colony of Sheikh Miskin, very gaunt in the moonlight. Its obstacle of water ditches muddled our thousands, so that we halted on the stubble plain beyond, for dawn. Some made fires against the penetrating mist of this clay Hauran: others slept as they were on the dew-slimy ground. Lost men went about calling their friends, in that sharp, full-throated wail of the Arab villager. The moon had set, and the world was black and very cold.

I roused my bodyguard, who rode so briskly that we entered Sheikh Saad with the dawn. As we passed between the rocks into the field behind the trees, the earth sprang to life again with the new sun. The morning airs flashed the olive-yards to silver, and men from a great goat-hair tent on the right called us to guest with them.

The parties of the night returned, full of spoil. Ezraa had been feebly held by Abd el Kader, the Algerian, with his retainers, some volunteers, and troops. When Talal came the volunteers joined him, the troops fled, and the retainers were so few that Adb el Kader had to abandon the place without fighting. Our men were too heavy with their great booty to catch him.

Auda came, boasting. He had taken el Ghazale by storm, capturing a derelict train, guns and two hundred men, of whom some were Germans. Nuri Shaalan reported four hundred prisoners with mules and machine-guns. The rank and file of Turks had been farmed out to remote villages, to earn their keep.

An English aeroplane flew round and round, wondering if we were the Arab force. Young spread out ground signals, and to him they dropped a message that Bulgaria had surrendered to the Allies. We had not known there was an offensive in the Balkans, so the news came orphaned, and as it were insignificant to us. Undoubtedly the end, not only of the great war, but of our war, was near. A sharp effort, and our trial would be over and every one loosed back to his affairs, forgetting the madness: since for most of us it was the first war, and we looked to its end as rest and peace.

The army had arrived. The groves became thronged as each detachment picked out the best vacant place and unsaddled, whether beside fig trees, or under palms, or olives, from which the birds burst out in frightened clouds, with a multitudinous crying. Our men took their animals to the stream meandering through green bushes and flowers and cultivated fruits, things strange to us during the years of our wandering in the flinty desert.

The people of Sheikh Saad came shyly to look at Feisal's army, which had been a whispered legendary thing, and was now in their village, led by renowned or formidable names—Talal, Nasir, Nuri, Auda. We stared back, in secret envy of their peasant life.

While the men stretched the saddle stiffness of riding from their legs, we went up, five or six of us, above the ruins, whence across the southern plain we should see the measure of security in store for us. To our astonishment we perceived, just over the walls, a thin company of regulars in uniform—Turks, Austrians, Germans—with eight machine guns on pack-animals. They were toiling up from Galilee towards Damascus after their defeat by Allenby; hopeless, but carefree, marching at ease, thinking themselves fifty miles from any war.

We did not give an alarm, to spare our tired troops pains: just Durzi ibn Dughmi, with the Khaffaji and others of the family, mounted quietly and fell on them from a narrow lane. The officers showed fight and were instantly killed. The men threw down their arms, and in five minutes had been searched and robbed and were being shepherded in file along the water-paths between the gardens to an open pound which seemed fit for our prison. Sheikh Saad was paying soon and well.

Away to the east appeared three or four black knots of people, moving northward. We loosed the Howeitat on them, and after an hour they returned in laughter, each man leading a mule or pack-horse; poor, tired, galled brutes, showing all too clearly the straits of the beaten army. Their riders had been unarmed soldiers fleeing from the British. The Howeitat disdained to make such prisoners. "We gave them to the boys and the girls of the village for servants," sneered Zaal, with his thin-lipped smile.

News came to us from the west that small companies of Turks were retiring into the local villages from Chauvel's attacks. We sent against them armed parties of Naim, a peasant tribe which had joined us last night at Sheikh Miskin, as appointed by Nasir, to do what they could. The mass rising we had so long prepared was now in flood, rising higher as each success armed more rebels. In two days' time we might have sixty thousand armed men in movement.

We snapped up further trifles on the Damascus road; and then saw heavy smoke above the hill which hid Deraa. A man cantered in, to inform Tallal that the Germans had set fire to aeroplanes and store-houses, and stood ready to evacuate the town. A British plane dropped word that Barrow's troops were near Remtha, and that two Turkish columns, one of four thousand, one of two thousand, were retiring towards us from Deraa and Mezerib respectively.

It seemed to me that these six thousand men were all that remained of the Fourth Army, from Deraa, and of the Seventh Army, which had been disputing Barrow's advance. With their destruction would end our purpose here. Yet, till we knew, we must retain Sheikh Saad. So the larger column, the four thousand, we would let pass, only fastening to them Khalid and his Rualla, with some northern peasantry, to harry their flanks and rear.

The nearer two thousand seemed more our size. We would meet them with half our regulars, and two of Pisani's guns. Tallal was anxious, for their indicated route would bring them through Tafas, his own village. He determined us to make speed there and seize the ridge south of it. Unfortunately speed was only a relative term with men so tired. I rode with my troop to Tafas, hoping to occupy a shadow position beyond it and fight a retiring action till the rest came up. Half-way on the road, there met us mounted Arabs, herding a drove of stripped prisoners towards Sheikh Saad. They were driving them mercilessly, the bruises of their urging blue across the ivory backs; but I left them to it, for these were Turks of the police battalion of Deraa, beneath whose iniquities the peasant-faces of the neighbourhood had run with tears and blood, innumerable times.

The Arabs told us that the Turkish column—Jemal Pasha's lancer regiment—was already entering Tafas. When we got within sight, we found they had taken the village (from which sounded an occasional shot) and were halted about it. Small pyres of smoke were going up from between the houses. On the rising ground to this side, knee deep in the thistles, stood a remnant of old men, women and children, telling terrible stories of what had happened when the Turks rushed in an hour before.

We lay on watch, and saw the enemy force march away from their assembly ground behind the houses. They headed in good order towards Miskin, the lancers in front and rear, composite formations of infantry disposed in column with machine-gun support as flank guards, guns and a mass of transport in the centre. We opened fire on the head of their line when it showed itself beyond the houses. They turned two field guns upon us, for reply. The shrapnel was as usual over-fused, and passed safely above our heads.

Nuri came with Pisani. Before their ranks rode Auda abu Tayi, expectant, and Tallal, nearly frantic with the tales his people poured out of the sufferings of the village. The last Turks were now quitting it. We slipped down behind them to end Tallal's suspense, while

our infantry took position and fired strongly with the Hotchkiss;
Pisani advanced his half battery among them; so that the French
high-explosive threw the rearguard into confusion.

The village lay stilly under its slow wreaths of white smoke, as
we rode near, on our guard. Some grey heaps seemed to hide in the
long grass, embracing the ground in the close way of corpses. We
looked away from these, knowing they were dead; but from one a
little figure tottered off, as if to escape us. It was a child, three or
four years old, whose dirty smock was stained red over one shoulder and side, with blood from a large half-fibrous wound, perhaps
a lance thrust, just where neck and body joined.

The child ran a few steps, then stood and cried to us in a tone
of astonishing strength (all else being very silent), "Don't hit me,
Baba." Abd el Aziz, choking out something—this was his village,
and she might be of his family—flung himself off his camel, and
stumbled, kneeling, in the grass beside the child. His suddenness
frightened her, for she threw up her arms and tried to scream; but,
instead, dropped in a little heap, while the blood rushed out again
over her clothes; then, I think, she died.

We rode past the other bodies of men and women and four more
dead babies, looking very soiled in the daylight, towards the village;
whose loneliness we now knew meant death and horror. By the outskirts were low mud walls, sheepfolds, and on one something red
and white. I looked close and saw the body of a woman folded across
it, bottom upwards, nailed there by a saw bayonet whose haft stuck
hideously into the air from between her naked legs. About her lay
others, perhaps twenty in all, variously killed.

The Zaagi burst into wild peals of laughter, the more desolate
for the warm sunshine and clear air of this upland afternoon. I said,
"The best of you brings me the most Turkish dead," and we turned
after the fading enemy, on our way shooting down those who had
fallen out by the roadside and came imploring our pity. One wounded Turk, half naked, not able to stand, sat and wept to us. Abdulla
turned away his camel's head, but the Zaagi, with curses, crossed

his track and whipped three bullets from his automatic through the man's bare chest. The blood came out with his heart beats, throb, throb, throb, slower and slower.

Tallal had seen what we had seen. He gave one moan like a hurt animal; then rode to the upper ground and sat there a while on his mare, shivering and looking fixedly after the Turks. I moved near to speak to him, but Auda caught my rein and stayed me. Very slowly Tallal drew his headcloth about his face; and then he seemed suddenly to take hold of himself, for he dashed his stirrups into the mare's flanks and galloped headlong, bending low and swaying in the saddle, right at the main body of the enemy.

It was a long ride down a gentle slope and across a hollow. We sat there like stone while he rushed forward, the drumming of his hoofs unnaturally loud in our ears, for we had stopped shooting, and the Turks had stopped. Both armies waited for him; and he rocked on in the hushed evening till only a few lengths from the enemy. Then he sat up in the saddle and cried his war cry, "Tallal, Tallal," twice in a tremendous shout. Instantly their rifles and machine-guns crashed out, and he and his mare riddled through and through with bullets, fell dead among the lance points.

Auda looked very cold and grim. "God give him mercy; we will take his price." He shook his rein and moved slowly after the enemy. We called up the peasants, now drunk with fear and blood, and sent them from this side and that against the retreating column. The old lion of battle waked in Auda's heart, and made him again our natural, inevitable leader. By a skilful turn he drove the Turks into bad ground and split their formation into three parts.

The third part, the smallest, was mostly made up of German and Austrian machine-gunners grouped round three motor-cars and a handful of mounted officers or troopers. They fought magnificently and repulsed us time and again despite our hardiness. The Arabs were fighting like devils, the sweat blurring their eyes, dust parching their throats; while the flame of cruelty and revenge which was burning in their bodies so twisted them that their hands could

ENTERING DAMASCUS

hardly shoot. By my order we took no prisoners, for the only time
in our war.

At last we left this stern section behind, and pursued the faster two. They were in panic; and by sunset we had destroyed all but the smallest pieces of them, gaining as and by what they lost. Parties of peasants flowed in on our advance. At first there were five or six to a weapon: then one would win a bayonet, another a sword, a third a pistol. An hour later those who had been on foot would be on donkeys. Afterwards every man had a rifle and a captured horse. By nightfall the horses were laden, and the rich plain was scattered over with dead men and animals. In a madness born of the horror of Tafas we killed and killed, even blowing in the heads of the fallen and of the animals; as though their death and running blood could slake our agony.

However, what with wounds and aches and weariness I could not rest from thinking of Tallal, the splendid leader, the fine horseman, the courteous and strong companion of the road; and after a while I had my other camel brought, and with one of my bodyguard rode out into the night to join our men hunting the greater Deraa column.

It was very dark, with a wind beating in great gusts from the south and east; and only by the noise of shots it tossed across to us and by occasional gun flashes, did we at length come to the fighting. Every field and valley had its Turks stumbling blindly northward. Our men were clinging on. The fall of night had made them bolder, and they were now closing with the enemy. Each village, as the fight rolled to it, took up the work; and the black, icy wind was wild with rifle-fire, shoutings, volleys from the Turks, and the rush of gallops, as small parties of either side crashed frantically together.

The enemy had tried to halt and camp at sunset, but Khalid had shaken them again into movement. Some marched, some stayed. Many dropped asleep in their tracks with fatigue. They had lost order and coherence, and were drifting through the blast in lorn packets, ready to shoot and run at every contact with us or with each other; and the Arabs were as scattered, and nearly as uncertain.

Exceptions were the German detachments; and here, for the first time, I grew proud of the enemy who had killed my brothers. They were two thousand miles from home, without hope and without guides, in conditions mad enough to break the bravest nerves. Yet their sections held together in firm rank, sheering through the wrack of Turk and Arab like armoured ships, high-faced and silent. When attacked they halted, took position, fired to order. There was no haste, no crying, no hesitation. They were glorious.

At last I found Khalid, and asked him to call off the Rualla and leave this rout to time and the peasantry. Heavier work, perhaps, lay to the southward. At dusk a rumour had passed across our plain that Deraa was empty, and Trad, Khalid's brother, with a good half of the Anazeh, had ridden off to see. I feared a reverse for him, since there must still be Turks in the place, and more struggling towards it up the railways and through the Irbid Hills. Indeed, unless Barrow, last reported to us as delayed in Remthe, had lost contact with his enemy, there must be a fighting rearguard yet to follow.

I wanted Khalid to support his brother. After an hour or two of shouting his message down the winds, hundreds of horse-men and camel-men had rallied to him. On his way to Deraa he charged through and over several detachments of Turks in the star-blink, and arrived to find Trad in secure possession. He had won through in the later twilight, taking the station at a gallop, jumping trenches and blotting out the scanty Turkish elements which still tried to resist.

With local help the Rualla plundered the camp, especially finding booty in the fiercely burning storehouses whose flaming roofs imperilled their lives; but this was one of the nights in which mankind went crazy, when death seemed impossible, however many died to the right and left, and when others' lives became toys to break and throw away.

Sheikh Saad passed a troubled evening of alarms and shots and shouts, with threatenings from the peasantry to murder the prisoners as added price of Tallal and his village. The active Sheikhs were out hunting the Turks, and their absence with their retainers deprived the Arab camp of its experienced chiefs and of its eyes and ears. Sleeping clan-jealousies had awaked in the blood thirst of the afternoon of killing, and Nasir and Nuri Said, Young and Winterton had to strain every nerve in keeping peace.

I got in after midnight and found Trad's messengers just arrived from Deraa. Nasir left to join him. I had wished to sleep, for this was my fourth night of riding; but my mind would not let me feel how tired my body was, so about two in the morning, I mounted a third camel and splashed out towards Deraa, down the Tafas track again, to windward of the dark village.

Nuri Said and his staff were riding the same road in advance of their mounted infantry, and our parties hurried together till the half-light came. Then my impatience and the cold would not let me travel horse-pace any longer. I gave liberty to my camel—the grand, rebellious Baha—and she stretched herself out against the field, racing my wearied followers for mile upon mile with piston-strides like an engine, so that I entered Deraa quite alone in the full dawn.

CHAPTER XXXV

JOINING THE BRITISH

NASIR WAS at the Mayor's house, arranging a military governor, and police; and for an inquisition of the place; I supplemented his ideas, putting guards over the pumps and engine sheds and what remained of tool shops or stores. Then in an hour of talk I built up publicly a programme of what the situation would demand of them, if they were not to lose hold. Poor Nasir stared in bewilderment.

I inquired about General Barrow. A man just ridden in from the West told us he had been fired on by the English, as they deployed to attack the town. To prevent such an accident the Zaagi and I rode up the Buweib, on whose crest was visible a strong post of Indian machine-gunners. They trained their weapons on us, proud of such splendidly dressed prizes. However, an officer showed himself, with some British troopers, and to them I explained myself. They were indeed in the midst of an enveloping movement against Deraa, and, while we watched, their aeroplanes bombed the luckless Nuri Said as he rode into the railway station. This was his penalty for losing the race from Sheikh Saad: but, to stop it, I hurried down to where General Barrow was inspecting outposts in a car.

He said he must post sentries in the village to keep the populace in order. I explained gently that the Arabs had installed their military governor. At the wells he said his sappers must inspect the pumps. I replied welcoming their assistance. He snorted that we seemed to be at home; he would take charge only of the railway station. I pointed to the engine moving out towards Mezerib (where our little Sheikh had prevented the Turks from blowing up the Tell el Shehab bridge, now become Arab property) and asked that his sentries be instructed not to interfere with our proper working of the line.

He had had no orders as to the status of the Arabs. Clayton did us this service, thinking we should deserve what we could assert: so Barrow, who had come in thinking of them as a conquered people, though dazed at my calm assumption that he was my guest, had no option but to follow the lead of such assurance. My head was working full speed in these minutes, on our joint behalf, to prevent the fatal first steps by which the unimaginative British, with the best will in the world, usually deprived the acquiescent native of the discipline of responsibility, and created a situation which called for years of agitation and successive reforms and riotings to mend.

Barrow surrendered himself by asking me to find him forage and food-stuffs. In the square I showed him Nasir's little silk pennon, propped on the balcony of the charred Government office, with a yawning sentry underneath. Barrow drew himself up and saluted sharply, while a thrill of pleasure at the General's compliment ran round Arab officers and men.

In return we strove to keep self-assertion within the bounds of political necessity. On all Arabs we impressed that these Indian troops were guests, and must be permitted, nay helped, to do anything they wished. The doctrine took us into unexpected places. Every chicken disappeared from the village, and three sowars carried off Nasir's pennon, having coveted the silver knobs and spike of its dainty staff. This pointed a contrast between the English General who saluted and the Indian trooper who stole: a contrast welcome to the Arab race-hesitation towards the Indians.

Meanwhile, everywhere we were taking men and guns. Our prisoners could be counted in thousands. Some we handed over to the British, who counted them again: most we boarded-out in the villages. Azrak heard the full news of victory. Feisal drove in a day later, our string of armoured cars following his Vauxhall. He installed himself in the station. I called with my record of stewardship: as the tale ended the room shook with a gentle earthquake.

Barrow, now watered and fed, was due to leave for his meeting with Chauvel near Damascus, that they might enter the City together. He asked us to take the right flank, which suited me, for there, along the Hejaz line, was Nasir, hanging on to the main Turkish retreat, reducing its numbers by continuous attack day and night. I had still much to do, and therefore waited in Deraa another night, savouring its quiet after the troops had gone; for the station stood at the limit of the open country, and the Indians round it had angered me by their out-of-placeness. The essence of the desert was the lonely moving individual, the son of the road, apart from the world as in a grave. These troops, in flocks like slow sheep, looked not worthy of the privilege of space.

My mind felt in the Indian rank and file something puny and confined; an air of thinking themselves mean; almost a careful, esteemed subservience, unlike the abrupt wholesomeness of Beduin. The manner of the British officers toward their men struck horror into my bodyguard, who had never seen personal inequality before.

I lay each night with my men upon the old aerodrome. By the charred hangars my guards, fickle-surfaced as the sea, squabbled after their wont; and there for the last time Abdulla brought me cooked rice in the silver bowl. After supping, I tried in the blankness to think forward: but my mind was a blank, my dreams puffed out like candles by the strong wind of success. In front was our too-tangible goal: but behind lay the effort of two years, its misery forgotten or glorified. Names rang through my head, each in imagination a superlative: Rum the magnificent, brilliant Petra, Azrak the remote, Batra the very clean. Yet the men had changed. Death had taken the gentle ones; and the new stridency, of those who were left, hurt me.

Sleep would not come, so before the light, I woke Stirling and my drivers, and we four climbed into the Blue Mist, our Rolls tender, and set out for Damascus, along the dirt road which was first rutted, and then blocked by the transport columns and rearguard of Barrow's division. We cut across country to the French railway, whose old ballast gave us a clear, if rugged, road; then we put on speed. At noon we saw Barrow's pennon at a stream, where he was watering his horses. My bodyguard were near-by, so I took my camel and rode over to him. Like other confirmed horsemen, he had been a little contemptuous of the camel; and had suggested, in Deraa, that we might hardly keep up with his cavalry, which was going to Damascus in about three forced marches.

So when he saw me freshly riding up he was astonished, and asked when we left Deraa. "This morning." His face fell. "Where will you stop to-night?" "In Damascus," said I gaily; and rode on, having made another enemy. It a little smote me to play tricks, for he was generous towards my wishes: but the stakes were high, beyond his sight, and I cared nothing what he thought of me so that we won.

I returned to Stirling, and drove on. At each village we left notes for the British advance guards, telling them where we were, and how far beyond us the enemy. It irked Stirling and myself to see the caution of Barrow's advance; scouts scouting empty valleys, sections crowning every deserted hill, a screen drawn forward so carefully over friendly country. It marked the difference between our certain movements and the tentative processes of normal war.

There could be no crisis till Kiswe, where we were to meet Chauvel, and where the Hejaz line approached our road. Upon the railway were Nasir, Nuri Shaalan and Auda, with the tribes; still harrying that column of four thousand (but in truth nearer seven) marked by our aeroplane near Sheikh Saad three busy days ago. They had fought ceaselessly throughout this time of our ease.

As we drove up we heard firing, and saw shrapnel behind a ridge to our right, where the railway was. Soon appeared the head of a Turkish column of about two thousand men, in ragged groups, halting now and then to fire their mountain guns. We ran on to overtake their pursuers, our great Rolls very blue on the open road. Some Arab horsemen from behind the Turks galloped towards us, bucketing unhandily across the irrigation ditches. We recognized Nasir on his liver-coloured stallion, the splendid animal yet spirited after its hundred miles of a running fight: also old Nuri Shaalan and about thirty of their servants. They told us these few were all that remained of the seven thousand Turks. The Rualla were hanging desperately on to both flanks, while Auda abu Tayi had ridden behind Jebel Mania to gather the Wuld Ali, his friends, and lie in wait there for this column, which they hoped to drive over the hill into his ambush. Did our appearance mean help at last?

I told them the British, in force, were just behind. If they could delay the enemy only an hour . . . Nasir looked ahead and saw a walled and wooded farmstead barring the level. He called to Nuri Shaalan, and they hastened thither to check the Turks.

We drove back three miles to the leading Indians, and told their ancient, surly Colonel what a gift the Arabs brought. He seemed not pleased to upset the beautiful order of his march, but at last opened out a squadron and sent them slowly across the plain towards the Turks, who turned the little guns their way. One or two shells burst nearly among the files, and then to our horror (for Nasir had put himself in jeopardy, expecting courageous help) the Colonel ordered a retirement, and fell back quickly to the road. Stirling and myself, hopping mad, dashed down and begged him not to be afraid of mountain guns, no heavier than Very pistols: but neither to kindness nor to wrath did the old man budge an inch. We raced a third time back along the road in search of higher authority.

A red-tipped Aide told us that over there was General Gregory. We blessed him, Stirling's professional pride nearly in tears at the mismanagement. We pulled our friend aboard and found his General, to whom we lent our car that the brigade major might take hot orders to the cavalry. A galloper hurtled back for the horse artillery, which opened fire just as the last of the light fled up the hill to its summit and took refuge in the clouds. Middlesex Yeomanry appeared and were pushed in among the Arabs, to charge the Turkish rear, and, as the night fell, we saw the break-up of the enemy, who abandoned their guns, their transport and all their stuff and went streaming up the col towards the two peaks of Mania, escaping into what they thought was empty land beyond.

However, in the empty land was Auda; and in that night of his last battle the old man killed and killed, plundered and captured, till dawn showed him the end. There passed the Fourth Army, our stumbling-block for two years.

Gregory's happy vigour heartened us to face Nasir. We drove to Kiswe, where we had agreed to meet him before midnight. After us came the press of Indian troops. We sought a retired spot; but already there were men by the thousand everywhere.

The movement and cross-currents of so many crowded minds drove me about, restlessly, like themselves. In the night my colour was unseen. I could walk as I pleased, an unconsidered Arab: and this finding myself among, but cut off from, my own kin made me strangely alone. Our armoured-car men were persons to me, from their fewness and our long companionship; and also in their selves, for these months unshieldedly open to the flaming sun and bullying wind had worn and refined them into individuals. In such a mob of unaccustomed soldiery, British, Australian and Indian, they went as strange and timid as myself; distinguished also by grime, for with weeks of wearing their clothes had been moulded to them by sweat and use and had become rather integuments than wrappings.

But these others were really soldiers, a novelty after two years' irregularity. And it came upon me freshly how the secret of uniform was to make a crowd solid, dignified, impersonal: to give it the singleness and tautness of an upstanding man. This death's livery which walled its bearers from ordinary life, was sign that they had sold their wills and bodies to the State: and contracted themselves into a service not the less abject for that its beginning was voluntary. Some of them had obeyed the instinct of lawlessness: some were hungry: others thirsted

From a painting by S. Carline

BOMBING THE TURKISH RETREAT IN WADI FARA
(Reproduced by permission of the Imperial War Museum)

for glamour, for the supposed colour of a military life: but, of them all, those only received satisfaction who had sought to degrade themselves, for to the peace-eye they were below humanity. Only women with a lech were allured by those witnessing clothes; the soldiers' pay, not sustenance like a labourer's, but pocket-money, seemed most profitably spent when it let them drink sometimes and forget.

Convicts had violence put upon them. Slaves might be free, if they could, in intention. But the soldier assigned his owner the twenty-four hours' use of his body; and sole conduct of his mind and passions. A convict had licence to hate the rule which confined him, and all humanity outside, if he were greedy in hate: but the sulking soldier was a bad soldier; indeed, no soldier. His affections must be hired pieces on the chess-board of the King.

About the soldiers hung the Arabs: gravely-gazing men from another sphere. My crooked duty had banished me among them for two years. To-night I was nearer to them than to the troops, and I resented it, as shameful. The intruding contrast mixed with longing for home, to sharpen my faculties and make fertile my distaste, till not merely did I see the unlikeness of race, and hear the unlikeness of language, but I learned to pick between their smells: the heavy, standing, curdled sourness of dried sweat in cotton, over the Arab crowds; and the feral smell of English soldiers: that hot pissy aura of thronged men in woollen clothes; a tart pungency, breath-catching, ammoniacal; a fervent fermenting naphtha-smell.

CHAPTER XXXVI

ENTRY INTO DAMASCUS

OUR WAR was ended:—even though we slept that night in Kiswe, for the Arabs told us the roads were dangerous, and we had no wish to die stupidly in the dark at the gate of Damascus. The sporting Australians saw the campaign as a point-to-point, with Damascus the post; but in reality we were all under Allenby, now, and the victory had been the logical fruit solely of his genius, and Bartholomew's pains.

Their tactical scheme properly put the Australians north and west of Damascus, across its railways, before the southern column might enter it: and we, the Arab leaders, had waited for the slower British partly because Allenby never questioned our fulfilling what was ordered. Power lay in his calm assumption that he would receive as perfect obedience as he gave trust.

He hoped we would be present at the entry, partly because he knew how much more than a mere trophy Damascus was to the Arabs: partly for prudential reasons. Feisal's movement made the enemy country friendly to the allies as they advanced, enabling convoys to go up without escort, towns to be administered without garrison. In their envelopment of Damascus the Australians might be forced, despite orders, to enter the town. If any one resisted them it would spoil the future. One night was given us to make the Damascenes receive the British Army as their allies.

This was a revolution in behaviour, if not in opinion; but Feisal's Damascus committee had for months been prepared to take over the reins when the Turks crashed. We had only to get in touch with them, to tell them the movements of the Allies, and what was required. So as dusk deepened Nasir sent the Rualla horse into the town, to find Ali Riza, the chairman of our committee, or Shukri el Ayubi, his assistant, telling them that relief would be available on the morrow, if they constructed a Government at once. As a matter of fact it had been done at four o'clock in the afternoon, before we took action. Ali Riza was absent, put in command at the last moment by the Turks of the retreat of their army from Galilee before Chauvel: but Shukri found unexpected support from the Algerian brothers, Mohammed Said and Abd el Kader. With the help of their retainers the Arab flag was on the Town Hall before sunset as the last echelons of Germans and Turks defiled past. They say the hindmost general saluted it, ironically.

I dissuaded Nasir from going in. This would be a night of confusion, and it would better serve his dignity if he entered serenely at dawn. He and Nuri Shaalan intercepted the second body of Rualla camel men, who had started out with me from Deraa this morning; and sent them all forward into Damascus, to support the Rualla sheikhs. So by midnight, when we went to rest, we had four thousand of our armed men in the town.

I wanted to sleep, for my work was coming on the morrow; but I could not. Damascus was the climax of our two years' uncertainty, and my mind was distracted by tags of all the ideas which had been used or rejected in that time. Also Kiswe was stifling with the exhalations of too many trees, too many plants, too many human beings: a microcosm of the crowded world in front of us.

As the Germans left Damascus they fired the dumps and ammunition stores, so that every few minutes we were jangled by explosions, whose first shock set the sky white with flame. At each such roar

the earth seemed to shake; we would lift our eyes to the north and
see the pale sky prick out suddenly in sheaves of yellow points, as
the shells, thrown to terrific heights from each bursting magazine,
in their turn burst like clustered rockets. I turned to Stirling and
muttered, "Damascus is burning," sick to think of the great town
in ashes as the price of freedom.

When dawn came we drove to the head of the ridge, which stood
over the oasis of the city, afraid to look north for the ruins we expected: but, instead of ruins, the silent gardens stood blurred green with
river mist, in whose setting shimmered the city, beautiful as ever,
like pearl in the morning sun. The uproar of the night had shrunk
to a stiff tall column of smoke, which rose in sullen blackness from
the store-yard by Kadem, terminus of the Hejaz line.

We drove down the straight banked road through the watered
fields, in which the peasants were just beginning their day's work.
A galloping horseman checked at our headcloths in the car, with a
merry salutation, holding out a bunch of yellow grapes. "Good
news: Damascus salutes you." He came from Shukri.

Nasir was just beyond us: to him we carried the tidings, that he
might have the honourable entry, a privilege of his fifty battles. With
Nuri Shaalan beside him, he asked a final gallop from his horse, and
vanished down the long road in a cloud of dust, which hung reluctantly in the air between the water splashes. To give him a fair start,
Stirling and I found a little stream, cool in the depths of a steep
channel. By it we stopped, to wash and shave.

Some Indian troopers peered at us and our car and its ragged driver's army shorts and tunic. I was in pure Arab dress; Stirling, but
for his head-covering, was all British staff officer. Their N.C.O. an
obtuse and bad-tempered person, thought he had taken prisoners.
When delivered from his arrest we judged we might go after Nasir.

Quite quietly we drove up the long street to the Government
buildings, on the bank of the Barada. The way was packed with
people, lined solid on the side-walks, in the road, at the windows
and on the balconies or house-tops. Many were crying, a few cheered

faintly, some bolder ones cried our names: but mostly they looked and looked, joy shining in their eyes. A movement like a long sigh from gate to heart of the city, marked our course.

At the town hall things were different. Its steps and stairs were packed with a swaying mob: yelling, embracing, dancing, singing. They crushed a way for us to the ante-chamber, where were the gleaming Nasir, and Nuri Shaalan, seated. On either side of them stood Abd el Kader, my old enemy, and Mohammed Said his brother. I was dumb with amazement. Mohammed Said leaped forward and shouted that they, grandsons of Abd el Kader, the Emir, with Shukri el Ayubi, of Saladin's house, had formed the Government and proclaimed Hussein "King of the Arabs" yesterday, into the ears of the humbled Turks and Germans.

While he ranted I turned to Shukri, who was no statesman, but a beloved man, almost a martyr in the people's eyes, because of what he had suffered from Jemal. He told me how the Algerians, alone of all Damascus, had stood by the Turks till they saw them running. Then, with their Algerians, they had burst in upon Feisal's committee where it sat in secret, and brutally assumed control.

They were fanatics, whose ideas were theological, not logical; and I turned to Nasir, meaning through him to check their impudence now from the start; but there came a diversion. The screaming press about us parted as though a ram drove through, men going down to right and left among ruined chairs and tables, while the terrific roaring of a familiar voice triumphed, and stilled them dead.

In the cleared space were Auda abu Tayi and Sultan el Atrash, chief of the Druses, tearing one another. Their followers bounded forward, while I jumped in to drive them apart; crashing upon Mohammed el Dheilan, filled with the same purpose. Together we broke them, and forced Auda back a pace, while Hussein el Atrash hustled the lighter Sultan into the crowd, and away to a side room. Then I looked round for Nasir and Abd el Kader, to set in order their Government. They were gone. The Algerians had persuaded Nasir to their house for refreshment. It was a good hap, for there were more pressing public things. We must prove the old days over, a native Government in power: for this Shukri would be my best instrument, as acting Governor. So in the Blue Mist, we set off to show ourselves, his enlargement in authority itself a banner of revolution for the citizens.

When we came in there had been some miles of people greeting us: now there were thousands for every hundred then. Every man, woman and child in this city of a quarter-million souls seemed in the streets, waiting only the spark of our appearance to ignite their spirits. Damascus went mad with joy. The men tossed up their tarbushes to cheer, the women tore off their veils. Householders threw flowers, hangings, carpets, into the road before us: their wives leaned, screaming with laughter, through the lattices and splashed us with bath-dippers of scent.

Poor dervishes made themselves our running footmen in front and behind, howling and cutting themselves with frenzy; and over the local cries and the shrilling of women came the measured roar of men's voices chanting, "Feisal, Nasir, Shukri, Urens," in waves which began here, rolled along the squares, through the market, down long streets to East gate, round the wall, back up the Meidan; and grew to a wall of shouts around us by the citadel.

They told me Chauvel was coming; our cars met in the southern outskirts. I described the excitement in the city, and how our new Government could not guarantee administrative services before the following day, when I would wait on him, to discuss his needs and mine. Meanwhile I made myself responsible for public order: only begging him to keep his men outside, because to-night would see such carnival as the town had not held for six hundred years, and its hospitality might pervert their discipline.

CHAPTER XXXVII

JERRY-CABINET-MAKING

WE SNEAKED back to the town hall to grapple with Abd el Kader: but he had not returned. I sent for him, and for his brother, and for Nasir: and got a curt reply that they were sleeping. So should I have been: but instead four or five of us were eating a snatch-meal in the gaudy salon, sitting on gold chairs, which writhed, about a gold table whose legs also writhed obscenely.

I explained pointedly to the messenger what I meant. He disappeared, and, in a few minutes a cousin of the Algerians came up, very agitated, and said they were on their way. This was an open lie, but I replied that it was well since in half an hour I should have fetched British troops and looked carefully for them. He ran off in haste; and Nuri Shaalan asked quietly what I meant to do.

I said I would depose Abd el Kader and Mohammed Said, and appoint Shukri in their place till Feisal came; and I did it in this gentle fashion because I was loath to hurt Nasir's feelings, and had no strength of my own if men resisted. He asked if the English would not come. I replied Certainly; but the sorrow was that afterwards they might not go. He thought a moment, and said, "You shall have the Rualla if you do all your will, and quickly." Without waiting, the old man went out

to muster me his tribe. The Algerians came to the tryst with their
bodyguards, and with murder in their eyes: but, on the way, saw Nuri
Shaalan's massed lowering tribesmen; Nuri Said, with his regulars in the
square; and within, my reckless guardsmen lounging in the ante-chamber. They saw clearly that the game was up: yet it was a stormy meeting.

In my capacity as deputy for Feisal I pronounced their Civil
Government of Damascus abolished, and named Shukri Pasha Ayubi
as acting Military Governor. Nuri Said was to be Commandant of
troops; Azmi, Adjutant General; Jemil, Chief of Public Security.
Mohammed Said, in a bitter reply, denounced me as a Christian
and an Englishman, and called on Nasir to assert himself.

Poor Nasir, far out of his depth, could only sit and look miserable at this falling out of friends. Abd el Kader leaped up and cursed
me virulently, puffing himself to a white heat of passion. His motives
seemed dogmatic, irrational: so I took no heed. This maddened him
yet more: suddenly he leaped forward with drawn dagger.

Like a flash Auda was on him, the old man bristling with the
chained-up fury of the morning, and longing for a fight. It would
have been heaven, for him, to have shredded some one there and
then with his great fingers. Abd el Kader was daunted; and Nuri
Shaalan closed the debate by saying to the carpet (so enormous and
violent a carpet it was) that the Rualla were mine, and no questions
asked. The Algerians rose and swept in high dudgeon from the hall.
I was persuaded they should be seized and shot; but could not make
myself fear their power of mischief, nor set the Arabs an example
of precautionary murder as part of politics.

We passed to work. Our aim was an Arab Government, with
foundations large and native enough to employ the enthusiasm and
self-sacrifice of the rebellion, translated into terms of peace. We had
to save some of the old prophetic personality, upon a substructure
to carry that ninety per cent of the population who had been too
solid to rebel, and on whose solidity the new State must rest.

Rebels, especially successful rebels, were of necessity bad subjects
and worse governors. Feisal's sorry duty would be to rid himself of

his war-friends, and replace them by those elements which had been most useful to the Turkish Government. Nasir was too little a political philosopher to feel this. Nuri Said knew, and Nuri Shaalan. Quickly they collected the nucleus of a staff, and plunged ahead as a team. History told us the steps were humdrum: appointments, offices, and departmental routine. First the police. A commandant and assistants were chosen: districts allotted: provisional wages, indents, uniform, responsibilities. The machine began to function. Then came a complaint of water supply. The conduit was foul with dead men and animals. An inspectorate, with its labour corps, solved this. Emergency regulations were drafted.

The day was drawing in, the world was in the streets: riotous. We chose an engineer to superintend the powerhouse, charging him at all pains to illuminate the town that night. The resumption of street lighting would be our most signal proof of peace. It was done, and to its shining quietness much of the order of the first evening of victory belonged: though our new police were zealous, and the grave Sheikhs of the many quarters helped their patrol.

Then sanitation. The streets were full of the debris of the broken army, derelict carts and cars, baggage, material, corpses. Typhus, dysentery and pellagra were rife among the Turks, and sufferers had died in every shadow along the line of march. Nuri prepared scavenger gangs to make a first clearing of the pestilent roads and open places, and rationed out his doctors among the hospitals, with promise of drugs and food next day, if any could be found.

Next a fire-brigade. The local engines had been smashed by the Germans, and the Army store-houses still burned, endangering the town. Mechanics were cried for; and trained men, pressed into service, sent down to circumscribe the flames. Then the prisons. Warders and inmates had vanished from them together. Shukri made a virtue of that, by amnesties, civil, political, military. The citizens must be disarmed— or at least dissuaded from carrying rifles. A proclamation was the treatment, followed up by good-humoured banter merging into police activity. This would effect our end without malice in three or four days.

Relief work. The destitute had been half-starved for days. A distribution of the damaged food from the Army store-houses was arranged. After that food must be provided for the general. The city might be starving in two days: there were no stocks in Damascus. To get temporary supplies from the near villages was easy, if we restored confidence, safe-guarded the roads, and replaced the transport animals, which the Turks had carried off, by others from the pool of captures. The British would not share out. We parted with our own animals: our Army transport.

The routine feeding of the place needed the railway. Pointsmen, drivers, firemen, shopmen, traffic staff had to be found and re-engaged immediately. Then the telegraphs: the junior staff were available: directors must be found, and linesmen sent out to put the system in repair. The post could wait a day or two: but quarters for ourselves and the British were urgent; and so were the resumption of trade, the opening of shops, and their corollary needs of markets and acceptable currency.

The currency was horrible. The Australians had looted millions in Turkish notes, the only stuff in use, and had reduced it to no value by throwing it about. One trooper gave a five hundred pound note to a lad who held his horse three minutes. Young tried his prentice-hand at bolstering it with the last remnant of our Akaba gold: but new prices had to be fixed, which involved the printing press; and hardly was that settled when a newspaper was demanded. Also, as heirs of the Turkish Government, the Arabs must maintain its record of fisc and property: with the register of souls. Whereas the old staffs were taking jubilant holiday.

Requisitions plagued us while we were yet half-hungry. Chauvel had no forage and he had forty thousand horses to feed. If forage was not brought him he would go seek it, and the new-lit freedom puff out like a match. Syria's status hung on his satisfaction; and we should find little mercy in his judgments.

Taken all in all, this was a busy evening. We reached an apparent end by sweeping delegation of office (too often, in our haste, to hands unworthy), and by drastic cutting down of efficiency. Stirling the suave, Young the capable, and Kirkbride the summary backed to their best the open-minded power of the Arab officers.

Our aim was a façade rather than a fitted building. It was run up so furiously well that when I left Damascus on October the fourth the Syrians had their *de facto* Government, which endured for two years, without foreign advice, in an occupied country wasted by war, and against the will of important elements among the Allies.

Later I was sitting alone in my room, working and thinking out as firm a way as the turbulent memories of the day allowed, when the Muedhdhins began to send their call of last prayer through the moist night over the illuminations of the feasting city. One, with a ringing voice of special sweetness, cried into my window from a near mosque. I found myself involuntarily distinguishing his words: "God alone is great: I testify there are no gods, but God: and Mohammed his Prophet. Come to prayer: come to security. God alone is great: there is no god—but God."

At the close, he dropped his voice two tones, almost to speaking level, and softly added: "And He is very good to us this day, O people of Damascus." The clamour hushed, as every one seemed to obey the call to prayer on this their first night of perfect freedom.

INDEX